Narrative Therapies with Children and their Families

Narrative Therapies with Children and their Families introduces and develops the concepts and principles of narrative approaches to therapeutic work and demonstrates how narrative-based approaches to practice provide a powerful and client-friendly framework for engaging and working with troubled children and their families.

Using clinical examples, each chapter develops a methodology around narrative practice and gives practical advice on working with narrative therapy in a variety of settings. Covering a broad range of difficult and sensitive topics, including trauma, abuse and youth offending, this book succeeds in illustrating the wide application of these principles in the context of the particular issues and challenges presented when working with children and families.

This practical, practice-based book will be welcomed by any professionals in the field of child, adolescent and family mental health who want to explore the benefits of employing narrative-based approaches in their work.

Arlene Vetere is Deputy Director of Clinical Psychology Doctorate training at Surrey University. She is President of the European Family Therapy Association and an academician in the UK Academy for Learned Societies in the Social Sciences.

Emilia Dowling is a chartered consultant clinical psychologist and family psychotherapist at the Tavistock Centre and in private practice. She is a visiting professor at the School of Psychology, Birkbeck College, University of London and member of the Institute of Family Therapy.

D0145623

Narrative Therapies with Children and their Families

A practitioner's guide to
concepts and approaches

Edited by
Arlene Vetere and Emilia Dowling

Routledge
Taylor & Francis Group

LONDON AND NEW YORK

First published 2005
by Routledge
27 Church Road, Hove, East Sussex BN3 2FA

Simultaneously published in the USA and Canada
by Routledge
270 Madison Avenue, New York NY 10016

Routledge is an imprint of the Taylor & Francis Group

Typeset in Garamond by RefineCatch Limited, Bungay, Suffolk
Printed and bound in Great Britain by Biddles Ltd, King's Lynn
Paperback cover design by Code 5 Design Associates Ltd

This publication has been produced with paper manufactured to
strict environmental standards and with pulp derived from
sustainable forests.

British Library Cataloguing in Publication Data
A catalogue record for this book is available from the British Library

Library of Congress Cataloging-in-Publication Data
Narrative therapies with children and their families : a practioners
guide to concepts and approaches / editors, Arlene Vetere and
Emilia Dowling.
    p. cm.
    Includes bibliographical references and index.
    ISBN 1-58391-826-4 (hbk) – ISBN 1-58391-827-2 (pbk)   I.
Narrative therapy. I. Vetere, Arlene.   II. Dowling, Emilia, 1941–
    RJ505.S75N375   2005
    616.89′165–dc22   2005001528

ISBN 1-58391-826-4 (hbk)
ISBN 1-58391-827-2 (pbk)

Contents

Contributors

Sara Barratt is a Systemic Psychotherapist and Social Worker at the Tavistock Clinic, London, where she is Head of Systemic Psychotherapy. She is a clinical supervisor and teacher on the family therapy trainings. Sara is a member of the fostering and adoption team, specialising in kinship care and working with families post-adoption. In addition she is consultant and trainer to local authority child care staff and a therapist in general practice.

Kirsten Blow is Co-Director of the Oxford Family Institute. She is an experienced therapist with particular expertise in working with children and families facing developmental crisis or transition because of family breakdown.

Charlotte Burck is a Systemic Psychotherapist, Senior Lecturer in Social Work and researcher at the Tavistock Clinic, London, and runs a Doctorate research programme there.

David Campbell is a Consultant Clinical Psychologist in the Child and Family Department of the Tavistock Clinic, London, where he works as a Systemic/Family Therapist and a course organiser, supervisor and teacher for various family therapy courses. In addition, he works as a consultant to teams and small organisations in the public services. He is the author of several books on the subject and co-editor of the *Systemic Thinking and Practice* series of books.

Alan Carr is Associate Professor of Clinical Psychology and Associate Dean for Research at the Faculty of Human Sciences, University College Dublin, and Marital and Family Therapist at the Clanwilliam Institute, Dublin. He has worked in Canada, the UK and Ireland. He has written more than a dozen books and 200 papers. He is married with two children, three dogs, and four boats and lives by the sea.

Jan Cooper, CQSW, MSc, is a UKCP Registered Family Therapist. She is Co-Director of Reading Safer Families with Dr Arlene Vetere. She combines clinical work, supervision and training in her private practice and is a Visiting Lecturer at Reading University.

Rudi Dallos is currently a Reader in Clinical Psychology and Programme Director on the Plymouth DClin Psychol training programme in clinical psychology at the University of Plymouth. He also works as a consultant clinical psychologist in Somerset specialising in work with adolescents and their families.

Gwyn Daniel is Senior Clinical Lecturer and Systemic Psychotherapist at the Tavistock Clinic, London and Co-Director of the Oxford Family Institute. She is author (with Charlotte Burck) of *Gender and Family Therapy* and (with Gill Gorell Barnes, Paul Thompson and Natasha Burchardt) of *Growing up in Stepfamilies*.

Emilia Dowling is a chartered consultant clinical psychologist and family psychotherapist (UKCP registered) at the Tavistock Clinic, London and in private practice, visiting professor at the School of Psychology, Birkbeck College, University of London, and member of the Institute of Family Therapy. Her interests include systemic consultation with families, schools and general practice and working with families during and after separation and divorce. In all areas of her work she is particularly interested in the children's perspective. She has published widely and co-edited with the late Elsie Osborne, *The Family and the School: A Joint System Approach to Problems with Children*, 1994 (2nd edn). She is co-author, with Gill Gorell Barnes, of *Working with Children and Parents through Separation and Divorce*, 2000.

Irvine Gersch is the Course Director for the professional training programme for educational psychologists at the University of East London. He has worked as a schoolteacher, counsellor, lecturer, educational psychologist, and as principal educational psychologist for a London Borough. He has published widely on pupil behaviour management, conciliation and mediation, School Systems, listening to the children, and the future of applied psychology. In 2002 he received The British Psychological Society's annual award for distinguished contribution to professional psychology. He has two adult children.

Gill Gorell Barnes is Honorary Senior Lecturer, Tavistock Clinic, London, and works privately as a couples, marital and family therapist. She specialises in work with separating couples and their children and acts as Consultant to Family Court Proceedings where alienation between parents is leading to estrangement between a parent and their child.

Myrna Gower is a Systemic Psychotherapist with many years experience of clinical practice, teaching and consultancy. She has a long association with the Tavistock Clinic, Prudence Skynner Family Therapy Clinic and Royal

Holloway, University of London. She is currently conducting research into Parenting Adult Children.

Rita Harris is a Consultant Clinical Psychologist and Systemic Psychotherapist. She is currently Chair of the Child and Family Department of the Tavistock Clinic in London. Her current clinical work is as part of a specialist fostering and adoption multi-disciplinary team. Here her research has focused on issues of contact for children with parents with whom they no longer live. She is particularly interested in ways in which their voice may be heard.

Sebastian Kraemer is a Consultant Child and Adolescent Psychiatrist at the Whittington Hospital, London and an honorary consultant at the Tavistock Clinic, London. His principal interests and publications are in parent and family therapy, infant mental health, paediatric liaison, the training of child and adolescent psychiatrists, the origins and roles of fatherhood and the fragility of the developing male.

John Launer is a GP and family therapist. He is a Senior Lecturer at the Tavistock Clinic, London, and Associate Director of Postgraduate GP Education for London. His interests include the use of narrative ideas and skills in GP consultation and in supervision. He is author of *Narrative Based Primary Care: A Practical Guide* (Radcliffe, 2002) and co-editor of *Supervision and Support in Primary Care* (Radcliffe, 2003).

Sue Rendall worked as a secondary school teacher for 10 years and as an Educational Psychologist in three different LEAs before taking up her present post as Consultant Child and Educational Psychologist in the Child and Family Department at the Tavistock and Portman NHS Trust, London, where she is also Course Director of Educational Psychology Professional Training and Vice Dean of Postgraduate Training.

Margaret Rustin is a Consultant Child and Adolescent Psychotherapist at the Tavistock Clinic, London. She has written widely on child psychotherapeutic practice, co-editing and contributing to *Closely Observed Infants* (1989), *Psychotic States in Children* (1997) and *Assessment in Child Psychotherapy* (2000). She is co-author, with Michael Rustin, of *Narratives of Love and Loss: Studies in Modern Children's Fiction* (1987/2001) and *Mirror to Nature: Drama, Psychoanalysis and Society* (2002).

Michael Rustin is Professor of Sociology at the University of East London, and a Visiting Professor at the Tavistock Clinic, London. He has written widely on psychoanalytic topics. He is author of *The Good Society and the Inner World* (1991), and *Reason and Unreason: Psychoanalysis, Science and Politics* (2001).

Gerrilyn Smith is a Consultant Clinical Psychologist and Systemic Psychotherapist. She heads up the Child and Adolescent Mental Health Services for Looked After Children in Liverpool which is based at Alder Hey Hospital. The chapter in this book reflects work she carried out while working at the Tavistock Clinic, London, much of it based in Haringey Child and Adolescent Mental Health Services.

Judith Trowell is the Project Director for the Childhood Depression Study, an ERC-funded study across London, Athens and Helsinki. This is part of her research and training activity arising from a long career of CAMHS clinical work, and she is now working in the West Midlands as Professor of Child Mental Health as well as at the Tavistock Clinic, London as a consultant psychiatrist.

Arlene Vetere, PhD, AcSS, is a Consultant Clinical Psychologist, and Family Systemic Psychotherapist, UKCP Registered, with Berkshire Healthcare Trust. She is Deputy Director of the Clinical Psychology Doctorate at Surrey University, Guildford, UK. Arlene chairs the Academic Research Committee for the UK Association for Family Therapy, and chairs the National Family Therapy Organisations Board of the European Family Therapy Association.

Patsy Wagner is lead practitioner and Principal Educational Psychologist of a London Education Psychology service which operates a consultation model based on interactionist, solution-focused and systemic perspectives. Narrative work informs her thinking and practice of working with schools, teachers, pupils, families, other professionals and the local education authority where she works. She is accomplished in classical equitation.

Chris Watkins has been an educator for 30 years, and is now leader of the MA in Effective Learning at the University of London Institute of Education. He uses narrative perspectives in professional practice, in understanding learning and in approaches to research. He is a legend in his own living room for lying under Land Rovers.

Jim Wilson is Consultant Family Therapist with Gwent Health Care Trust (sessional). He is Staff Training and Development Consultant for Foster Care Associates and Co-Director of Partners for Collaborative Solutions, an international training and consultation organisation.

Bernadette Wren is Consultant Clinical Psychologist in the Child and Family Department, Tavistock Clinic, London, and Systemic Psychotherapy Research Teacher and Supervisor at the University of East London. She co-chairs the UEL-Tavistock Doctorate in Systemic Psychotherapy and works clinically with families where a parent has mental illness. She is the Editor of *Clinical Child Psychology and Psychiatry*, an international peer-review journal.

Foreword

Charlotte Burck

This is a very timely book. The editors have conceived its task as elaborating ways in which systemic and narratives theories enhance each other in work with children and their families. In order to do so, they have gathered together a range of experienced and skilled practitioners who draw on and combine both theoretical traditions in their work. The result is a volume which addresses significant absences and gaps in the literature of therapeutic work with children, offering vivid examples of trustworthy treatment approaches for the mental health and social care services.

Just as systemic family therapy approaches profoundly changed psychological and psychiatric treatments for children and their families in the 1960s and 1970s, narrative approaches brought energising radical perspectives to the systemic field in the late 1980s, generating enormous clinical creativity. However, accounts of mutual recriminations in the literature between the systemic and narrative approaches led to tension and standoff between them. These have included among others, a critique of the loss of an interactional and family focus in the narrative approaches (Minuchin 1998) and criticism of the neglect of power within systemic approaches (White and Epston 1989). This rather unhelpful polarisation between systemic and narrative approaches contributed to a paucity of writing in which 'narrative-systemic' approaches were developed. This is one of the gaps this book tackles: the clinicians gathered here have, in Bertrando's (2000) phrase, focused on both text and context – they work with narratives within the complex texture of their relational contexts.

The clinicians who present their work in this volume are united in their ability to 'work' the tensions between systemic and narrative theoretical frameworks in their practice. This allows us to experience the richness of clinical strategies of hybridisation. These engagements between narrative and systemic ways of thinking and practice encourage the possibilities of other encounters across difference – the ability to create hybridisations where neither perspective is disqualified or omitted which belie the blandness so often associated with concepts such as eclecticism.

However, it is the placing of children centrally in their relational contexts, fore-fronting their voices, their play, their dilemmas, their stories, which will, in my view, ensure that this book makes a significant contribution to professionals working with children in whatever setting. As the editors point out, there has been a surprising paucity of texts on working with children in the systemic and narrative approaches. Children's voices so easily get lost in the work and in the literature. In these authors' theoretical and clinical approaches, children claim their place as active agents.

The seduction of narrative, of stories, is to capture us through and in language, and as Gerrilyn Smith, one of the authors, notes 'children and stories go together'. These clinicians offer many examples of ways in which they engage with children's stories. However children also privilege other modalities of communication and invite family members as well as clinicians to pay attention to their embodiment. Authors remind us of these rich resources – play, theatre, puppets, drawing and photographs – through which they develop understanding and generate alternative perspectives collaboratively with children and their parents and carers.

What many of these clinicians do so well in describing their clinical work is to demonstrate the complexities involved in supporting and privileging children's ways of expressing themselves, alongside keeping their parent/s or carers engaged in therapeutic ways, particularly when children's narratives 'trouble' adults' perspectives and positions. The ability to elicit children's perspectives safely, utilising the interrelatedness between play and serious-ness, is elaborated in many of these chapters. Work with children highlights most starkly issues of power – the inequalities of age difference – in families and in therapy. It is the acknowledgement of differences of perspectives and the ability to work across them, to interweave these narratives in ways that do not perpetuate the inequities between adults and children, which is so well addressed here. These are illustrations of clinical work striving to be 'dialogi-cal' in theory as well as in practice. Here too particular attention is paid to the interconnectedness of the personal and social for which the systemic and narrative approaches, separately as well as in combination, are noted.

The authors have developed their theoretical approaches in working with children in troubled circumstances in a wide range of different settings, not only in child and adolescent mental health services, but also in youth offending teams, primary care, schools, and for the court, among others. The contexts within which these children live include those of parental mental illness, of divorce, of foster families, of violence within family and of war. To have access to such a variety of practice should itself inspire the reader to further develop their own work with children.

Included here is luminous writing of skilled and inspiring clinical work, which is moving and emotional as well as rigorously underpinned by a theor-etical framework. Many of these writers offer vivid case examples and specific therapeutic interventions juxtaposed with clear consideration of the contexts in which they are engaging with children and their families. There are also chapters in which authors have distilled and condensed guidelines from their own work to aid other professionals. The book therefore invites practitioners to be influenced on a number of different levels – those who are inspired by witnessing others' work, communicated as nuanced, sometimes poetic accounts of clinical encounters, as well as those who privilege principles derived from evidence-based accounts.

Children on the whole call on us to use more aspects of ourselves, personally and professionally as clinicians, than adults do. What this book achieves on their behalf is to provide fine examples of work – provocations for us to take up these invitations.

Acknowledgements

We would like to thank all the contributors for making this book possible, the many colleagues and trainees who have inspired us with their ideas and the families we have worked with, who have taught us so much by sharing their dilemmas and strengths with us. Our special thanks go to Kathryn Middleweek for her invaluable help in keeping track of the various drafts and acting as an anchor point for all the contributions. To Graham McManus for his painstaking checking of references and inconsistencies throughout. To John Dowling for his continuous support and encouragement, and last but not least, to Mike Coombs who started the conversation about this book.

Arlene Vetere and Emilia Dowling

Introduction

Arlene Vetere and Emilia Dowling

'Stories are our dreams, really. That's why we tell stories. They're what makes us interesting and what connects us with one another.'

(Ewan McGregor in *Big Fish*, the film)

Why we think this book needed to be written

This book represents our attempt to bring together the richness and variety of the application of narrative ideas to the work of professionals in the child and family mental health field. Our particular interest as editors is to highlight the ways in which the different uses of narrative can be applied to work with children and families and to explore the specific connections between narrative ideas and systemic practice.

The use of narrative has been of common interest to all psychotherapeutic modalities: that is, a central tenet of therapeutic work has been an interest in stories, accounts, narratives, and biographies. However, as Sween (1999) points out, different types of psychotherapy focus on different aspects of life as the unit of experience. Therefore the emphasis will vary according to the therapeutic approach. Behaviour will be the focus in behaviour therapy, cognition in cognitive therapy, the connections between current and early experiences in psychoanalytic psychotherapy, while systemic therapy will emphasise relationships and interactions – essentially what takes place between people.

The family systems field, broadly speaking, has tried to link social and individual accounts and experiences of distress, such that consideration can be given to the interaction between personal accounts, wider social discourses, and relationships. Although the use of stories in therapy is not new, the emergence of the narrative approaches is characterised by the commitment to focus on the meaning these narratives have for the client, that is, their actual lived experience in describing their own story. Epston *et al.* (2002: 97) define story as

> a unit of meaning that provides a frame for lived experience. It is through these stories that lived experience is interpreted. We enter into stories;

we are entered into stories by others; and we live our lives through these stories. Stories enable persons to link aspects of their experience through the dimension of time . . . it is through stories that we obtain a sense of our lives changing.

In the context of individual psychotherapy with adults, McLeod (1997) has summarised three main elements to the narrative approach: (1) it is the way in which the client's early life story is told which is of significance; (2) the constructs through which the person makes sense of their world are structured through the use of stories; and (3) the therapist–client encounter involves constructing a new story, often called 're-authoring', which is compelling and useful for the client. This is an attempt to foreground the client's story over and above therapy theory, where theory is used in the service of the co-construction of new meanings and understandings, rather than driving the therapy conversation as such. In this approach we work with the client's story, the therapist's story and the story of the therapy itself. Systemically speaking we would pay attention to the interaction between these stories, and when working with family groups, we can see the potential for multiple interactions, both within and outwith the therapeutic system. Rudi Dallos, in his book, *Interacting Stories* (1997), explores the therapeutic potential of the rapprochement between constructivism and systemic thinking and practice.

Within the narrative and systemic approaches, people are seen as culturally embedded, which helps us view therapeutic practices as cultural practices. For us, this means that therapists will bring their own stories into the therapeutic encounter, which has special significance for our therapeutic work with children and families. The variety of stories that can be co-constructed within the therapeutic setting offers different perspectives, and helps people create some psychological distance, or space for reflection, in the face of overwhelming emotional experiences. Within the family systems field, as with many other psychotherapeutic approaches, the opportunity to develop a thoughtful approach to life's dilemmas, and to harness resources and strengths, has long been appreciated. What we wish to focus on in this edited collection is how we are developing these ideas in relation to our work with children and young people and their families. Thus we hope to emphasise the child's point of view, how to elicit their stories and understandings, to promote their contribution to the development of new meanings, while not losing sight of the embodied nature of experience, and the importance of nonverbal communication in relationships, including the value of observation and play in the therapeutic encounter.

What this book offers – multiple meanings and multiple perspectives

A systemic narrative approach, in our view, attempts to combine the listening to different stories and the gathering of the multiple perspectives on a situation with promoting interactions between the participants, encouraging them to co-create new realities through the therapeutic conversation. If social realities can be said to be constructed through language in interaction, the therapeutic milieu can be an ideal arena to develop new and richer stories, incorporating the common as well as the particular themes. Diversity is contained within stories as much as between them. Our task is to explore how children and their parents or carers may approach some common problems within different and shared perspectives, while always trying to keep our curiosity alive, as Cecchin (1987) would say! This book represents different authors' approaches to the task of exploring childhood experiences, something that is close and personal to them, yet cannot be taken for granted in others. 'On being a stranger in your own land' could have been an alternative title for this book!

We have organised the work in four parts. In Part I, Chapter 1 provides an introductory framework to the use of narrative approaches in Child and Family Mental Health work. For the other chapters in this work, we feel privileged to have been able to bring together the contributions of very experienced practitioners who have described the application of narrative ideas to the specific context of their work. As all authors draw heavily on their clinical experience, all case material has been anonymised and names and details have been changed in order to preserve confidentiality.

Part II is about 'Narratives of childhood'. It begins with Margaret and Michael Rustin's chapter exploring the intimate connections between narrative theory, systemic family therapy and psychoanalysis. In Chapter 3 David Campbell and Judith Trowell examine the benefits of narrative-based approaches informed by both systemic and psychoanalytic perspectives in the treatment of childhood depression. Gerrylin Smith (Chapter 4) gives a moving account of her work with traumatised children and Arlene Vetere and Jan Cooper (Chapter 5) describe their work with children who have witnessed violence in the home. Part II ends with Chapter 6 by Jim Wilson, describing his creative approaches to the engagement of children in the therapeutic process.

Part III, 'Narratives of working with families', focuses on the application of narrative ideas to work with particular family constellations and situations. Sebastian Kraemer's chapter on the relationship between fathers and sons (Chapter 7) is followed by Gwyn Daniel and Bernadette Wren's description of the dilemmas for children living with parents with a diagnosis of mental illness (Chapter 8). They document the use of narrative in working with young carers' support groups. Sara Barratt and Rita Harris's chapter illustrates the way in which narrative approaches help children in fostering and adoptive families to maintain and make sense of their connections to multiple families (Chapter 9). Part III ends with Chapter 10 by Myrna Gower, Emilia Dowling and Irvine Gersch on parenting adult children, an under-represented topic in the systemic family therapy literature.

Part IV of the book refers to 'Narratives in Special Contexts'. In Chapter 11 Kirsten Blow and Gwyn Daniel address the complexities of working with children involved in contact disputes, and Gill Gorell Barnes (Chapter 12) describes a novel way of using clinical skills in the legal context when providing assessments for the courts in situations where violence has been part of the proceedings. John Launer (Chapter 13) describes the application of narrative ideas in the primary care context and in Chapter 14 Rudi Dallos illustrates the use of a narrative approach by a Youth Offending Team. Patsy Wagner and Chris Watkins (Chapter 15) focus on the use of narrative in the educational context and Sue Rendall (Chapter 16) documents the narratives of pupils, parents and teachers in relation to permanent exclusion from school. In Chapter 17 Alan Carr describes work from a 'positive psychology' point of view in working with families when other contexts might have lost hope.

Part I

Narrative concepts and therapeutic challenges

Chapter 1

Narrative concepts and therapeutic challenges

Emilia Dowling and Arlene Vetere

Putting the family back into narrative work

The family therapy field has recognised it is sometimes not enough to expect children's problems to change just because the systemic meaning for the family has been addressed, or because the parents have been helped with their problems. 'Playful' approaches that directly focus on the child's problem have been developed within the narrative therapy approaches to balance earlier systemic practices that may have risked ignoring the child's perspective. Balance, though, is the key word for us. Now the field has recognised the need for direct work with children, and the potential for working with children's stories, it is important not to throw out earlier systemic ideas and approaches (Vetere and Dallos 2003). The systemic paradigm enabled us to shift the focus from intra-psychic pathology to interpersonal relationships and their contexts. Conceptualising people's difficulties in terms of patterns of interaction has been one of the most productive contributions of systemic thinking to the understanding and re-construction of mental health problems. The recognition that different levels of context can give different meanings to behaviour and relationships helped us think about wider social and cultural influences on people and their relationships, while also considering how relationships themselves can change lived experience and influence more widely held beliefs.

Children's problems are often not theirs alone! The systemic adage that children's behaviour is reactive to their social and interpersonal contexts and that problems can be directly related to other stresses in the family is still helpful to us in understanding how problems arise and where solutions might lie. Children can be said to learn ways of managing anxiety and coping within family systems, and family members may be involved in creating anxieties, for example, where a child is worried about the well-being of a parent, or where a child is frightened and at risk of direct harm in the family.

Systemically speaking, family groups, households and extended kin members filter wider cultural messages to children, and provide the context in which these cultural influences are understood and given meaning. The systemic tenet of paying attention to the interpersonal context in which the problem behaviour occurs may have been forgotten or at least marginalised within the narrative therapy literature. We believe it is important to bring this back and incorporate it into the dominant discourse of therapy. Sal Minuchin in his seminal paper, 'Where is the Family in Narrative Family Therapy' (1998) raises important questions, arguing that as narrative therapy highlights context and culture, paradoxically the theory seems to have misplaced the family and returned to a focus on the individual. Questioning what the losses are, he asks:

> What are they shedding? First, the observation of dialogues among family members and their effects on interpersonal patterns. Second, the spontaneous and induced enactments that transform a session into a live scenario . . . Third, a recognition of the therapist's knowledge as a positive force for healing.
>
> (Minuchin 1998: 403)

When using a narrative approach as the focus of the therapeutic encounter, we must be aware that we might be returning to that individual focus on the story from one person's perspective, and that decisions about who we see might mean who we listen to and therefore whose voice might remain unheard. A particular danger for therapists might be the temptation to privilege adult over children's voices. For example, George was referred by the school for being 'aggressive', after repeated attempts on their part to discuss the situations with the parents. The contact between the school and the family had fallen into a pattern whereby the teachers presented the parents with complaints about George's aggressive behaviour both in the classroom and in the playground. George's stepfather would get enraged by the complaints and would arrive home to give George a thrashing for misbehaving at school. This had led to paralysis in the teachers who worried about the consequences for George if they communicated their concern to the parents. Communication between the family and the school had virtually ceased.

A family–school meeting was set up to try to 'widen' the narrative about George in the family and school context. When his mother was asked if George was good at anything, she described how artistic he was and how he used to love drawing with his father who is an architect. Not any more though – his parents are separated and George's contact with him is very erratic. One of the teachers confirmed how she had seen these abilities in George during design and technology lessons and wondered whether it might be possible for George to re-connect with his father. With these new elements to enrich the story about George's aggression it was possible to begin to make connections between his angry outbursts and the feeling of loss of his father. The teachers showed an interest in engaging George in tasks which could develop his artistic talent, and his mother and stepfather, in the light of new understanding about George's behaviour, were able to take active steps to promote contact between George and his father on a more regular basis.

The family systems field has helped us focus on family members' strengths – often success in therapy involves tapping into family resources (social, behavioural and psychological). In our view this process involves both thinking and action, within a feedback process that helps us fine-tune our responses towards desired ends. Narrative therapists, for example, work on 'discovering' children's abilities in the face of serious and distressing problems, and in the face of problem-saturated stories. Freeman *et al.* (1997) give some examples of what we think are excellent facilitating questions to ask about children: 'If I were shipwrecked on a desert island with your son/ daughter, what would I come to respect about him/her? What would I come to depend on him/her for as time went by?' However, where we think the narrative approaches have parted company with systemic thinking is in the understanding of emotional experience and the emphasis on interpersonal process. A social constructionist view of emotions is that the emotions that are described in therapy acquire their meanings by being situated within a narrative plot. While we agree with this, and also agree that a task of therapy is to bring a language to experience, we think there is more to it. Emotions, for us, go beyond words. They are embodied experiences and can be profoundly interpersonal, such as in attachment relationships, and in therapeutic relationships.

Anderson and Levin (1997) talk about multiple co-existing stories where therapists and clients, adults and children are equal contributors in a collaborative therapeutic approach. This does not mean that there are no contradictions or discrepancies: 'New meaning occurs as thoughts are expressed, clarified and expanded. As each person talks others listen. Outer and inner dialogues occur simultaneously and overlap' (Anderson and Levin 1997: 266). Refreshingly, they take an interactional perspective of narratives co-evolving in conversation: 'Any narrative, therefore that may be attributed to someone is not that person's internal property but rather a social, multiple voiced and dynamic product' (p. 276).

Challenging the dominant discourse of 'separation' in adolescence, Weingarten (1997) invites parents and young people together, giving the message that they can benefit from listening to each other's perspective and be a resource for each other. A basic premise of family therapy revisited.

We understand the social constructionist position on language to be that it constructs the means by which thoughts, feelings and behaviours are produced, and because these are all historically and culturally situated, they are not seen as static truths (Gergen and Kaye 1992). For us, the systemic position is crucial in our thinking and practice; that words and language derive meaning from the relational contexts in which they are used. Systemically speaking, meanings and words and their use in language are iteratively constructed over time, mutually influenced by the richness of nonverbal communications in relationships. We would suggest that social construction-ist narrative approaches have helped systemic practitioners stay light on their toes in relation to theory and observation, but that without systemic think-ing, the ideas contained within social constructionist narrative approaches lack practical application. Thus, for us, a rapprochement between systemic thinking and practice and the critical perspectives of narrative-based social constructionist approaches, offers a solid, ethically accountable base for our practice.

In concluding this section, we have some concern that the recent 'turn to narrative', so to speak, runs the risk of losing sight of some of the benefits of a systemic approach to thinking and practice. However, we think the narrative approach to exploring children's stories in therapy, as espoused by White and Epston (1990), can be made systemic. Vetere and Dallos (2003) outline three ways in which this can be achieved: (1) by exploring the connections between the beliefs and stories about relationships and events from everyone involved in the network of concern; (2) by generating multi-perspectives about these events; and (3) by exploring the fit between older and more current stories or accounts about self, others, events and the connections between them. When moving beyond therapeutic exploration of these stories, we can maintain our systemic focus in the co-construction of new stories, by: (1) exploring children's and family members' preferred ideas about events and relationships; (2) sharing our professional knowledge to support these good ideas; (3) encouraging further reflection on the fit between the different ideas generated from different perspectives; (4) addressing the relational and psychological implications of these preferred ideas; and (5) exploring the implications for action (Fredman 1997).

A hierarchy of discourses?

The stance the narrator takes in relation to the story

When working with children and families, mental health professionals are called to intervene when someone in the relational system is concerned about one of their members. The concern may come from school if a child is not performing or is exhibiting behavioural difficulties, from a GP or social ser-vices if there are concerns about the child's physical or emotional welfare, or family members themselves may wish to consult about their own concerns about family functioning. In exploring these concerns, professionals informed by narrative ideas will help their clients to identify a range of stories that will help to widen the narrative, which is often initially presented as a problem-oriented dominant story.

Altschuler (2002) in her work with families and chronic illness, quoting

Zimmerman and Beaudoin (2002), summarises the narrative approach as one where:

- The client's experience is privileged over that of the therapist or referrer in defining the problem;
- Questions are asked to separate the client from the influence of the problem story;
- Emphasis is placed on exception: current and past experiences that contradict the problem story are noticed;
- Subsequent questions explore the meaning of these less noticed experiences, with the goal of helping clients re-author an alternate story so that it becomes more influential than the problem story (pp. 12–16).

The key question however, when working with families, is *whose story remains the dominant one*, and how do we as professionals enable the less powerful members of the family, often the children, to contribute to or even challenge the dominant story as told by the adults. Fredman (2002) describes her narrative approach as participating in the 'co-creation of preferred stories with people that have a good enough fit with their lived experience and are meaningful and coherent for themselves and those in significant relationship with them'. The question for us in Child and Family Mental Health must be, how are we able to incorporate the children's perspective, enabling their voices to be heard?

Gorell Barnes and Dowling (1997) describe their work with families during and in the aftermath of divorce as the telling and re-telling of different stories, allowing different voices to be heard. These stories, maybe initially conflict laden, often full of resentment and hostility, gradually evolve and thicken to incorporate positive elements and affectionate memories often produced by the children when their voice is helped to emerge. This can result in a re-writing of the story in a way that permits a more balanced and therefore more coherent account of the lived experience, allowing family members to move on to develop a new story of the family in its current form.

Who are the other participants?

Professionals working with families are often faced with the dilemma about whose voice is privileged over whom. Is it the referrer's who emphasises the 'index' patient's need for 'treatment' because of his or her 'problems'? When making basic decisions about who to invite to a first session are we implicitly silencing or marginalising those who are not asked to attend? Might an older brother deemed to 'have left home and therefore not involved' not have some crucial stories to tell about his relationship with the younger sibling 'in trouble'? The meaning of the problem behaviour from his perspective might contribute to a much richer understanding of the young person's difficulties.

A decision by a professional to work with a family presenting a child with a school-based problem might leave out a crucial voice, the teacher, or even when a teacher is included, what about the head teacher or other members of the school community such as peers, teaching assistants, and so on. The list is endless and it would be totally impractical for mental health professionals to include everyone in their work. But we must be aware of those voices we are not hearing, of those stories that remain untold and therefore are marginalised from the emerging dominant story.

An example of narrative and post-divorce work

In the course of work with families post-separation and divorce, Dowling and Gorell Barnes (2000) describe as a therapeutic goal, helping the family to co-construct an ongoing overall post-divorce family narrative. This would allow the acknowledgement of different views of equal validity, without marginalising or privileging any one version. The hope is that children would no longer be required to falsify their own experience in the service of each parent's reality. They pay particular attention to the child's voice, knowing from clinical experience how often children are required to privilege other views above their own. The work involves developing richer narratives of the family experiences, including positive as well as negative elements of the relationships, and emphasising the ongoing importance of parent–child relationships even if the marital relationship has come to an end. For the parents it is important to develop a new narrative of a co-parenting relationship in the service of the children.

In the course of the work they identified three main groups of parental relationship narratives:

> The first grouping contains ongoing conflict laden relationships, which include narratives that disqualify the child's experience in favour of a personal slant preferred by one parent. The children have to develop parallel narratives to 'fit' with each parent and are left with a loyalty dilemma as to which to believe and therefore whom to please. A higher order organising construct of their experience becomes 'not to upset the other parent'.

> The second group lacks narratives and denies the children in the family a right to a story. The main features of this group are:
> a)   An intransigent silence involving a refusal to talk about areas of the child's experience that relate to the other parent.
> b)   A refusal to clarify or develop explanations for the child about the processes taking place around them. The absence of shared meaning between parent and child about their daily lived experience and the falsification of family memory contribute to unmanageable confusion in the child's mind.

The third grouping consists of parents who have remained entangled with their spouses, preoccupied with the care offered to the child by the other parent. Stories may be full of reproach and the ongoing desire to reform the other and 'convert' them to the view of the storyteller. The children take on the task of keeping conflict at bay, filtering information from one parent to the other in order to keep the peace. This requires a considerable amount of mental energy, which may result in difficulties to concentrate and learn at school. Their own wishes and views become submerged.

(Gorell Barnes and Dowling 1997: 185)

Gorell Barnes and Dowling draw attention to two important conclusions arising from their work in relation to the hope of arriving at a collective coherent story. First, the recognition that some parents' stories are irreconcilable. Second, coherence itself as an attribute of post-divorce experience may not be an appropriate metaphor given the complexities of the different emerging narratives. Therefore it seems more useful to talk about 'multiple stories'; coherence in this context refers to the parents' joint wish to do the best for their children.

Bringing forth the voice of the child

'Childhood is a negotiated process where children are active in constructing their own social worlds, and reflecting upon and understanding its meaning and significance to their own personal lives' (France *et al.* 2000: 151). As practitioners we are interested in learning from children. More recently, as we have realised that adult preconceptions of children might say more about the adults than the children themselves, we have sought children's accounts of their experiences directly from them. This bringing forth the voice of the child is part of a greater emphasis within clinical practice and clinical research on children's participatory roles. It is seen by many as an ethical position that challenges practices of 'othering' (Kitzinger and Wilkinson 1996) and enables us to be better informed about children's issues and how they understand them.

Mullender and her colleagues (2002) argue that a deficit model of developmental psychology has led to the marginalisation of children as a source of information about their own lives. Traditional developmental theories, they argue, conceptualise children as 'growing up into the adult world' as if they are somehow incomplete, or not yet competent because of their maturational stage. They suggest that child care policies and practices could be enriched if children were consulted around the design and delivery of services. Their research, interviewing children of junior and secondary school age, about the effects of living with domestic violence, presents us with an example of how children's experiences of active coping under duress can be used both to challenge and to direct statutory and voluntary service interventions for children and their families.

Within this participatory model, children are seen as agents, actively constructing meanings about what happens to them, and what might happen to them, much as Kelly (1955) suggested adults do! Thus the confluence of biological maturation, social and cultural influences and children's search for meaning forms the platform on which we explain ourselves to children and involve them in decision making that affects them and their families.

What happened to the voice of the child in family therapy practice?

Our task is to help and support children and their families in dealing with serious problems – how to encourage children and young people to make a contribution to the family work, so all are equally engaged? Yet it would seem that, despite our best efforts, a few studies are suggesting that we do not always find ways to involve the children in the work, in a meaningful way for them. For example, Cederborg (1997), working in a Swedish child psychiatry clinic, used a word space analysis to analyse the video tapes of family therapy sessions with seven families. She found that children produced 3.5 per cent of the words spoken during the sessions, with parents speaking for 56 per cent of the time, and therapists for 37.5 per cent. Similarly, Mas *et al.* (1985) found that children spoke far less often than their parents and, when they did speak, tended to express themselves in terms of agreement or disagreement. Dowling (1979) in her research on therapists' behaviour in family therapy found that, although therapists considered 'bringing in' the children highly desirable, in practice this particular behaviour was rarely displayed in family sessions.

Vetere and Dallos (2003) recently reviewed studies that surveyed how the needs and views of children were included in family-oriented services and approaches. Their conclusions were simple: involve the children in the therapy, and find ways of engaging them with the use of activities, games and tasks! For example, Strickland-Clark and her colleagues (2000) interviewed a small sample of children, immediately following their family therapy sessions, and asked them about their experiences of helpful and unhelpful events during the therapy. Some major themes emerged from the analyses, such as valuing being heard and being included in the therapy process, as well as being pleased to be asked for their views by the researchers! In particular, the children told the researchers how difficult it was for them if they thought they were not being listened to, their worries about saying the wrong things, and their apprehension about coming to the therapy if they thought it was designed to reprimand them for bad behaviour. Similarly, Stith *et al.* (1996) asked children about their experiences of therapy and what helped them settle. They found that children appreciated child-centred activities that directly involved them, open discussion of family difficulties that affected them directly, and when a screen and team were used, a proper explanation of the process, and active participation of the team in the therapy.

Some ethical concerns?

What are *our* responsibilities as therapists to children and parents in family work (Combrinck-Graham 1985)? How do we agree the rules for conduct in therapeutic sessions, and how and to what extent are limits consistently enforced? Who gives consent to therapeutic work? Do children and young people give consent or assent?

Have we been too reliant on words and questioning in our systemic practice and when working with families? Is spoken language the main communicative medium for children? What about adolescents? We often use genograms in our practice, as ways of both getting to know the family and their culture, and helping people engage with the work. We think genograms are very good in helping to focus their attention, especially when the adolescents are involved directly in constructing them and hearing stories about their parents as children. A visual medium can help make words meaningful, and develop coherence in narratives in such a way that elicits curiosity about what happened, and why that might be relevant for now.

What contexts influence how we talk to children?

Kirsten Blow (1994) identifies several factors that may influence how we as practitioners think about children, how we talk with them, what we ask them, and how we make sense of their issues. These factors may have a profound effect on the therapeutic context of safety that we create for children and their families.

Our theories of child development, moral development and attachment and resilience

When working with children's narratives, therapists adapt their style to the developmental stage of the child – augmenting words with images and drawings, using objects, showing through behaviour and paying careful attention to the child's nonverbal behaviour as an important means of communication. Rober (1998) suggests asking a child to bring an object to the therapy session that can help the therapist understand who they are. Often, talking and looking at these objects, opens up opportunities for children and their parents to tell stories that have not yet been told.

Sanders (1985) writes about her systemic work with younger children and their families, in an article entitled, ' "Now I see the difference – the use of visual news of difference" '. She found that circular questions sometimes confused children. This made her task, to tease out a recursive understanding of interactions between children and parents, for example, too difficult. She developed the use of visual scaling questions, popular among solution-focused therapists. For example, asking children and other family members to place an X on a line with two polar opposites at either end, to indicate behavioural progress at each meeting, or how their views might change, or how they see things differently at the start of meetings. Use of these rating scales can both engage children in the therapy process, and help with setting goals and monitoring change, in a way that keeps them engaged in the process.

Barry Bowen (personal communication) in his work with children refusing to attend school, as a result of bullying, for example, would draw the home–school diagram. This is a line picture, with a house drawing at one end, connected by the journey to school, then the school yard with the school at the other end. Children are asked to indicate with an X where the problem occurs. This strategy again helps children to articulate a view early on in therapy when they might otherwise choose not to speak.

Ellen Wachtel's work on the 'language of becoming' (2001) is another example. It is a way of talking with children that helps them see themselves as constantly changing, and helps parents notice and reflect back the specific ways the child is 'becoming'. For example, 'you are becoming better able to control your temper' means the parent is choosing to focus on the child calming down and the ways they achieved that, *more* than on the loss of control and temper outburst that preceded it. She suggests this is liberating for parents too as it helps them pay attention to desired outcomes and reinforce desired behaviours. Parents are not value free in this project! Children are believed to look to parents for judgements about what is and is not valued. It seems to us this approach builds on good behavioural work with parents and develops further the idea that personality is evolving and there is some choice over behaviour. Wachtel thinks this helps break vicious circles of self-fulfilling prophecies, self-perpetuating beliefs, mutually reinforcing negative cycles of behaviour and belief and, as such, needs to be grounded in understanding the stages of a child's cognitive development, such as the construction of beliefs about self, causation, and so on.

The key question in therapy is how to encourage and strengthen new ways of acting. New narratives about the self are thought to be more likely to take hold if there is some evidence that supports the new perspective, or if they chime with some aspect of self-perception already developed. Developmental theorists have put forward ideas that can guide our work with children here. Susan Harter (1999) argues that 'because the self is a cognitive construction, the particular cognitive abilities and limitations of each developmental period will represent the template that dictates the features of the self-portrait to be crafted'. Mead (1934) put forward the view that from a very early age, children discover their 'self' by what is reflected back from parents/carers, as if 'seeing' yourself through the eyes of others – the 'I' and the 'me'. Winnicott (1971) developed the metaphor of mirroring in child development, for example, the young child babbles with delight at something and the parent/ carer who is sensitively attuned, interprets their pleasure with words, ascribing meaning to the child's experience.

Piaget (1977) and Harter (1999) summarise some aspects of child cognitive development in stages. For example, the preschool child aged about 3–5 may describe their self in terms of concrete observations, perhaps about preferences and possessions. The child in the age group of about 5–7 is learning to categorise and represent objects and ideas. The older child, aged about 7–11 is learning to think in terms of higher order categorisations and to describe their self in terms of personality attributes. Unlike younger children, they may hold competing views of their self at once and make overall judgements about their self-worth.

Children's beliefs and knowledge about adults, for example, what adults prefer children not to say, cannot bear to hear . . .

Clinical experience in working with families post-separation and divorce shows that sometimes parents have made bids for their children's loyalty in oppositional ways, presenting persistently discrepant stories, leaving the children confused and unable to reconcile the differences imposed on them. The following is an example of such conflicting narratives.

Neil, aged 9, lived half the week with each parent after their separation. During his time with each parent, he would constantly hear denigrating stories about the other parent and the message to him was that neither parent was to be trusted to have his best interests at heart. This left him confused and angry, unable to concentrate or make friends at school.

Adult's beliefs about what is best for children, for example, during separation and divorce

Sometimes parents in the post-separation phase believe it is better to have 'a clean break' and sever contact with the out of house parent. This is particularly the case when a new partner arrives on the scene and the adult's wish is to consolidate the new family and leave behind the previous partner, not only physically but also in the minds of the children. This situation creates loyalty dilemmas for the children, who find it difficult to reconcile the different versions of their current life and delete crucial elements of their life story. The therapeutic context can provide a setting where children have the opportunity to remember, even if it is painful, and a narrative can be developed including both positive and negative experiences and memories.

For example, Mrs T consulted about her 7-year-old son Tim who was having unexplained temper tantrums and was underachieving at school. The first family interview was attended by Mrs T, Tim, and his 2-year-old sister Daphne. During the interview it became evident that Tim had a very fragmented story about family life before his father 'disappeared'. His mother believed Tim was very lucky having her father around providing a male role model for him. Tim was in a dilemma: if he insisted in enquiring about his father he would appear disloyal to his granddad whom he dearly loved. On the other hand he longed to have an explanation about his absent dad. The dominant discourse in his mother's family was 'you just get on with it'. That was certainly what her mother told her when her husband finally left after many infidelities. She now wanted Tim to 'get on with it' and do well at school. She also wished him to be easy going like Daphne. During the family sessions we worked towards co-constructing a new story that incorporated elements of getting on with it as the family had had to after the father left, but also included new opportunities to wonder about the past and feel cross and sad about it at times. As Mrs T grew stronger and more able to manage the rage and resentment she felt towards her ex-husband, she was able to differentiate between her son's feelings and her own. During a therapy session the mother helped her son compose a letter to his father, asking some of the questions she felt unable to answer. The therapeutic context provided a safe place to experiment with re-writing a story of hurt and silenced feelings. A reply came some time later and Tim brought the letter proudly to the session. We could then work on the theme of the father–son relationship developing even if the marital relationship had ended.

Power issues – children may be at the bottom of the hierarchy – they need to understand how 'upper levels' work in order to survive; children as 'parent watchers' and issues of trust and therapeutic engagement

Narrative therapists have worked hard to find ways to engage children around weighty problems and in developing a therapeutic relationship that draws on children's knowledge about themselves, and their resources. For example, they advocate beginning a therapeutic session by getting to know the child apart from the problem (Freeman *et al.* 1997). They engage parents and children in short, positive stories about the child, and then make room for parents' worries about the child. Thus the child knows we are interested in their positive side, as much as we might be interested in their difficulties and dilemmas. Freeman *et al.* have developed some lovely questions to engage children in talking about themselves and their problems, such as 'what would you like me to know about you first?', or 'what would be a more fun way of talking about this?', 'could we come up with a magic way of solving this problem you're facing?', or 'could we talk about it (or play with it) another way – can you show me with a sand picture, or by writing a story about it, or talking about it with puppets?'

In family work it is important to pay attention to the hierarchy of discourses in a family, the way in which certain stories about children's lives and parental functioning dominate over other stories, and the effects of such dominance on potential stories, which have become silenced or submerged. We find an example in work with Sophie and her family.

Sophie's parents had separated when she was 7 following a number of violent incidents from her father to her mother. Sophie vividly remembered the occasion when her father had smashed the front door and left the family home. Her mother had been traumatised by the violence and found it impossible to talk about the separation to the children in a way that could allow them to have a coherent story about their father's leaving. Instead, their questions were met with reluctance and silence. Sophie had developed aggressive behaviour at home and at school and got into frequent fights with other girls and constant arguments with her mother. During a therapy session it was possible to help Sophie make connections between her unexpressed anger towards her father and her frequent outbursts directed at others. Gradually it became possible, in the family sessions, for Sophie and her siblings to develop an understanding of the end of their parents' marital relationship. The therapeutic context provided a safe place for their mother to talk to the children about the situation, having had the opportunity to process her experiences in separate individual sessions with one of the therapists.

Our personal experiences of childhood, for example, gender issues, sibling relationships, our position in the birth order

Narrative therapy approaches, by definition, invite self-disclosure in the form of story telling, based on personal and professional experience, from the therapist. This usually conveys what a similar experience was like for the therapist, in the hope the client finds this of interest to their own learning. Both client and therapist attribute meaning to the self-disclosure which further unfolds their developing relationship. When working with children, it may be appropriate for us to tell stories from our own childhoods, those of our children, and from other children and families we have known. Family therapists who work with intergenerational relationships will often ask how parents dealt with similar dilemmas in their own childhoods (when relevant), or how their parents/carers responded to them at times. We find children are often intrigued to be reminded their parents were young once, and like to hear how they managed and coped. For us, this serves the purpose of fostering learning across the generations, and we too play a part in this process.

For example, both authors of this chapter, AV and ED, have migrated across continents. As a child AV's experience of migration in both directions was taken for granted, and her experiences of culture clash were not openly discussed, either at school or at home. This informs her approach to working with children who migrate, and she will often refer to her experience as a way of helping children begin to explore their own reactions, for example.

ED was named after her paternal grandmother who died a few months before ED was born. The family story was that ED had been born 'baptised'. That is, there was no option but to name her after her grandmother. In the therapeutic context she is always curious to find out stories about names and their meaning for both children and parents.

How what we say to children is important, it might carry them through a difficult period

The issue here is how we help children use their imagination and their ability to play when faced with serious and distressing problems (the both/and approach, as it is sometimes called). When a statement is made by someone we like and respect, it can have a transforming effect, 'even a chance statement can take hold and have an enormous effect, such as a compliment' (Wachtel 2001: 371). Wachtel calls these statements 'emotional life preservers in stormy seas'. Narrative approaches that focus on a search for the child's competence, such as the solution-focused approaches, offer us other examples: 'If I were a "fly on the wall" of your daughter's everyday life, what would I admire about her, that only those that live with her could know?' (Selekman 1997: 44).

In our therapeutic work with children, we can help them 'name' and articulate their distress and worries, and so on, in ways that might not have been said. This challenge to the unsaid and the unsayable might unhelpfully put children under the spotlight and arouse fears of betrayal and abandonment. On the other hand, we are trying to create new meanings together that respect the pacing and sensitivities of all family members. Our attempts to place descriptions of vulnerability and madness in a context of sense rather than nonsense, for example exploring the meaningfulness in apparently 'crazy' behaviour, may be the first step in a long journey towards a more constructive view of their self. A therapeutic context that promotes the safe exploration of reciprocal meanings also helps reframe 'shaming' problems as challenges that can be faced, for all family members, not just for the child alone. The therapeutic technique of externalising has been developed for use in some narrative approaches to help separate the child from the description of their problem (White and Epston 1990). Using this technique, the child is seen in relationship to the problem, such as problems with temper, soiling, or anorexia, and other family members are recruited to help the child defeat the problem. We would sound a note of caution against the widespread application of the technique of externalising without careful assessment of the context of the problem. Externalising as a technique is not designed to explore causes for behaviour that sometimes are crucial to understand, for example, soiling as a behavioural response to sexual abuse. So, although recruiting parents and carers to help a child battle against a problem may be less pathologising and more liberating for children and parents, it may inadvertently play down the role and responsibilities of adults in creating anxieties for children.

Our views of children as learners – how do children develop a coherent story about themselves?

'What should I know your daughter has got going for her to set against the problem, whatever it may be?' Such an enquiry can pave the way for discussion of a child's strengths and resources, which may create a context in which worries can be expressed.

Sometimes it is helpful to differentiate explicitly between adult and children's concerns and free the children from a position of 'parent watchers'. In a session with an 8-year-old boy suffering from headaches and chest pains and his mother, we needed to make a list of adult worries, putting the mother in charge of those, and child worries such as homework and friends which legitimately belonged with the child and were age appropriate.

We take the view that children need to be able to express their feelings, particularly negative feelings, such as anger, disappointment and sadness about difficult experiences in family life. Parents may find it difficult to accept these expressions, as they may feel responsible for the circumstances that have contributed to the children's feelings. If feelings are not allowed to be expressed they may find a way out through psychosomatic symptoms or behavioural difficulties (Wood 1988). Alternatively a child's ability to concentrate and pay attention may be overtaxed by demands in the family and any unexpressed worries. We find an example in the context of domestic violence, where a child's ability to learn can be temporarily impaired (Koenen *et al.* 2003).

Some useful techniques

Interviewing children

It is essential when interviewing children on their own to create a context in which children feel safe and therefore free to talk about their thoughts and feelings. In systemic work, individual interviews take place as part of the overall work with the family, therefore it is important to make clear to the children that the individual interview is an opportunity to explore their worries and find ways, with the help of the therapist, to convey these worries to the parents and work towards solutions in the family context. Children are seen with their parents or carers in the first instance and an age appropriate explanation of the purpose of the individual interview is offered if the children are going to be seen on their own. With all children, but especially with younger ones, it is important to make sure that they are clear about the boundaries of the interview: where it will take place, for how long, where the parent will be and how they can be reached should the child become distressed. In our practice we encourage parents to remain available rather than leave the premises as this can create anxieties in the children. It is important that the children are clear that the therapist will help them articulate their anxieties, worries, fears and hopes and enables their voice to be heard back in the context of the family session.

Children and parents need to be clear that the information obtained in the interview will be used with the parents *in order to make the children's life better*. This may cause initial anxiety and the professional concerned will have to explain fully that they are acting on the children's behalf. In our experience, most children feel relieved that a responsible adult is going to help them voice their worries, or do it on their behalf, until they feel ready to do it themselves (Dowling and Gorell Barnes 2000).

Use of play in therapy

In systemic work, play is seen as the place where children and adults meet, where it is possible to suspend a too quick search for meaning and just play with the things children bring to therapy (Rober 1998). According to Andolfi *et al.* (1989: 65), play is 'an effective tool for connecting the world of the adults, which is rich in abstract thought and words, with the world of the children, full of nonverbal expressions and concrete images'. Play is about interaction, connection, pleasure and, eventually, understanding.

In order to create safety for a child in therapy, so that play can happen, it is important to have a good working relationship with the parents or carers. Our attempts to understand how the parents have tried to make things better, and may well feel disappointed and let down, having failed themselves and the child, affirms their attempts to find solutions. For us it is important that people have tried, not that they have succeeded. We try to balance understanding and acknowledgement of their efforts with drawing forth accounts of resilience and earlier attempts at problem solving. Such an approach privileges the therapeutic relationship and draws on ideas found in most child- and family-centred therapeutic approaches, so while not unique to systemic or narrative approaches, it creates a context for the development of this work.

Use of drawing in family sessions

The purpose of using drawings in the context of family therapy sessions is to provide an opportunity for children to use an alternative to words in order to communicate their thoughts and feelings. The therapist can help the family make sense of children's preoccupations as they often find it easier to communicate them in a pictorial way than to put them into words.

However we must be cautious not to impose our own interpretations, and our comments as to their meaning need to be put as a possibility rather than as a fact. The therapist's focus is to assist the child in telling a story through their picture and to help them to convey the meaning of their own story. Neutral rather than leading questions in relation to the drawings will enable the child to elaborate on what it means for them. Drawings will have a symbolic meaning which may or may not be decoded depending on the context in which the drawing is taking place and the experience and confidence of the professionals. Drawings are not necessarily a concrete representation of children's reality.

Play materials

Play materials facilitate communication with children and help professionals get a sense of the children's preoccupations. The use of dolls and farm animals can help children construct stories reflecting their state of mind and their experience of relationships. Aggressive play and negative interactions with the toys will provide some clues as to the child's range of responses to situations. Expression of aggression, lack of care, and negative interactions expressed through play with these small objects will provide clues as to what is going on in the child's mind. On the other hand, fantasy play featuring positive and caring attitudes, people or animals able to care for each other will throw light on the kind of experiences a child may have had or may long for. However, it is not always useful to feed our impressions back to the child. What is important is to *try to understand the meaning of the stories children are telling through their play*.

Story telling

Children sometimes find it easier to talk at 'one removed'. Using puppets or dolls to tell a story can be a useful way of establishing an interactive context which helps engage the children. The telling and re-telling of stories enables children to practise negotiating relationships and experimenting with managing and resolving conflict, and enables them to experience a range of emotional experiences through make-believe games. Encouraging children to develop alternative stories enables them to practise with different scenarios which lead to different outcomes. Bullying characters can be found to have a vulnerable and kinder side, fights can be followed by making up and the strong can help the weak. It is useful to ask children to imagine different endings to the story so that they may develop a sense of agency in relation to the stories they create.

Impact of working with children on the worker

An important aspect of the work with children is paying attention and making sense of the impact their communications have on workers. Children's behaviour can be irritating, attention-seeking, provoking or aggressive and workers need to be able to make sense of this behaviour in interactional terms in order to manage it. Working with children can be invigorating, fun, enjoyable and enormously satisfying. Many of us enjoy the work because we can take part in children's lives, help promote their well-being and that of their family members, and help 'untangle the developmental knot', to use Winnicott's term. But this is not always the case. We can be touched and saddened when things go wrong for children, and we all face the risk of secondary traumatisation when we listen to dreadful stories of harm and abuse, sometimes on a daily basis. An important aspect of the work with children is paying attention to and making sense of the impact their communications have on us. Irritating, attention-seeking, risk taking, provoking, or aggressive behaviour can be extremely stressful to manage and tolerate. However trying to make sense of it in interactional terms and seeing behaviour as a communication that needs to be understood can be very helpful. All of us can remember our childhoods, and we may well be parents and grandparents. The potential for personal resonance in our work with children is enormous. It is essential, therefore, to create opportunities for rest and thoughtful reflection by regular use of debriefing, supervision or peer consultation. Thus can we begin to address the emotional impact of the work on us as workers.

Part II

Narratives of childhood

Chapter 2

Narratives and phantasies

Margaret Rustin and Michael Rustin

Narratives are fundamental to the 'talking cures', whether psychoanalytic or 'systemic' in all their many variants. In these forms of psychotherapy, patients come and talk about aspects of their lives, past and present. Therapists offer a space for them to talk, listen, and in one way or another suggest fresh ways in which they can think about themselves, from reflections on what they have said, or communicated in other ways. Although the differences between psychoanalytic and family systemic traditions can, from close-up, seem very preoccupying, they are small by comparison with what divides all these 'talking cures' from those which 'objectify' human beings, and aim to change them by interventions (pharmacological or behaviour-modifying) which bypass or ignore their understandings of themselves as complex sentient beings, or as participants in ongoing conversations with themselves and others.

In this chapter, we are going to explore some of the intellectual origins of this 'narrative perspective' as it is relevant to all these 'discursive therapies'. We will note the particularly intimate connection there has been between narrative theories and systemic family therapy, and also the influence the 'cultural turn' in the social sciences has had on psychoanalysis. We will explore the similarities and differences between psychoanalytic and systemic approaches to psychotherapy, in the hope of promoting more dialogue between these actually near, but sometimes subjectively distant, clinical neighbours. Finally, we will look at the extraordinary best-selling phenomenon of J.K. Rowling's *Harry Potter* stories from the point of view of both these perspectives, to test out our suggestions about their overlapping insights into the developmental experiences of children and families.

Why narrative?

Narrative perspectives have become important in some of the social sciences, and in their practical therapeutic applications, in recent years. A shift to qualitative methods in research (of which narrative methods are one example), advocacy of attention to the 'whole person' in the health and social services, and rejection of some of the overweening claims of scientism especially in its human applications, have all contributed to this development. Although some view narrative methods as specifically 'post-modern' and 'relativist' in implication, narratives and stories are central to any process of reflection, and the therapies that are based on this. We do not see narrative as a point of contention between psychoanalytic and systemic approaches to psychotherapy.

Nevertheless, some of the enthusiasm for narrative in psychotherapeutic circles derives from the idea that it provides an alternative to the understanding of the clinical material provided by clients via theories felt to be imposed on them, as it were, from above. Imposed, perhaps, by psychoanalysts who seem to claim access to deeper truths than those accessible outside analysis, because of their belief in unconscious aspects of the mind. Advocates of narrative methods argue that they are inherently democratic, especially in contrast with classical psychoanalysis.[1] They hold that the propensity to construct narratives, including narratives about the self, is a universal one, and is the way individuals define their own particularity and uniqueness. Respect for the narratives elaborated by individuals thus carries with it respect for persons, as their authors. Insofar as therapeutic interventions provide enhanced opportunities for individuals to reflect on and reconsider the narratives they construct about their lives, they are an aid to their freedom. Therapy within families has the additional advantage that it can take note of contradictions between the narratives of different family members, and also of the fact that a role assigned to a family member in a family narrative may not be the same as the role he or she would choose for him or herself, if the question were made explicit. Narratives may be constructed and told by individuals, but their scripts usually allot parts to others who are linked to them by emotional bonds. Thus the clarification of different narrative lines, overt or covert, actual or potential, within a family, seems likely to clarify differentials of power. Therapists working with these assumptions can feel that they are doing no more than bringing out the implications of the scripts described or enacted for them by their therapeutic subjects. They can adopt the role of mediators, clarifiers, or even umpires where disagreements have to be negotiated. What they seem to dispense with is a higher-order theoretical framing of their subjects' experience, or the idea that this is likely to relieve anyone's suffering or enhance their well-being.

Narratives have a social and a cultural dimension. Individual subjects find themselves positioned by narratives which attribute capabilities, dispositions, and indeed deficits, to persons on grounds of their membership of a class or group. Narratives of class, gender and ethnicity all have the power to circumscribe the identities of individuals. Power is exercised in part through master narratives evolved by dominant groups, within whose shaping definitions individuals' own life-narratives are perforce constructed. Challenging such narratives, revealing the limits they impose on those who are assigned roles within them, has become a political dimension of narrative methods, in relation to all three of the dimensions of inequality mentioned above, and in others besides. In the social and cultural domain, the idea of narrative has thus become linked to critique, to the articulation of alternative or subordinate narratives in opposition to the narratives of the powerful. An attraction of this position is again that no higher-order theory of societal development or latent human possibility is needed to make critique possible. If an individual or a group is enabled to construct their own narrative and explore their own hopes, a condition of greater equality and justice can be expected to ensue. The interpreter or facilitator of narrative in this context takes the position of a midwife of change, not its procreator. Within the contrasting roles of 'legislators and interpreters' formulated by the sociologist Zygmunt Bauman (1987) in his critique of modernism,[2] the narrative therapist adopts the role of interpreter.

The position sketched out now has a significant place across the whole field of the psychotherapies, within the psychoanalytic field as well as the field of family therapy. It is sometimes counterposed to classical and, in Britain, particularly Kleinian psychoanalysis, which is seen as prescriptive and absolutist. By contrast the narrative or 'constructionist' perspective is held to be open-ended and pluralist, supporting clients in developing their own narratives. The distinctive quality the psychotherapist brings to this facilitating process is a trained capacity to listen, to refrain from moral judgement, and to be sensitive to the multiplicity of levels of meaning through which their clients communicate with them. A narrative view of the analytic process, drawing on Roy Schafer's (1992) and Donald Spence's (1982) ideas, casts the analyst 'in the role of helpful editor or provisional amanuensis' (Bruner 1990: 113). Adam Philips, who sees himself as outside the psychoanalytic orthodoxy, titled one of his books *Terrors and Experts* (1997), thereby linking classical psychoanalysis with other modernist projects which set out to transform human nature and society.[3]

There is no doubt that the emergence of narrative as a central idea in the lexicon of the contemporary social sciences is of great importance. It is part of a paradigm shift which has taken place, in which the difference in their methods from those of the natural sciences has been insisted on. The claims of a unified scientific methodology, seeking to establish general laws governing all phenomena, which became dominant in the earlier part of the twentieth century on the basis of a reductive atomism applied to all objects of enquiry, have been in partial retreat for many years. Both the objects of study of the sciences (their ontology) and their methods of study (their epistemology) have come to be seen to be more differentiated and variable than formerly. The historical and sociological study of the sciences has contributed to this change of perspective, since Thomas Kuhn (1962) and his successors revealed that scientific methods did not conform to a set of unitary principles, nor was the evolution of scientific ideas a linear progress towards an all-encompassing truth. Instead, scientific ideas were shown to be constructed by social actors in accordance with their various purposes, and while their findings were constrained by the properties of the objects they investigated, scientific ideas were not simply, in Richard Rorty's (1980) term, the 'mirror of nature'.

The cultural turn in the human sciences

An important dimension of this 'pluralisation' of the sciences, and a contributor to it, has been the 'cultural turn' in the social sciences. By this is meant the recognition that societies are inherently constructed through languages and symbols, and can only be understood and explained where due weight is given to their symbolic dimensions. A game of chess, to take the example cited long ago by the Wittgensteinian philosopher Peter Winch (1958), cannot be understood independently of its rules – the physics of the movement of the pieces is of little or no relevance to understanding the game. Material production, held by Marx to be the foundation of human societies, also takes place according to norms governing who is entitled to what property, and indeed why and how participants in the process of production should do what they do.[4] The behaviour of individuals can only be understood, and indeed predicted, if one understands their beliefs and desires. 'Action' rather than 'behaviour' becomes the primary object of attention and explanation.

Academic psychology was one of the last social sciences to be influenced by this change of orientation, having been previously among the most committed (along with economics) to reductive atomism and the search for laws of constant conjunction between phenomena. But in recent years a good deal of development has occurred, with approaches that give weight to norms and cultures having found a significant, if minority, place. Social constructionism and discourse theories are two of the genres the new culturalism has made possible in this discipline.

Psychoanalysis and systemic therapy have both found greater freedom and academic toleration in this more pluralist climate. This both because of the acceptance that individuals' own beliefs and states of minds are relevant data if one takes the trouble to understand them, and because of the recognition that effective methods of research must necessarily be related to the nature of the objects they are attempting to investigate. That is, one methodological size does not fit all.

The place of narrative in the cultural turn

The recognition of the role of narrative in the understanding of human lives has been a vital part of this 'cultural turn'.[5] The most important philosophical theorist of narrative, Paul Ricoeur (1984–88, 1991)[6] developed his approach as a critique of the excessive scientism of one of the spearhead doctrines of the cultural turn, namely structuralism. The new saliency of culture and media as a field of study was taken by some theorists as an opportunity to develop a new kind of science, which would reclaim this field from the grasp of the humanists. They developed methods of systematic cultural analysis drawing on semiotics and information theory among their resources. The structuralists, following the cultural anthropologist Claude Levi-Strauss, held (in the 'strong' version of this rationalist programme) that cultures were universally structured by means of binary classifications. The function of their organising myths was held to be to resolve the contradictions that these oppositions symbolically registered. They located in the long and complex narratives they studied, repeated patterns of binary opposition, such that these patterns became the essential meaning of the narratives.

For Ricoeur, however, narration has a primordial role in human lives, and narratives cannot be reduced to the recurrent manifestations of the contradictions from which they could (sometimes) be seen to be constructed. This is because in Ricoeur's view human beings necessarily live their lives in time, and organise their experience of themselves in relation to temporality and what unavoidably follows from it. Human lives are finite, ending in death, and the passage from birth to death and its various implications and symbolic analogues is central to human beings' understanding of themselves. Ricoeur, who drew on Heidegger in his account of the centrality of experience lived in time in the face of mortality, thus reasserted a kind of human-centredness to a debate about culture which was in danger of losing sight of its human subjects.[7]

Thus a weakening of the boundaries between the humanities and the sciences was taking place during the 1970s and 1980s. On the one side there was a reassertion of dimensions of meaning and action, rejecting the inappropriate sway of science in the human sphere. On the other side was a reassertion of the claims of sciences made more inclusive and powerful by their invasion of the cultural and information spheres. Ricoeur opposed this unification, holding that it mainly serves the ends of instrumental rationality and control. There remain, he argued, distinct and different modes of access to the truth, those that are scientific in form, which refer to actual entities located in space and time, and those that are imaginative, which refer to hypothetical or possible entities. There can be as much truth in fictional discourses, he argued, as in factual ones, so long as one remains clear about the different nature of their respective truths. Indeed fictional or hypothetical discourses are the means by which our world is continually imagined and reconstructed by human subjects. Ricoeur provides an impressive justification for the exploration of literature as part of psychological inquiry.[8]

The systemic and the psychoanalytic

What are the implications of this debate, and its recovery of the importance of narrative in the human sciences, for the practice of psychotherapy? In this discussion we will be considering principally psychoanalytic and systemic family therapies, and the ongoing dialogue that continues between them – for example, at the Tavistock Clinic in London where much of the work on which this book is based takes place. We are primarily interested in these two therapeutic traditions because both share the presupposition that it is meanings generated by patients themselves, in an open-ended 'therapeutic space', that are the primary focus for understanding and intervention. Both of these therapeutic approaches resist the more 'objectivist' and conventionally scientific methods of many psychological interventions (such as the widely influential cognitive behaviour therapy) on grounds that these ignore underlying structures of motivation and belief, and work instead with more segmented models of mental process in order to make possible more closely targeted kinds of intervention.

The question we wish to pose is the following: how far does an understanding of the importance of narrative – stories – to human lives differentiate systemic from psychoanalytic approaches to psychotherapy, and how far does it by contrast unify them? Or does it both unify and divide them, in different respects?

First, to the aspect of unification. By definition, the 'talking cures' are based on conversations between therapists and their clients on troubling aspects of their lives. Even though patients/clients[9] are free within this therapeutic context to talk about whatever they want, they have come for therapy, and that is what therapists aim to provide. If they are working in the public sector, therapists will be under considerable constraint to focus on this task, not least because of the pressure of waiting lists and the abundance of mental pain with which their clinics are surrounded. Uniting these perspectives is a commitment to attend to what troubles the patient, and to help him or her understand what this is, and find ways of moving beyond it.

Second, within these therapeutic practices there is a primary interest in meaning and sense-making. Both therapeutic traditions seek to enable patients and clients to reflect on aspects of their own mental process, and to achieve change through greater self-understanding. Both provide spaces within which such reflection can take place, through a dialogue with therapists. Both assign initiative to their patients in deciding what is to be the subject of conversation and reflection. They differ, however, as we shall show, in their conception of what it is most central to reflect on, and how such reflection is brought about.

Third, these two interlinked traditions are characterised by a commitment to 'therapeutic enactment' as the necessary basis for discovery, reflection and change. Each in its different way holds that some of the crucial aspects of the patients' mental experience have to be manifested and 'lived' in the consulting room, in the therapist's presence, if they are to be adequately communicated and understood. Neither systemic nor psychoanalytic psychotherapy consists merely of patients talking *with* therapists *about* some aspect of themselves, whether this is located in the past or the present, though such conversations do take place in all psychotherapeutic encounters. Psychotherapy is sometimes thought of as the recall by patients of past traumatic episodes in their lives, which are then interpreted by therapists as the source of their current difficulties. But this is not how either psychoanalytic or family therapy functions, for the most part. Instead, some aspect of the patients' mental life has to be demonstrated or enacted in the framed space of the therapy setting. It is this enactment which enables interpretation and reflection to address experience and its representations in the emotionally charged way that is necessary for understanding and change to take place. This process has a dramaturgical quality, more obviously so in the 'staging' of family therapy interactions with one-way mirrors and interruptions for reflection, but in a different way with a cast of players from the patient's 'internal world', in the case of psychoanalytic psychotherapy.[10]

In both kinds of psychotherapy, systemic and psychoanalytic, the therapist is at the same time a participant in this enactment, and its observer. In psychoanalytic psychotherapy this is through the phenomena of the transference and the counter-transference, which the psychotherapeutic setting is designed to 'produce'.[11] Psychoanalytic psychotherapists make themselves available as the 'objects' of patients' 'enactments' of their feelings and beliefs, and it is through the experience of patients' state of mind in the therapeutic encounter that they try to gain and convey an understanding of them. The transference relationship, as both observed and felt (in the 'counter-transference') is the scene of these 'enactments'.

Systemic therapists are also active participants in their therapeutic interactions, not primarily through facilitating transference-based relationships (though these must be present to a degree), but through questioning taken-for-granted beliefs and assumptions, in ensuring that all members of a family group have a voice, and through the 'dramaturgical' construction and management of the therapeutic 'setting' as a space designed for mutual learning. The ongoing discussion between family therapists, both inside the therapy room and outside it, and the 'experimental' procedure whereby interventions are considered, attempted and reviewed, is another aspect of their active role in these enactments.[12] Systemic therapists take a more interventionist role, and have more active therapeutic techniques, than psychoanalytic psychotherapists. The latter believe that access to unconscious states of mind requires that they leave patients to initiate communication for the most part, following Freud's precept of 'free association'.

A precondition for both these therapeutic approaches is the 'containment' provided by therapists. A therapeutic relationship and its setting have to be such that patients will be willing to risk the self-exposure necessary for self-understanding and change to be possible. Patients have to feel understood and accepted if they are to make good use of their therapist. 'Containment' has been most fully theorised in the psychoanalytic tradition, but its function and importance seem to be equally central to the work of systemic therapists, and indeed probably to other kinds of therapeutic intervention too, whether or not this is explicitly acknowledged.

The elements of 'enactment' (the participant observer role would be its analogue in research) in both these therapeutic traditions help to explain the distance between the procedures by which they generate and develop their knowledge-base, and that of more conventional scientific methods, which insist on the 'objectivity' and indeed 'impersonality' of researchers, and their separation from the phenomena being studied. The strengths of the stance of objectivity are obvious enough, and for many areas of scientific study this has of course been hugely productive and transformative. What systemic and psychoanalytic psychotherapists however contend is that there are some human phenomena which simply cannot be accessed by such 'objective' methods, but are only rendered visible through an emotionally engaged interaction with the therapist-observer. It is because introspection, which is proscribed as a resource for understanding by most scientists, has always been a central means of accessing reality for creative artists and writers that the arts have probably taught human beings more about their minds and feelings than the sciences.

Now let's give some attention to the divergences and differences between psychoanalytic and systemic approaches, having noted many points of convergence between them.

In systemic therapy, the first therapeutic task is to make manifest the different definitions and meanings there are within a family that has in some way become extremely unhappy, precarious, or simply stuck. Unhappy families are places where thinking and communication have become difficult. Meanings have become coercive, forms of unwitting domination. What needs to be seen as an *interpretation* or *belief* about how things are, whether it be held by one family member alone or shared by others, has instead become reified as the way things *really* are, such that no other way of thinking about them has become conceivable. Sometimes such interpretations assign particular roles and definitions to individual family members. In performing these roles (it may be to be ill, or 'difficult', or omnipotently capable of looking after everyone) such an individual may be maintaining the family system by sustaining the definition of reality on which it has come to depend. But this may be at a devastating cost to them, and perhaps to everyone else in the family. It is sometimes when such costs have become apparent that families ask for help, though they may initially be asking for help only for one member who is breaking under the strain, not for the whole family.

The idea that reality is 'socially constructed' ('social constructionism') begins for family therapists with the family itself. Families are deemed always to be socially constructed in discourses and narratives. Sometimes the construction has gone badly wrong and has led to great unhappiness. It is necessary then to go back into the process of social construction, to make manifest that a family exists through shared or unshared definitions, and that if these are reflected on it can become different, and can be 'constructed' or reconstructed, or indeed deconstructed, in a different way. One could say that systemic therapy, and narrative and social constructivist approaches in general, defined themselves against 'essentialisms' of all kinds, including the essentialism of the 'canonical' (Bruner 1990) or normative family. Sartre's aphorism 'existence precedes essence' is a founding principle of this tradition.

As we have suggested, this critique of essentialism extends to the supposed essences of gender and race, as well as to normative family forms and roles. The 'social constructionist' and 'discursive' foundations of systemic approaches thus connect its therapeutic theory and practice with important developments in the cultural and social sciences. Systemic therapy applied these new theories and methods of study (including close attention to texts) to the therapeutic setting. Systemic approaches have thus remained connected with these wider scientific and cultural debates, whereas psychoanalysis has developed more through practices and ideas internal to its own professional community. It is interesting to note that the respective emphasis given to the 'external' and the 'internal' in these two intellectual traditions, normally referring to the social and interior dimensions of the person and the mind, also characterises their respective patterns of intellectual development.

Psychoanalysis also concerns itself with differences of meaning, and focuses on narratives in exploring these. But the discrepancies of meaning of particular concern to it are between those meanings that are shaped by 'internal' unconscious templates, and those that are the conscious and overt beliefs of the subject. The intersection at the heart of the psychoanalytic tradition is between the 'internal' pressure of 'desire' and the external forces of 'reality'. It is the interface between unconscious and conscious mental processes which psychoanalytic therapies are designed to explore, with the transference and counter-transference, and the interpretation of dreams and unconscious phantasy as their particular resources.

Psychoanalytic psychotherapy sets going a process of narrative construction in its patients, just as systemic therapy does. What is specific to the psychoanalytic approach is its attention to the relation between the story-lines elaborated in reports and associations and the 'internal stories' which shape the patient's picture of reality. In psychoanalytic child psychotherapy, toys and drawing materials are provided as resources in the therapy room, and the stories children elaborate in playing and drawing (for example, of a boat being attacked by angry crocodiles) are then reflected on. These narratives may proceed in parallel, with child patients remaining absorbed in their own stories about what is happening in their play, while still paying attention and responding to their therapists' reflections on their underlying meanings. These concern the child-patient's primary 'object-relations' – his or her phantasised inner world of relations between aspects of him or herself, parents and siblings – and also the child's relations with the therapist-in-phantasy. The therapist is on the surest ground in being able to think about discrepancies between the 'real therapist' and the therapist experienced by the patient (for example, as a cruel or abandoning parent). This transferential dimension of the patient's enactments is the most powerful instrument for psychoanalytic understanding, not just because it looks 'deeper' (into the unconscious) but also because the contrast between phantasy and reality can be more clearly attended to in this 'here and now' encounter than it can when a patient is talking about events outside the therapy room, past or present, about which therapists have no direct knowledge.

Certainly the natural story-making and story-telling proclivities of both child and adult patients are fundamental to this process. If patients did not want to talk about their lives as they unfold, and children did not like to give accounts of what is going on in their play, there would be little for psychoanalytic therapists to work with. Indeed patients whose ability to tell stories about themselves or others is inhibited, or who are afraid or incapable of expression, pose a particular problem for psychoanalytic therapy.[13] The 'narratives' that provide materials for analytic reflection and interpretation are nearly always fragmentary ones, whose patterns continually reform and dissolve. Children's play in therapy sessions often wanders all over the place, and it may be difficult for therapists to keep up with it. Finding some coherence and meaning in what is being said and done is what the therapeutic work is about. Bion (1963) talked about the 'selected fact' as an organising point of coherence in this process, and Edna O'Shaugnessy (1994) has further shown the clinical relevance of this idea. The perspectives of 'complexity theory' may be useful as a way of thinking about the process by which meaning can be located in apparently chaotic material (Moran 1991; Quinodoz 1997; Miller 1999; Rustin 2002b).

Psychoanalysis, at least in the object-relations tradition, presupposes a deep mental structure and a process of 'psychic development', and these provide reference points for its work of understanding and interpretation. This theoretical 'realism' – the positing of deep generative structures in the mind – is a major point of difference between systemic and psychoanalytic therapies. The vicissitudes of the Oedipus complex, and the complex transitions and oscillations theorised in this tradition between the paranoid-schizoid and depressive positions, and their various narcissistic half-way houses in 'borderline states' are central organising principles of psychoanalytic psychotherapy, which seem to have no ontological equivalent in systemic family therapy.[14]

Some years ago, and perhaps still in the minds of some, the distance between a perspective which posited such 'universal' and 'essentialist' principles of mental functioning in the manner of Freud and Klein, and one based on social and discursive construction, seemed unbridgeable. Indeed, getting away from the prescriptive certitudes apparently embodied in the psychoanalytic account of 'normal psychic development' was one of the motivating forces in the development of family therapy.[15] Today, however, this gap may be less difficult to bridge. On the psychoanalytic side, late Kleinian theorists like Ronald Britton (1998, 2003) have emphasised the impermanent nature of all 'settlements' between paranoid-schizoid and depressive functioning, arguing that fluidity and oscillation between them can be a source of creativity, and does not merely risk psychic regression. The development of the concept of 'containment' in current psychoanalytic thought, originating in Bion (1962), emphasises the relation of container and contained as an ongoing exchange, which involves continuous mental processing. The container is seen as a protected space for psychic development, not as a box. 'Multiple voices'[16] figure in psychoanalytic as well as systemic therapy, though in the former case this refers to the many parts of the minds of therapists and patients that are present in psychoanalytic psychotherapy, and not mainly to the liberated or newly discovered voices of different family members. But between these conceptions there is a significant overlap, as the literature shows.[17]

Richard Rorty, a leading post-modern philosopher, brought out the affinities between contemporary psychoanalysis and discursive models of society and culture in his essay on Freud (Rorty 1980). He defends Freud's conception of the unconscious by arguing that it is reasonable to assign many different 'selves' to an individual (he draws on Davidson, 1982, in this), and also to see psychoanalysis as a way of bringing these into communication with one another. (Kleinian analysts refer to the different 'parts' of the self.) The conversation of different aspects of the self that Freud has made possible, is seen by Rorty as analogous to his conceptions of philosophy and democratic society as ongoing conversations about meanings and values in which it is pointless to look for foundational truth.[18] Conflict and difference have thus become incorporated into the thinking of contemporary psychoanalysts, not merely as unavoidable and unwelcome facts of life, which is part of the spirit in which Freud first brought them to our attention, but also as inherently desirable sources of psychic life.

Another new source of 'difference' in contemporary psychoanalysis can be seen in the implicit place of 'gendered positions' in the formation and elaboration of its ideas. We can say that Freud was preoccupied with the Oedipal relationship between father and son, in the context of the triangular relationship of both with mother. Klein focused much of her writing on the pre-Oedipal dyad of mother and baby. But the emergence of a new generation of psychoanalysts within the Kleinian tradition has 'brought Oedipus (and the father) back in', such that the elaboration of how to live creatively with two internal parents has become a criterion of psychic creativity. Britton's work is particularly significant in this respect. It is paradoxical that both Kleinian and systemic therapies, though antithetical to each other, were in different ways both reactions to gendered kinds of domination, and that both traditions are now in a position to be more open-minded and inclusive about these issues, probably as a consequence of the broader changes in gender balance that have taken place over recent decades.

Finally, there is the question of the ethical commitments of these two different traditions of psychotherapy. A stereotypical view holds the psychoanalytic tradition to be committed to be absolutist in its commitment to developmental norms, and moralising towards its patients in its practice. On the other hand, if systemic therapists were *only* social constructionists, they might find it difficult to pursue any therapeutic goals for their patients, unless patients themselves proposed them. These are ideal-typical representations of an absolutist modernism on the psychoanalytic side, and of a relativist post-modernism on the systemic side.

However, neither view states the whole truth. Psychoanalytic therapists are committed to their patients' capacity for choice and change, as well as to their being able to sustain reciprocal and loving relationships. Systemic therapists hope that their clients will discover sympathy and understanding for each other, and will suffer less as a result of their therapy. The psychoanalytic tradition has a more elaborate theorisation of the origins of anxiety and mental pain than the systemic, but the differences in their practical goals are less than between their theoretical models. Many systemic therapists have become interested in the developmental models of attachment theory, whose vocabulary of secure and insecure attachment parallels in its function the psychoanalytic conceptions of containment.[19] We can conclude by saying that both these therapeutic traditions hold that individuals develop and thrive in the context of relationships of understanding and affection, and that their therapeutic practices are each designed to facilitate these states of relatedness.

Understanding Harry Potter

We have tried to clarify some of the similarities and differences between these two psychotherapeutic traditions. Each offers a way of thinking about families, and a therapeutic practice for helping them when they encounter difficulties. We have suggested elsewhere (Rustin and Rustin 2001) that a psychoanalytic approach, brought together with a sociological awareness of context, can help in the understanding of fictional writing for children. We have sought to show how the best literature for children explores their primary experiences of development, and especially the anxieties of becoming more independent of parental care as they grow older, even while continuing to depend on it in both internal and external reality. Our approach has perhaps always had an implicitly 'systemic' as well as 'psychoanalytic' dimension, since it has given attention to cultural context as well as to unconscious phantasy. Both family context (the permanently or temporarily absent parents ubiquitous in writing for children), and the broader cultural and social world present in the stories (e.g. the repressive patriarchy of the war-time Wales of Nina Bawden's

Carrie's War; the immigrant melting pot America of Russell Hoban's *The Mouse and his Child*) frame our discussions of the emotional experiences of the central figures of these stories, boys, girls, and in some cases their animal surrogates (e.g. E.B. White's *Stuart Little, Charlotte's Web*, and *The Trumpet of the Swan*).[20]

Here we are going to look at a spectacularly successful series of books for children, J.K. Rowling's *Harry Potter* novels, and try to look more directly at the implications of a psychoanalytic and systemic therapeutic perspective for understanding them. The stories will thus be a way of testing out our reflections on the convergences and divergences of these approaches. We will begin with some psychoanalytic reflections.

Freud explored the important distinction between fantasy untrammelled by reality, which he linked with the self-idealising omnipotence of day-dreams, and phantasy rooted in unconscious preoccupations, anxieties, wishes, hopes and beliefs. This is visible particularly in our dream-lives, a mode of mental life which is not under the sway of self-serving omnipotence, but which gives us access to our internal worlds. This theme has interested modern psychoanalysis, and some of the best psychoanalytic writing about literature (Britton 1998, 2003; Sodré 1999; Byatt and Sodré 1996) derives from this valuable clarification of the nature of imagination. For all the extravagance of its inventions, and the importance of wizardry and magic to its narrative, we think that the Harry Potter stories do connect deeply with the imaginative and unconscious worlds of children, and this is one reason for their remarkable success.

Harry's capacity to evoke intense reader-involvement in his various quests is based in part on the universal appeal of what Freud called 'the family romance'. Like many fictional heroes in children's books, Harry is, or so it appears, on his own. He is literally an orphan, but also when we first meet him deeply out of step with the Dursley household at 4 Privet Drive. He looks different from them, he thinks about different things, and as he is so often in trouble because of his unwelcome unconventionality, so it is hardly surprising to learn how he dreams of being rescued by unknown relations from the dreary and depriving atmosphere of his aunt and uncle's establishment. Freud suggested that the childhood wish to belong to a family other than the one we actually have whenever we are disappointed by it, is a good example of the power of wishful thinking. This wish is delightfully represented in many traditional fairy tales, as well as in children's phantasies and dreams. The desire not to be who we are is transformed into the conviction that we really are someone else, of an altogether superior sort, like the frog who is really a prince. Everyday realities can be set aside as we imagine ourselves discovering our 'true' place in the world. Well, Harry's lowly position in life is turned upside down when he finds out just how important he is in the wizard world, and so the story starts.

The place of magic in these stories functions at many levels. One important theme is that magic is to do with what we do not understand. This is in fact the basis of the anxious and obsessional Mr Dursley's hatred and fear of wizardry. Rowling does not allow her child wizards to use magic powers to get out of ordinary life problems, or at least not to any serious extent. So these are not like the superheroes of a comic strip. There is a discipline to the use of magic, and its has proper and improper possibilities – it is not there to avoid things like homework, or school rules, or problems with friends. It is a more serious aspect of life than that, and it requires long hard study before it can be well used. Indeed, it is the educational purpose of Hogwarts to teach magic, both its powers and its responsibilities. When Harry arrives at Hogwarts he realises that his new school has its own terrors for him. At Privet Drive, it seemed to be Mr Dursley or Dudley who couldn't bear anything out of the ordinary and who got into a panic so easily. But Harry has to cope with his own panic when the boring certainties of the local primary school and life at the Dursleys are replaced by the mystery of Platform 9½ (where is it, will he miss the train?) the terror of the Sorting Hat's decision (which House will he be placed in? Will the balance of his character be judged benignly so he can be in the House he admires, or will his less admirable Slytherin-like traits be not only discerned but also taken as the basis of a judgement?). He can no longer project his unease into the conveniently available Dursleys. The agonies of the 11-year-old's first encounters with secondary school are the background resonances for Harry's readers. This is a child moving out of a more protected world into a larger more competitive environment and wondering if they can make it on their own.

Harry's trials are quite clearly a serious matter from the start, however much fun there is along the way. He has to face the deepest human anxieties of death, and the fear of extinction, of abandonment and of a failure to uphold one's values. In the Quidditch game, in the nightmare visit to the forest, and in so many other places as the stories unfold, Harry does not know if he will survive, whether anyone will help him, and whether he can keep going. He is fearful of external attack, and fearful too of betraying himself. He does not understand the blinding pain of his scar, although he knows that it is something that links his inner experience of past and present and that the pain has a meaning. As a baby he learns he survived Voldemort's attack because he was a loved child. His mother's love protected him because it was more powerful than Voldemort's hatred and envy. His task in the wizard world is to take on the responsibility of protecting something which will be subject to repeated attacks. It is the existence of a circle of creative love from which Voldemort feels excluded that drives him to such destructiveness and to his unrelenting pursuit of Harry. In a later volume we learn the appalling tragedy of Voldemort's childhood which has turned him from victim to monster. Hero and anti-hero are both given complex characters and each is shown to have an identity based at depth on an inner relationship with lost parental figures. Harry's survival and development depend on the growth of his imaginative contact with representations of a loving parental couple, who can provide the basis for stable identifications.

Now to some more systemic reflections. The ongoing seven-volume series allows Rowling to tell her story of the profound pains of growing up in the frame of 7 years of school. The stories are as attentive to the relational context of Harry's life as to his own thoughts and feelings. In a novel for children, this could hardly be otherwise. The significance of the larger family environment is in fact a kind of common ground between psychoanalytic therapy undertaken with children, and systemic therapy, even though each has a different approach to work with parents and families. It is hard to undertake successful therapeutic work of any kind with children in a contemporary Child and Adolescent Mental Health Clinic without keeping the family, of whatever kind it is, firmly in mind. Harry's move into adolescence, with the changing patterns of peer friendships, interest in girls, and the deep unhappiness of young adolescence – a sort of depression fuelled by self-doubt – are all there as comfort for Rowling's readers, who feel less alone for knowing that Harry too feels left out, jealous, guilty, disloyal, and cowardly at times. The potential for this developmental saga depends on Harry's discovering various parental and sibling figures on whom he can depend. These are arranged in interesting pairs, echoing Harry's profound pre-occupation with his lost parents – Dumbledore and Professor McGonagall, Hagrid the giant and Hedwig the owl postman, Mr and Mrs Weasley, Hermione and Ron. Harry is a 'looked-after child' who actually does get looked after. Well-fed, well-educated, nursed when ill, but above all kept in the minds of people for whom he is a person who needs support, friendship, protection, and space to find himself.

The substitute family of Hogwarts is close at times to the ideal of a child's imagination. The magnificent feasts, the cosy House rooms, the intense loyalty within the Houses, the attentiveness of the teachers, is a secure base indeed. In fact, when Hogwarts and Dumbledore are threatened in later volumes it is truly the end of innocence for Harry and his friends. The richness of the mix of adults and children also makes it a very interesting place to be, so that it combines security and the excitement of new experiences in equal measure. It is only when he is safely ensconced in school that he can start his emotionally turbulent inner journey. Life at the Dursleys was a sort of prolonged place of waiting which he revisits each summer perhaps to get his breath for the next stage on his journey.

Finally, it is worth taking note of the much broader social world that, often implicitly and metaphorically, becomes part of the stories and which gives them much of their capacity to surprise and delight their readers. Modern literary criticism has tended to focus on questions of discourse, code and context, at the expense of an earlier literary interest in character, and especially moral character. This tendency has made some forms of psychoanalytic criticism, where it remains concerned with questions of personal development and relationships, seem quite out of step with academic fashion. The closer to clinical practice such writing is, the further it tends to be from the norms of contemporary literary criticism. Critics tend to ask of a piece of writing, 'How does it work?', psychoanalysts to ask, 'How does it complement or add to the insights of psychoanalysis into human lives?'

But attention to the cultural codes and genres J.K. Rowling has absorbed and transformed in writing her novel-series is illuminating. Part of the success of these novels is due to her feeling for many styles of writing already familiar to her readers, in one way or another, since they are so embedded in our culture. The school story, with its typical heroes and villains; the gothic romance, with its thrilling sense of the uncanny; the modern adventure fantasy familiar to readers from fictional precedents and their reinvention as computer adventure games; and the Roald Dahl-influenced subversive story of appalling family life (at 4 Privet Drive), are but four of the genres which Rowling melds together in her narrative. But she is imaginative in her own right too, and even though many elements of her books bear traces of their literary forerunners, the totality is original and repeatedly delights the reader with its inventions. We have also already suggested how the context that Rowling has created provides a more-than-adequate container for the exploration of Harry's personal development.

Codes and genres have been of interest to modern critics not only because of their interest in literary technique, but also because of their function as bearers of ideological meaning. This is one link between the de-mystifying and critical roles of social and cultural constructionism, systemic therapy, and and literary theory. Some critics of Rowling's work (Blake 2002; Gupta 2003) have adopted this perspective, looking for connections between the narratives and the ideological currents (the market, New Labour) which have been dominant during their period of amazing commercial success. The first half of Gupta's critique concerns itself with the commercial promotion and reception of the stories, not the fictions themselves. The cover of Andrew Blake's book makes a point against the commercial promotion of best-sellers like Rowling's by carrying the disavowal 'This book is not endorsed or authorised by Warner Bros, J.K. Rowling or Bloomsbury Publishing plc,' though one wonders if this is not a marketing ploy in itself. Gupta makes the interesting point that Rowling's feeling for 'brands' and the linguistic tropes which market them mirror or anticipate the commercial appeal of her own books. But we see this not as an indication of Rowling's own adeptness at branding, but rather as an aspect of her sensitivity to children's contemporary experience, whose pleasures and anxieties she surely has to grasp if she is to win their interest.

Many social distinctions are explored in the Harry Potter stories. Hogwarts has a class structure, in effect mapped by its four Houses. Hermione is a 'scholarship girl', and is not even of wizard blood. Malfoy represents the reactionary top end of the social spectrum, and belongs to a snobbish and racist family, if we think of contempt for muggles by those with wizard blood as a metaphor for racism. But though the wizards represent a kind of privilege of birth, in its treatment of more ordinary racial differences the story is liberal and enlightened. Since Hermione is the cleverest and most hard-working of the three central children, and is deeply loyal to her friends, it is also hard to criticise these novels on grounds of their attitudes to gender. The stories are compassionate towards rebels and deviants from the established order (Hagrid, Sirius Black), and express a hatred of cruelty, for example as represented by Azkaban, the feared prison which inflicts a terrible spiritual death on its inmates. The tabloid press is delightfully sent up in the person of Rita Skeeter (at one point turned into a beetle), and the self-deceiving and time-serving official establishment is exposed in the person of Cornelius Fudge, the Minister for Magic. All in all the sympathies of the novels seem distinctly to the left, somewhat to the discomfiture of radical critics who have been so dismayed by the vast marketing success of the series. The books do however place the saving of the world in the hands of an enlightened elite, led by Dumbledore. They do not set much store by popular democracy.

But it is hard to see these social themes as the most important aspects of these novels, nor perhaps would one expect them to be given the age-range of its intended readers. We think the books are primarily about childhood and its anxieties, and about what happens to children as they live through the experiences of growing older. They give life to a child's point of view, at a point in our culture when this is being invaded by adult demands for children to be competent rather than exploratory, to passively consume rather than do things actively, and to watch television rather than to read or play. In this respect these novels, like those of Philip Pullman, should be welcome to psychotherapists of both psychoanalytic and systemic hues, since they encourage the lively minds and passionate feelings that both seek to release in their therapeutic endeavours.

Chapter 3

Narrative perspectives on childhood depression

David Campbell and Judith Trowell

Introduction

Depression in children is a growing concern among mental health workers and therapists. The age of onset is steadily decreasing and the incidence of childhood depression in the child mental health services is rising (Angold *et al.* 1998). The ideas presented in this chapter are based on a large-scale outcome research project which compared individual child psychotherapy to family therapy for a sample of depressed children and their families across three European cities (Campbell *et al.* 2003; Trowell *et al.* 2003).

Many therapists today utilise the basic principles of narrative therapy, such as: (1) describing a patient's experience within a chronological story line; (2) identifying dominant and subjugated stories the patient has drawn on to construct their story; (3) building on expectations to the dominant and 'problem-saturated' story; and (4) enabling a patient to 'step back' or externalise the problem narrative in order to muster their resources to challenge it.

When we look at the literature to consider how other researchers have understood childhood depression we learn that they are very troubled and difficult to help groups of young people (Rutter *et al.* 1986; McCauley *et al.* 1995; Brent *et al.* 1997). Mitchell *et al.* (1988) reported that subjects with combined depression and anxiety were more severely depressed than those with major depression alone. Simonoff *et al.* (1997) found that 77 per cent of depressive subjects demonstrated one other common mental disorder. Depression in children and adolescents is significantly concerned with anxiety related disorders, separation anxiety, simple phobia, normal phobia, agoraphobia and overanxious disorder. These certainly apply to the young people in this study.

Kovacs (1997) and Kovacs and Sherrill (2001) emphasise that depression in young people is associated with co-morbid psychiatric conditions (anxiety or conduct disorder generally) which complicate the treatment. They also state there is frequently family dysfunction which can 'derail specific treatment goals' (Coyne 1990). In this study there were, in the London families, cases with considerable co-morbidity and family difficulties.

However, in this field there are still many unanswered questions about how narratives are constructed and the extent to which they reside with us as fixed narratives, or are being constantly negotiated within the ongoing relationships around us. This research study compared individual and family perspectives, and since we authors have come from the two perspectives (individual: JT; and family: DC), it gives us the opportunity to shed some light on these unanswered questions.

First, a brief description of the research design should help readers appreciate where some of our ideas have come from. Within each European city (London, based at the Tavistock Clinic, Helsinki and Athens) approximately 24 cases (total = 72) were screened for major depressive disorder or dysthymia (a milder but chronic form), and then randomly allocated to two treatment groups: individual child psychotherapy up to 30 weekly sessions plus separate parent support sessions up to 15; and family therapy up to 14 sessions, approximately every two weeks. Individual therapists worked alone whereas family therapists worked as co-therapy or observer pairs, and regular supervision was provided throughout the treatment. Baseline measures of depression and anxiety, and other measures of functioning were then repeated at the end of therapy and at 6-month follow-up (Puig-Antich and Ryan 1996). The therapy was also monitored using questionnaires administered monthly during the treatments.

The referred patients, the depressed young people, in all three countries were predominantly boys and the families were small, with an only child or two children, very few with three or more. There had been few health problems for the mothers during pregnancy but the rate of parental mental health illness including depression was about 45 per cent in London with some depression in the extended family as well.

Note for the reader

We are aware in reading this chapter that the reader will have to straddle treatment modalities, but perhaps more challenging is the attempt to unite a deficit-based, problem-centred paradigm with a resource-based, solution-centred paradigm. Our starting point for this study was the identification and diagnosis of childhood depression, which is clearly based within the deficit-based, 'something is wrong' paradigm. (This is the paradigm that organises mental health services and which brings distressed children to our attention.) Yet we hope to demonstrate that a narrative model enables children (and their therapists) to move beyond this paradigm to appreciate new ways of seeing the world and new ways of constructing relationships which become part of a new narrative. The different models for exploring a child's life will allow new thoughts to emerge both in the context of a relationship to an individual therapist and in the context of new patterns of behaviour among family members.

The therapeutic work

One of the therapeutic tasks was therefore to encourage, either in the family session with the therapist present or with the parent and young person seen separately, the individuals and families to work towards sharing and trusting, and to help them listen to each other; to help them find new words to construct new narratives. In the individual work, there was a considerable amount of naming for the young person; naming feelings, states of mind, and for the parents acknowledging their own issues, their feelings, but above all to help them see the young person as separate and not an extension of themselves. In family work the therapist encouraged sharing the painful, problem-saturated narratives and exploring the alternative perspectives within the family for new narratives.

Individual therapy

Looking at the individual-focused psychodynamic psychotherapy and parent work, the therapists, the parent workers and the supervisors – as well as the young people, their parents and families – had a story or problem: depression, rather than conflicts or difficult behaviours. The professionals particularly had to construct a new story or understanding that adapted their own feelings and responses. They had the new demanding context of the research design, including a baseline assessment with a research team prior to therapy – a research assessment. The young person and parent(s) were then seen monthly during therapy, and the end of therapy assessment and follow-up interviews were carried out after the usual conclusion of the work.

The narrative this created was both positive and negative. Initially it was intrusive, disturbing the usual clinical practice of clinical assessment and move to therapy. The research also determined the duration of therapy rather than this being a case-by-case clinical decision, and this created a hierarchy giving more power to the research team than the clinicians; a new story where clinical judgement usually was seen as the final arbiter.

The positive narrative was slower to emerge. The supervisors had experience of previous research and so could anticipate the process and were aware that many young people prefer and benefit from time-limited work. They also knew that if need be clinical judgement could cut across the research parameters if the risk to the young person escalated beyond a safe state, for example if the young person was actually suicidal or becoming psychotic.

The individual child workers had more problems, trained in long-term open-ended therapy, they were distressed that such needy young people were required to terminate. However, as the cases increased and the 6-month follow-ups were done, the situation changed. Many of the young people were much improved and were getting on with their lives. This surprised and pleased the therapists and led to a reappraisal of the project and their usual clinical work. The importance of the follow-up for the families and the therapists needs recognition, the families value the continued interest and concern and the therapists are able to learn from the outcome.

The research study did therefore create a shift in the individual therapy narrative; brief focused work can be very beneficial, even with such troubled young people, follow-up is valued by most families, and professionals can learn a great deal.

The individual therapists were able to manage the powerful emotions generated by this very demanding work using their psychoanalytic understanding both of themselves and of the young person. Their ability to observe and reflect restored their capacity to think and stay in touch. The supervision could be seen as a space for a different narrative story to emerge, one where the therapist was encouraged to develop ideas and so emerge as a thinking, competent, therapeutic resource rather than an individual overwhelmed by the distress and despair or rage of the young person.

Alongside this, the work with the parent(s) was creating a different story for them too. Their own needs were acknowledged, their pain, distress and shame. They were helped to rediscover themselves as a functioning parent who had concerns about their child. The young person's need to attend school, have friends and for the parent(s) to have their own life was the new story. But again the work was sustained by the psychoanalytic understanding of the parent workers that enabled them to manage and understand themselves and the parent(s) when the negative feelings were very intense.

The following examples are offered to help understand this process of 'staying in touch' with each other and with the emotional content in the session; and suggest practice implications.

Mother and young person 'in touch'

R aged 10 years lived with his mother and the two were locked together in their hopelessness and despair. Neither went out unless it was essential. R was absent from school and this led to referral, but once referred and engaged, R could use his own therapy and his mother, with a great deal of help from her worker and the professional network, could encourage his move back to school and out into the world. They were both able to grasp the therapeutic opportunity.

This could be understood in several ways. R, at 10 years, was still of an age where he could be obliged to attend. There were also professionals in the network keen to help and support. Particularly important was the capacity of the parent-worker to engage and support mother, so that R felt able to move out of the home and mother would survive. Mother also had enough concern and resources to be able to let her son go.

What the children and parents said

R AGED 10

Before therapy:

> Everything is hopeless, nothing can change. I am useless, I am no good at anything. I'm stupid, I never go anywhere, I have no friends. I just stay in the flat and watch TV all night, and sleep all day.

At follow-up:

> School is OK, I go out with friends two or three times a week, lessons aren't too bad. I hope to go to college. It's still difficult with mum but a bit easier. I have my own bed now.

R'S MOTHER

Before therapy:

> I am desperate about R, I can't get him to school, he just won't go, and before he was bullied a lot, so I'm not happy about him going to that school and they won't find him another. He has difficulties with the work, and he needs a lot of extra help. It is very hard as he is at home round my feet all day, sitting around or sleeping, and I know he is very depressed. He clings to me, won't let me out of his sight, we get on each other's nerves a lot, and we have a lot of rows.

At follow-up:

> R seemed pleased to come to therapy, and with the help of the education social worker, he's back at school now. The school have been quite good, and have been giving him extra help where he's behind. There are times when we fall back into the old ways, and I find it difficult to get him to go to school, but on the whole it's much better. I've been depressed myself, and on medication; I'm very up and down, and sometimes we still have big rows, but it's much better, and I'm relieved that he's back in school, and has some friends, as it has worried me a lot.

Mother 'out of touch' with young person

In this family, S, aged 14 years, was seen as impossible, there was very great concern but also helplessness. No one could help S, she seemed to be completely in control of herself and her family.

S herself felt she could not go on and she saw no point in coming to therapy, but agreed to come, perhaps to confirm how useless it was. She was definite it would not help, it would fail. Also she would never return to school.

Once established in therapy the extent of her disturbance emerged, as did her fear and panic that no one could help her. She oscillated from arrogant omnipotence, to contempt for her therapist, to weeping, vulnerable, needy dependence.

This contrasted with her mother's view which was apparently one of considerable relief that they had been accepted into the project. Her anxiety and worry rapidly settled and she saw her daughter as improving dramatically. But perhaps more significantly, once the daughter was settled in therapy, the severity and complexity of the family dynamics and the marital issues became overwhelming. The parent worker struggled to find a way of working that could move the family and the parental couple forward.

This pattern could be understood as a young person acutely aware of the family and marital difficulties. She tried to take control of herself and the family, and as this increasingly failed, she became very troubled. The therapy did enable the young person to move forward, but the parental couple found it hard to use the help offered and remained preoccupied with their own conflicts.

What the children and parents said

S AGED 11

Before therapy:

> It's all awful, I want to be dead, there's no point in anything. I can't get out of bed, can't go to school. I keep hearing voices, I know it's in my head, but it sounds like my friend telling me to do things – cut, run away. I stay in bed instead. I can't eat anything.

At follow-up:

> I have a few friends and I go out with them a lot. They got me into college, school was hopeless, they all called me names. I like it there, and I try to get there two or three times a week. It's my mum who needs help: I'm OK. I want to be a better shape. I suppose I quite enjoy my life now.

S'S MOTHER

Before therapy:

> I've done everything I can for S, but she shuts herself in her room and won't go to school. She says the other girls call her names, and I'm not happy to make her go if that's what's going to happen. The school send people round to take her, but she won't go. You can't force her to go, it'll make her ill. She's very depressed, and I can't get her to eat, and I worry about that. We shout at each other a lot at times. I'm very depressed myself, under the doctor, and my partner and I have lots of rows. S doesn't get on with her dad.

At follow-up:

> Things are much better with S, they've found her a college, and she seems to like it, and she gets herself there most days. She still sees the social worker. She seems much better in herself, and she's out with her friends a lot, more than I like really. I've been very bad myself, my partner has left. I've missed coming to the clinic, it helped to talk: I've been under the doctor again with my nerves, and he's found me a counsellor, but it's not the same, and I guess I miss S when she's out.

Mother 'too in touch' with young person

In this family, A, a 10-year-old boy, had profound problems managing his relationship with his mother following the break up of the parental relationship. Both mother and son engaged in the work and were very enthusiastic and committed. However, the time-limited contract provoked distress and anxiety in the mother, and the son was perceived to be deteriorating. Pressure to continue was immense and the cruelty of the research parameters was stressed. The therapist also found the research constraining and tried to find a way to change the termination point. Managing this anxiety was not easy for the therapists or the research team. The anger at the absent father became directed at the rigid, distant research director who seemed to be indifferent to the young person's need and the mother's anxiety. This can be understood as projection of the depression leading to the masked anxiety and anger in the mother and the anger in the young person emerging in the therapy narrative.

What the children and parents said

A AGED 10

Before therapy:

> It's really hard, I never see my dad now. My sister has a boyfriend, and
> my Mum is always busy. She gets very angry and keeps yelling at me. It
> all seems hopeless. I can't concentrate at school thinking about Dad
> and Mum.

At follow-up:

> Things are better, but it's really bad at school, they keep on at me, and
> I lose it, get angry and slam out. I get fed up with my Mum too, but
> we've been getting on better. I still don't see my Dad enough.

A'S MOTHER

Before therapy:

> I'm very worried about A. He's clearly so unhappy, he's very
> irritable a lot of the time, and he's doing badly at school. He takes
> things very hard, and seems to feel responsible for things which aren't
> his fault at all. My husband and I are in the middle of a difficult divorce,
> I don't know what the outcome will be for me and the children, and we
> are having a lot of rows about his contact with the children. I think
> I know that A has taken this all very badly, he feels very responsible for
> me, it's had a bad effect on him. I've been depressed myself, and
> I've had trouble with my nerves on and off for a while.

At follow-up:

> A seems much brighter in himself, and we're getting on much better
> at home, though he still seems to be finding things difficult at school,
> finds it difficult to sit down and concentrate, and finds the work difficult.
> The school sometimes contact me to talk about him, but they seem to
> like him, which is a good thing. The divorce is settled, and he sees his
> Dad regularly now. I don't quite know how things are going to work
> out for me, I still feel angry and depressed at times. I'm still on
> medication, and I haven't sorted out what to do. But things are a lot
> better, and I don't think A worries about me quite so much as he did.

Family therapy

A family therapy approach provides the opportunity to break the patterns of relating which maintain the depressive feelings in children and other family members; and to create new patterns which promote a more positive or hopeful view of relationships and life in general (Diamond and Siqueland 1995; Focht-Birkerts and Beardslee 2000). The patterns are maintained by the stories we tell ourselves about how we and others 'should be', and the stories are embedded in larger discourses maintained by our families and by the societies we live in. For example, there are discourses in our society about 'how parents should treat children' or 'how one should respond to sadness', which promote values and give us a range of options for how we may behave. Each family will take a position within the range of possibilities, and the positions are made explicit through the stories, incidents, examples and bits of behaviour which family members choose to tell each other – these become the family narratives.

For some of our families, we became aware fairly quickly of a family story or narrative which seemed to hold relationships in stasis. These tended to be broad, all-encompassing stories which connected many people over a long period of time, such as a story about the parentage of a child, the death of a sibling or the meaning of a divorce. The family seemed to us to be living in the shadow of the narrative which did not offer alternatives that would lead to the creation of new relationships. The therapist's work consisted of revisiting the original narrative and listening for inconsistencies or contradictions or small openings in the narrative flow which allowed for questions to be inserted. The questions open the narrative and take it in new directions, and when this happens there are possibilities for reinterpreting the family behaviour associated with the depression.

A family narrative

Barney is a 10-year-old boy living with his mother, stepfather and his younger sister from this new union. There is a powerful story that Barney should maintain a relationship with his distant, biological father, which seems to preserve a barrier between him and his stepfather and to leave him feeling frustrated and powerless to influence a relationship that is beyond his control. Here is an example of the therapist unpicking this story, to create the possibility of an alternative.

THERAPIST: And is the relationship [with your biological father] something you want to carry in a different way, and is it OK to do it your way?

B: I just do not see why it has to be up to me . . .

T: [looking at parents]: What does B mean when he says it's up to him?

B: [his voice becoming whiny]: Everyone says to me, 'why don't you write to him, why don't you write to your grandparents? It's not really my problem . . .'

MOTHER: I think it's a very difficult situation for B. I told his dad years ago, and it just fizzles out, it does not really happen. Nothing happens. Nothing happens and it's extremely difficult for B . . . I sort of started to think, N [stepfather] and myself have been leaving a space for his dad to be B's father in our life . . . I think what it has done, it sort of prevented them [pointing at N and B and little sister] just being a unit. Because what N does, to all intent and purposes is a father's job, and yet it never happened that B called him 'dad', and yet N has been there since B was 2½ years old.

T: And R [biological father] came into the picture later than that?

B: He never came into the picture.

T: It's very interesting to hear what you are saying in respect of previous conversations we had about the importance you both gave to the 'biological father'.

N: Yes

T: And the position that you both accepted, that you, N, are not the father; that something must happen between B and R while now you are saying that you have always been there and you have been doing fatherly things.

N: Yes, I suppose that if C [mother] had not left a gap, I would have filled this gap sooner.

MOTHER: But in many ways you have done, but in our mind we did not do it.

So, as therapists on this project, we have looked for powerful stories about 'how relationships should be' that we believed were constraining individuals and making it difficult to move beyond sadness, frustration and depression. And when we completed the research project we looked back over our work to identify some of the powerful narratives influencing our families.

A family narrative about worrying

In the above case of B, this 10-year-old boy protested throughout the 14 sessions of therapy about having to take part in the family sessions. He said he was feeling sad at the beginning but after a few sessions he felt better, largely due to a change of school, and there had been no point in continuing for the remaining 12 sessions. The sessions often made him cry and 'think about things he didn't want to think about'.

The parents had a view that they had in fact gained from the sessions. Mother said, 'Initially B felt we came here for him, but as the problems were unwrapped, the problem wasn't just about B being happier at school, but about my worry, and maybe worrying too much about school'. N, the step-father, said he had gained enormously from the sessions and felt he had matured as a father during the therapy. So the therapist and family were left with two contrasting stories about the value of the therapy sessions, and this led the therapy team to think again about what it meant for B to be seen as the child who 'brought the family to therapy with his depression'. What kind of responsibility would fall on this young boy's shoulders?

The therapist pursued mother's comments and the idea that she and B had developed a close relationship built around her worry and attempts to make B happy. B's part in the interaction was that he and his mother would have a close relationship enhanced when he could provide things for her to worry about.

This was a successful piece of therapy for this family, and among the hypotheses about what was helpful is the idea that N's 'increasing maturity' enabled him to be a more active participant in family life, and to represent a slight 'outsider's' view of the relationship between B and his mother. He actually said near the end of the therapy, 'there's nothing worse than somebody worrying about you'. We think that when this position is available within a family narrative about responsibility, it gives everyone, and in this case mother, the opportunity to re-examine the narrative she is using to guide her behaviour with her son. She thought carefully about her level of worry and how it contributed to the depression her son was describing. So within this formulation we would say N's more active positioning with a family narrative about responsibility has allowed others to take new positions and shift the narrative.

B was drawn into a position in which he both did and didn't want to be responsible for family problems and the focus of his mother's worry. He *did* in the sense that this kept him in an important and close relationship with his mother, but he *didn't* because he also realised this tied him to being a child to be worried about, at a time when he was also fervent about spending more time with his friends and making a good effort at his new school. (He had a very whiny voice which makes one think about a child who is being positioned by others in some way that is at odds with how he would like to position himself, and is left, above all, feeling trapped.)

A family narrative about absent parents

The majority of the children in our study came from families in which one parent, usually the father, was absent from the family due to separation, divorce or death. We speculated that this contributed to making the children more vulnerable to depression in several ways. It left one parent less supported in trying to manage depression in the family, which meant they would be less resilient as they tried to overcome negative views of the world in themselves or their children. It also deprived a child of a second source of identity formation. With two parents the child has the opportunity to build an identity which incorporates two ways of seeing the world, and particularly two ways of dealing with life's inevitable disappointments and frustrations.

If there is only one view of disappointments, and if that happens to be a negative, sad outlook, it is harder for a child to find alternative resources to overcome his or her own struggles.

When seen in the family context, the child's absent parent becomes the parent's absent partner. The absence of the partner will have its own separate meanings for the marital partner. It may represent a bitter sadness, an unresolved grief, a relief, an angry ongoing struggle, or an attempt to start a new life with a clean slate. The parent's story or narrative about the separation interacts with the child's narrative, which may be completely different. In most cases, where the child has not been the victim of abuse, the child's story is one of personal loss and longing. When these two narratives interact, it is difficult to create a truly 'incorporating narrative'.

It is important here to make a distinction between the concept of a coherent narrative, in which parts of a story fit together into a coherent whole, and in 'incorporating narrative' which includes many different ideas, some of which will contradict each other. The 'incorporating narrative' seeks to acknowledge the discontinuities and discomforts rather than necessarily seeking coherence.

For example, if an absent father is held in great bitterness by a mother who has received years of abuse, the family narrative will struggle to contain a picture of the father which meets the child's sense of emptiness. We had one such case in our project that helps to illustrate this point:

Alex was an only child of parents who separated when he was three. His father drifted into a serious drug habit and contact with Alex declined dramatically. This left Alex with a mixture of feelings which he found difficult to express. He was deeply upset and angry that his father appeared to care so little for him. He was ashamed to tell anyone what was worrying him, including his mother who was emotionally detached from her ex-partner after abusive experiences and years of trying to keep him engaged. When Alex shared this private and painful story in a family session in the presence of his mother things began to change for him. Acknowledging these feelings seemed to help Alex come to terms with the reality of his father's life and to relinquish some of his hope for a better dad. The therapist helped him to grieve for the father he once had.

We have found that some of the single parents in our study blamed themselves for leaving their child without a parent, yet had powerful reasons for breaking up their marital relationship in the first place. Part of our work became focused on helping these parents create a new narrative about the marriage and why it was dissolved, which was not built around self-blame. This allowed parents to tolerate and even encourage a more open discussion of the absent parent, as they really were.

A family narrative about despair

It was characteristic of families in our study that they were demoralised by the effects of coping with the child's depression. This affected them in different ways. For example, the sense of failure in many families was palpable, and this led to loss of confidence and self-esteem. Other families were very angry that they had tried to do many things without success, and seemed to be slapped down again and again by an implacable force. Still others spoke about the toll that family life had taken on the marriage.

As therapists we found it was helpful to identify the theme of a 'family depression'. This perspective can lift some of the burden from the shoulders of the depressed child, and locate the depression within the network of relationships. For example, one family had drifted into a very negative, angry, blaming pattern directed toward their depressed 13-year-old son, and this led to many arguments and a break down of communication. The therapist established that everyone was feeling so demoralised that their 'cognitive style' was built around the perception that life was bleak and they were helpless to change anything. It became difficult to use the therapy and absorb different ideas about their family relationships. The therapist had set some tasks which the family could not carry out. They seemed despairing, and no one person was able to act in a way that would shift the attitude of the others.

The therapist gradually talked about this attitude which gripped everyone. No one person was responsible because each was dragged down by the attitude within the whole family. No one was available to offer alternative views, and no one was available to hear them. A vicious cycle of despair, rather than one depressed child, was the focus for therapy.

A family narrative about attachments

Two observations seem pertinent here. One was that the therapists working with these cases felt that even though they approached these families as they would any family they see in their own service, and even though they put the same effort into engaging and drawing the family into the therapy, there was something different about the quality of the attachment between them and the families. There seemed to be more distance and a slight wariness about getting engaged with the therapist. It is unclear how much the therapists were 'keeping their distance' to avoid getting sucked into depressive feelings, and how much the families were wary about making new relationships. However, what does seem clear is that attachments of this sort are complicated and need further thought.

The second, related observation was that we found children in these families were attached to their parent or parents with unexpected strength. For example, they generally sat through family sessions as though they were 'fully paid-up members of the adult generation'. Unlike most children of this age, our group seemed to be glad to be at the meetings, there were very few missed appointments, and they took a strong interest in what was being discussed. In one case the child protested bitterly about coming, yet came to every session. We speculated about why these children should be so interested in their parents' lives and came to the conclusion that they may also have felt some tenuousness about staying attached (see Sexson and Kaslow 2001). They may have acquired a type of vigilance which keeps them close to their parent/parents' life and which also draws them in to trying to help solve the problem of depression. The nature of depression may also play a part in this because it is behaviour which shuts out the world and if the parent you love is unavailable or depressed (as some of the mothers in our sample proved to be), the child may work harder to break into the parent's inner world.

What emerges then is a picture of a family with a particular narrative about attachments, and how these may work within the family between parent and child; and outside the family where they make connections to the 'helping agencies'.

Mother/child interaction

One of the challenging questions posed by narrative theory is how a narrative is created in the interaction between a parent and child. For example, how is the creation of a narrative affected by a mother and child who have a similar view of the child's experience, as opposed to a mother and child who give different accounts of a child's feelings and moods?

This study provided data which allowed us to compare the young person and mother's accounts of the young person's own feelings.

As part of the research battery the young people and their mothers were asked to complete the Moods and Feelings Questionnaire (Angold *et al.* 1995). This was at baseline, at the end of therapy and follow-up, and at intervals during the therapy and therefore provides a record of the young person's view of their state of mind and the mother's new understanding of their child, as she answers the same questions but from her perspective about her child.

There is thus the possibility of comparing the narratives of a young person and their progress through the project alongside that of the mother. One young woman and her mother both saw her as quite depressed. At the start the girl continued to rate herself as depressed whereas mother quickly felt all was well. When her daughter acted on her despair mother was briefly very aware of this but again rapidly returned to seeing her as fine. The daughter herself did progress, and by the end of therapy review she was no longer rating herself depressed.

Another girl was depressed with serious symptomology and her mother rated her as depressed but then quickly rated her within normal limits. The daughter deteriorated, becoming more and more depressed. By the end of the project she had improved and was functioning at school and outside but was still as depressed as most of the others when they entered the project. Mother seemed unaware of the state of her daughter.

Many of the boys started off with fairly low depression scores and these gradually decreased as they saw themselves as less depressed. The mothers were relatively closely in touch with them. Interestingly two mothers whose sons had been seriously depressed suddenly saw these sons as relapsing as the end of therapy approached, whereas the sons themselves were continuing their steady improvement. Both these mothers had crises in relation to the fathers of the boys which coincided with the end of treatment.

How can we understand the narrative these results give us? Mothers seemed to experience considerable relief when their daughters were in the project and no longer saw them as depressed (troubled). Or was it that they took the opportunity once the daughter was receiving 'help' to explore their own very difficult circumstances, and then lost touch with their daughter's internal state?

The mothers closely 'in touch' with their sons needed to be able to allow the son out of his bed and out to school; in other words, needed to separate. Were they 'too in touch'? The mothers of the other boys seemed to panic as the end approached and their own issues surfaced, and they needed to involve their sons.

The boys whose mothers were aware and in touch used their own therapeutic space to consider the need to separate; to realise that their role as a partner or parent to their mother could be changed. The parent workers could enable their very depressed mothers to understand or accept the needs of their son. But the mothers were also helped to find more appropriate support elsewhere. Depression ran in the family, but change was possible.

The girls were seriously depressed but they were in families where the marriage was very dysfunctional and acrimonious and the girls were labelled as difficult. These girls were struggling and their therapy became the place to contain this and find a way through. The mothers were preoccupied while being concerned and could use their work to tackle some of their problems.

The seriously depressed boys grasped the opportunity the therapy provided and they worked hard on the problems, making progress while their mothers struggled. The mothers' depression was worrying.

Depression and anxiety

Alongside the diagnosis of depression which led to inclusion in the study, the most frequent co-working condition was anxiety, as rated by the Birmaher Anxiety Scale (Birmaher 1998). The depression and anxiety could be seen as more internal and relationship-based, rather than due to deprivation or poverty, in the light of the surprisingly positive responses to the questions about physical environment.

In London and across the three centres the random allocation for depression resulted in the young people that came to family therapy being more anxious than those allocated to individual therapy. Family therapy resulted in a definite reduction in this anxiety. These results show a trend as the numbers were too small to be able to establish significance. The therapeutic narrative in family therapy did seem able to address directly the anxiety-provoking issues such as loss, uncertainty and the transition to adulthood. However, after the end of therapy the family therapy cases did start to deteriorate; that is, the anxiety level began to increase. The individual therapy and parent work did not relieve the anxiety to the same extent, but after the end of therapy the anxiety level continued to fall, so it would appear that the narrative of this therapy enabled the internal and external dialogues to continue beneficially.

These findings raise important issues which require further exploration. For example, children's anxiety may be more quickly relieved because family therapy offers opportunities for sharing internal anxieties with family members, and 'reality checking' which allows a parent/parents to give the child different feedback about their anxious behaviour or anxious state of mind.

The fact that children in the individual treatment continued to have lower levels of anxiety suggests that a focus on the children's own internal thoughts may sustain the child in a changing environment, and also suggests that family therapists might consider extending their work beyond the reduction of symptoms by offering, for example, 'top-up' sessions.

Conclusion

There are a number of practice implications that can be drawn from the study so far. Time-limited therapy does enable many young people and their families to engage in treatment. The young person and parent both need to engage, and in family work this is a core component. In individual work, again, the parallel work with the parents is essential (Rushton and Miles 2000). Parents and mother can be very supporting and enabling despite their own difficulties. But where there are unresolved relationship difficulties and considerable anxiety and anger in the parent, then the young person can be a part of this in the mother's perception. The young person will have their own anger and anxiety, but this may be different from the mother's in its focus. Young people can be very perceptive and in touch with parental difficulties and need professionals to work with the parental problems in order to free the young person. In the family context we have seen that a child's depression is related to concern about relationships and the ability of family members to understand and care for each other.

In the study we have been struck by the importance of work with parents to alleviate a child's depression. Yet we are also aware that there is a dearth of appropriate services for parents. Increasingly services for parents have been reduced. At the conclusion of family therapy, or the conclusion of the young person's individual therapy, very troubled parents remained. Where are there appropriate services? The number of these services seems to be part of the problem – services such as work with parents looking at parenting issues, psychotherapy with parents looking at how past family emotional issues impact in the present, individual or couple psychotherapy looking at how early experiences for the adults impact on their relationship and their parenting, and then there is parental guidance, group work and counselling. The project indicates the young people use what they are given; services for parents emerge as the issue.

Given these reflections, the recent study set itself a very challenging task and the improvements after therapy are even more impressive.

The young people lived in families that were struggling, either with parents who were on their own and depressed or in adversarial marriages where there was some depression but mainly anger and conflict. The interplay between the environment and families and (genetic) innate differences makes it hard to do more than remark on the resilience of the young people and their capacity to use the intervention offered.

Acknowledgement

We would like to thank Gillian Miles for her contribution to the work and thinking about parents.

Chapter 4

Children's narratives of traumatic experiences

Gerrilyn Smith

Lear to the eyeless Gloucester: Yet thou doth see how the world goes.
Gloucester: I see it feelingly.

(*King Lear* (iv 6) by William Shakespeare)

'Once upon a time' or so the story goes. But of course it isn't once but repeatedly as if by sheer force of repetition we could derive comfort and solace, absorb its message. Upon is a relational and directional preposition meaning above and in contact with or supported by – but it connects once with time. A time is not 'this time' or 'that time' – a specific time – but 'a time' – an unspecified time. These English language constructions signal to the listener that we are about to tell a story, something fictional, not 'true'.

I love words – by themselves, with others, in sentences, paragraphs, pages, chapters, books . . . I love the sound of them and some I like to write – loopy ones usually. I like the feel of words in my ears and my mouth[1] . . . so it is no surprise to me that words have played such an important part in my therapeutic work.

I like to play with words. Systemic concepts such as 'reframing' and the 'use of metaphor' came easily, leading me to work as a strategic therapist. And now as time has moved on, I can see that I could be construed as a narrative therapist.

Therapeutically this narrative play frame (Bateson 1972) can be helpful in allowing children to voice and write their lived experience, to operate cognitively and emotionally on that static encapsulation – to process it. Or in the case of traumatic narratives to turn it into the process it should be rather than keeping it as a static defining moment in their life when everything suddenly and abruptly stopped – when they were scared to death but lived to tell the tale.

I want to describe my work with children who are recovering from traumatic experiences. It is informed by many years of working with family violence, sexual abuse, rape, and institutional abuse with adults and children alike. When I reflect on these years of experience, some of the most important lessons I learned are the simplest.

Naming

First, naming and speaking aloud what has happened are the most important starting points – the external manifestation of an internal experience. Often these traumatic stories are mentioned in referral letters or written about in case notes but have not been openly talked about in the family or within the therapeutic arena.[2]

For example a 13-year-old UK white girl was referred because of violent behaviour towards her mother. The referral letter and supporting papers talk of an allegation of sexual abuse made some 7 years earlier by the young girl against an older stepsibling when on contact with her father. This was investigated but no further statutory action happened. The turning point in therapy came about when the therapist was able to raise this allegation directly with the mother and the maternal grandparents – the young girl had refused to attend therapy. It was clear that because no further action had resulted the adults didn't know what to believe. Furthermore the young girl had made additional disclosures. These involved her stepmother being cruel to her and pulling her by the hair. This was exactly the same kind of behaviour the young girl was now doing to her mother. Having previously told and suffered dire and negative consequences – the threat of never seeing her father again – it seemed the young girl now enacted her experiences on her mother who clearly was getting the wrong message. In effect she was telling without literally telling.

Talking about these past traumatic experiences with the significant adults in the young girl's life allowed them to see her behaviour differently and re-opened conversations about how much they wanted to protect her and help; how let down they too felt by the lack of statutory investigation. This in turn led to a discussion about how to make her time with her dad as safe as possible. These conversations occurred first between the adults and the therapist but moved on to include the young woman, who did finally attend the final family session and where with all of them together these issues from the past were discussed.

The ideas and experience I gained in working with sexual violence, have influenced the work I have been doing recently with children and their families from Kosovo. All the children described in this article have left Kosovo as a consequence of war. They all have had undeniably traumatic experiences in their journey to the UK. I began working with them some 4 years after they arrived, by which time they all spoke English well enough for me to work with them directly without an interpreter. However I chose, despite having no prior experience of working with interpreters, to start by talking to the parents and obtain a clear idea of what they were most worried about in relation to their children. This also fits with the importance of engaging families in the therapeutic process (Tribe and Raval 2002) and exploring their understanding of the reasons behind their child's current symptoms (Stratton 2003). I wanted to strengthen the generational hierarchy and keep the parents fully involved in their child's recovery/healing experience. This is the same view that informed my work with non-abusing parents where sexual abuse had been an issue, as well as when working with foster parents and adopters of children with traumatic experiences (Smith 1994, 2003).

As a therapist working with children, I do not wish to replace the primary caregiver as central to the change process. I believe this helps with engagement. I am mindful of encouraging a good therapeutic fit between my model of working and that of the clients who seek treatment. With children this means their primary caregivers.

Naming and validating traumatic experience is often a crucial first step in re-storying that experience. After years of doing this work I realise how easily I can now converse about awful things. This I suspect is a skill to make the uncommon seem commonplace and, most importantly, available for discussion. I use 'peak episodes' as metaphorical encapsulations of the whole experience and 'mine' them, if you like, for alternative views, introducing complexity and affective nuances to the traumatic narrative.

Ariola 10, Emmanuela 14, and Freddie 13 and their parents have all given permission for their stories to be told. They wanted a wider audience to understand what it has been like for them leaving Kosovo and coming to the UK. The young people also wanted their first names to be used. Meeting them has had a profound effect on my son and me.

Professional and personal support

In conversation recently with my colleague Robin Solomons, Social Worker in Tavistock Children and Families Department, I talked of my ruminations both as a child and as an adult about what I would have done as a gentile if confronted with the issue of hiding Jews during the Nazi genocide campaign. We were discussing ethical issues about professional boundaries in our work and in particular attending court on behalf of our clients as therapists rather than as expert witnesses. I told her I had come to realise that ruminating on past events might mean that I was missing something far more important – I realised that my time was now and it wasn't in this case Jews fleeing persecutions but 'ethnic Albanians' fleeing genocide in Kosovo or previously children where sexual abuse had been an issue.

I was reminded of Stephen Frosh daring to ask in 1997 – 'Does anyone still believe that it is possible for a therapist to offer something personal in therapy, to use her or his own imaginative capacity to lend a thinking presence to the other?' (p. 93) and I want him to know that yes I do believe this is not only possible but necessary if therapy is not just talking or telling stories, but something truly transforming and healing. Repeatedly we are informed by research on therapy that the relational aspects of the therapeutic interchange account for a more significant amount of change than skills or techniques.

I prepare myself for my 'walk through the valley of the shadow of death'.[3] In working with children's traumatic narratives 'my capacity to think and work in the margins of experience – to be empathically connected to the traumatic narrative must be sustained by you, my professional brothers and sisters'.[4] So my conversations with Robin (and others) are a very important part of my clinical work.

I realise that my work clearly spills over into my personal life despite a lifelong commitment to keep personal and professional boundaries in place. This came home to me when my son (13) wrote the following poem for a school assignment:

> *Forgotten Children*
> We sit in what is left of our home crying
> Wishing it would end
> Explosions are everywhere
> Death is near, we can feel it
> A playground once filled with happiness is a smoking crater
> We are the forgotten children of Kosovo
>
> We are huddling in our school terrified
> Fearing what might happen next
> Gunshots can be heard
> Death is here, we can see it
> A girl once filled with joy is lying dead on the floor
> We are the forgotten children of Palestine
>
> We are lying in the street starving
> Wondering if there is a better world out there
> Screams reverberating in our heads
> Death has been here, it has touched us
> Our parents once filled with love were executed in front of us
> We are the forgotten children of Afghanistan
>
> We are the forgotten children of the world[5]

I was shocked at what he had written, moved by it and pleased that he can see a world beyond his own experience and wants to put it into words for himself and for others.

I am intrigued by the unsaid, the unspoken but felt experience. 'All this endless talk does not really liberate because it misses the point . . . language is self referential, caught in a closed symbolic circuit. As Freud knew [and Frosh clearly] language only hints at what is there' (Frosh 1997: 91). Jeremy

Woodcock (2001) wrote 'that which is unacceptable in atrocity may be hidden in the most revealing way' (p. 142). This takes courage to address/to name in the therapeutic work.

Frosh goes on to write 'all this narratising is a defence against something else' (1997: 93) and this is nowhere more true than in the traumatic story – one that the client carts around to all and sundry to tell, sometimes ignored or often repeated almost verbatim to any one who would listen. It becomes a mind numbing experience – having already numbed the mind of the person who experienced it and then spreading its frosty mist to the minds of those who hear it. We need to acknowledge our resistance to engage empathically with traumatic narratives (Smith 1996; Woodcock 2001) and to recognise that doing this type of trauma work increases enormously the risk of secondary post traumatic stress disorder or compassion fatigue (Figley 1995).

Multifaceted story telling: increasing the repertoire of self

Renos Papadopoulos and John Byng-Hall (1997) make the point that essentially all 'talking therapies' are narrative. For children, stories form a special place within their childhood experience and any parent can attest to the fascination and fads their child goes through with regard to certain themes and ideas often captured in their books. So working with children and using stories to help them and their parents/primary caregivers make sense of what has happened to them fits into the normal developmentally appropriate range of experiences.

Children and stories go together but the stories that will be shared in this chapter will be terrible ones. Yet they still require the repetitive treatment given to those best loved ones. This helps to dilute their awesome paralysing, mind numbing power. I hope that you, the reader, will be able to see how the seeds of strength and resilience hide in the folds and creases of the words – the unspoken story; the song of silence.

All stories require a reader – they are written or told to be read and heard. This relationship between reader and writer, teller and listener, therapist and client is the creative transforming energy of change, motion and lively curiosity – the impetus to be alive.

Often when working therapeutically with children, you as the therapist are both the reader and writer simultaneously. I encourage the child first to tell the story orally (here the child is the narrator and I am the listener), then together we write the story (here we are co-authors and sometimes I function as the English scribe). I often get the child to read the story aloud to their parents (the child as narrator to their parents as listeners) or if they feel unable to do so I will read it to their parents on their behalf (I am the reader with parents and child – providing two levels of listening). The child hearing their account can begin to make meta cognitions about it.

I will over time not lend myself to this process encouraging the child/ young person to develop these aspects of self – to be reader, writer and listener to their own life stories.[6] Jim Wilson talks about this idea of performance in his work with children (Wilson 1998).

I may ask questions about the story and we may write a number of different endings to a particular story we have been working on. I am trying to introduce complexity and diversity into an experience that has come to be all defining and to avoid frozen narratives (Blow and Daniel 2002).

Children move easily between languages in multilingual families, understanding the contextual cues that indicate another language is needed here. For example in working with Emmanuela who is telling as opposed to writing the story of her running from danger:

> When I saw all those people lying down,[7] I said to myself 'Am I going to be like that?' I couldn't think about anything – just to get out of there. I was talking to myself and saying that 'I can do this.' At this point I interrupted Emmanuela's oral story and asked her, 'Did you say this in English?' She looked at me as if I were stupid – 'No' she said. 'Can you say it in Albanian for me? I would like to hear it.'

In doing this I am picking up a thread of resilience of strength, weaving it in English and Albanian – the message of 'I can do this' in both the child/young person's new language – English – and their previous language, in this case Albanian.

When a child is multilingual I have the story translated and get them to read it to me in the language in which it happened.[8] This language incompetence on my part means the child becomes the reader and writer of their story which I cannot understand because I do not know their language. It demonstrates their competence and highlights their superior fluency. I listen to these languaged stories not with my ears but my heart and it is often in this other language that the emotions – the fear, terror and sadness – are locked. Often the translated experience (i.e. the English version) does not have the same emotional power that the languaged experience does (De Zulueta 1984; Karamat-Ali in press; Burck 1997, 2003).

Clearly, being heard and having your experience reflected back to you accurately is part of a healing process, which is why I repeat the message in all the languages the child has access to – so it is not just one languaged self that benefits from the intervention. I would also use written and oral repetition for unilingual children as a means of bedding down the therapeutic story, if you like, in a number of modalities and increasing the neural associative connections that are made.

Moving between different frames

Children move easily between play and what is real. Bateson saw the para-doxical play frame as an essential part of the development of communication (Bateson 1972). Children signal to us as adults that they understand the difference as part of the developmental process of incorporating the adult view of the world. For children where trauma has played a part in shaping their world view, this play frame can suddenly move from a game to a real-life nightmare experience. All the children talked of how normal playground interactions often triggered traumatic memories to their war experiences. Freddie described how his dreams turn to nightmares. He has an awareness that the story starts out as fictional but then turns only too terrifyingly true.

> I am dreaming that I am walking in the woods. I see a huge tree trunk. It is bloodstained. [Real-life memory] I wonder how this has happened. I think maybe a sword and then I see a Horseman [fantasy]. But the horseman becomes a Soldier in uniform and there are guns everywhere including a machine gun [real life and the story begins to run away] I run in the woods. [Real] There is a narrow passage where the horse cannot squeeze through. [Fantasy] The Horseman gets off his horse and shoots in the trees. I keep running. I hide behind a tree. I peak around the tree to the right – no one is there. I peak around to the left and the Soldier is there. I wake up. I notice I am sweaty, and my heart is beating very fast.
>
> Freddie

Freddie tells me the dream is a mixture of a movie he has seen and his own real-life experiences of war. I ask him how the movie ends, choosing at this point to emphasise the fictional account rather than the real. He tells me it recounts a story of a warrior who has to abandon his troops during battle. All his soldiers are killed. He is also killed and has his head chopped off but he haunts the place of the battle looking for his head. He cannot rest until 'he and his skull are reunited' and he 'regains control of his spirit'. Tempting as it might be for me to move into the metaphorical connection between Freddie and his own dilemma of reuniting his body and mind, I move instead to the real-life dilemma he was confronted with. I think the separation between 'real' and 'fantasy' can be helpful and choose to focus on the external reality he has presented. I believe he is dealing with his mind–body split but that I must not draw too much attention to it. I ask him how he would have liked to deal with his real-life experience of being shot at in the woods. By moving back and forth between real and fictional accounts I am aiming to increase narrative flexibility in what I know to be a frozen and traumatic narrative.

I am also not sure if Freddie was indeed shot at in the woods. But thera-peutically, truth does not matter here. He has witnessed shooting in the woods and seen the dead bodies the next day being buried in mass graves.

Like many males who witness or experience violence the stories they tell often involve examples of them 'vanquishing the foe' instead of the feelings of helplessness they had at the time – the masculine experience of victimisation is unconscionably alien – that is, female.

Freddie tells me 'I would have liked to take a gun and shoot him.' His unexpressed anger is still palpable after 4 years. In our discussions together about the moral dilemmas that war brings up, Freddie also tells me 'I can't believe I'm here. I'm meant to be here but I don't know why yet? The thing about me is I have lots of spirit. Everybody loves me. I would tell people – Don't be afraid. Do what you think is right and your spirit will grow strong.' He goes on to talk about how he has learned to manage his feelings of fear and terror: 'I do my breathing exercises and I talk to myself.' I ask, 'What do you say to yourself Freddie?' (In writing this chapter I am aware that I did not ask Freddie what language he spoke to himself in.) 'I've done this and defeated it before. I am the master of my own destiny. I survived. Don't look back, look forward. I can calm myself down.'

This moral struggle of what to do when confronted with hatred and violence recurs in many of the discussions I have had with survivors of traumatic abusive experiences. For both boys and girls, it connects to the discourse of masculinities as it is overwhelming males who perpetrate the violence.[9]

I recognise that it is for the child to define what the traumatic experience is for them. Emmanuela's story below has many traumatic elements, but the peak episode she returns to and dreams about every night despite ongoing treatment is of a soldier who threw a stone at her while she was running away.

Emmanuela's story

I was playing with my brother, then my dad came home and my mum said, 'We have to get out of here.' And we did. I went back to get a teddy of mine that was really special to me and someone hit me with a stone. Then I ran and caught up with my mum, dad and brother. I was bleeding. I saw people lying down on the floor and soldiers shooting and I saw smoke and heard gun noises.

I was so scared and I thought what might happen to us. When I saw all those people lying down, I realised they were dead. I said to myself 'Am I going to be like that?' I couldn't think about anything, just to get out of there. I was talking to myself and saying, 'I can do this. I am going to be just fine'. I touched my forehead and there was blood all over my head.

Emmanuela has a recurring nightmare about this experience, especially of the soldier throwing the rock at her. She remembers feeling the blood running down her forehead. She has the scar to this day and sees it every time she looks at a reflection of herself, a potent reminder of this traumatic episode. When Emmanuela first came to see me she was having night terrors three or four times a night. This disrupted her sleep and meant she was too tired to go to school. She had no memory of what she was dreaming. Her parents described her actions and what she would say as she shouted out. These night terrors have now become nightmares and more recently dreams. This is evidenced by her conscious recollection of them, the reduction in frequency, intensity and duration of each dream sequence. Rather than re-enacting a dream sequence, she is now waking from her sleep. All these physiological signs, reported to me by her parents through an interpreter, tell me she is processing her traumatic material. Additionally the fear component has also reduced. She still has two to three dreams per week; these involve the soldier who always hides his face. She speaks to him. 'Pse?' she says [Albanian for 'why?']. He speaks back but it is unintelligible – it is in Serbian. At first she was too frightened to speak in her dream. She also saw herself as little whereas now she is more her own age and she is not only speaking to him but also shouting at him. Most recently she told me she was angry with him. We have written and discussed the soldier's point of view – his shame at throwing stones at children, his fear that she will not be able to forgive him, as well as her desire to understand a senseless act of cruelty amid an overwhelming backdrop of atrocities.

I have talked with many of the parents and encouraged them to provide, if possible, an explanation of what happened in Kosovo to facilitate their child's understanding of what has become a significant and life-changing event.

The following story by Ariola was supported by a watercolour. I had used a standard 'Life graph' and 'Life path' blank work sheets[10] to help her think about her life so far. Although I had heard the story of the 'spooky woods', it was not until she had done her painting that I realised the enormity of it. The spooky woods literally blocked off everything.

Ariola's story

> One dark night my family and I had to sleep in the spooky wood. We tried to escape from the war. It was a horrible night. We were so frightened. There was banging and shooting. My spirit got out of my body because he was scared. We managed to go to England. We were okay but my spirit wasn't. My spirit tried to look for me every day but he did not find me. One sunny morning, my spirit came to London and still looked for me. In London there was no shooting or bombs. We were all ok. The next morning my spirit found me and we lived happily ever after.

I asked Ariola some questions about her story – how did her spirit find her? She replied, 'At first he didn't know where I was. He looked everywhere for me. He needed the sun to see me. Spirits know where their bodies are. They always try to get back to their bodies.' What did her spirit look like? 'My spirit is white, long and thin. It came out of my tummy because it was scared and went back in the same way it came out.' How do you feel about your spirit leaving you? 'I feel angry with my spirit for leaving me.'

The Life graph marks out a significant event for each year of her life. You can see that life before the war was generally 'good'. She was 5 or 6 when war broke out. Getting to England was an improvement but when she was referred to me at age 9 things at school were 'bad'.

This involved teasing by other pupils, which took on a racial element including name-calling and taunting Ariola for being a gypsy. This had significance and was one of the reasons her parents fled Kosovo. A previous traumatic stress reaction increases the likelihood of future acute stress reactions developing. So while other children may have weathered name-calling in school, for Ariola it was unbearable and she was miserable. After much discussion and thought her parents moved her to a new school and life is now at least 'good'. Figure 4.1 shows Ariola's Life graph.

Figure 4.2 is a black and white reproduction of Ariola's watercolour. There is a sniper in the tree to the right. He is shooting people. One is lying under the tree bleeding. One is dead to the left. Several are fleeing in the woods. 'Where are you sweetheart?' I asked – and she pointed to the little face in the bush to the very right of the picture – the horrified and silent observer to this atrocity.

At the end of this session I talked through an interpreter with Ariola's father. He remembers the night of the scary woods only too well. The men were separated from the women and children. The sound of shots was heard all through the night and everyone had to wait until it was over – 2 days – to

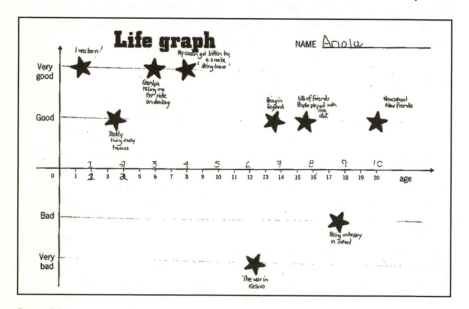

Figure 4.1

Figure 4.2

go and find their loved ones. Ariola 'slept' in the woods without her parents, surrounded by bleeding and dead bodies for two days. When I talked with Ariola's father I wanted to focus his attention on the fact that Ariola was 'now out of the woods' but that her life path still seemed to be obstructed by the experience. I invited him to help me think how we could, as adults, convince Ariola that she need not observe life from behind a bush – that it was indeed now safe to come out.

Characteristics of the traumatic narrative

A traumatic experience freezes time, and the story trapped by frozen time is often one of simple sensory fragments disconnected from associative material and devoid of the hope, light and resilience that make life positively joyful. The power of traumatic stories is overwhelming. It can be difficult to stop the narrative from tumbling out as it does in some circumstances but it tumbles fast and furiously with little or no punctuation – laden with emotion or strangely devoid of it.

Features of traumatic narratives include dichotomous views of the world. For example within sexual abuse stories, people are categorised as either victims or perpetrators with no room for any other category, which is neither victim nor perpetrator. This can also be seen in Emmanuela's story where the soldier has no real identity. He is simply – the other.

Traumatic narratives often demonstrate a 'failure of imagination' and the role of the therapist is to facilitate or lend their imagination to the creation of new narratives (Frosh 1997).

Life cycle transitions provide opportunities to re-examine and edit our 'life stories' in light of new experiences and different ways of viewing ourselves. For the children I am working with, life in England has opened a whole range of different life experiences and a new language with which to articulate and process not only the new experiences but also the old ones. So the movement back and forth between their different languaged selves is important. This is something I impress on their parents, who often are not as fluent in the new language and so are missing out on the child's discussion of new experiences and who often avoid talking about Kosovo because of the painful memories it brings up – part of the traumatic avoidance of the war. I encourage them to reclaim the positive parts of their Kosovan identity and to help their children remain 'strong in their roots' rather than begin 'growing afresh from the knees up' – both metaphors I have used and left for my sensitive and intuitive interpreters (Leonora Hashani and Fittore Zhurie) to interpret for me.

Traumatic narratives have an absence of the 'fine gradations of affect' present in other narratives. Gill Gorell Barnes (1995: 74) has written 'when systems of power become absolute, no space for the child's developing mind to include any sense of volition or active organisation of their own thinking' can occur. Hence part of the reparative experience – the 're-storying' – must be both improving the child's sense of personal agency and facilitating the meta cognitions that will allow them to organise and extract meaning from their traumatic story. Our role here as therapists has to be helping children develop 'minds capable of thinking and reflecting on experience rather than being able to respond to events through constraints induced by former terror'.

Resilience should foster 'multiplicity of self accounts with no commitment to one' (Gergen 1992: 180). The impact of trauma deletes the multiplicity of the accounts and consequently reduces the child and the family's resilience. As the families I have worked with have begun to process their traumatic material, other aspects of their former lives have emerged – stories of the land, their families, and their work. As part of the therapeutic exchange I have traded words with the children. At the end of each session they give me an Albanian word. My vocabulary has increased but it reflects our connections – 'goodbye' was the first word I learnt – followed by 'thank you'. This part of the session – our ending ritual – has been a very important part of bridging the cultural divide.

Seeing traumatic experiences from different viewpoints is the beginning of the 'thawing process', as in the example of Emmanuela seeing the story from the soldier's point of view or looking at herself and seeing if she is still a little girl or now the teenager she is, when she talks to him.

In helping children to develop coherent life stories, I try to remain attuned to the strategy of living your life 'as if' nothing has happened. This doesn't necessarily mean that the child thinks nothing has happened; it may just be the best way to carry on at this point in time. Usually symptomatic behaviours signal that some transformation is required because the 'pretend forgetting' isn't working anymore. Again in Emmanuela's case her night terrors were so frequent they disrupted her sleep and she was unable to attend school because she was too tired.

Resilience research (Rutter 1999) informs us of the importance of education and peer relationships, especially at this age, so this became one of my primary foci – to get Emmanuela back to school and with her friends as quickly as possible. The same was true for Ariola where the teasing and bullying at school kept her traumatic material alive. Her change of school made a significant difference.

Creating new stories

Can one word in a story make a difference? If we listen closely 'listening at the level of the word to the possibilities for a story to pivot at any point' (Weingarten 1998: 3) then yes it can be the beginning of something different – the beginning of generating new solutions to old problems; a different point of view, learning new meanings, exploring ways to go on living connected to our past but not unhelpfully, living in the present and simultaneously forging a way forward.

For example, working with a woman who had been raped by three men, she told me they took her spirit away. I stopped her story at this point and asked if her spirit had been taken or had it, in its infinite wisdom, left? In doing this I am elaborating on the spiritual theme introduced by the client so she can derive maximum benefit from her spiritual beliefs – a factor we know to be associated with resilience – and also looking for a pivotal point – the difference between theft of a soul and the voluntary flight of a soul. This caused her to think and in the course of her therapy to consider issues such as how she might encourage her soul/spirit to return to her. This could be seen as a 'transformation event' (Coulehan et al. 1998) in that it shifts the clients' view of her problem leading to the possibility of different solutions (White and Epston 1990). I continually search for elements in stories that are amenable to challenge, redefinitions or alternative interpretations.

Engaging parents is crucial but needs careful consideration as often the parent is also traumatised and for them to hear their child's traumatic stories can reinforce their own feelings of guilt for not having protected them in the first place. Assigning specific tasks for them to carry out, such as recording the frequency of night terrors, helps to engage them in the reparation and establishment of the safe context the child needs in order to be able to move on and through their traumatic experience.

There are other times when as a therapist I will be told that the child has forgotten the traumatic experience or they were too young to remember it.

This frequently comes up in fostering and adoption work and occasionally with refugee children. In these cases I will explain to primary caregivers the nature of a traumatic memory and help them recognise that early traumatic experiences unlanguaged can still manifest themselves in the most obvious way through bodily memory or behavioural enactments. I then encourage them to help the child 'word' the experience. I am seeking to create flexibility of self-identification and working towards life stories as opposed to a single life story, and stories that they can live with rather than something that has no dynamic quality about it but remains fixed and immovable.

By emphasising relational aspects of the stories being told or written, through the obvious therapeutic relationship but also by working in tandem with the parents, I am hoping to encourage resilient characteristics of the child/young person's identity to emerge and for their parents to guide me in finding and nurturing them between the sessions through homework tasks. This aims to avoid the traumatic configuration of self from taking over and seriously impairing the child/young person's quality of life.

In recognition of how spiritual beliefs contribute to our resilience, I have become more curious about children's beliefs about spirit. This is demonstrated in the examples and by the following discussion with Ariola:

GS: What are spirits for?
ARIOLA: They help us get through life by sticking with us. When my spirit was far away, I was weak and scared. When my spirit is with me I feel I have more energy and I am not weak anymore.
GS: What do you feed spirits?
ARIOLA: I would like to feed my spirit with happiness, kindness and courage.

The new stories become increasingly removed from the fixed and terrible moment around which a narrative may or may not have been constructed. In helping to explain to children how they react to fear and stress, I have used the metaphor of 'going turtle' where you withdraw into your shell to protect yourself. We often begin sessions with physical exercises I do with the children that are designed for 'coming out of your shell' and 'spreading your wings'. I explain we need our wings so we can fly high above our experience, get a good look at it and not be frightened by it anymore. This is the power of a good story.

Chapter 5

Children who witness violence at home

Arlene Vetere and Jan Cooper

Any act or omission committed within the framework of the family, by one of its members that undermines the life, the bodily or psychological integrity, or the liberty of another member of the same family, or that seriously harms the development of his or her personality.

(Definition of physical violence in the family, Council of Europe 1986)

In our work with children and their families where violence is of concern, we often find that the child's version of events has been neglected. This is not to say that adults are not concerned about children's experiences and do not try to talk to children about their experiences, but rather that somehow, telling others about what happened is something that children are not always asked about or even able to do. This can be for many reasons. We have found that adults vary a lot in their ability to hear what children are saying, because it is so hard to hear and to take action around children. Similarly we have found that children dare not speak, may not trust adults enough to speak, but can speak if they think they will be heard. In this chapter we want to explore how we, as practitioners, can help create the conditions that allow children to talk about their experiences of seeing one loved family member hurt another loved family member. And how, in talking about their experiences, they can be helped to confront their anxiety, process their emotional responses and develop their understanding of the meaning of these events.

Children are at greatest risk of harm in their own homes, either at the hands of their parents and carers, or through the effects of knowing about and watching other family members behave violently. Moffitt and Caspi (1998) estimate that children who witness domestic assault are four to nine times at greater risk of being assaulted themselves. The British Crime Survey (1996, 2000) estimates that one third of reported violent crime is domestic assault, with men more likely to assault their women partners, and more likely to cause physical injury. Straus and Gelles (1990), writing in the USA estimate that one in three women will be physically assaulted by their male partner over the course of their relationship. Renzetti (1992) estimates similar high levels of assaultive behaviour in her sample of lesbian women. Violence in intimate relationships is not a problem that requires a short-term solution; it needs a sustained community response dedicated to understanding the effects of transgenerational trauma, continuous trauma, and immediate trauma on children and their families – often endured in silence.

Trauma and its effects

> People are more likely to be killed, physically assaulted, hit, beaten up, slapped or spanked in their own homes by other family members than anywhere else, or by anyone else in our society.
>
> (Gelles and Cornell 1990: 5)

Osofsky (1997: 98) offers us a definition of trauma, as an 'exceptional experience of powerful and dangerous stimuli [that] overwhelm a child's capacity to regulate emotions'. We shall consider the effects of aggression on a young child's adaptation to their emotional context, in terms of their physiological and emotional development and the development of attachment systems in the family. Attachment behaviour is a developmental process of social regulation of emotion and behaviour, deeply embedded in family care giving (Bowlby 1984). Much of what socialises young children often takes place in a family context, where adults filter wider cultural messages about childhood, family life, gender expectations, and so on. Young children have no basis for comparison and adapt to their family environment as best they can. Living in a family atmosphere where violent behaviour is commonplace, or constantly threatened, can make it harder for children to learn to regulate their own emotional arousal and aggressive responses (Browne and Herbert 1997). When parents and carers are frightened or frightening, or both, they find it harder to be mindful of their children; they may be volatile or inconsistent in their caring responses, and the children are put in a double bind where their signals of distress and fear might go unnoticed. Children are impelled to seek comfort and security, yet they cannot trust it because the parent trying to give it may not be safe. This could restrict a child's capacity to learn to play and lead to the creation of defences against anxiety, such as creating an illusion of safety by identifying with an aggressor. It would seem that children show the same signs of distress when exposed to violence as when they are physically abused (Osofsky 1998).

Children who do not appear to learn constructive means of problem solving around conflict and rely on aggressive behaviours, will often face rejection by their peers, and exclusion from school. They may seek comfort and acceptance from other peers who are similarly socially excluded, but feelings of isolation and/or anger may form. Their reputation for aggressive behaviour may grow. Engaging with the education system and other societal institutions of support, such as found within faith communities for example, may be harder if the child is not learning a developmentally appropriate consideration of the needs and feelings of others.

On the other hand, resilience can be fostered within a secure attachment with someone outside the violent household, if security is not to be found at home. The securely attached child is helped to think about thinking. This has a protective function in the face of frightening events and people. The child can think about intentions and motives that may lie behind others' actions in an empathic way (Fonagy and Target 1997). This could serve to reduce the catastrophic nature of witnessing or being caught up in a parent's or carer's violence, and paves the way for a child to engage in positive relationships within social institutions outside the family, such as school. School life and, later on, employment, can offer social experiences of belonging and the development of a sense of personal competence.

Children may react to trauma exposure in a number of ways: regression to earlier behaviours, the development of new fears, loss of trust in adults, emotional instability and distress, behavioural changes, difficulty concentrating, repetitive play, and sleep difficulties, including nightmares. Any gender differences in children's responses might show in girls tending to develop more internalising problems, and boys tending to develop more externalising problems. Living with a parent or carer who is unpredictable causes anxiety and tension – like 'treading on eggshells', as one young person described it to us. Younger children are more likely to 'lose' skills, such as with toileting and use of language, whereas older children are more likely not to show their feelings about anything, such as an apparent lack of emotion in teenagers. The major defence a child may use is not to want to talk about it!

The effects on children of exposure to domestic violence can depend on a range of mediating and interacting factors, such as: (1) the characteristics of the violence (a single event or chronic violence, which can have the worst effects); (2) the developmental phase of the child and other resources and supports available to the child as a result of their age; (3) the child's proximity to the violence; (4) the child's familiarity with the victim and perpetrator (in our work we have noticed that when the child has a more meaningful relationship with the man who hurts their mother, the more harmful can be the effects on the child); (5) the availability of family and community support; and (6) the responses to violence exposure by the family, the school and wider community groups, including mental health services for children and families. This list shows why the effects on children of domestic violence are so devastating and why service providers need to consider the implications of risks and protective factors when planning and delivering services to children and their families.

Thinking about children's safety

As practitioners, we may not always know that a child is living in a context of domestic violence. However when we see a pattern of behaviours that includes loss of interest in activities, somatic symptoms, distractibility and high activity levels, repetitive play and numbing, and sleeping difficulties, we should consider whether witnessing violence might be the cause. Hester *et al.* (2000) suggest a number of helpful questions we might ask when we suspect a child is experiencing domestic violence: (1) what happens when your mum and dad (stepmum/stepdad/carer) disagree? (2) what does your mum/dad do when she/he gets angry? (3) did you ever hear or see your dad hurting your mum? What did you do? (4) who do you talk to about things that make you unhappy? (5) what kind of things make you scared or angry? and (6) do you worry about your mum and dad? If the child indicates that domestic violence is happening, Hester *et al.* (2000) suggest a series of further areas of enquiry, needed to help develop a safety plan for the child: (1) what was the most recent incident of violence? – ask the child for details; (2) were any weapons used, or threatened to be used? Have weapons been used or threatened in the past? (3) was their mother locked in a room or prevented from leaving the house – has this happened before? (4) was any substance use involved? (5) how often do these incidents occur? (6) have the police ever come to your house – what happened? and (7) what does the child do when violence takes place – do they try to intervene? what happens? where are their siblings at the time? Often children make the decision to call the neighbours or the police.

In developing a personal safety plan with the child, a number of factors need to be considered: (1) who else knows and is taking action? are statutory services involved? (2) agree with the child a safe place for them to go if there is further violence; (3) agree who the child can go to when they need to, and who will check how the child is faring; (4) make sure the child knows how to contact emergency services if necessary, but make sure they understand it is neither safe nor their responsibility to intervene actively to protect their mothers; (5) be clear with the child what your relationship is with their mum and dad, and whether you will or can speak to them about safety; and (6) ensure the support offered takes account of the child's particular cultural needs (Hester *et al.* 2000).

We have written elsewhere in detail about our approach to the management and assessment of risk in the aftermath of family violence, so we shall summarise here some key points (Vetere and Cooper 2001, 2003). We are asked to undertake risk assessments of further violence, family re-unification, couples and individual therapy, and preventive work. We prioritise safety in a number of ways. We hold perpetrators responsible for their violent and intimidatory behaviours. We work hard to help people develop accountability for their actions. We would not undertake therapeutic work of any nature if we could not see in their actions or in their talk some recognition and understanding of their interpersonal responsibilities to others, for example, both for stopping violence and for safety. We undertake therapy and re-unification work in collaboration with our referrers or some trusted professional who provides a third perspective. Thus if family members tell us violent behaviour has ceased, we use our regular reviews with our 'stable third' to corroborate what we are being told. Usually this person knows the children and visits the house on a regular basis; for example, a health visitor, faith or community leader, social worker, or a trusted grandparent. We share the risks of doing family work with the family members themselves, including extended family where appropriate, and within the professional network of family support. We do not offer confidentiality in our work, but rather negotiate confidentiality around issues that do not concern violent behaviour and its effects on family members' well being. We are very clear with family members about our duty of care, and our moral position on the use of violent strategies of social control. We recognise that those who harm others may well have been harmed themselves, both in the past and in the present, but we do not begin intensive therapeutic work on these issues until safety can be shown to be prioritised within the family by the perpetrators of harm. Finally, we ask perpetrators of violence to agree to no-violence contracts at our first meeting. We establish a safety plan in response to our detailed and careful understanding of previous violent episodes, which takes account of more immediate triggers to violent escalation and stressful circumstances that the family might be experiencing. It is essential that all family members understand the safety plan and agree to its implementation. If the no-violence contract breaks down we convene a meeting with the family and our stable third, and decide how and whether to proceed with our work. We may do some individual work with the perpetrator at this point, or we may work in parallel with another agency; for example, we do not undertake drugs and alcohol counselling ourselves. We do not see children with their parents until we are assured that their parents can take responsibility for the children's safety. We give parents credit for their efforts, even if the outcomes are not always as hoped!

Therapeutic responses

Our most important response as practitioners is to prioritise safety in our work with children and their families. Our first task is to help the child feel safe. This can be achieved in a number of ways. We can help the child and their carers to return to normal routines as soon as possible after a traumatic event. The pacing and timing of interventions are important. We can support relationships and help strengthen new relationships; for example, in post-adoption consultation work where the adopted child has come from a family of origin context of domestic assault, helping the new family settle down into its routines. The intensity of a one-to-one therapeutic relationship may be too threatening for a traumatised child at this time.

Knowing *how* to talk to young children and their parents affected by exposure to family violence, even though we may not always know the answers, is important. Patience and cultural attunement are needed to understand children's responses and to help people cope. When children talk to us, they need to know our anxieties are both contained and containable. Young children need reassurance, protection, simple answers to questions, and understanding for 'clingy' behaviour. Children need realistic answers to questions, help with maintaining their routines and structured, non-demanding tasks, and gentle, firm limits for their behaviour. Adolescents need factual answers, discussion opportunities, help with linking thoughts to feelings, encouragement to take up community based activities, and some involvement in emergency issues and decision making. Families need practical and/or faith-based support, help in resuming their routines, and therapeutic help with longer term adjustment problems.

Parents themselves may be traumatised, and may not want to listen to their children because it re-evokes their own traumatic experiences. In looking for strengths, we join with parents in the places where things go well, while acknowledging the awfulness and the distress. Parents and carers need to trust the information we give them, hence multidisciplinary collaboration needs to be seen to be happening. We can support parents in listening to children, and our multidisciplinary colleagues can create a context of support for us in this difficult work. We all value talking and listening. For some children living in a context of domestic violence, most support may be offered through their schools. As community practitioners we can help raise awareness of the effects of domestic violence on children and help parents and caregivers pay attention to the effects on children in developmentally appropriate ways. As child and family mental health practitioners, we bring an understanding of people's sensitivities, of how people communicate, how things can go wrong in family relationships, and the development of resilience, which may be helpful to other professionals who come into contact with children who witness domestic assault.

Case example one: Kate and Sue Rivers

When trauma and its effects remain undetected

Witnessing a parent's violence to the other parent can affect a child's social and emotional development, their ability to trust, to learn, to manage anger and regulate emotion, to play and explore, and their developing sense of their self-esteem. Living in a household where family members behave violently means living with fear, abuses of power, threat and intimidation, betrayal of trust, and the creation of family secrets. Children learn that violent behaviour is 'tolerable' and that adults get away with it.

In the following example, we explore the effects of unacknowledged trauma in the children. We were jointly instructed to undertake an assessment on twin girls, aged 12, with respect to whether their mother was fit to look after them, and whether their father should have contact with them. The family was a white Welsh family living in the suburbs of a large metropolitan city. At the time we met the girls, Kate and Sue, and their mother, Mrs Rivers, they had not had contact with their father for over a year. We read the court papers released to us and learned that their father had tried to kill their mother. Both girls had overheard the attack and, as far as we could see, no one in the legal and child care system had paid attention to this in any way that had been written down. Mr Rivers had been found guilty and was sent to prison. It seemed he had been released after 3 months, earlier than the girls and their mother had expected, and they had not been warned of this. The first they knew of his release was when Kate saw her father sitting in his car at the bottom of their road.

In undertaking our assessment we met with both girls, separately and together, Mrs Rivers, Mrs Rivers and the girls, Mr Rivers, the social worker, and other professional staff, such as teachers. There were no extended family members living locally. In the period following Mr Rivers' arrest and imprisonment, Kate's behaviour had escalated in seriousness and caused serious concern to the adults around her. For example, Kate accused her mother of harsh and unusual punishments, such as tying her wrists and lashing her to a tree in the garden; and she accused the school staff of kicking her and tying her wrists. Mrs Rivers was concerned by stealing within the home, attributed to Kate, and the repeated and worsening cutting of Kate's clothes. Concern about Kate during this period had escalated to the point where social services took her into care, and she lived with six foster families in 3 months. She was returned home at the point we met the family, partly we believe because she would not settle in foster care and insisted she wanted to return home. Our instruction showed that Mrs Rivers was suspected of deliberately harming her daughter.

Once we started the process of meeting and interviewing the different family members and professional staff, we realised that no one had understood the effects on children of living in a home where their father had intimidated and assaulted their mother over an extended period of time. The girls' voices had been marginalised as professional energy seemed concentrated on showing the mother to be unfit, and supporting the father's wish to see his daughters. On talking to the girls and their mother, we discovered that following their father's release from prison, both girls insisted on sleeping in the same bed in the same bedroom, forsaking their earlier sleeping arrangements. Kate insisted on tying up her bedroom windows with an elaborate arrangement of rope and refused to open the window despite the seasonal warm weather. This behaviour had been interpreted within the professional system as further evidence of the bizarre practices within Mrs Rivers' home, and her inability to manage her children. We could not find an appreciation of the effects of chronic domestic violence on a woman and mother, either in the court papers or in talking to the professionals.

Through talking to the girls on their own and together, we slowly pieced together an account of their reactions following the assault on their mother. Kate had come into Sue's bedroom once the attack started, and then wanted to rescue her mother. Sue prevented her, holding her hand over her mouth, in case she should cry out and draw their father's attention to them. Both girls hid under the covers while their mother managed to escape and rouse the neighbours. We learned that both girls struggled with the guilt of not saving their mother from an awful attack. They both reported significant anxieties and fears subsequently. We learned that much of the stealing within the home had in fact been done by Sue, and not by Kate as assumed by her mother and social services. Kate in her younger years had been a very fiery child, whereas Sue was always seen as somewhat demure in her manner. This served to deflect adult concern away from her at a time when she too needed it. We learned that Mr Rivers left sexual bondage magazines in the bathroom where both girls had been able to see them, despite Mrs Rivers' attempts to hide them. Kate told us she knew her father had tied up her mother and had always feared for her safety. Kate admitted cutting her clothes and told us that a gruff male voice in her head had told her to do this.

Both girls were clear that they did not want contact with their father at this time. They were very frightened of him, and of what they thought he was capable of doing. When we spoke to Mr Rivers, we asked him how he would take responsibility for his behaviours with his girls, how he would talk to them about his imprisonment and past treatment of their mother, and how as a father, he would think about their safety and well-being. Mr Rivers was of the opinion that he had served his time, and did not need to consider the effects of his past behaviour on his daughters' emotional development and relationship with him, now or in the future.

We worked towards a different narrative in the context of assessment, by meeting the girls separately, together and with their mother. We helped them begin to make sense of their thoughts, feelings and experiences. We advocated for them in conversation with professionals and in professionals' meetings. Our report recommended further therapeutic work for Mrs Rivers and both girls, separately and together, to understand and process the effects on them, individually and in their relationships, of Mr Rivers' assault on Mrs Rivers and her struggle as a mother to re-establish her authority and to look after herself and her children in the aftermath. We recommended a change to different professional personnel, who could repair damaged relationships with professional systems, and where the workers had an understanding of the long-term effects of domestic violence and trauma on individuals and family systems.

Case example two: the Brown children

The use of scaling questions with children

In this second case example, we discuss a court assessment and the framework we created when talking to the children that ensured they were all treated with equity and in age appropriate ways. The family included Mrs Brown, Sue 13 years, Jane 10 years, Alice 8 years, and Samantha aged 6 years. During the assessment Mrs Brown discovered that she was pregnant with a baby boy. This was a complex case with professional involvement spanning a number of years. A large number of professionals were involved, with some holding the history of the case and others, like us, reading the papers and meeting those involved for the first time. When we read the court papers we could see that social services had been concerned about the children because of neglect and inconsistency in their care. At the same time, the social workers commented on Mrs Brown's warm relationship with her daughters and their very affectionate sibling relationships. Therefore, as well as their concerns, social workers also acknowledged they felt ambivalent and 'pulled in two ways' when making difficult decisions about taking the girls into the care system. Part of their concern was the inconsistency of various carers, including blaming and ambivalence between Mrs Brown and her mother, Mrs Green, as to who was the responsible carer. Although domestic violence was not specifically mentioned in our instructions the social workers' reports commented on the short- and long-term effects on the children as witnesses and victims of domestic violence.

Mrs Brown was married to Mr Brown, the father of Sue and Jane, for 5 years before they separated. Mrs Brown had been in short-term relationships with the fathers of Alice and Samantha and with the father of her unborn baby. During her marriage, Mr Brown was consistently violent to her, and his two daughters were both witnesses and also victims of his abusive attacks. Since their separation, Mr Brown had travelled around the country but regularly came back to the house, without any prior agreement, about four or five times a year. These visits were unpredictable. The trigger was most often alcohol abuse and the visits took the form of violent and frightening episodes that resulted in Mr Brown trying to break into the house, smashing windows and shouting both sentimental and insulting abuse. During these violent episodes Mrs Brown would run away or hide with her daughters. More recently Mrs Brown had been encouraged and empowered by her social workers to manage the situation with regard to safety. At the time we met her she could give us evidence (supported by the social worker) that she did not hesitate to contact the police and she cooperated with them in a monitoring system. In addition, Mrs Brown did not let Mr Brown into the house and she could pay attention to the effects of this abusive behaviour as well as try to manage her own fear. However, she could not stop Mr Brown coming to the house nor could she or anyone else predict when he would come. She felt she was being held responsible for his behaviour and we agreed with her.

Earlier, the two older girls had been taken into the care of the local authority and had been placed in a children's home for 18 months, and the younger girls had been taken into care and placed in a foster home for 6 months. At the time of the assessment, supervised contact between Mrs Brown and her children took place every 2 weeks, shared between the two sets of girls. The sisters had monthly contact together.

The local authority care plan placed before the court proposed that Sue and Jane would be placed with long-term foster carers and proposed adoption for Alice and Samantha. Mrs Brown was contesting the local authority plan. The local authority asked for experts who would work from a systemic point of view. Our instructions from the court were as follows: (1) to assess Mrs Brown's commitment to her children; (2) to assess the nature of the attachment between the children and their mother; (3) to advise how often contact should take place; and (4) to assess Mrs Brown's potential for working in cooperation with social services and foster carers.

In reading the court documents and considering our instructions, we proposed a three-part assessment with a report to the court following completion of each part. Part One concentrated on our meetings with Mrs Brown and Mrs Green. If Part One resulted in a positive assessment, we proposed that in Part Two we would meet with Sue, Jane, Alice and Samantha and this would lead into Part Three in which we would meet with the professionals involved. The whole process was set out in the following way: (1) six sessions with Mrs Brown, including a meeting with Mrs Brown and her mother Mrs Green; (2) two individual sessions with each of the four girls; (3) one session with the children at each carer's home; (4) two joint sibling sessions at the local authority children's home; (5) one meeting with the Children's Court Reporter (CAFCASS); (6) one session with the local authority social workers; (7) one session with the local authority residential care workers; and (8) one session with foster carers. This strategy enabled us to widen existing narratives to incorporate multiple perspectives. Such action enables a thoughtful process that brings forth marginalised voices, while maintaining neutrality and keeping the children's interests and well-being in focus.

Because of the long history of this case, the complexity, and the strong differences in professional opinions and representations, we were clear that whatever recommendations we wanted to make would need to be the result of some very robust thinking. Our thinking needed to be as transparent as possible so that we could defend it, both in the way we structured our assessment process, and theoretically. Thus the following questions and tasks formed the core of our interviews with each of the girls on their own, together in pairs, and all together. The interviews took place within an 8-week period. The questions were adapted and made flexible in age appropriate ways. We encouraged Sue, Jane, Alice and Samantha to ask us questions as well as encouraging their ideas and comments.

Questions and tasks in our first interviews with the girls

- Question 1. Who had told them about our visit? Did they understand all that was said to them? Could they ask questions if they were not sure?

Informed consent and understanding confidentiality is always a complicated process when working with children. As this was a court case we could offer no confidentiality, and we could be clear with them about this and tell them the reasons. We started by asking them a 'who?' question, as a way to a systemic understanding about who supported them, who gave them information and who they thought they could trust. A court assessment necessarily means that the practitioner does not have time to get to know a young person, but has to ask important questions. Using a table top with a few objects it is possible to set out the 'players' representing the Judge, Court Reporter (CAFCASS), us, social workers, and so on, and also including the person named as the 'who' person. Setting it out in this way we could talk about the 'players', who the players talk to and what decisions they have to make. We could also tell the story of how we became involved and how we decided to ask them all the same questions so it would be a fair process. We encouraged them to talk together about their conversations with us if they wanted and needed to.

- Task 1. We asked them to do a family drawing showing who was in their family.

All the sisters put the same people in their drawings.

- Task 2. We asked them to position themselves on a scale of 1–10, number 1 being 'I want to go to live with Mum' and number 10, 'I don't want to live with Mum'. Added to this we asked their opinions about the views of all their sisters and where they thought their sisters would place themselves on the same scale.

This question allowed us to think about their individual responses but also to develop an understanding of their sibling relationships. Interestingly they all knew the opinions of their sisters and they were all accurate in their predictions.

- Question 2. We asked them to tell us about themselves and some of the things they both disliked and enjoyed at the present time.

This question was asked around everyday things and events. We wanted them to tell us about their lives in the children's home and in foster care from the time they went to live there. They could give us an analysis of the good, difficult, sad, happy and everyday events and we could begin to think about the future with them.

- Question 3. We asked them to consider three possibilities if they went back to live with their mother; (1) what would they look forward to; (2) would they be worried or fearful about anything and if so, what would that be; and (3) how did they think their mother would manage to look after them? We asked them to tell us by giving everyday examples.

This continued the previous question but with more specific answers to our questions and allowed them to talk about Mr Brown. The important question about fearfulness and safety was talked about by all of them except the youngest who did not want to engage in that subject at all. In an assessment in which the practitioners are always working against the clock, the dilemma about having a conversation about fearfulness is in avoiding making the young person more anxious and fearful than they were in the first place. We understood from their descriptions that they were all fearful of Mr Brown and his visits. The explanation of the two oldest girls was that it was not him, it was the alcohol. They did not want to live with him, but they did want to see him from time to time and they predicted that if we asked their mother, she would say the same.

- Quesion 4. We asked them to think about what would happen if they did not go back home, and what would they wish for in the immediate future.

During all this questioning, we reassured them that we were not looking for the 'right' answer. We wanted to know what their ideas were.

- Question 5. We asked them to think about their experiences and knowledge of themselves: (1) if you feel sad what do you do to cheer yourself up; and (2) if you feel angry who can you talk to or what do you do when you are angry?
- Question 6. We asked them to think about their family contact and specifically what kind of contact they had with their family. For example, did they want to have any contact with their grandmother, Mrs Green?

This question allowed them to think about their wider family, and the tempestuous relationship between their mother and grandmother.

- Question 7. We asked them to think about who was closest to whom and how they got on together, again with everyday or historical examples.

These questions allowed us to learn about the complexity of the sibling group. It also allowed us an opinion about the two oldest and youngest in relation to the proposed care plan that would separate them. The issue of open or closed adoption was in our minds as well as future contact.

- Question 8. We recommended that they should ask their carers to call us if they had questions after we left.

Questions and tasks in the second interviews and sibling group meetings

In these interviews we re-asked task 2, and questions 3, 4 and 7. This allowed for verification of the answers and allowed the girls some time to reflect on their answers and make changes if they wished. We also added and expanded the following questions:

- Question 1a. We asked them to think about who had been most helpful to them in discussing our visits.

This question allowed us to think further about their relationships with their carers and their capacity to work with or see professionals as potentially helpful.

- Task 2 was re-asked and expanded. We asked again about their views and expanded into the possibility they might want to make changes, or their sisters might make changes. This also offered them an opportunity to elaborate on their answers.

This task allowed us to understand further their individual needs and those of the sibling group and family, including their mother, grandmother and unborn brother. It gave an opportunity to answer questions over time and to reflect on their answers. Again we were trying to offer them opportunities rather than wanting the 'right' answer.

- Question 2 was re-asked. We asked them to bring us up to date about themselves and some of the things they enjoyed or disliked.

This question was expanded into more detail, including adding or changing their original ideas.

- Question 2a was new. We asked them to consider the questions, 'If you can't live with your Mum: (1) how often would you like to see your Mum and/or Grandmother; and (2) how often would you like to see your sisters?'

- Question 3a was new. We asked them all to consider how they would manage if they all went home to live with their mother, and then what difference the new baby would make.
- Question 4a new. We asked them individually and together what they would have to do if they went home to live.
  We asked them to expand on question 4. In question 4 we asked them to think about what would happen if they did not go back home. If this happened how would they advise us to write our assessment?

For example, in relation to their understanding of fairness and equity, we asked them to comment on either one of them going home, all of them going home, or in different combinations. This opened up the important possibility that they might want to go home but they also might believe it would not work and they would not be disloyal for saying it.

- New task. As a whole group task we asked them together to draw a picture of themselves as siblings.

This was by far the most popular request of the whole assessment and was very enjoyable. The two older sisters included the unborn boy baby.

It seemed to us that the unpredictability of Mr Brown's visits to his family home had been influential in making the family and professionals believe there was nothing they could do about it. Therefore, the violence and intimidation were not talked about openly and a fierce family loyalty that could be described as 'it's us against the world', developed. We thought it would be helpful for family and professionals alike to have the subject openly discussed in terms of continuing risk assessment, safety plans and understanding the emotional response to trauma. It is helpful for any practitioner in a case like this to ask themselves, 'what are the effects on the children when the professionals feel hopeless and/or scared by someone in their family?'

We found Sue, Jane, Alice and Samantha to be appropriately responsive to us; that is, initially unsure, but warming to us as we engaged with them. They were cooperative, well informed and very aware of one another's needs and opinions. They knew and understood far more than the court reports indicated. Although the reader may find our questions rather formal, when we were engaged in the process we found them helpful in enabling us in a mutual quest for all points of view, and they demonstrate the importance of a framework for interviewing children. When we talked to the other professionals in Stage Three, our description of the process allowed the girls' voices to be heard in a way that minimised professional rivalry and differences of opinion.

Secondary traumatisation

Figley (1995) notes that powerful feelings can be evoked in therapists and practitioners who work with children exposed to violence. Thinking about children can evoke our own childhood experiences and our wish that children should not see certain things. When dealing with the effects on young children, Figley argues that we are at risk of being overwhelmed by our own responses. These feelings, while expected, if left unexamined or unacknowledged can get in the way of our work. For example, they can lead to a loss of professional boundaries, and to an intensification of our efforts to be helpful on the one hand, or to burnout and reduced effectiveness on the other hand. The risks to us as practitioners can be found in too heavy a caseload, and too much time spent listening to traumatic material, with little or no supervision and support.

In our work with traumatised children and their parents/carers, we try to balance our own needs with our commitment to understanding the importance of prevention and early intervention. We employ a range of strategies and approaches, underpinned by our beliefs about the right to live in safety and without fear of harm from those you love and who look after you. Our beliefs sustain us, and help us persist in the face of disappointment and discouragement when things do not go well for children and their families. Our persistence is supported by reflective supervision practices, collaborative interdisciplinary partnerships and joint working where possible, trying to set realistic goals and expectations, keeping up with the research literature and attending conferences, and engaging in preventative work.

Conclusion

We close this chapter by drawing out some of the practice implications. We hope we have made explicit how our work contributes to the development of richer narratives which incorporate empowerment, a sense of agency, a sense of being heard and an entitlement to feel safe. Clearly the early years matter and early intervention matters. Children and young people need consistency, warmth and personal safety in their relationships with their caregivers. Both positive and negative experiences shape the development of children, so our task is to raise the awareness of caregivers and responders to the importance of prevention and early intervention when violence in the home is known, or suspected. Similarly, we need to try to influence the legal system of decision making, using our awareness of children's needs and the systemic implications of violent relationships in the way we write our reports and talk to judges. In planning and offering our services, we need to balance risk and protective factors, to support parents in listening to their children, and to support each other in our commitment to listen to what children have to say.

Chapter 6

Engaging children and young people

A theatre of possibilities

Jim Wilson

> Our work is always a meeting point between us as persons, not between us as an experiment. The subject for study is intercommunication between me and the patient meeting on equal terms, each teaching the other and getting enriched by the experience of involvement . . . What we do in our work is to arrange a professional setting made up of time and space and behaviour . . . and we see what happens. This is the same as form in art . . . which allows of spontaneous impulse, and the unexpected creative gesture. This is what we wait for and value highly in our work, and we even hold back on our bright ideas when they come, for fear of blocking the bright ideas that might come from the child or adult patient.
>
> (Winnicott 1970: 278, cited in Shepherd *et al.* 1996)

Clara, aged 6, is telling me about her friends and the games they enjoy playing in school. She tells me how she can skip, and sing while she skips, and there is a great deal of pleasure in the way she describes her play. Her mother, also present in the room, looks downcast and depressed. She is going through a divorce with a great deal of tension and argument over how often Clara should be allowed to see her father. She is worried about how Clara is managing this very tense time and has brought her for help. This is our third meeting and my impression is that Clara is a very resilient child who is more worried about her mother than herself.

As I try to engage the mother in talk about her worries for her daughter, Clara spontaneously moves towards the white board in my room and adopts the posture of a teacher. 'I am the teacher and you [pointing to me] are called Tommy, and you [pointing to her mother] are called Scarlet . . . and you are not to talk!'

She announces this with some authority. Her mother looks slightly perplexed but Clara has immediately given me an opportunity. I put my hand up to ask permission to speak. Clara, the 'teacher' says, 'Yes Tommy?' I notice I am role-playing a young child and so my voice changes its tone to try to convey to Clara that I want to enter into this new classroom theatre she has created for us:

'Please miss, I have a question. Some children tell me that when their parents don't live together any more the children try to find ways to help so it doesn't upset them so much. Please Miss, can you tell me what are the best things to do to help when your parents don't live together any more?'

In her initiative she had provided an opportunity to create a different context that engaged her more fully and permitted me to shift my position from therapist to 'therapist as pupil' just as Clara had moved from client to 'client as teacher'. Throughout her improvisation Clara's responses were intriguing: she mentioned how she found it important that children should not think all the time about 'the bad things' and try to do other things to make them feel less sad, although 'the monsters can sometimes come at night'. Clara thus gave an example of a distraction strategy often used by children of her age in coping with difficult emotions (Harris 1989). I could see from Clara's mother's surprised expression that she had never heard her daughter speak in this way before. We had begun to create a more improvisational space within the meeting.

I set out here to present three dimensions to the process of engaging or joining with children and young people in therapy. These dimensions are:

1   Engagement and the improvisational therapist.
2   Engagement; finding useful theories and an inclusive orientation.
3   Engagement skills; a theatre of possibilities.

I take therapy as a theatre of possibilities as my working metaphor because of its connotations with play, symbolism, and the association of forms of theatre with the idea of improvisation crucial to effective engagement (Boal 1979, 1992, 1995). Revising and challenging orthodoxy in theory and practice provides opportunities to improvise fresh thinking and skill development, illustrated through the anecdotes that follow (details of which have been altered to preserve anonymity). The exploration ends with tips for a more improvisational orientation to practice.

Engagement and the improvisational therapist

Winnicott's aim of attempting to create 'a meeting point between us as persons' is informed by his study and deep allegiance to the psychoanalytic framework. Since my background is in systemic approaches, it follows that the reflection on my activity as a therapist will be explained through this perspective. For example, if I use puppets in a session my study of systemic family therapy and the developments in narrative and social constructionist theories have more than a hand in dictating how the puppets behave and what they talk about (though to date none of the puppets have been called on to describe their theoretical influences to their young clients). Earlier chapters in this book have elaborated the theoretical influences in family therapy and so I will limit discussion to a brief account (for a fuller, general orientation see Wilson 1998).

From scientific systems talk to language-in-action

I owe much of my early theoretical influences to the ideas of the Milan Associates (Palazzoli *et al.* 1978, 1980a, 1980b) and specifically to Gianfranco Cecchin (1987; Cecchin *et al.* 1992, 1994) and his ongoing consultations over many years with my colleagues at The Family Institute in Cardiff. This training taught me the art of influential questions and the capacity to value the systemic logic in any given situation. His teachings (though he would never refer to them as such) interrupted any tendency I may have had towards believing too firmly about how families *should* conduct their lives and solve their problems. Instead I learned to apply an attitude of playful curiosity and serious irreverence towards orthodox practices and the limitations of grandiose theories.

In recent years, like many other family therapists, I have opened my eyes to the possibilities in more collaborative influences to practice (Hoffman 1981, 1993, 2002; Anderson and Goolishian 1998; White and Epston 1990; White 1995; Smith and Nylund 1997). These practitioners employ the metaphor of 'conversation', 'narrative' or 'story' for therapy and focus attention on how language creates reality/ies. The emphasis on language, story and conversation certainly influences my practice but it is important to include how this shift has obscured the role of communication *through action* and *activity* in therapy. Many family therapists are trained to adopt a largely sedentary position – conducting a session from the one position and expecting clients to do the same – unless, of course, there are some young children in the room. In such circumstances a number of toys (if available) may be placed in the corner of the room and the children invited to contribute from a safe distance. This is perhaps a caricature but there are still too many colleagues completing family therapy training without much direct experience of interacting therapeutically with children in the presence of their parents or on their own. Yet, without entering into the potential and often real experience of discomfort and/or satisfaction of trying something different, new skills will not develop and practitioners will 'play safe', failing to realise their potential as practitioners or to tap the creativity that may be resting in the child's mind if only we could make a move towards them.

It is because of the potential to enrich practice with children and parents that the dominant metaphor of therapy as a conversation has its limitations in practice if not, strictly speaking, in narrative theorising. However the words 'language' and 'conversation' have dominated the grammar of therapy and the words 'drama' and 'action' have had only bit-parts in recent years, possibly because, in Britain at least, the action-oriented approaches associated with early structural therapies were considered old-fashioned, redolent of patriarchal values and a 'therapist-knows-best' attitude towards family functioning. This trend in the culture of family therapy has contributed to an overemphasis on therapy as a talking medium.

The spoken word is invisible but the term, *language in action* allows for much more flexibility of physical movement – as well as movement of thought and word. These are inextricably linked. Ideas inform action and movements towards more improvisational possibilities. As the Norwegian sculptor Gustav Vigeland (1869–1943) advises (in an inscription at the Vigeland Sculpture Park in Oslo): 'choose your words, they become actions. Understand your actions, they become habits. Study your habits, they mould your character.'

In addition to a consideration of language and action the practitioner must be aware of opportunities for improvisation. This principle applies equally to experimenting with new techniques and can lead to a more 'alive' practice and practitioner. So the engagement of children and young people is facilitated by a therapist who is willing to explore what is possible while at the same time being mindful of his or her own limitations and the constraints of the working context. Engagement is not down to technique alone: it comes from a sensitised connection with the context in which the meeting between client and therapist occurs.

The aim of trying to introduce a 'not too unusual difference', along the lines of Andersen (1990), means attending to our feelings of comfort or discomfort and paying attention to the signs of comfort or discomfort shown by our clients. This helps us to gauge the capacity of all concerned to make the therapeutic session safe enough to improvise (Byng-Hall 1995). Our capacity to engage with children includes a consideration of the possibilities and limitations of our professional identity and how our agencies or job-remits construct a professional protocol within which certain ways of behaving and acting with clients are acceptable or unacceptable. Professional prejudices organise practice such as a belief that family therapists should not meet with individual children or use creative arts techniques since these practices are the domain of other professionals. It is easy to fall for orthodoxy when, in fact, certain orthodoxies are constraints to creativity. Prejudices against creativity can also infiltrate family therapy training programmes.

The danger of forgetting old ways

Once I was offering a consultation to experienced family therapists to explain my ideas about more improvisational possibilities in working with children. At the coffee break one of the group approached me to tell me that he trained as a play therapist many years ago. However when he later entered into his family therapy training he put aside those skills, techniques and methods that had informed his repertoire as a play therapist in order that he might focus on the procedures necessary in becoming a family therapist. This division of disciplines into specific professions is perhaps understandable, yet it raises an important question: do we limit our potential resourcefulness as therapists and hence the potential connections that we can make with children by adhering to ideas of how one *should* conduct oneself as a professional family therapist? Adherence to an assumed orthodoxy can limit possibilities of making the therapeutic encounter more creative for everyone in the meeting. Feedback from children in therapy (e.g. Stith *et al.* 1996) indicates that the therapist who is not patronising and who shows a capacity to use activities as well as words in the encounter will make for more active participation by children. The child's feeling of being understood, so that his or her difficulties are taken seriously, is crucial to good engagement. It is also vitally important that the therapist makes every effort to try to understand the situation from the child's perspective – to enter the *playground of ideas and activities* familiar to most children. This playground includes such activities as art, music, play, pretence, storytelling, games, and playful ritual. The dramatic compositions in play can be used to shape the meeting into a theatrical domain not only for the child but for each participant in the session. The therapy door can become a potential proscenium arch: one in which the actors and the audience shape their various positions and in which the systemic therapist's job is to maintain a safe improvisational context.

Engagement skills: the ability to decentre and take a new position

The ability to decentre (Donaldson 1978) refers to our capacity as adults to try to imagine how the world is experienced by the other, as if to see from behind the eyes of the child. The almost inescapable consequences of working from within social services and health service communities are that children referred to these services soon acquire definitions of their identity shaped by the adults and professionals who surround them, creating a form of sediment that chokes off a child's identity and capacity for resilience. This influence can hold an almost hypnotic power over us if we are not careful. Frequently a tension exists between the perspectives of adult carers, therapists and other definers and it is this tension of perspectives that creates the material for the systemic improvisational context. If we do not also engage with the gatekeepers of the child's identity we may risk losing a therapeutic hold on the work.

Engaging with the emotional context: finding the music in the words

In one family session a father was so angry with his daughter, berating her and pointing his finger accusingly, that I almost stopped the session. I had also lost sight of his desperation to find answers to his child's challenging behaviour. I needed to make a more useful connection with the father in order for him to allow me to make a more useful connection with his child. In this case I was eventually able to talk with him about the effect of his recent diagnosis of diabetes and the restrictions this meant for his life. He talked about his stresses at home and about his money worries. When we talked about his life and his uncertainties only then were we able to create a different conversation around his daughter. This attention to the music of uncertainty in the man's words of complaint helped me to move away from becoming the opponent of the parent.

The need to try to create an imaginative connection with the child's perspective is therefore related to the therapist's ability to engage the parents (and/or other significant players). To do this requires a search for a resourceful context from within which a novel idea or behaviour or feeling can emerge. This means actively seeking out a connection with aspects of our clients' lives that hold potential and strength without challenging the negative identities too soon. These negative self-descriptions and descriptions of others are often familiar dependants that need to be understood rather than chastised. In addition, the systemic therapist needs to look to his or her 'inner talk' (after Andersen 1990) for direction and connection. Because the playful context is a delicate domain systemic therapists who plan and think too hard beforehand may find their good intentions trip them up. Yet we must also allow ourselves to think: to have 'little theories'; to attune ourselves to the emotional context (the mood and feel of the session); to consider both our physiological and intellectual responses; and to notice, observe and reflect on what position the child is offering. The systemic improvisational therapist has to wait to see what might emerge while at the same time holding on to ideas informed by the complex context of relationships within which the interplay develops.

Engaging in practice: a theatre of possibilities

Augusto Boal (1995), the theatre practitioner, considers that the knowledge-enhancing power of the theatre is due to three essential ingredients which I will illustrate through case examples. The first of these is '**The property to magnify everything allowing us to see things which (in more distant form) would escape our gaze**' (Boal 1995: 26) (author's emphasis).

The boy who lost his laugh

Alan has just turned 5 years and he is already suspended from primary school for hitting other children, spitting at teachers and refusing to obey the rules in the classroom. His mother and father are very worried. They explain to me in the course of our first meeting that Alan has always been a very protected child. He had many medical complications when he was first born and he still requires regular medical checks for some possible developmental problems. I learn that Alan had an older sister who died in hospital when she was only 10 weeks old. In the course of our meetings the death of this first child begins to be discussed and the intensity of feelings of loss, and anger about her loss, is palpable, immediate and moves all of us to tears. Later in the meetings the parents, Sian and Neil, wonder if Alan would find it useful to meet with me on his own. I agree that this may be a useful step.

(An aside: Sometimes parents who see a family therapist about a child-focused problem will also feel that their special child needs special attention on his own and Alan was no exception. In these situations I try wherever possible to engage the parents as my consultants to the individual sessions with the child. In this situation I arranged for the parents to observe my play with Alan from behind a one-way screen and at a later date organised a meeting (sometimes on the telephone) to share our impressions of my session or sessions with their child. I find that in most situations parents are immediately interested in their role as consultant/observer and feel much more involved in the therapeutic process as a result. This requires a certain amount of courage from all parties, not least the therapist who may feel awkward at being observed or worried that he or she will do so well in the session as to deflate the parents even more. In my experience this is unlikely to happen when sufficient honesty and trust have been established between parent, child and therapist. Expertise is easier to acknowledge when it is reciprocated. Sian and Neil were pleased to be asked and Alan was delighted to be playing in the room with me.)

The play was partly shaped by my desire to introduce themes that seemed relevant to the boy's experience and also, implicitly, to the parents. In school he had been bullied; he had been in many arguments with teachers; he had had repeated visits to the hospital; he had recently separated from his mother in order to start school; he was finding it difficult to make friends; and perhaps he and his parents were living in the shadow of his dead sister.

We created a story in which he was a doctor, 'Dr Alan', giving advice to a character called 'Chicken Boy' who had many of the difficulties that Alan himself had experienced. But in the play I was trying a little too hard and I needed to relax more, to think less, and pay more attention to what was happening in the moment-to-moment interaction with Alan to see where he might wish to direct the play. When I slowed down my endeavour I noticed that throughout the play I could not recall Alan smiling or laughing. Neither could I recall him smiling or laughing in any of the previous sessions. This created a new idea. I said, 'Chicken Boy has one other thing which he is worried about. Do you know what this is? I'll tell you. He's just noticed that he's lost his laugh. Do you have any idea where he put it?' (I put my hands in my pockets to search and I look concerned) 'Where has his laugh gone?' Alan and I then spent some time searching for the lost laugh and eventually I said, 'I wonder what this laugh will sound like when it comes?' and I offered some funny sounds hoping that my silly imitation laugh might lead to some genuine giggles. The giggles didn't come but eventually a smile came across his face. It was remarkable because of its unexpectedness.

Soon after this we ended the session and when the parents came out from behind the screen I could see that Neil was moved by the play, but I did not want to enter into a conversation at that stage. This would have created a clash of contexts between the imaginative playful domain and the context of analytic talk by the parents and me *about* the play session.

(An aside: This stage is variously referred to as 'parent business meetings' or 'telephone conferences' or 'shared impressions meetings'. The parents in the role of 'consultants' create an atmosphere that can dispel expectations of the therapist as the Wizard of Oz. Parents will sometimes remark on patterns of interaction between child and therapist that reflect their own struggles. Rather than this being construed as a failure by the therapist to work their magic it is more often the case that this pattern of connection becomes a source for further joint exploration of possibilities. This more useful frame is made possible by creating a context in which the parents participate actively in the child's play sessions. Defensive postures are less likely and the myth of therapist as Superman is dispelled without the therapist's credibility being lost. The aim of creating a useful improvisational context takes precedence over the desire to show off one's expertise.)

Reflection on the boy who lost his laugh

'The boy who lost his laugh' could be seen as a metaphor for a family that had lost its sense of joy in life. It was as if this moment in the play with Alan created a connection between the child and the pattern of sadness that seemed to impregnate this family. This was only part of the work with Alan; his school-related problems have involved a wider systemic network including the head teacher and an educational psychologist. Yet Alan is making changes too and his parents describe the atmosphere at home as 'much lighter'. Alan's parents followed the session with a wish to talk about the loss of Anna their daughter and their subsequent years on antidepressants.

Engaging children in therapy is a multi-level systemic process which takes account of the perspectives and concerns of parents and other professionals involved with the child (Carr 2000a, 2002; Fonagy *et al.* 2002). Unless there is a general context of concern and mutual respect between professionals and family, the therapist and family will be unlikely to make full use of these collaborative endeavours.

The second essential ingredient of the knowledge-enhancing power of theatre is **'The doubling of self which occurs in the subject who comes on stage . . . which enables self observation'** (Boal 1995: 26) (author's emphasis).

The family as director, and therapist as actor of inner talk

A social work colleague, Sonia, was invited by me to offer her reflections on the conversation I had just had with three family members, a mother in her 30s, a boy called David aged 15 living in foster care, and his younger sister Jennifer aged 11 who was living with her mother at home. The session had been full of tension, with the mother complaining about the boy's lack of understanding and the boy similarly complaining that his mother never did enough to get over her depression and 'sort out her life'. Despite this tense atmosphere it had been a lively session and there was some hope that the boy would, in time, return to his mother's care.

When I asked Sonia for her reflections she spoke passionately in support of the mother and criticised the boy for not understanding his mother, raising her hand and pointing a finger accusingly. It was clear that she chose to be the mother's advocate in this session. I had not anticipated this response and realised that as she spoke I had become a secret ally to the boy. I had noticed my feelings to identify with the boy's perspective were stronger the more my colleague was advocating passionately for the mother, so how could we use these positions in some way to benefit the family? My initial temptation was to defend the boy but that would have led to an escalation between my colleague and myself and would have become an enactment of their inter-action and difficulty. So, instead, I took a risk and suggested that my col-league Sonia and I might try something. I wondered if Sonia would be able to advocate from the position of the mother while I took the position of the boy and together we might try to improvise our associations drawn from the anger between David and his mother Rebecca.

To my relief my colleague entered into the spirit of the improvisation and we asked the family if it would be possible for them to comment on our attempts to talk together as if we were talking from each of their perspectives to try to understand what might *also* be present in the angry exchanges. What is important about this technique is that it moves beyond a representation of behaviour and words as enacted in a typical role play. Instead it is an imagina-tive excursion into the supposed inner and, as yet, unexpressed talk in order to help expand the possibilities in the therapy. To do this sensitively requires the therapist to judge how much of a risk to take. We have to judge how much of this imagined inner talk would be heard and responded to in a useful way and how much of it might be seen as overly intrusive and overly reveal-ing such that the integrity of the clients is threatened. So there is a fine line in scripting these inner/outer conversations within a safe enough discomfort zone. The second consideration, which is fundamental to this sort of impro-visation, is that the clients are actively involved in modifying and shaping the expression of this reflecting theatre. Our feedback is received with a sense of professional humility, one that allows for corrections to be made and yet also permits some debate to be entered into with the family. In this particular example it took a few minutes before my social work colleague and I could enter into a 'first person' narrative.

Edited excerpt (taken from video records):

Son's inner talk (JW): [in response to an accusation of selfishness made by Sonia as the mother] Yes I am selfish. You're right but I have learned to be selfish. It is important for me to look after myself because over the years we've had so many moves and so many things have happened that I am frightened that if we are to get back together again the same old problems will arise and I just don't want that to happen. I don't want yet another one of these moves.

    [Later the tone of the theatre begins to change from anger to sadness and apprehension at the fear of further failure]:

Mother's inner talk (SONIA): Yes I think you're right and I feel that it's important that we try to make it work this time because we can't carry on the way you've been going.

Son's inner talk (JW): You're my mother and I'll always love you but it's got to be different this time.

Mother's inner talk (SONIA): Maybe I also have to think about the changes in the future but you have to stop thinking about what *you* want and what *you* need now to think about what *we* need and *we* want!

Son's inner talk (JW): Well maybe you are right but maybe I also need to be a bit selfish to protect myself.

The dialogue developed further and led to a discussion later, after the performance, with the family about the breakdown in family relationships some years earlier from which they had never recovered. The themes of loss and hurt had been apparent yet never revisited or re-articulated, and instead the anger between the boy and his mother had become a persistent and repetitive scene in a one-act play. Our attempt to enter the improvised 'inner talk' of the mother and son stopped the symmetrical escalation of the arguments and broadened the narrative to include other related yet unexpressed themes. In so doing the play shifted the interactions between me and my colleague. We talked less from opposition and instead developed a different narrative that expressed itself in more appreciation of the other's point of view. By creating, metaphorically speaking, a proscenium arch around the therapy room, we had found a new way to talk and, more importantly, a new way for the family to comment on that talk: to reflect for themselves on the meanings which might be relevant from within the conversation.

    The improvisation stopped the escalation between myself and my colleague as it also did between the boy and his mother. Being part of the audience to observe the interaction somehow united the mother and son. They then become part of the team of script writers and directors in order to offer their impressions and suggestions for corrections to our script. The interaction between us became more like a collaboration of directors and actors than a formal therapy session. Both my colleagues and I were able to reappraise our positions within this domain, not just the family members. We could all consider our positions and shift them while saving face in the 'as if' world of systemic improvisational theatre.

While the above example represents a more conscious use of the metaphor of theatre in therapy, the next example is an illustration of how one can also apply this orientation by creating a context that plays with time. This is the third essential ingredient of the knowledge enhancing power of theatre: '**The unfettered exercise of memory and imagination, the free play of past and future'** (Boal 1995: 26) (author's emphasis).

Time travel talk

Jonathan is 13 and his mother Shauna feels she can no longer tolerate his aggressive oppositional behaviour. In the course of our work we learn that Jonathan's mother feels everything went wrong after his father left when he was 8 years old and since then, 'every argument we have seems to play back to that time'. Jonathan agrees that at least some of the arguments about the past were about his father leaving. I ask the mother about this:

JW: I imagine you must have tried to explain to Jonathan when he was aged 8 why his father left and what happened to him.

SHAUNA: No I didn't because I became very depressed and everyone was left dangling.

JW: So does that mean there have been many questions your son may have had in his mind and many responses you didn't have a chance to give to him because you were so depressed?

SHAUNA: Yes it was impossible and I feel that was a time when everything went wrong after that.

Reflection on time travel talk

It was difficult for the boy and his mother to talk about the father leaving without her becoming defensive and Jonathan becoming the angry accuser. But how might it look if we were to create an opportunity to travel in time to allow the questions to be asked and to allow the mother a chance to respond to her son? I asked Jonathan if he could, 'Please help me to try something a little different.' His mother and he agreed to 'let me pretend, as it were, to be Jonathan aged 8 and to return to those days 7 years ago in order to ask those questions of your mother that had never been able to be asked and in order to allow your mother the opportunity to respond and explain.' Jonathan shrugged his shoulders and agreed it would be 'OK' to try and his mother, although apprehensive, also wanted to try.

This shift from the reality of here- and-now talk about the past to a theatrical improvisation placed the past and present together to allow the expression of questions and responses which had been impossible to voice in the harsh present reality of therapy.

So as Jonathan (aged 8) I asked my mother a number of questions that I imagined it would be helpful for the mother to respond to. I enquired as to why my father left, and if it was my fault that he left, then asked, 'Why couldn't you have worked things out and made it better?', and then the most difficult question of all: 'So if it wasn't my fault that he left, was it yours?' When I asked each of these questions I paid attention to each of Jonathan's mother's responses. I could see she was finding the exercise upsetting but she wanted to persist and when I asked the last question she became very tearful. This released her to explain that after her husband had left she had met another man who physically assaulted her son and herself. She had never forgiven herself for this and felt that her son blamed her for what happened.

The time travel talk allowed for new expression while maintaining the integrity of the participants. When I returned to her son to ask his impressions he was supportive of his mother. He criticised my performance by saying it was too complex: 'When you're 8 you do what your parents tell you to do. The world is made of black-and-white.' I agreed with him that 'When you're 15, of course, you begin to see the world as full of grey areas too.'

In this above example the position of the therapist is a flexible one. It is playful in a serious fashion; it is theatrical but has the purpose of relieving human suffering. The creativity generated is purposeful and goes beyond entertainment (which in its own right may also be educative). However the therapist is not play-acting with people's lives and so the spirit of the encounter has to be shaped by professional ethics and a desire to be helpful – the performance is an aid to the therapeutic process, not an end in itself.

Engagement and children's views on what works

If we listen to what our young clients tell us about what matters when they meet with a professional therapist the responses are reassuringly obvious and reachable. The quality of the practitioner to appear authentic and non-patronising is crucial; the skill of paying close attention to the use of age-appropriate language and being able to provide a combination of talk and activity with younger children, with the aim of creating a sense of safety and trust, and the capacity to work with the young client's own concerns are all qualities common to good engagement from whatever theoretical base. The ability to take the young person's perspectives seriously and to explore their views is essential. It means entering into a trusting debate at times, offering alternative problem-solving strategies (Kim Berg and Steiner 2003) and supporting them through the changes they intend to make (Carr 2002). It also requires flexibility in stances from facilitator across a spectrum of repertoires to 'difficult-ator' (Boal 1995) at the other extreme.

In my work with older children and teenagers the therapy room becomes a workshop. We may use drawings to depict problem sequences, attempted solutions and records of inner and outer resources, impediments to finding solutions and images of alternative futures (Selekman 1997). For some young people who are not at ease with direct conversation, it is more effective to use less direct methods to communicate, such as creating journals and diaries, poetry and letters, or stories about their lives, or to write songs, or to compose videos and use other media. One colleague recently showed me an animated cartoon created by children of asylum seekers to express their views and experiences of making the transition to life in the UK. Such contributions from the playground of ideas provide the therapist with opportunities to engage and collaborate with the young persons in both exploring the context of their lives and difficulties and then finding the next steps forward.

The boy who bounced for Ireland: starting with the obvious connection

Seamus is 13 and in the first session his mother and father seemed to be emotionally wrapped around every minor concern in his life. They said he was being bullied in school and he agreed.

The father had repeatedly contacted the school and had had a series of meetings with the head teachers, yet the bullying continued. It seemed in this family that everybody breathed with the one set of lungs – a suffocating protectiveness that restricted opportunities in life, as though the boy's horizons were being shaped by his parents' worries. I learned that Seamus complained to his mother each day when he came home from school. In the session she looked a very worried woman who held her head down, frightened to speak out against her husband. After the first meeting I asked to see Seamus alone because I needed some breathing space and I needed to hear from Seamus about his ideas on solving the bullying problem. In our search for useful resources I learned that he had a technique called 'Silent Tim', which allowed him not to respond to the bully's jibes. We agreed that this was a useful resource to use and I asked him more about his life outside school. I discovered he was a good trampolinist and enjoyed being coached, so I suggested that I could be his coach to help him deal with the bullying problem. He was to keep a journal of his 'Silent Tim technique' and how effective it could be, but I suggested that he was not to tell his parents each day when he came home about his school life or to discuss any troubles that arose. Instead he was asked to keep this diary secret from them. (I later explained this task to the parents and said it would help me greatly if they would support their son in his private enterprise.) The school-bullying problem had disappeared by the next session. However his tone was still sad and defeated. He explained that the bullying was no longer a problem, but that he was very concerned about his father and mother arguing and he asked me if I could I help them because they were talking about separating.

This disclosure does not happen very often in my experience but with Seamus it led to a discussion with the parents about the son's concerns for them and they agreed to have marital sessions to explore their longstanding difficulties.

This is an illustration of the need to connect with the specific problems identified by our young clients, and how useful it is to try to create a context that is familiar to them and reminiscent of a resourceful context already apparent in their lives. It was also important for me not to rush ahead of my thinking. It had occurred to me that the father's overbearing attitude towards his wife and son was a form of bullying and what was being presented by the boy was a metaphor for a problem elsewhere *as well as* a real problem in his life. It is also slightly comical to recall that when I spoke to the parents about their son's concern for his parent's troubled marriage, the father managed to correct me by saying, 'You made a mistake at the beginning by simply focusing on the school problem. You should have asked more about our marital relationship instead of just acting on our opinion about Seamus and the school!' I was happy to be corrected by him because this allowed the mother and particularly the father to maintain their integrity. The son's confidence in me opened the door to tackling very longstanding marital problems.

Reflection on the boy who bounced for Ireland

This case would tend to suggest that the boy's problem represented a problem elsewhere in the life of his family. While this was a useful idea on this occasion it is not used as a universal application. Wachtel (1994) suggests we should be mindful of considering the assumption that each child's problem *must have* its systemic origins somewhere else in the family. The danger with this prejudice is that it implicates other family members and risks their disengagement. It also pushes the therapist's focus away from the child's own concerns when this may well be a useful place to begin. In Child-Focused Practice (Wilson 1998, 2000a, 2000b, 2003) the concern is always to hold in one's mind the need to hear the perspectives of the child and to treat them seriously, and also to place these alongside those other perspectives of family members and significant others in the child's life. This creates an expanded system within which the child's perspective can be understood.

Collaboration, expertise and a theatre of possibilities

This chapter illustrates a collaborative orientation to work that implicitly debunks the unhelpful mystique of the expert in psychotherapy with children and families. Repositioning practices include the examples above as well as other action methods not elaborated here, such as reversals, mini-sculpting, playful mind reading, children as consultants and therapists and sibling groups as co-researchers. All these methods aim to shift the physical and, hopefully, the experiential and cognitive responses in client and therapist. Repositioning practices create shifts in the context of the child in therapy. The job of the therapist is to look for ways to promote expertise in context (our own as well as our clients').

Many very capable and creative colleagues working in the helping professions still hold on to a utopian idea that there is an expert somewhere who will be able to treat their young clients just as the Wizard of Oz was expected to provide answers to the problems of the travellers on the yellow brick road. Belief in the expert assessor is necessary when the Expert has made a sound judgement. But, at times, the Expert's words and opinions go unexamined, and the resourcefulness and potential elsewhere in the professional and family network are overshadowed by uncritical deference.

Many children 'looked after' in the state care system benefit most from an approach in which a context of care is provided over a long period of time, together with periodic support and advice as required (Fonagy *et al.* 2002). Therapeutic engagement is not a 'one-off' event but a process that extends beyond the relatively narrow focus of the therapy room. The systemic improvisational orientation explored here opens out the apron stage and pulls aside the curtain on therapeutic secrecy that was so much a part of earlier traditions. By creating opportunities for children and their families to become active collaborators/consultants reflecting on their child's progress and participating directly in creating solutions, the stage is set for a more egalitarian adventure which humanises the therapeutic connection with children and their carers. Using collaborative ways of working with clients is not a matter of strategy alone; it is, in essence, a way of demystifying the therapeutic process. This approach to therapy deals with the ideas brought from systemic and related concepts, and creates an improvisational practice that attempts to liberate new ideas, stories and actions and shared ownership of the process of change. The improvisation of thought moves us to a consideration of ideas beyond the norms of received theories, and the improvisation of practice moves us beyond the orthodoxy of received techniques.

With the proviso that no interaction can be fully instructive, here are some ideas to promote an improvisational attitude to engaging children and others in therapy.

Ten suggestions for the improvisational therapist

(Alternatively devise your own list.)

1 Study one theoretical approach in depth so that it becomes second nature, just as a musician needs to learn scales until he or she can play naturally without thinking about them.

2 Once fluent, look at other approaches and methods to incorporate into your practice, and ensure that your attitude is shaped towards the development of new possibilities for the benefit of clients and not the self-aggrandisement of the therapist.

3 Consider those aspects of yourself that seem to inhibit opportunities to take steps into your own discomfort zone. These may be beliefs about not wanting to embarrass yourself by playing with children or talking with reluctant or aggressive young people in therapy, especially if the parents are observing/participating. Look out for those ideas that marginalise children from the therapeutic context. These are ideas that will allow you to rationalise not seeing children when, in fact, it is your shyness, embarrassment or fear that stops you from staying with the struggle, especially when the sessions may be messy or oppositional.

4 Try to develop a professional support group that values your experimentation and takes care to ensure the practice is reflected on in a serious manner.

5 Consider ways in which your life is inspired by creative processes outside your work, such as theatre, reading, playing a musical instrument, writing stories, playing a sport, and so on. Then ask yourself: in what ways may these personal resources be usefully translated into my practice with children and families?

6 Try to ensure that you develop a 'not too unusual difference' in your practice. This means exploring theories, methods and techniques and practising them until you feel they belong to you – or rejecting them if the difference is 'too unusual'.

7 Try to establish a practice that allows you to become an expert in creating expertise in context. This usually means developing a sense of systemic humility about what is possible, especially in the presence of young children where the most creative stance may be to become artfully incompetent; let your clients correct you and allow yourself to make mistakes so long as you have created a safe enough environment in which to do this. This will inspire your clients to take risks as well.

8 Do not give up on theoretical rigour. Continue to study theories and read as widely as possible from inside and outside the family therapy field.

9 Remember that our clients are not looking for a 'wonder therapist' or an Oscar-winning performance. They are concerned to find someone who has the capacity to connect with them emotionally and who conveys a sense of expertise and competence.

10 On certain occasions be prepared for the long haul and always look to establish a resourceful context rather than feeling obliged to provide all the resources yourself since this is likely to lead to dissatisfaction and burnout.

The rest is practice . . .

Note

It is difficult to be precise about the development of an idea in a session since all writing about our recollections is post hoc. Even in the above examples where video tapes provide accurate dialogue, we are still in the realms of memory and imagination. Boal (1995) argues that 'an idea flies at the speed of light but its articulation . . . in words plods along like a horse and cart' (p. 61).

Acknowledgement

This chapter is dedicated to the memory of Dr Gianfranco Cecchin for his contribution to the field of family therapy and the vitality, wit and humanity he brought to his training and therapy practice.

Part III

Narratives of working with families

Chapter 7

Narratives of fathers and sons

'There is no such thing as a father'

Sebastian Kraemer

Fathers are just as important to their children as mothers are. This is not so much related to the level of involvement that a father has with his child, as to the child's imagined link to him. Men and women become fathers and mothers when their offspring is conceived, creating both biological and psychological systems, and the setting for a family drama.

On this stage sons are not uniquely different from daughters, but are in childhood more vulnerable to parental failures. The paternal function interrupts a boy's exclusive bond with his mother. If father is unable to do it, the task may be performed by anyone, even by the mother herself.

In therapy the play is brought to life by the actors, family and therapist alike.

'Merely players'

> The theatre, more tangibly than any other art, presents us with the past . . . In the theatre you never leave the present.
>
> (Berger 2001: 548)

We are a storytelling species, but the telling of stories is not simply narrative, it has drama too. People telling stories in family meetings have an audience. They do not quite know what they are going to say, so the play is improvised and the audience is also the cast. A father gives an account of a train journey across Britain he took alone at the age of 7. His son is listening, but only just, as he is 3 years old and very overactive. Part of its drama was created by my expression of amazement that he could have travelled so far alone. 'How did you get across London?' I asked incredulously.

Theatre and therapy are connected. If effective, both create space for new experiences, bringing them to life. Plays grew out of rituals and stories developed by our ancestors long before anything was written down. As for humanity so for each human: some of our earliest memories are of sitting spellbound on a parent's lap listening, sometimes to the same story told again and again. Tribes, nations and religions thrive on mythical stories of creation and heroism[1] (Spencer and Wollman 2002), which give meaning to the present. The capacity to make sense of the past, in particular of the motives of one's parents and other caregivers, has now become a tool of psychological enquiry. Being unable to give a meaningful account of your own personal life history is seen as a deficit. The Adult Attachment Interview (Hesse 1999) is designed to assess how the subject values attachments and is scored on the basis of its narrative coherence. This is closer to poetry than to logic, requiring creative thought. People who have had a very disturbed and disrupted childhood often fail to make any sense of it. They are the ones most likely to repeat the cycle when they come to have children of their own. Yet those who have, through luck or talent, found a way of understanding their parents' actions and attitudes[2] are more able to break the cycle of deprivation and damage. This is an active conversation with people who may already have died or disappeared.

The most powerful narratives describe irreversible changes in people's lives, neatly summarised by Shakespeare as 'exits and entrances'.[3] Children grow into adult sexual beings and then into parents themselves. Meanwhile the original parents age and die. An early biblical narrative (Genesis, ch. 10) simply lists these arrivals and departures like the text of an old fashioned title deed, without much drama. Fathers begat sons, who then inherited their possessions. Mothers and daughters were bystanders, even chattels, in spite of visible daily evidence of their major role in procreation, education, nutrition and childcare (Kraemer 1991; Zoja 2001). Until the twentieth century a struggle between generations was seen as exclusively man's work, representing the old and the new generations (Gosse 1908; Turgenev 1861).

Mothers and fathers, fathers and sons

The picture thus created is of an engagement between two people, but clinical work with families is not like that. Fathers I have met in family consultations have been, like most parents, keen to help their children, *but always with an eye on the mother*. Relationships, except the most infantile, are essentially triangular. Though he is not immediately aware of it,[4] the infant's entrance is what sets the scene. The eternal triangle – of love, jealousy and betrayal – is older than any psychological theory but Sigmund Freud was the first to state that the child's desire for each parent is at least as strong as, or even stronger than, their desire for each other. He noted how the father's presence prevents Oedipus' fate: 'The little boy notices that his father stands in his way with his mother' (Freud 1920).

From the infant boy's point of view, a father is at first a less immediate figure. The mother is all around him while he is inside her but, once he is born, this experience is gradually diluted by the entrances of other people, adults and older children, who take over from time to time. The speed of this process varies greatly, but the direction does not. The luckiest children get to know their father as an intimate early on. Most cultures tell us that the sexes are opposite so it comes as a surprise for new parents to discover that the infant requires more or less the same kind of care from both. Males experience hormonal changes when their partners have babies. A fall in testosterone makes them more maternal. Yet the differences, however small, are significant. The father never had his child inside his body and he does not have to give much, in terms of volume of genetic material and of time, to produce him. He does not even have to survive until the child is born.

Babies have little concept of gender at birth but usually develop an identification with the mother, since she is the primary caregiver. To the others around him gender is of enormous importance and the little boy soon discovers that he is male, which is not the same sex as his mother. 'Disidentification' a term coined by Greenson (1968), is the painful process of becoming 'not female', a repudiation of femininity which is a familiar feature of most boys. 'I am not like her', he thinks; but then; 'who am I like?' What follows is an identification with masculinity (see Frosh *et al.* 2001). This is an uneven journey for most boys, who will make exaggerated efforts at being superman at one moment and become helpless infants the next.[5]

Traditionally fathers came into their own when the child was older. For sons this was also the shift from mother's apron strings to an apprenticeship with father and his craft. In the modern world the presence in a small boy's daily life of real men, as opposed to stereotypical heroes in cartoons and stories, will help him to find a more balanced sense of gender (Pruett 1993). The term 'role model' is often applied here, but is inadequate. Identification is much more than imitation. A famous footballer may be a role model, but real identification can only be acquired through personal contact. The boy needs a rounded character, not a cardboard cut-out.

In non-human primates there is relatively little connection between male parents and their offspring, but as humans evolved, the sharing of food and pairing[6] led to the possibility of father–child attachments, even in infancy. But, except in the rare case when the mother is absent, the male partner does not get far as a parent unless he is trusted by the infant's mother. He may not be the father at all, and even if he is, the mother may not want him. His role is optional, whatever anyone may wish or feel. Yet in spite of the contingent place of fathers they are of immense importance because we make so much of the reproductive process. It matters profoundly to a child, as to his parents, who made him. Human imagination makes tasks into things, but a father is nothing without a mother and a child, and the same applies at each point in the triangle.[7] He is both participant and witness, both player and audience.

Long before reproductive knowledge and gender identity are issues for the child, attachments to caregivers are being formed. Attachments to each parent are independent and develop at different rates (Steele *et al.* 1996).

Recent studies seem to support the traditional sequence in which father becomes more important after 10 or 11 years (Lamb and Lewis 2004; Steele and Steele 2004) but this turns out to be dependent on early intimate contact between father and child, such as bathing the baby. The Steeles found that fathers who have not understood their own life stories, and who have not mourned their losses, are less engaged as parents. These men are more passive in their thinking and their children become less confident and less sociable. Grossmann and her colleagues (2002) show how fathers in conventional families, where mothers spend much more time with the children, have a unique role in helping them to explore the wider world from mother's secure base. A specific connection between fathers and baby boys is highlighted by Feldman (2003). She notes sex differences in the rhythms of intimate contact so that fathers are more in tune with sons, and mothers with daughters. 'The coregulation formed between father and son during the first months may be essential environmental inputs that facilitate the formation of self regulatory capacities' (Feldman 2003: 17). Father's attentive care of his baby son seems helpful in its own right, not just as an adjunct to mother's.

When mothers are depressed following the birth it is their male children that suffer the most lasting effects, particularly in self-regulation (Morrell and Murray 2002). Some of these boys become dreamy or hyperactive, even at primary school age, long after the mother's depression has lifted. Here, an involved father can minimise, or even prevent, developmental harm. Similarly if the mother is physically ill after the birth, for example a premature delivery or an emergency caesarian section, a father might come into his own as a primary parent. There is nothing, apart from social prejudices and the lack of functioning breasts, to stop men from caring for babies effectively (Pruett 1993). But in the absence of early intimacy he becomes more like a teacher, or coach. Studies on modern fathers show that they are most useful for the child's social and mental development when they are engaged in parallel with the mother, rather than 'taking over' when the child is older.

In recent decades in western and western-influenced societies, equal parenting has for the first time been considered possible. It is unusual in historical terms but it is not 'unnatural'. In some hunter gatherer societies men take an equal and active role in parenting,[8] and this arrangement may have been more prevalent for the hundreds of thousands of years that hunting and gathering was our only way of life. It is now socially acceptable for a man to be closely involved in the care of his infant, occasionally more so than the mother. But familiar distinctions between parents still prevail, so that when a child is ill at school, for example, the default response is to call the mother. Segregation of roles — 'father's money for mother's domestic service' — was the norm in many mid-twentieth century societies, but this is now in competition with a more complex notion: 'fair shares for adult parents'. The spectrum of parental roles is now greater, with some men as primary caregivers at one end, and traditional breadwinners who stay away from the nursery, at the other. In the middle, both parents may be earning money *and* caring for their children each day. All this offers richer variety and choice for families, but more opportunities for parental arguments.

When development goes well enough the players negotiate their triangular life in small steps. Toddlers have tantrums and both parents respond more or less effectively. Alongside the quality of their teamwork the capacity to do this comes from their own experiences of care in infancy. When our own rages have been calmed by bigger and more patient adults we carry within us a belief that loss of control can be managed. It is easier for two to deal with an explosive child than one alone, but it can also lead to conflict. One familiar sequence is an exhausted mother saying to the father 'you deal with him now!'

When things go wrong

Children with behavioural and emotional disorders almost invariably have a history in which this kind of containment has not happened. Even if the primary problem is mainly biological, the formation of a secure attachment between child and parents, and other caregivers, is the most important ingredient of mental resilience. Security does not depend on having their own two parents caring for them, but it does depend on having one or more faithful caregivers who can manage powerful feelings of love and hate between themselves and the growing child. It may not be fair that the mother carries a greater burden of responsibility for promoting secure attachment, but she usually does.

Many cases of postnatal depression occur when a lone mother has no confiding relationship with another adult. If she has to care for a child on her own, she is deprived of adult company and emotional support. Neither has a break from the other. Whether this is idyllic or maddening it cannot be good for either. The same applies where a man has to do the task alone, which is increasingly common. Babies thrive when they have a small number of familiar and loyal caregivers so that the child does not have to have an exclusive relationship with only one. Some of the pioneering family therapists would teasingly refer to that state as a cross-generational 'marriage' (Whitaker 1977; Palazzoli *et al.* 1978, ch. 15). Jay Haley was the first to describe the 'secret coalition' (1976, ch. 4), whose mischief has continued to preoccupy family therapists.[9] Families in therapy usually contain more than two people, but enmeshment[10] between one parent and a symptomatic child is a common theme. The props on the family stage include a bedroom door which may, or may not, shut out the child at night when he or she reaches a certain age.

Paternal function: making up the numbers

In the triangular drama, exclusion and inclusion are not fixed positions. Each player is at the same time a partner in a couple, and also alone on the outside looking in, occupying a third position, or metaposition.[11] It is a paternal function to make such experiences and reflections possible. It provides 'an alternative point of view' as one 16-year-old boy who never knew his father elegantly put it.

There are of course many lone parents who can support a healthy independence in their children, but this is likely to depend on the parent having both internal and external supports. If this is the mother, in her mind there are parents who can work together, and in her life she will have secure adult friendships (with people who can also do some babysitting). Both maternal and paternal functions will from time to time be performed by the same person, by parents of the opposite sex, or by people who are not parents at all. The Oedipal challenge is, after all, more about generation than about gender. Babies can't make babies.

Absent fathers

In his own mind no child is 'without a father'. In the absence of a given story he will make up his own. Nowadays fatherlessness is no longer regarded as an automatic disadvantage, nor is it rare. Some women choose to have children without involving the father after conception. Others find single parenthood preferable after trying to collaborate with the father or with another adult male. The findings of social science and developmental psychology show associations between variables, such as single parenthood and social difficulties, but these can be misused to make prescriptive statements about how families should be,[12] or to criticise parents who do things differently; for example, raising a child with no word or sight of father. During the last decades of the twentieth century single mothers in Britain and the USA became political targets, as if all social problems were their fault. Yet there is statistical evidence to show the benefit of having two involved parents[13] (Cabrera et al. 2000), even if they are not together.

Cooperation between parents is more difficult, but probably more important, if they are separated. Although parental separation is usually painful for children, most harm occurs when there is unresolved and relentless conflict between them, together or apart (Kelly 2000; Booth and Amato 2001). Although they may think their child does not notice it, the quality of the parents' relationship is always a matter of fundamental significance for any child. Careful agreement over contact, education and money is enormously hard work, especially when there are new partnerships, but it is a priceless gift to children when they do not have to feel responsible – like in-house marital therapists – for the way their parents get on with each other.

When the father is rarely or never seen, a child depends on his mother or other relatives to inform him. If a boy with no contact with his father hears from his mother only that he is a bad man (perhaps along with all other men) he will feel that he is descended from someone who not only could not stay at home to care for him but also would not, and therefore does not love him. This, though not necessarily wholly true, is painful and disturbing to the child's self-esteem (as much for a girl as for a boy). If the mother says good things about the absent father, that when they were together there were some good times, and that father loved his baby or his partner, or both, then the child has the chance of a good father in his mind.[14] This requires brave and active mental work on the mother's part. She may despise him, or feel nothing for him, but it is possible for a mother to make sense of her broken relationship with the father, much as parents can make sense of their own parents' deficits. A bad father can still be understood, and not just rejected out of hand. The same applies to missing mothers. These are therapeutic tasks (Dowling and Gorell Barnes 2000). Some fathers are more helpful out of the picture (Jaffee et al. 2003) and sometimes there is very little good to tell.

Father waits in the wings for his entrance between mother and son

Though some modern young couples without children may hope to discard traditional roles, once the baby is born an asymmetrical triangle is created. Biological realities do make a difference, and cultural prejudices about men and women do not simply disappear when we want them to. With few exceptions the mother is still the primary parent, while the father follows. This sequence is in many families much quicker than it was even 20 years ago but in others it is still traditional, with father seeing little of his children in the early months or years, and always deferring to mother when he does. Whatever the sex of the child, the mother tends to be the gatekeeper for his relationship with that child[15] (Allen and Hawkins 1999; White 1999); she introduces the father and child to each other, or fails to do so. And for boys there is the potential for comparisons, even rivalry, between son and father, while mother is the referee.

The triangular predicament for boys is not unique but there are developmental differences between the sexes that make boys more vulnerable to both biological and emotional stress in the early years. Because of this fragility (Kraemer 2000) boys take up most of the time of child mental health services, while girls predominate in adolescent clinics. Whatever the underlying problem – such as an inborn tendency towards anxiety, restlessness, inattentiveness, clumsiness, learning difficulties, social aloofness, or depression – the quality of triangular relationships has a powerful influence on the outcome. Clinically a case can be made for the familiar hypothesis that: *many younger boys with emotional and behavioural difficulties have powerfully enmeshed relationships with their mothers from which the father is to some extent excluded.*

Ben, a very bright and articulate child aged 8 frustrates his parents terribly, but his mother more than his father. He was referred because of poor coordination and learning problems. He had already had psychological and psychiatric assessments, and was regarded as very bright but with specific spelling and reading difficulties and borderline ADHD (attention deficit hyperactivity disorder). He had not received medication at his mother's request. Everything he is asked to do generates a self-righteous tantrum. His mother pleads with him and the noise increases. Father wants to intervene but mother keeps him away saying he is too harsh. While the boy has his own weekly individual sessions with a psychoanalytic child psychotherapist,[16] work with the couple uncovers a familiar story. Mother and baby did not have a good start together. He was born after a long labour, was often ill as an infant and mother felt oppressed by his demands. Her experience of men in her family of origin was that they always had problems. Her brother was clumsy and dyslexic and could not hold down a job and her father died in uncertain circumstances, possibly by suicide. Father's own father was distant and autocratic. The couple are loyal but it has been a struggle for them to work together for this child, especially since his younger brother was born, and had a much happier start. Ben is furiously jealous, accusing both parents of loving his brother more than him.

The child's therapist and I worked 2-monthly with the parents together. These sessions were lively, affectionate and personal. All four of us in the room have different nationalities, and much was made of our differences, but also the fact that all of us have sons.[17] The therapists are a man and a woman. Ben's weekly individual sessions demonstrated his frustration at not being able to make things happen his way. He is very competitive with the therapist, wanting to sit in her chair. He asserts that he is in the Trojan horse and she is being invaded by him. She experiences this as a strong desire to get inside a maternal figure. He is enraged when the therapist comments on his omnipotence and tapes up her mouth to silence her (dramatic indeed).

He was very engaged in his own therapy, but its effectiveness depended also on the quality of our contact with the couple, and on our active encouragement of the need for change in the way they manage Ben's outbursts. The telling of the story outlined above is not in itself therapeutic. Therapy, like theatre, happens in the present. Mother's imitation in these sessions of Ben's whining and her pleading responses is a vivid enactment of their entwined, but ambivalent, relationship. We wanted to show in particular how Ben is aroused – even sexually – by his mother's reaction to him. In the meantime mother, who had at first insisted that Ben should have special education, now became convinced that all his symptoms were due to ADHD, in spite of the fact that emotional outbursts are not part of the syndrome. I interpreted this as her desire to have a paternal prescription from someone like me, explaining how powerful – patriarchal even – a doctor feels when he has a drug up his sleeve.[18] But we rehearsed alternative scenarios for the three of them, showing how a child can be calmed when he knows that his parents are working together for him, rather than undermining each other. As I was soon to leave the clinic, I gave mother a pair of children's scissors, to cut the umbilical cord, from the play box in my room. She was amused and took them everywhere with her after that.[19]

Father was now able to make his entrance. Within a few months Ben was getting gold stars for effort at school. It became clearer to what extent he has specific spelling and reading difficulties, which may need equally specific help. But he is far less troubled and troubling. His therapy continues, and in his play he becomes more preoccupied with his masculinity and rivalry with his father.

A father may be less useful at home than away from it. In a different family a 9-year-old boy who terrorised his mother with insults and kicks got little reaction from his father, much to mother's annoyance. We made some progress in family meetings exploring the child's early life and the parents' past family histories, but not much. It then turned out father was having an affair (with mother's best friend) and so had to leave the home. After many months of justified rage from the mother, he broke up with her friend and lived alone. The boy then settled, and went to a new school. Mother said at the end that she was proud of the way father now dealt with their son 'in a way that only a man can do'.

Drawing a line

'Drawing a line' describes the setting of a boundary. Among prehuman primates the male tends to beat the bounds of the band to keep out intruders. In humans, this is a familiar and traditional paternal role too, protecting the family, but there is also a line to be drawn through the middle of it. The making of distinctions is the beginning of logical thought, and of morality too; the patriarchal Abrahamic God creates the world by marking the boundaries between sky and earth and between night and day. Gregory Bateson saw this process as the essence of mind, that knowledge is news of difference.[20] Again it needs emphasing that this is not something only men (or God) can do. The paternal function is not exclusively father's.

The particular line that has to be drawn in families is one showing the difference between generations. The Oedipal struggle is not so much a symmetrical contest between father and son for mother's love as one in which a truth has to be established; namely that the boy is not the sexual partner of the mother; the father is, or was.[21] The boys I have failed to help in clinical practice did not get this message. Between them the mother and father managed to stifle it, leaving the child and mother to consume each other with intrusive thoughts and actions, with very disturbing results. These are boys who may be clever and charming but at the same time subject to violent or perverse impulses, to lying, or to terrors that from time to time overwhelm them. The importance of Freud in this context is his emphasis on the intimate passion between mother and son. However disguised, seduction is an essential part of the drama.

This, sometimes tragic, outcome is the legacy of several generations of parental failure. From a therapeutic point of view, there is no point in blaming anyone for it. The constellation of hostile, humiliating or neglectful parents whose children then become parents is a familiar narrative in most child mental health clinics. The young woman becomes a mother – perhaps in defiance of her own – with a man who is not able to support her. He may bring in money or be generous in other ways but he cannot manage the emotional complexities of triangular life.[22] This pattern occurs in many different cultures and social classes. Education, intelligence and money are no protection. The quality of care may on the face of it seem good, with a comfortable home and a good school, but clinical stories told by parents are often heartsinkingly predictable: 'My father didn't care for me, he was only interested in his work [or other compulsive activity]. I just wished he would love me . . . My mother was depressed, she preferred my sister to me, I never felt really accepted, she was always trying to change me.' A particularly destructive pattern is where the mother has been sexually abused in childhood. She grows up feeling contaminated and has no trust in men, yet she forms a partnership with one (or more) and has some children. The relationship is not strong and breaks down. The boy child takes the father's place, perhaps by sleeping with mother, or by fighting with her. Accounts of stories like this test the patience of any therapist, and some are just too terrible to tell. Family and narrative therapies rightly prize our focus on family strengths, but these cannot be invented, any more than a mother can sanitise for a boy the disappearance of his father. The clinical struggle is to rescue shreds of competence and love from a scene which feels to the therapist like a catastrophe.[23]

Early intervention at the weakest link in the life cycle

I have met many parents with whom I can have lively conversations, and whose courage and intelligence I can admire, but whose ability to keep their actual child in mind is very limited. Instead the child is experienced through a veil of projections from past relationships, and treated accordingly. This is a dilemma for systemic therapies. It is possible to engage parents in therapy who might never get any help in their own right, yet not be able to change the 'basic fault' if the damage has been too great. Thirty years ago Selma Fraiberg coined the phrase 'ghosts in the nursery' (Fraiberg *et al.* 1975, see also Fonagy *et al.* 1993) to describe the persecutory experiences of new parents, in particular mothers, when confronted with their baby's desires and demands. What breaks through at this fragile moment in the mother's life is her experience of her own mother a generation before, when she herself was an infant. If that was 'good enough' (i.e. the best it can or should be) then the flashbacks are helpful, as if her mother were with her now supporting her. If they were bad, for example if her mother was withdrawn, or intrusive, then her view of her baby is taken over by these involuntary and usually unconscious memories, so that the baby is no longer an innocent child but someone with a grudge, or worse, against his or her caregiver. This is a terrible start, and can set in train a series of misfortunes that are increasingly hard to reverse.

A father, or other family member, has his own ghosts to deal with too – and rarely any opportunity to reflect on them (Walters 1997) – but the chances are that between them two parents will have different strengths and weaknesses which make it easier for them to overcome these threats. Given the more powerful effect of mother's care in the early months, this is the point in the life cycle at which another caregiver can modify its course. This is a paternal function, but someone else may perform it. Whoever it is, the haunted mother needs an intimate to support her. Besides that (and sadly a grandparent in such a case may in reality not be helpful) what is also required here is skilled help from health visitors and therapeutic professionals (Fonagy 1998; Barnes 2003), to prevent a vicious spiral of alienation and mistrust between mother and child, and between mother and father. This is the time to tell the story in all its painful detail. It is live, like a stage play waiting to start. The adult attachment interview, a research tool, can be adapted for clinical use to elicit it (Steele and Steele 2000). In the most serious cases clinical therapeutic interventions may otherwise come too late.

Because of the mother's pivotal role, a narrative of father and son will always include the woman in between them. The triangular drama gives depth and meaning to the relationships between the participants and to others that follow. Clinical interventions are likely to be more effective while the story is being created, rather than years later when it has become an established saga, in which the players have become attached, or even addicted, to their parts.

Epilogue: the therapist as actor

Some clinical stories would lead a passive audience to take sides with the victim, the one who seems the most hard done by. A therapist, in contrast, becomes an actor, part of the play. He or she can take sides but not for long. In the early years of family therapy much was made of 'the end of blaming' as if this could be done by will power alone. Technique is required to do this. 'Positive connotation' was devised to help the family systems therapist to be on no one's and everyone's side at the same time. In early use it could seem insincere, but practitioners gradually discovered that it made sense; that the effort to see some virtue in what appeared to be destructive was not a trick but an interpretation of deeply buried wishes or the celebration of unexpected consequences.

This conflict-avoiding strategy is easily misused. It is patronising to say 'well done' to someone in therapy when one feels just the opposite, but it is therapeutic to change your own perceptions so that you no longer feel critical. Although Ben's family story was not a tragic one, it was painful enough. His mother expected us to blame her, because she felt so guilty and had been, implicitly or explicitly, accused by others – perhaps even by her husband – of causing Ben's difficulties with her excitable temperament, as if she were drawing him into fights with her for her own purposes. This was a tempting hypothesis to make in the heat of the moment, but in family therapy it is a useless observation.[24] We had to see how the addictive quality of these rows was an expression, however distorted, of the passionate love between them, not of its denial. Once we had taken this step, which is based on a theoretical assumption about Oedipal triangles, we ourselves felt different about her and her husband's predicament. From the way we were talking she could feel that we did not think she was a bad mother, or that father was derelict in his duty. From this position it was now possible to challenge the parents to do things differently, because it came from hard-won affection rather than frustration or criticism, easily experienced by family members as contempt.

The effort to do this is not unlike the actor's method as he or she gets into a state of mind that he or she cannot yet quite believe in. It seems wrong to think of a therapist as acting, which implies being false. Yet in order to get past the ordinary reactions of sympathy and blame, therapists need a method of responding which is both genuine and also unexpected. One way of doing this is to look out for the unacknowledged positive desires that drive what seem to be irritating attitudes. Love can be twisted into unrecognisable shapes. I have found repeatedly that positive connotations can seem fanciful or absurd while I am uttering them but almost immediately, because of the reaction they receive, begin to have a truth of their own, surprising me as much as the recipient. 'In ordinary life truth is what really exists, what a person really knows. Whereas on the stage it consists of something that is not actually in existence but which could happen' (Stanislavski 1937: 129). 'Truth on the stage is whatever we can believe with sincerity, whether in ourselves or in our colleagues' (p. 130).

Acknowledgements

I am grateful to Wilhelmina Kraemer-Zurné for helpful comments on earlier drafts of this chapter, and to the families who have given permission for clinical material about them to be published here.

Chapter 8

Narrative therapy with children in families where a parent has a mental health problem

Gwyn Daniel and Bernadette Wren

Introduction: our own perspective and context

Working in an area defined in terms of 'illness' means that, as systemic therapists, we constantly need to position ourselves within several intersecting and often contradictory narratives. Engaging with, while not fully endorsing, a category defined as 'parental mental illness' means that we need to be mindful of how compelling is the medical discourse, both for families and for the professionals who work with them. While the research evidence (e.g. Rutter and Quinton 1984; Duncan and Reder 2000) clearly suggests that it is the behaviour rather than the diagnosis of parents which impacts on their children's lives and wellbeing, nevertheless the totalising category of mental illness can constrain clinicians from the creative attention to the detail and meaning of interactions that is the hallmark of effective therapy. Additionally, when working with children within a context where child protection issues are likely to loom large and where we may be affronted by the reversal of generational tasks, by the marginalisation of children's needs or by their involvement in psychotic worlds, there are likely to be challenges to a systemic approach that promotes positive connotation and encourages a sense of agency.

The context for this chapter is a clinical project we have been engaged with in the Child and Family Department at the Tavistock Clinic in London for the past two years, where we have seen families in which a parent has been involved with adult mental health services, whether or not a child has been defined as having a problem in their own right. In taking on these referred families, we have typically found ourselves working preventatively with children who are often living with recurrent family instability or in the midst of very severe family conflicts that generate high levels of anxiety.

Our motivations for undertaking this particular project are diverse, but the shared area of interest also came from each of us having specialties in two different but connected areas; Bernadette in work with children of transgendered parents (Wren and Di Ceglie 1999), and Gwyn with children whose parents are involved in legal disputes over contact (Blow and Daniel 2002 and

Chapter 11 in this volume). We each have many experiences of conversations with children who have been subjected to drastic changes over which they have no control, where they may be caught up in the continuing drama of their parents' lives and have had to adopt strategies to manage what we have come to call 'precarious parenting'. Working with the families of mentally ill parents seemed to be a logical extension of our existing work as we had strong feelings about the lack of attention paid to children's needs within adult mental health services.

We find that working with these families provides challenges to our commitment to work collaboratively. Child and Adolescent Mental Health Services (CAMHS) are routinely referred families where the behaviour of both children and parents troubles the conventions. In families where *children* are identified as having problems, while this may be shaming for parents, clinicians can engage and work collaboratively with parents within the canon that adults should help children. In families where it is primarily *parental* behaviours which are seen as problematic and where children may have taken up more or less explicit caregiving roles, parents may have a very strong wish to deny that their children are experiencing difficulty. Therefore referral to a CAMHS, while based on sound professional 'joined-up practice', may carry the added connotation for parents with mental health problems that, if their child requires this service, the child has been damaged. While our professional narrative is of preventative work and the promotion of resilience, for parents, referral may represent the most dreaded narrative – that their children have been contaminated and will in turn become ill. We therefore need to tread carefully the path between, on the one hand, providing a service for children whose parents are vulnerable, where 'precarious' parenting may have exposed them to harmful experiences, and on the other, not implying a 'cascading' effect of inevitable damage and thereby undermining the resilience and coping strategies of such children.

Children in this context are often described as 'parentified' (Byng-Hall 2002; Earley and Cushway 2002); however our conversations with children and their parents lead us to be cautious about the use of this term. Our concern is that it tends to subsume a whole range of experiences into one category, which also carries a negative and potentially pathologising connotation. As clinicians, so much of our assessment of what children can and cannot manage and at what age, is value-laden and dependent on social, economic and cultural contexts, that the term, though widely used, needs to be carefully deconstructed. It is important for us to reflect on our own professional and personal narratives about childhood, to question our assumptions about the expectations that should properly be placed on children. We constantly face the question of what constitutes good-enough parenting in this context and what are the short-term and long-term effects of taking up a 'parental' position in childhood. In our work we are interested in the ways that children construct their relationship to their parent's mental illness and with the strategies they employ to manage what can be highly stressful and frightening experiences. We are interested in how at certain times children and their parents adopt the positions of 'child-as-carer' and 'parent-as-patient', and then return to more conventional child/parent interactions. Parents are often aware that the involvement of the child in emotionally demanding tasks is seen as inappropriate, and can be aware of shifting between a 'problematised' narrative and a normative or canonical narrative. At other times, it is we, as the professionals, who take it on ourselves to 'trouble' the parental narrative if the child's active contribution to managing the emotional wellbeing of the family seems too burdensome. We try to find ways of standing outside fixed narratives – either the parent's passive acceptance of the child-as-carer or the canonical discourse that implies disapproval. We do this by exploring children's own narratives, and learning what enables each individual child to feel a sense of agency and self-esteem, and what erodes it.

We have been inspired by the innovative work of Alan Cooklin and the Camden and Islington Family Service Unit 'Kids Time' workshops, many of which we have been privileged to attend. These meetings convinced us of the benefit to children and to their parents when the parents are able to be honest enough to talk in a group setting about the impact of their psychological difficulties on their parenting, and brave enough to listen to their children's experiences (Royal College of Psychiatrists 2003).

In this chapter we outline our theoretical commitment to working within a narrative approach and its implication for practice in this area, and then explore some professional narratives about children and parental mental health, briefly reviewing the research and clinical literature. Following that, we highlight some of the narratives that we have identified from our work with children (including adult children) and that inform our ideas for change in families. We show how, within a narrative model, we use a range of interventions to amplify the voices of children, while engaging with the parental aspirations of highly vulnerable and troubled adults.

A narrative approach

The powerful message for clinicians in the narrative model is that the capacity to tell a coherent and lucid story about one's relational life and to be aware of different perspectives seems to be a critical part of resilience (Byng-Hall 2002; Walsh 1998; Fonagy *et al.* 1994). 'Coherent' here involves both plausibility and a fair degree of internal consistency, coupled with a tolerance for some uncertainty and contradiction.

Integral to this narrative approach for systemic practitioners is the idea that the narratives that lend unity to the experience of everyday life develop through multi-layered conversations (real or imagined) with significant others, as well as between aspects of the self (Vygotsky 1978; Bahktin 1981; Crossley 2000). We also acknowledge a range of variable 'selves', any one of which may do the telling, selected from a multiplicity of personae that individuals switch between as they go about their lives (Riessman 2003; Harre and van Langehove 1999). Axiomatically, the stories we tell about ourselves will not encompass all our experience; there will be gaps where things cannot be remembered or recovered into language; and alternative stories told about a particular experience at a different time might each make a good fit (Shotter 1993). Indeed, it is precisely the potential for seeing oneself differently, using different narrative accounts, that can be seen as essential for psychological change (Schafer 1992; White and Epston 1990).

Working clinically within this model, we can listen to our clients' accounts and ask how each person positions themselves and others in the stories they tell, and ask what are the implications for action of such a story. Although the plots in the lives of our clients mean that the teller is constrained in the range of possible plausible tellings, many circumstances do permit fluid positionings that imply different pictures of the self and different understandings of the world, and offer different choices for behaviour. We are curious, for instance, about whether people are performing an identity in which they are victims of circumstance, or as powerful agentic beings able to act purposefully. Or do they shift between positions in different contexts?

The parents we see are usually keen to be, and to be seen to be, 'good' parents according to the canons of their social world. They fear being judged adversely by powerful professionals and often struggle to present a narrative of the parenting relationships which explains away any apparent problems. Does this mean that if we work in a narrative model, therapists will do no more than support clients in the telling of their stories, employing a narrative strategy that supports the legitimacy of their choices and hopes, omitting awkward or intolerable events and experiences? How, as therapists, do we decide what counts as a 'better' story for all family members?

A narrative needs certain qualities to convince us of its integrity and authenticity. For example, we will look at connections among the series of stories that any individual constructs over the course of clinical sessions. A new and 'better' story needs in some way to be continuous with preceding stories and to explain what was omitted or glossed over previously; the details of the story will be more complex and varied than those of its predecessor (Rosenwald 1992). The narrative transformations we expect to occur in the course of our work chiefly come as a result of helping families to negotiate around their competing understandings of the place of the parent's illness-related behaviour in the life of the family. Generally, we hope that more views and understandings enter into people's narratives, with recognition that different perspectives exist of the same event. We hope for outcomes in which parents develop a less monological story (Lysaker *et al.* 2003) about their difficulties and come to incorporate elements of the child's experience into their story of illness and its effects. Relative to their developmental level, children can also come to incorporate elements of the parent's experience into their story.

We promote this chiefly through exploration of particular painful or troubling incidents, encouraging parents and children to articulate and critically examine beliefs and emotions around these incidents. In this way, a child can articulate beliefs about the parent's illness and has the chance to process puzzling or frightening events into a more meaningful and manageable story. Anxieties about the response of others to one's account can be explored in a safe context. We also strive to help parents and children identify in their stories positive or more 'normal' parent–child interactions when mental illness is not dominating the relationship. Times when parenting goes well, as well as difficult times, can be incorporated into a richer, more complex account of family life. With this broadening of the narrative possibilities, we also hope that parents and children may feel less powerless, and come to embrace a more realistic sense of agency.

The Edwards family's story – part I

In the Edwards family, the four boys were able to tell their mother how frightening and upsetting they found her behaviour when she shut herself away from them, when she had got into such a state in the car that she began to drive dangerously or when she interpreted facial grimaces as a hostile signals. It seemed to be the mother's trust in the therapist and the therapist's constant reiteration that she was being helpful to her children by allowing them to speak like this that enabled her to continue to listen to their concerns and think about how to act on them.

In this family the children took different positions around their willingness to express fear and anxiety. The oldest, John, who lived away from home was able to talk to his mother in a very challenging way without becoming blaming; the second boy, Terry, aged 15, who was especially close to her, found it extremely difficult and did his best to distract the others. The third son, Paul, took a more critical stance and the youngest, Darren, aged 11, was the one who showed most distress. It is very helpful in working with siblings to ask about how the position each child takes affects the position others can be free to take, implying the idea that narratives are relational. Working in this way also helped break up a potentially monolithic narrative of 'the mother versus the children' in which Terry, in particular, might have needed to show his loyalty in more covert or bullying ways.

Within this framework, we then employ a wide variety of other therapeutic techniques aimed at supporting families to make changes. Interventions may involve whole family or individual work, or both; we may work closely with the network of professionals or simply acknowledge their role as providing a (psychiatric or legal) frame for therapy; we may see siblings as a group; we may do symptom-focused work with a child. Our approach is systemic in its insistence on the therapeutic value of ensuring that multiple perspectives in the family are heard, and what gives it a narrative dimension is our close exploration of the complex, evolving and interweaving stories that family members narrate.

Professional narratives about children and parental mental illness

The literature on the effects on children of parental illness has burgeoned in recent years as the extent of the neglect of this group of children has become more apparent (Department of Health 2000). The discourses around these children's needs are various, and in this section we highlight some of the tensions that can exist between them.

One obvious tension is found in the way that professionals may indicate the complexity and urgency of work in the field by highlighting how the issue of parental mental illness intersects with other areas of concern including substance misuse, violence and sexual abuse. This often means, in the psychological literature, that those other invariable intersections – the impact of racism, social marginalisation, poor skills and poverty – obtain less prominence. Little research goes into understanding how far the isolation of families with a parent identified as psychiatrically ill may be intensified by poverty and racism, and how children may miss out on chances for acquiring social skills through lack of funds for recreational activities, while a parent's sense of incompetence and failure can be underlined by a truncated education, unemployment and the difficulty in providing materially for their children.

Another tension arises from the tendency for the 'risk to children' discourse to treat parent–child influence as unidirectional. From a systemic viewpoint, parents and children are features of each other's environments, where each person's input is significant. If aspects of the child's temperament or behaviour put him or her at particular risk when an exhausted or anxious parent feels repeatedly antagonised by those behaviours, where is the responsibility for change? In other situations, the child's willingness to take on emotional and practical tasks may be just what makes the family unit viable. If encouraged to free the child from these tasks, the parent may risk damaging the fragile structure of their lives together. Indeed, some authors have pointed to the benefit of caregiving in childhood as offering opportunities for greater sensitivity and individuation to develop (Walker and Lee 1998), where support and respite are available from other family members. For other authors, caregiving which involves cross-generational boundary transgressions is seen as troubling because too often these patterns of relating re-occur in families as individuals try to make up in adult life for the deprivations and over-burdening they experienced in childhood (Boszormenyi-Nagy and Sparks 1973).

A further tension is found in reviewing early diagnosis-driven research work in the field, where different diagnoses in parents have been linked with particular patterns of difficulties in their children. While this work has high-lighted some serious risks to children, the assumption can be made that all diagnosed parents are likely to show harmful parenting. Greater complexity in professional understandings has brought an acknowledgement that parenting troubles may not neatly follow DSM-IVR or ICD-10 categorisation. Several researchers have pointed out the possibility that parenting difficulties among depressed parents and schizophrenic parents, for example, may not strictly be a function of the psychiatric illness at all but rather stem from the impairments in the parents' social functioning and responsiveness – moulded within a particular social and emotional context – that might have placed them at risk of mental illness in the first place (e.g. Mufson *et al.* 1994; Goldstein 1988). Complementary to this work are studies which suggest that competent parenting can mediate the effects on children of most other risk factors associated with drug-abusing parents (Dawe *et al.* 2000). This means that we are able to conclude that a child is at high risk where intense hostility is directed at him or her, or where the parent's care is utterly chaotic and inconsistent (Berg-Nielsen *et al.* 2002). But in less clear-cut situations, we can only observe particular patterns of risk factors and protective factors in which outcomes for particular children can be predicted with much less certainty.

When we consider how interventions with this group of mentally ill parents are conceived, two main clinical approaches emerge. Much helpful work has been aimed at trying to support joined-up thinking between adult and child psychological services, encouraging professionals in adult work to consider particular ways to improve the safety and wellbeing of their patients' children (Falicov 1998; Duncan and Reder 2000). This work has been sub-stantiated by a growing empirical literature in the field (see Leverton 2003) that attempts to build on family (and professional) resources by providing, for example, better key worker support to families and more educational input on mental illness. This work may best be carried out at a neutral location between adult and child services where neither the adult's turmoil nor pos-sible risks to the child are the exclusive focus. Such families can often be helped in a group setting that supports honesty about parenting difficulties and where other group members can offer insights and suggestions from their own struggles.

This kind of endeavour overlaps, but in limited ways, with the kind of therapeutic work we discuss in this chapter where we aim for more substantive change in aspects of family members' self-narratives and relational identities. In the context of a more upbeat and pragmatic discourse, what can go unacknowledged is the extent to which particular features of family relational patterns create particular difficulties for the operation of successful therapeutic work – narrative or otherwise.

One pattern is the parent's degree of preoccupation with their own dramas, which are felt to be more vivid and more compelling than anything that may be happening in the lives of their children or partners – associated with difficulty in thinking reflexively about the perspective of others (e.g. their children) and acting with that perspective in mind. These are precisely the aspects of psychological-mindedness that permit people to be readily engaged in talking therapy. In adapting to their parent's intermittent self-preoccupation, children may learn to behave in ways that comfort or distract or enliven the parent. This adaptation may not involve domestic tasks like shopping or childcare, but may involve responsibilities covertly imposed on the child which bind him or her to conform to the parent's affective mapping in ways that distort the child's social and emotional development. For professionals trying to explore these relational patterns, the parent's dread of blame, when their child is under scrutiny for indications of distress, may drive them to see all offers of help as a form of intrusive surveillance and refuse to engage with child mental health teams.

These are the kind of predictable difficulties in a subset of people parenting 'precariously' that make working therapeutically in the field very problematic, and may also account for the paucity of studies which document in any detail what this challenging clinical work can involve. Indeed, it is instructive to read in a recent review of the field (Leverton 2003) that despite the growing body of clinical and research work on helping professionals identify risks to children, there is little detailed information on the ways on which parental mental illness impacts on children and little about the reciprocal relationships between parents and children.

One way in which we have come to link these many professional discourses is to focus on the idea of resilience. Resilience is defined by Masten *et al.* (1990) as the process of, or capacity for, an outcome of successful adaptation despite challenging or threatening circumstances. There is plenty of evidence of what are the robust indicators of resilience – any of which may be markers for far more complex processes (Rutter 1985). Individual factors include an 'easy' temperament, interpersonal awareness and empathy, and a willingness and capacity to plan. Family factors include firm parental limit-setting, warmth (Garmezy 1993), cohesion, flexibility (Olson *et al.* 1970) and a willingness to be open about painful and conflictual issues (Focht-Birkerts and Beardslee 2000). This approach allows us to think about each family's own particular pattern of vulnerability and protective factors – and the interplay with what occurs in the relevant economic, social and racial climate – and it connects us to narrative therapy by the central theoretical notion in resilience research that the effect of stressors has to be considered in terms of *meaning*. Rutter (1985) has placed particular emphasis on the way a child attaches meaning to events and incorporates them into his or her belief system and set of self-concepts. We can think of narratives as providing the structure within which we organise events into a meaningful – if also partial and inconsistent

– pattern. A systemic and narrative orientation helps us to interpret key findings of the resilience literature (e.g. Werner 1993) as demonstrating that self-esteem and self-efficacy are promoted essentially by supportive relationships in which positive and coherent understandings of events can be transmitted to a child. The resilience model also connects us to the importance of professionals exploring the child's own understanding of the situation (Cooklin 2001; Fredman and Fuggle 2000; Bibou-Nakou 2004). To make an assessment of the extent to which their caretaking duties may be burdensome, to assess their level of confusion or fear in the presence of a disturbed parent, and to understand the attributions they make about the odd behaviour, we need to open and maintain a dialogue with children.

Learning from children

In this section we highlight some of the understandings we have reached about children's perspectives on parental mental illness, based on our therapeutic conversations with referred families and on life story interviews with adults reflecting back on their experience of growing up with a mentally ill parent. We have clustered these into the following themes:

* Deconstructing and contextualising 'illness'
* Moral discourses and accountability
* Responsibility and blame
* Agency and competence
* Protectiveness, loyalty and caring.

This description of discourses highlights themes in the accounts of the young people we see. In the subsequent section, we give a fuller picture of our clinical approach.

Deconstructing and contextualising 'illness'

We are aware of how a medical discourse lends itself to explanations which are reductive, which locate the illness within the person rather than interpersonally and which are likely to be expressed in terms of certainties. The process of communicating with children about their parent's unpredictable, withdrawn or volatile behaviour often augments these features. However, children are usually great allies in the deconstructive process (Cooklin 2001). Our experience of conversations with children leads us to see them as natural systemic thinkers. They subject received wisdom to intense scrutiny, explore its meaning within their own social and relational context and deconstruct the totalising categories handed to them by adults. Part of this questioning of received wisdom lies in the nature of young children's developing mental worlds where they have to construct explanations for so many new things without the benefit of experience. This means that their responses will often reach to the very heart of adult evasions.

However, children are usually at the receiving end of adults' beliefs about what they are capable of understanding, which often lead to the type of bland rational generalisations that, while designed to reassure, are least likely to fit with a child's mental map. An example of this is the statement that a parent's mental illness is nothing to do with anything a child has done. This is clearly a very important part of therapy, but at the level of daily living simply clashes too much with what children observe for it to be discounted altogether. A child's subjective experience that a depressed parent will display even more unhappiness if the child plays up cannot be avoided or discounted, although the extent of the child's influence can and should be challenged.

Young children will often opt for explanations for parental behaviour which centre their own thoughts and actions. Thus the narrative about mental illness that is considered by many professionals to be a 'better story' for children may locate the explanation within the adult – so naming depression or mania as an illness which is amenable to treatment (Focht-Birkerts and Beardslee 2000). While this can help children to be more informed about the reasons behind their parents' behaviour and counteracts the negative interpretations of mental illness prevalent within mainstream culture, a rationalised medical discourse can leave gaps and uncertainties for children whose experience of ordinary illness does not prepare them to apply similar concepts in this case.

Caroline's story

Caroline, whose mother had a psychotic breakdown when she was nine and convinced her children that the world was about to end, remembers her mother explaining to her after her period of treatment in hospital that the breakdown was caused by a chemical deficiency (she was diagnosed as having bi-polar affective disorder). Caroline remembers not overtly questioning this explanation but wondering to herself at the time, how exactly did having a chemical deficiency lead you to think the end of the world was nigh?

The over-use of a rational, medicalised discourse by adults may leave gaps which can then often be filled by children with moral discourses of accountability and blame.

Moral discourses and accountability

Children are also likely to want to locate the illness within a moral discourse and while not necessarily blaming, because most children are intensely loyal to their parents, they either want some accountability for behaviour or treat as inadequate or self-serving some of the explanations given. We are interested in the dilemmas and contradictions for parents and children as they address the difficult question of the extent to which parents with a mental illness can be held accountable for their behaviour towards their children.

The Edwards family's story – part 2

In the Edwards family, where the mother had had a psychotic breakdown several years before, she asked to have a session with her four sons in order to talk with them about her illness and the effect it had had on them. She felt able to do this from a safe distance in time but she also had fears about what her husband, from whom she was separating, might have said to them about her and how he might use it against her. Although the boys were prepared to talk about the previous episode and we had a useful conversation about what each of them knew and from what source, it became clear that they were much more interested in confronting their mother about her behaviour in the present. Some of this behaviour clearly continued to frighten and worry them. This was a much more difficult conversation for the mother to sustain because it revealed in front of the therapists the extent to which she was still organised by paranoid thinking.

Kyle's story

Twelve-year-old Kyle, in refusing a totalising illness discourse for his mother, preferred to describe her as bossy and interfering when she obsessively cleaned the house, including Kyle's room, and he challenged his stepfather when he begged Kyle not to make a fuss because his mother had a 'cleaning illness'. Kyle believed, perhaps, that his mother had choices about whether she did this or not. In expecting his mother to be responsible, he was aided by his stepsister, who, from a more detached position, reiterated that, however ill you were, you could still listen to other people and did not need to shout.

Responsibility and blame

As clinicians know, there is often an inverse relation between willingness to take responsibility and a sense of being blamed. Parents who feel criticised are more likely to blame their illness, a family member or inadequate services for their behaviour than they are to take responsibility for it, a responsibility that feels especially overwhelming if it conflicts with their ideals and aspirations for parenthood. Conversely, 'refusal' to take responsibility in itself generally leads others to become more blaming.

Mattie's story

It was very important for Mattie, aged 18, that her mother, Joan, understood how much of her childhood she had lost when Joan was hospitalised with severe depression on several occasions. Mattie was struggling to cope with her life and felt she was owed support and help now that her mother was more settled in her life.

While Joan was able to listen to Mattie's account, when she began to feel blamed she would evoke the fact that Mattie's two brothers had not expressed similar feelings to Mattie and therefore her illness could not have had as serious an effect as Mattie was saying. This in turn led Mattie to become more angry and blaming because it not only left her feeling her experiences were not being taken seriously but also evoked memories of how both her brothers had been protected in ways that she had not.

The most helpful way forward in therapy for Joan and Mattie was when we explored these gender issues and the expectations they had of themselves and each other as women.

The relationship between blame and responsibility is also influenced by the position taken by other adults in the system, which in turn affects the narratives available to children.

This is an especially charged issue when parents are separated and the child resides with a parent who is diagnosed as mentally ill. If this parent fears that an ex-partner will use mental illness as an opportunity to gain residence, there may be a strong incentive to deny behaviour that upsets children or to involve children in secrecy. Alternatively a parent who has residency may exaggerate instances of 'irrational' behaviour on the part of the other parent as a reason to stop or reduce contact.

Hannah's story

In work with 11-year-old Hannah and her mother, where the father, who at that time had residence, constantly interpreted everything his ex-partner did or said in terms of her 'craziness', it was harder to address the impact on Hannah of her mother's depression. Hannah's mother insisted that her depressive breakdown was only caused by her ex-partner's abusive treatment of her and then used by him as an excuse to gain residence. In this context it was difficult to develop a conversation between mother and daughter about the impact of depression in the family, the way Hannah had tried to take care of her mother when the family was still together, and the fears that Hannah had for herself, given that three generations of women before her had had this problem.

The topic of depression was explored in further individual sessions with Hannah, who described the influence of her mother's experience. She described her fear of hospitals, which she attributed to visiting her mother in a psychiatric hospital, and she began to share her fears about 'catching' depression herself. She described how, whenever she felt sad or 'moody' she would take herself immediately to task and go in for positive thinking to keep it at bay. She found it helpful when we developed a metaphor of 'inoculation'; to think about allowing herself some sad feelings and that these could be seen as a small dose which could protect her against her fear of a 'bigger dose'.

Agency and competence

The evidence from the literature seems to suggest that children can undertake considerable caring duties and responsibilities without ill effects, provided that they receive recognition for doing so and that what they are expected to do is not totally beyond them.

Caroline's story

Caroline, in her life story interview, described two memories of this. One was of being greatly valued and praised for her competence when her mother had a manic episode and she looked after the household and got her brother to school. She also remembered the extreme anxiety of feeling that she was just a step ahead of total chaos and how her sense of being responsible could at times overwhelm her. Both emotional experiences, of being proud of her competence and also of being fearful of chaos lurking, survived with her into her adult life.

Clearly many other factors are influential here, such as the presence or not of other caring and responsible adults, the degree to which the parent's mental illness is a secret or is known by other people in the child's life, such as school teachers, and the nature of sibling relationships. As stated earlier, the ability of a separated parent to act as a trusted confidant will depend on the nature of the relationship; if there is conflict or competition over the children, then a child may choose not to confide in a parent who is also a critical and hostile ex-partner, because of fears about how such information will be used. However, one of the greatest barriers to children's contributions being acknowledged by parents is that for children to undertake such tasks clashes strongly with the entire ideology around parenting, which is that parents should care for children and not the other way round.

Martine's story

In the Little family, there was a very hostile and conflictual relationship between 13-year-old Martine and her mother which centred around whether Martine was prepared to accept her mother's authority or not. Martine had a very powerful narrative about being the only one who held things together when her mother had a breakdown after her father left. It seemed essential for her that this story should be acknowledged and yet her mother always accused her of lying when she relayed this information to the therapists. The only thing her mother could acknowledge was that Martine had been helpful to her younger brothers at this time. This seemed to fall within the realm of appropriate older sibling responsibility and did not transgress a generational hierarchy. It seemed that for Martine's mother, her daughter's constant referral to this time was an example of her maliciousness and desire to undermine her rather than a desperate wish for recognition.

Protectiveness, loyalty and caring

We are all familiar with narratives of loyalty, protectiveness and caring from children to their parents. In therapeutic work with families, parents are often astonished and deeply moved to learn about how much their children observe, think and worry about them. Helping these narratives become explicitly acknowledged can be enormously helpful in the therapeutic process. However, both parents and professionals have at best an ambivalent and sometimes a negative or even pathologising response to these narratives because it is not supposed to be that way round; this can become another area where children can be subtly deprived of their agency

Protectiveness of one parent can also be experienced by another parent or by a sibling as an attack on them.

Adam's story

Seventeen-year-old Adam, whose father experienced extreme swings in mood and behaviour, had frequently stepped in to support his mother when she found his father's behaviour getting out of control. His father, George, however, had very strong views about respect being owed fathers by sons, Adam would be blamed for doing this and his father would then try to find a way to enforce his parental authority.

Loyalty may take the form of silence, especially when there is a fear on the part of the parent about their illness becoming public knowledge; therefore school teachers may remain unaware of the responsibilities a child is handling at home. More subtle forms of loyalty and protectiveness might involve a child feeling they do not have the right to show happiness when a parent is severely depressed. Conversely, a child may feel he or she must act in a way that cheers a parent up or at least rouses them to anger, even if that anger is directed at the child.

Helpful clinical interventions

In this section we will discuss how we have found it helpful to intervene clinically with children and parents. As noted earlier, our narrative orientation frees us to plan a very wide range of interventions, but at the heart of the work is a belief in the priority of exploring how different family members narrate, both separately and in each other's presence, their experience of living with parental mental illness. Our work is far from following a neat format, but we can often conceptualise it as falling into several more or less distinct stages:

- Creating a context where everyone's narrative can be heard
- Helping parents reflect on what has been said
- Helping parents reflect on their parenting values and the dilemmas these may create
- Helping parents make the relevant changes.

Creating a context where everyone's narrative can be heard

As has been made clear, we find that making space for parents to hear children – while self-evidently a part of all therapeutic activity – is crucial and particularly challenging in this context. We need to return to this theme frequently, trying to evoke the parent's curiosity about the child, creating openings for them to learn something new about how their child sees the world. This may involve the therapist very actively taking control in sessions, making rules that everyone will have a turn to speak and that people do not interrupt. Establishing this kind of turn-taking – crucial in all systemic family work based on feedback – allows the family members to have a different experience of each other's presence. We try always to do this collaboratively, often working to gain family members' ideas about how this kind of turn-taking can be maintained both in the sessions and at home. In actively taking charge in the session and sometimes limiting and interrupting the parents' talk, we show that, despite being respectful of their claims to parental authority, we can energetically exercise our own authority if it permits the conversations to progress and the presenting problems to be tackled. Here the therapist needs to work persuasively, with confidence and humour, indicating optimism that the family members are willing to help and support each other. In working this way therapists can be cast – often quite helpfully – in the role of benign grandparents.

Parental domination of conversation can point not only to the parents' self-absorption but also to problems in the parents' capacity to see the child as separate, as capable and as entitled to have a different perspective. We often find that the parent is over-identified with the child, 'knowing' confidently what the child thinks and needs. Parents may be particularly convinced that younger children have no worries about their parent's wellbeing as these children often demonstrate a form of anxious compliance, unable, with limited language skills, or unwilling to put unhappiness or confusion into words. We use drawings and other materials to help them communicate a more complex picture of how they see their world and the relationships in it.

Helping parents reflect on what has been said

Just ensuring that parents hear their children's accounts is not enough. Parents may need support if they are to give serious thought to what their children are saying and begin to incorporate what they hear into their understanding of family life. Clearly providing a safe and supportive therapeutic environment is crucial for this, since vulnerable parents have to face hearing some very painful and unwelcome accounts from their children. The work of Focht-Birkerts and Beardslee (2000) has been important here in providing a context to challenge the belief that if a parent hears that they have hurt their children this will make them a bad parent. We might say to parents that there is good evidence from research and from our clinical experience with other families that allowing their children to express pain and distress is helpful. Therefore, by doing this they are in fact being good parents.

Earlier, we discussed how this kind of intervention can raise issues of loyalty and secrecy, with children uncertain about what will be the cost of openness in terms of the parent's hurt or anger after the session. If the therapist feels that family members may be too easily wounded at any stage, separate sessions to explore these matters are arranged, and preparations laid for how sensitive material might later be shared. Then, in carefully managed family sessions, children can be helped to contest a parent's denying or minimising account of the distress caused by the parent's psychological difficulties. When there is no agreement on how to refer to the parent's troubled thinking or behaviour – and therefore no possibility of 'storying' it together – it can be helpful to discuss one particular recent episode in detail and to spend time trying to negotiate with the family a shared vocabulary for the incident so that it can be talked about more openly and its impact on each person discussed.

The therapist needs to be attuned to this and to tackle it as a crucial aspect of process, exploring how far family members can agree that therapy provides a 'protected' space in which people may find words to say difficult and potentially painful things.

Helping parents reflect on their parenting values and the dilemmas these may create

Part of this reflective work with parents involves making connections between the values and principles they bring to parenting and their own experience of being parented. We ask about parents' memories of childhood and the history of the relationship with their own parents. Such conversations need to be carefully boundaried: we are not offering the parents individual therapy. The aim is to explore where their hopes and aspirations as parents might have come from and then to connect these to their aspirations and their behaviour towards their own children.

We enquire about how their beliefs about parenting have evolved as they have gained experience as parents and as their children have grown. We look at shared parenting values with partners and explore particular points of conflict. In our experience, parents typically articulate very clear, often quite rigid, ideals for parenting and for their hoped-for relationships with their children. If their childhood memories are positive, they are likely to sound somewhat idealised and unrealistic. More often their aspirations relate to the importance of offering whatever they felt was denied to them as children. Many of the parents we see report childhoods of exposure to abuse, neglect and violence and they are determined to provide something better for their own children. Their aspirations might be for a particularly close and confiding parent–child relationship, with no secrets and no distance, or for a very open relationship without hierarchy or authority, or it might be a wish to above all protect their child from harm. In promoting change we go on to explore the dilemmas for parents when their hopes as parents are considered dispassionately in relation to their achievements. Parents can find that the aspiration that means so much to them – if that aspiration is too rigidly held on to – is precisely what is undermining their parenting.

Lena's story

Lena, very disabled by anxiety and psychotic depression, had made allegations that 6-year-old Pansy's father had sexually abused the child and she was still preoccupied with Pansy's safety. We learned, after meeting Lena alone, that she had been sexually abused by her own father as a small child. We came to understand her accusations as expressing concern about Pansy's vulnerability at an age when she herself had felt unprotected. Our understanding was largely shaped by Lena's increasing willingness to talk about her fear that she herself had exposed Lucy to risk and damage during the years that she had cared for her.

She came to see she was in a dilemma. While she remained preoccupied with risk and harm, she could never be easy in Pansy's company and enjoy her time with her child; she was constantly interrogating her and looking out for signs that she had been harmed. As her thinking about her own story of vulnerability and blame became clearer and she was able to see the impact of her experience on her parenting, she was willing to give up her hyper-vigilance and take the chance of spending more relaxed and rewarding times with Pansy.

Parents may find that the narratives of aspiration compete problematically with their narratives of actual experience. Sometimes this is acknowledged, with the blame placed squarely on the child for being too challenging and troublesome. We try to identify with parents the lack of fit between the aspirational narrative and the narrative of actual parenting and to explore how far this clash can be responsible for setting up repetitive patterns of conflict. We aim to help parents construct an account of their parenting that is less polarised between ideal and reality. It is important to work collaboratively on this, welcoming and validating the parent's own insights into this process and giving parents responsibility for developing solutions.

Helping parents make the relevant changes

When families establish the areas where they want to make changes, we often work in quite practical ways to help them achieve change. We usually need a direct and clear approach to identifying target beliefs and behaviours, but this work needs to be done with a very lively awareness of the complexity of the family dramas.

For example, in working on the idealised parenting/achievable parenting split, we typically find ourselves engaged in encouraging families to work on ordinary parenting tasks – not arguing in front of children, not persisting with repeated interrogations of children, being consistent with boundaries, and so on. Reporting back to the therapist on success or difficulties with these tasks can be a reassuring process for very vulnerable parents who fear change. Parents can be helped to develop simple pieces of self-talk to keep them connected to the changes they want to make. Signs that risky times are approaching need to be identified so that plans can be made to manage a crisis, for example identifying protective relationships that can be called on when the parent becomes distressed. Parents often need help to know how to take care of themselves, but also need to recognise how those strategies are distinct from moves to ensure that their children are also taken care of.

Summary and conclusions

In this chapter we have described therapeutic work with children and parents, both interventions with parents and direct conversations and play with children, exploring the ways their different narratives interweave and overlap. We have noted that often the parents find it hard to work collaboratively alongside therapists on developing ways of helping their children or to give children the opportunity to voice their anxieties or fears without interruption. The question of to what extent parents who are caught up in their own intense emotional dramas are able to attend to their children's needs, reaches right into the very heart of the therapeutic process. The children we see appear to be anxious to discover whether we are capable of listening to their narratives through challenging, but not blaming or pathologising, their parents. The narrative process is thus always fluid and shifting, with parents and children taking up different positions in relation to each other's and the therapist's emergent narratives. This is not a context where therapists are easily likely to experience great therapeutic 'successes', as change is more likely to occur in small incremental ways and with improvements in relationships easily undermined by changes in a parent's state of mind, over which both children and therapists have very little control.

The rewards for therapists, in our experience, lie in the small observable shifts in either beliefs or actions which create the foundations for different kinds of narratives between parents and children, or at the very least lay down moments which can live on in the memory when times get hard again.

Chapter 9

The changing context of permanency

Unifying stories in the context of divided loyalties

Sara Barratt and Rita Harris

Introduction

We all carry with us ideas and experiences, which determine how we think about families and roles within them. We have different expectations about what it means to be a mother, father, son or daughter. These have a profound influence on how we understand and work with the experiences of how others should be and how we want them to be. In this chapter we aim to discuss the narratives that people bring to the role they play in fostering and adoption. We describe our work in this area; some of the themes that arise from it and ways that using narrative have been helpful. The work described draws on our experience as members of a multidisciplinary adoption and fostering team. Central to this work is finding ways of respecting painful and difficult stories in ways that form a basis for the development of future narratives.

Changing social attitudes and beliefs about children and families have influenced the context in which children and young people are cared for away from their birth families. The work we are undertaking is conducted against a backdrop of radical changes, which have given rise to beliefs about family and childcare. This has led to an increase in the number of adoptions, kinship care arrangements and expectations of contact with biological families. The Children Act 1989 (Department of Health 1991) emphasised the importance of children placed away from their birth parents having contact with their families of origin, and the Adoption Act, among other things, highlights the need for greater post-adoption support for families.

Children who are removed from biological families usually suffer several changes of carer in pursuit of a permanent home, either through adoption, fostering or kinship care. We are therefore working with a group of children and young people with complicated histories leading to disrupted attachment relationships and consequently impaired social functioning. Given the complexity of the task carers undertake, we are reminded continually of the personal strengths and resourcefulness they bring. We are impressed by the ability of carers to commit to children who take them to the edge both physically and emotionally to test this commitment, and of children to begin to put their trust in adults when they have little reason to think that adults can be trustworthy.

Children come into 'permanent' relationships in different ways. Sometimes the carers hold parental responsibility, for instance with adoption; sometimes it is the local authority and sometimes it is shared, as with residence orders, often used in kinship placements. There are many routes to permanence, which is a changing concept. When we first started in this field of work over 30 years ago, most children who were adopted were white babies. Parents were accustomed to telling children the story of having been chosen by them at the hospital; in the past 20–30 years, however, this has changed and adopters cannot talk about choice in the same way. Now adoption of children is a complicated journey in which adopters may feel that they have little choice and have been increasingly in a position where, if they don't take the child offered they believe that there may not be another chance. Overseas adopters have often adopted despite agencies – but having come to adoption independently it is more difficult for them to access services.

The story of contact

We are often asked to give an opinion on contact in the context of many players; some of whose views may be more privileged and therefore hold more power than others. Our views, like those of others, influence the dialogue that takes place between the participants. There is an interactive process that creates the material on which our conclusions are based. Each person's contribution is influenced by their beliefs and stories of families, and so on. These arise from personal and family experiences, socio-cultural backgrounds and professional experiences and trainings. When children are placed at a distance from their birth families the hard-pushed social worker feels able to concentrate on the other worryingly unsafe children on her caseload. Placement far away makes contact difficult and a sense of trust and respect needs to be developed, nurtured by the social worker, for contact to be containing for the child. Where there is a belief that parental contact is essential for children and it is well managed, children benefit from the opportunity to connect the strands of their lives and can be protected from the distress of feeling that they are disloyal to the different aspects of themselves.

For some, identity is defined by membership to a family of origin and the loss of connection with them is equal to a loss of identity. This can be coupled with the idea that lack of contact with the family of origin results in a loss of knowledge and understanding of their family history and thus seen as damaging of the child's ability to make new relationships. Some professionals believe (Harris and Lindsey 2002) that contact maintains a sense of identity with the family of origin and consequently with stability of placement. Within the professional discourse, supported by family rights groups, there is often an idea that for children to maintain a sense of identity, contact with biological parents or other members of the family of origin is essential.

In our view, identity is a dynamic, evolving process, formed within the context of ongoing relationships. It is quality of *these* that will be important in determining how children feel about themselves. Therefore a positive identity can only be developed within a relationship that supports that identity. Part of our work is to help those deciding on the question of contact to ascertain whether the contact will facilitate this process or undermine the carer's ability to sustain and nurture relationships that support the child's sense of belonging and identity. In addition, in order to be positive, contact needs to support rather than undermine the carer's sense of entitlement to parent the children.

The point at which contact is discussed is often one where the children are feeling an acute sense of loyalty to their parents. This sense of loyalty often takes precedence over their fears for their own safety. Similarly, in our experience, social workers who have been working closely with birth parents are agonised by the pain of the parents' loss and their own feelings of having failed to keep the family together. The challenge for us in listening to these accounts is getting a balance between what the children and adults believe to be best while ensuring the children's physical and emotional safety. We often do this by linking stories about the past to what they need in the present. It is difficult for them, at this stage, to think about the future. We have to be mindful that children, professionals and birth parents operate within different time frames; in practice this means listening carefully to the pace at which people can contemplate an idea of themselves in a new context.

Janine, aged 11, is the only child of an elderly White British father and a young Black British mother. Prior to her father's death 2 years earlier he was her main carer as her mother was a heavy drinker, often needing hospital admissions. The social worker sought alternative care for Janine and tried to maintain her contact with her mother, their rationale being that this gave the mother hope. The mother and her sister chose the carers, feeling that they would help Janine maintain contact with her biological family. There is evidence (Fish and Spiers 1990) that when biological parents are involved in choosing alternative carers for their child they are more likely to support the placement. Contact with the mother stopped following a number of visits during which it became clear that Janine was not safe as her mother was found unconscious during a contact visit. We were concerned to help Janine maintain a positive identity as a young black girl, which the White British carers supported by allowing the mother to their home for defined periods, with the condition of sobriety. They also fostered a closer relationship with her maternal aunt living in Spain to ensure that Janine could develop a positive narrative about this aspect of her identity.

The question of contact is complicated; social workers can make strong relationships with families and often struggle with their concern for the pain experienced by the biological parents. As in the case example, the social worker believed that if Janine's mother ceased having contact with her daughter she would give up the will to live. Professionals always have to maintain a balance between ensuring the safety of children and the importance of maintaining contact with people with whom they have close emotional ties.

Adoption

Children who come into the care system have suffered abuse and neglect, which has often impaired their ability to form attachments. The structure of the child protection system, with duty, short-term and long-term teams means that children are processed by a number of different professionals. In our experience the way in which the childcare system is structured appears to undervalue the importance of relationship for children. Thus a child who has been through the gamut of social service hoops, often living with several different carers, may arrive at an adoptive family with little expectation that these people will commit to them. This is in sharp contrast to the expectations of adoptive parents who enter the relationship with hopes that the child will have a sense of belonging. It is in this context that parents and children can become disappointed and unable to understand the responses of one another.

Coupled with this is the wish on the part of social services departments to close a chapter for themselves and the child on the difficulties that brought them into care; this can lead to an overoptimistic view of an adoptive placement which does not allow for the exploration of anticipated difficulties. The different expectations that come from the time frame that professionals, carers and children hold is often a feature of our work. Caroline Lindsey (1997: 178) says: 'Time is a crucial ingredient in the creation of new family stories'. Unlike a biological family, which will have some idea of a family life cycle based on their own social and cultural norms, the family adopting an older child struggles with time in a variety of ways. It is hard to predict when or whether the child will be able to accept that they are there to stay and to see the adoptive parents as their own. For many children, the past is ever present.

Lindsey (1997: 180) continues: 'Families always find that the task of family integration takes much longer than they expect. They are shocked by the professional's ready acceptance of a time frame of several years for this adjustment, which may be intolerably long for them. They would like the children to forget the past'.

Children who have come to the attention of the care system carry a heavy story of difficulty. Their experiences, as defined by the adults whom they meet, are open for discussion and definition. We know that children have a strong capacity for resilience but when there are difficulties in their placements it is easier to look at children's past experience and the effect of this on their ability to make relationships within their new families. The narrative of the 'wish to adopt' story can sometimes be difficult to tell in front of the child – and for the child to hear.

We work initially with adults to talk about the reason for infertility, their feelings about the loss of a birth child and how this has affected their views of themselves and their partner. We also talk about what they bring from their past experiences to the adoption relationship so that they can access their own losses and pain and work on the impact on their current family relationships. Couples who adopt have come to the decision by debate and discussion. Rarely are both partners equally committed, so when the child arrives and disrupts the balance of what is usually a well established, long-term relationship, tensions can be diverted to focus on the child's behaviour.

Families are referred to us to find ways of responding to their children; there is little permission to talk about the couple relationship and its impact on the children. For the couple post-adoption, the focus is on the child and the child's behaviour – the story behind the wish to adopt has been lost or changed as a result of the changes that parenthood has brought. Children also value the space to speak to someone on their own about what *they* bring. These conversations can often enable the adults and children to work together in family sessions to develop narratives about their past which influence their behaviour towards one another in the present.

While adoptive parents struggle with the changes that older children bring to their lives and revisit their lost hopes, the children are also confronted by the lost past, experiencing the distress and rejection of their biological parents. We find that adoptive families usually talk about the greatest difficulties being between the parent who holds the 'mother' role and the children. We have to remember that for children there have been several, sometimes many, mothers before they are adopted; for the mother there have rarely been other children and so the expectations that they carry of the permanency of the new relationship are quite different.

Learning

When children start to settle in the family, parents think they can get on with concentrating on schoolwork. Again, they have a different time frame for the child and they believe that the trauma is over so 'normal' life can begin. However, it is when a child starts to feel settled that they begin to revisit their past, and this can become a preoccupation which can be difficult to share. This often only comes to the attention of adults as they notice children having difficulties in concentrating. They may have managed at primary school but secondary transfer brings a number of changes that make this more difficult. These may include the loss of a familiar peer group, the expectation of greater self-sufficiency, biological and developmental changes and increasing academic demands. We hear parents in a continuous struggle with children about doing their homework. They say that their children seem to be unable to put their minds to schoolwork and this creates increasing tension in the house. We find ourselves in the middle of the battles, usually including the school, in helping the family find a way forward.

Adopted children often have difficulties managing intimacy. They may be uncertain about how to form safe, close relationships. This can mean that when friendships at school are difficult their preoccupation with their sense of self, particularly in their peer group, will take precedence over learning. It takes time for children to start to form attachments; for many it is impossible. This is further complicated for children who have not had sufficient time to attach to their adoptive parents. Perhaps it is inevitable that, just as many biological children struggle with learning and relationships at secondary level, this is the most difficult time for adopted and looked after children too.

In the team we see adoptive parents who are worried that their children are not functioning as well as they had anticipated and that they are failing to meet their needs. An idea that often emerges is that these children have suffered such severe harm that talking about it would only lead to further damage. Children may experience this as proof of their unspeakable badness and that they are intrinsically unlovable. Much of our work involves creating a context where these stories can be shared.

For example, James aged 11 and Susan aged 9 were referred with their adoptive mother who was concerned that Susan had started soiling again. The children were the second and third in a family of five biological siblings received into care following extreme neglect. In their adoptive placement both children were thriving. However, following a sexualised incident between Susan and a boy at her school both Susan and James began to disclose very serious intergenerational sexual abuse of all five children in their family of origin. Susan's behaviour deteriorated significantly; she started soiling, lying and stealing food, and her mother felt that all her work had been undone. Our work focused on helping the adoptive mother understand that this was not a failure of her care but that the disclosure of sexual abuse would inevitably lead to difficulties that had to be faced. The effect of witnessing the distress of these children was overwhelming to all concerned. The task for the therapist lies in finding ways to help people begin to tell their stories. In this instance it felt appropriate to begin with their experiences of school because Susan was experiencing issues such as name calling, as before. Our work enabled the children to tell us what had happened in their biological family and for the mother to hear from the child how to respond in a way that did not have resonance with the past.

Managing ageing incoherent narratives

Dallos (1997) introduces as one of the aims of his book, *Interacting Stories*, 'to consider how family members can be seen to hold stories in common and in opposition to each other – the differences between them' (p. 2) He says 'we might argue that the concept of difference – of competing, interacting, stories – is necessary to capture the dynamics and tensions fuelling the evolving nature of family life' (1997: 2). For families with a shared history, this process reinforces the connections that define their system and facilitate development. For the children we see there is no one holding an overview of their life – their experiences can feel fragmented and incoherent – within this context family members' competing stories can be experienced as frightening and potentially destructive. In addition the dominant discourse is generally the adult discourse.

Families come for therapy because their lived experience is too painful to bear and they take the risk of trusting professionals by describing their feelings and experiences. Lives are not only lived through narrative; children entering the care system do not usually have the language to describe their experience – it takes more than the telling of a new story to help to develop a new description of themselves and their feeling of responsibility for the breakdown of the family of origin. In our work with children dislocated from their biological parents the idea that change can come about by changing narratives is naïve. The relationship with the therapist and the hard work that is undertaken to help people change their relationship to one another and their ideas about themselves are a crucial part of this. Stephen Frosh in his chapter in *Multiple Voices* (1997: 94) says:

> Psychotherapy, including family therapy, does well to heed postmodernism's critique of rationalism. But it goes nowhere if all it learns from postmodernism is that people's lives can be construed in narrative form, a completely banal discovery in any case. *Of course* lives are narratives; some kind of story can be told about anything. Actually, postmodernism reveals the limits of all narrative and debunks the idea that simply replacing one story with another will move people anywhere at all.

Children who have been taken from their birth families and who have come to the attention of a child protection agency will have gathered a strong narrative told by the adults who have come into contact with them and their families. For a decision that a biological parent cannot provide adequate care, the stories that will dominate will be those which support the deficits in that parent and the belief that the children need alternative care. Children's experience of their parents will usually incorporate positive as well as negative experiences and aspects of their relationship, but the story of abuse or wrongdoing by the parent will be told and re-told in reports and in the Court. Good carers reinforce to the children the story that the parent is responsible for what went wrong and not the child themselves, so there is little scope for the child to tell and re-work a different narrative.

The task of therapy

The task of therapy here can be twofold. First, space has to be allowed for the child's marginalised story to be told. Second, a relationship has to be developed that allows children to reconnect with their lived experience. The team we work in comprises people with diverse professional narratives. The different theoretical beliefs in the team allow us to hold and respect a number of perspectives. It is through our differences that we have the flexibility to respond to the diverse needs of this client group. It is here that child psycho-therapy and systemic psychotherapy come together, with the former offering a relationship with children in which experiences can be explored through play enactment and language, and the latter bringing these experiences into current relationships within the family. For families without a shared history, family life has not evolved and the stories are different and essentially conflict-ing. Children's and parents' past experiences have often been dramatic punc-tuations; narratives about particular events are different and the difference between children and adults has to be allowed. It is often the pain of the child's story that is so difficult to hear. We frequently work with carers and adopters who hold the belief that it will make things worse for the child to talk about the past – and for many of our children very little is known about the detail of their lives – so a silence is maintained which gets bigger. Our task involves careful work with the adults to help them practise listening within the session in a way that enables the child to talk. Interruptions or false reassurances can be silencing to children.

Problems may arise when these differences of expectation between children and adults are too great to coexist, particularly when children arrive with the burden of distrust, abuse and severe neglect, feeling that no choices are open to them. Narratives are ways of bringing together and ordering memories, however these are selected and constructed in an interactional way. Whereas remembering in families can be seen as a joint, collaborative activity, for many of the children we see this process of remembering events and the *meaning* of them may have happened in a context of attempts to distort and deny actions. Children who have been abused can be confused by the accompanying distortions – such as 'discipline is good for you' in cases of serious physical and emotional abuse, or 'this is our secret – it is because I love you' in cases of sexual abuse. Sexual abuse usually takes place without lan-guage and children do not have the language to describe their experience. This leaves a gap in the coherence of the children's story, which is com-pounded by injunctions from the person perpetrating the abuse that the child must talk to no one about what is happening. The power of the secret and the need to protect the biological family from criticism mean that some aspects of memory remain locked within children and the development of a coherent narrative is difficult to begin to create. It can be easier to forget and remain loyal to the past carers/abusers and their definition of you.

In one family in which the biological mother was drug dependent and involved in serious violence, there was enormous anxiety that if her children knew the reason for coming into care there would be serious consequences. The adults involved had created a story for themselves that the children were unaware of their mother's past and that John (aged 15) would become overwhelmed and his sister, Stella (aged 13), would become violent like her mother. John was already withdrawn and it was feared that he would cease all normal activities and more than likely kill himself. For Stella, the reverse was the case. Stella wanted to track down her birth mother and to learn more about her origins, while John did not wish to know anything. It seemed like an 'all or nothing' situation. However, by beginning with quite simple questions about what the children knew and remembered from their past a more manageable exploration seemed possible, and the adults had to listen to what the children did in fact know. This was the starting point for a piece of work that was painstakingly slow but allowed the possibility for all voices to be heard.

When talking to families there is a feeling that asking about the past will give rise to too big a story which cannot be put back in the box and as a result everything will go wrong – but, as therapists, we suggest it is the small questions which give a child the idea that their past is part of who they are. So questions such as 'did you eat this when you were with your mummy?' or 'where did you sleep?' may lead to an answer that is difficult to hear – but at least it gives the child the idea that the adult is interested in *them* and in hearing about their experiences rather than expecting them to fit into what the adults expect them to be.

We worked with Sue, the aunt of Lara, aged 6, whose mother was drug dependent and leading a chaotic lifestyle; the mother was turning up at Lara's school. Sue had gone along with the idea that she was Lara's mother and was worried that the school and other parents would hear the truth. Although it was a difficult conversation, Sue began to talk about the tensions for her in keeping up the pretence with the fear that someone at school, the biological mother or a family member would say something that meant that Lara would learn the identity of her biological mother and judge her aunt for having been dishonest with her. We rehearsed with Sue how to talk to Lara about her biological mother and the responses to anticipated questions; she came back to say how relieved she felt; she had opened up the opportunity for new conversations with the little girl and they felt much more at ease with each other. She had not discovered whether Lara had already been aware of her origins but they were now developing more realistic narratives about the context for their relationship.

Children often come to new relationships without a coherent story of their own. They may have experienced many changes in their lives with information having been lost or too difficult and painful to remember. Adults often cannot know what children have experienced and may create stories that confuse children because they do not fit with their lived experience. By unpicking some of the assumptions and beliefs held by those involved we find that children, young people and their families develop a sense of understanding of the past as well as writing new possible stories that they can all contribute to.

Kinship

An increasing number of children are cared for by members of their extended families and networks. This can provide more continuity of relationships for children and a greater sense of entitlement to parent for the adults than adoptive parents. In many ways this can enhance the children's feelings of belonging. They are also a cheaper option for social services departments (Laws 2001) in that they are paid significantly less than foster carers. On the other hand kinship care requires carers to manage complicated relationships within the extended family. The involvement of social workers is sometimes seen as supportive and sometimes emphasises children's feeling of rejection by biological parents. Children who have been 'given' to the carer by the parent may feel they have permission to settle and form an attachment to the carer. Children who have been 'taken away' may still feel disloyal to the biological parent. We wonder if the involvement of a statutory agency gives children a greater sense of being rejected – that they were not wanted or given, but that they became, in some way, the property of the state.

From our experience the current relationship with the biological parents is central. For example, in families where biological parents have a continued presence, carers have to struggle with meeting the needs of the children and the relationship with the parents whose interruptions they may resent. For the children, the often-unpredictable appearance of their parents can be unsettling; they often experience feelings of divided loyalty and responsibility for their parents. When biological parents are absent, either through death or disappearance, they may become idealised. While this gives rise to feelings of loss, when the parent has died children start to feel more settled. In the case of an absent parent our work often involves facilitating a discussion about fears and fantasies concerning them and their well-being.

It seems that kinship carers who have a supportive family network that provides some respite care do best. For many that we see, for example where the biological parent is a drug user and also dependent, the carer is in a difficult position in terms of loyalty. The family may be divided, with some members supporting the parent and others feeling more concerned about the child, as in the example of Toby that is described below. Greef (2001) talks about the position of the birth parent in the family system: 'thinking of family systems we must ask what function does the "disappointing child" (the parent) play in the dynamics of the wider family system. It could be that grandparents and others in the family bolster their own self-esteem by patronising and looking down on the parent' (p. 51). He goes on to say that, at a more extreme level, the parent may become the family scapegoat and find it difficult to re-establish her position in the family as parent to her child. This may be an important point; parents are often presented to us as alcohol or drug dependent and, despite help from rehabilitation units, have been unable to maintain a stable lifestyle for themselves or their children.

The families we see referred by social workers have usually been awarded shared parental responsibility; while this further disenfranchises the birth parent it provides some security for children in that they can have a degree of certainty that they will remain with the carers. The children we see do not often talk about their worries about their biological parents at home because they feel disloyal to their carers. In our family sessions we find that children always respond to our questions about their life (usually with their mother) by talking about feeling unsafe; they tell stories of moving house frequently, stealing food, and learning to live with their mother's different partners. These children often have little memory of their biological father but some recall experiencing some stability when their mother was living in a relationship. When we ask about physical characteristics the carers are often able to say what the biological father looked like, something which can be very important for children of dual heritage. For example, when speaking to Toby, aged 6, about his mother, he said that she came to see him last week and took him out. His grandmother, Gwen, corrected this optimistic story and said that it had been a month ago and she had been told to take him out to a school fete. We wondered if he looked like her and he didn't reply. Toby's grandmother is Welsh and his grandfather, Biko, black South African. When asked what he knew about his father Toby looked to Gwen who said she had met him once and that he was Welsh. We have continued to talk about his identity in further sessions but this conversation gave him the opportunity to ask about his father. Toby has been enthusiastic in talking further about the traditions the family hold when they are in South Africa and when they are in Wales. It seems that Toby and his brother Jo (aged 4) showed some relaxation on being able to ask questions. Toby is, however, mindful of Biko's wrath at his daughter's neglect of her children, which means that he does not talk to her when she visits the house. This may support Greef's (2001) hypothesis that the scapegoat daughter can be further alienated from her children by the reception she is given when she visits. In our work we have been encouraging Biko to think about the way his behaviour towards his daughter affects the children.

The family initially self-referred at the suggestion of the school because Toby was disruptive in class. Biko and Gwen have different styles of parenting and differing views about their daughter, the mother of the children. Gwen is described as strict; Biko thinks she is too strict and that there should not be rules. He thinks the children's mother has let them down badly and does not want her in the house. When she visits he refuses to talk to her.

The children's mother lives elsewhere and visits from time to time. She seems to lead a very chaotic lifestyle but Gwen and Biko are reluctant to consider the idea that she may be on drugs.

This is an extract from a very rowdy session in which the children only calmed down and participated when their mother was discussed:

TOBY: My mother is my mother.

BIKO: I don't want to see their mother coming to interfere because she doesn't really do anything at all for them.

TOBY: [shouts] YES SHE DOES!

BIKO: What?

TOBY: She takes me out.

BIKO: Only out . . . [Silence]

THERAPIST: [to Biko]: It seems that he has loving feeling to his mum and you have different feelings . . . I wondered whether Toby feels he has to defend her and maybe when he feels she is criticised, that it is a criticism of him and he may feel he has to look after her. What do you think about his response?

GWEN: A difficult situation for them if we are honest. Lucy [mum] is persona non grata in the house but she's still our daughter and she's still their mother. I have tried to get in touch with her.

Biko's opinion of his daughter is similar to that described in David Pitcher's (2002) study of grandparent carers. He says that for one third of grandparents in his study the difficulties they experience are caused by poor reliability and the disruptive behaviour of the children before and after visits (Pitcher 2002). His study confirmed the experience of carers we meet in our clinical work in that, for the majority, both grandparents and other relatives are caring for children whose parents have heavy drug involvement. Carers, therefore, are struggling with their own views of the parent and helping the child to make sense of their experience. It can be difficult for the children to allow themselves to be cared for when they have been the main caretakers of drug and alcohol dependent parents. Our work involves helping children to talk about or demonstrate through play their experience of life with their biological parent. The carer may have strong feelings about the parent whom they may feel has let them down in different ways, for example by stealing or lying. This is a pressure that non-related carers do not experience. We find that children are often hopeful that their carers will also parent their parents. It is a complicated task to help carers and children find a way to talk about their relationship with the biological parents and for the child to start to feel less responsible in order to regain their childhood.

Kinship carers who are grandparents seem to carry more authority than siblings. While the sibling carer may be seen as the 'good' child, they often see themselves as the least favoured. We have worked with a number of families of different racial and ethnic backgrounds who are caring for their nephews or nieces. Sibling carers often express resentment that their own parents are more supportive to the drug/alcohol dependent sibling than to them. They often say that they have always been expected to manage with little or no family support. The parent who is usually living a chaotic lifestyle is seen as favoured over the carer. For example, Rosa was living on benefit with her two children in a council flat with two small bedrooms when she took on the care of Sumi who, like her daughter, was 12 years old. Sumi's behaviour was troubling the other children in the family, for example she took or spoilt their belongings when they were out of the house. Rosa was clear about her commitment to Sumi and would not want to relinquish her care; but she saw her own mother as providing sanctuary and financial support to her sister while Rosa was increasingly isolated in the family.

Our work involved negotiating with local authority services around housing and education while working with Rosa, Sumi and other family members to help them support one another as a family. Children such as Sumi have not experienced intimacy and closeness in their relationships; she was accustomed to saying what needed to be said to get her out of a hole (usually described as lying). Rosa committed herself to this child with little support and with the dilemma that to involve the local authority social worker could lead to decisions being taken that would be out of her control. There may have been resentment about the expectation that they have given up parts of their lives to care for the child of a relative but their commitment to the child, either from a sense of family obligation or to protect the child from the care system was very strong.

Discussion

The children, young people and families we work with have a diversity of experience and narratives about their lives. These are often, particularly for the children, extremely painful, and include experiences of fear, abuse and neglect. The adults, whether adopters or carers, have had their life cycle interrupted. This may be the result of infertility or the requirement to care for members of their extended family when they had other plans. Whatever the circumstances that bring them to therapy, we remain impressed by the ability of the families we meet to struggle together in their quest for a new family.

In all aspects of our work we bring our views and expectations, and these affect how we understand the stories we hear and how we contribute to their telling, by our choice of questions and the feedback we choose to follow. Our views and those of other adults may be more privileged and hold more power than those of the children concerned. This is often in a context in which adults fear that the child's story may be too painful to bear and, if told, will lead to further damage. In our work it is essential to allow space for the child's voice to be heard, respected and given credence. This can be felt acutely when the question of continued contact with biological parents is being addressed. The point at which this is discussed is often one where children are feeling an acute sense of loyalty to their parents, which can take precedence over their fears for their own safety. We struggle to achieve a balance between what the children and the adults believe to be best, while ensuring the children's safety. We have found linking stories between the past, the present and the future helps to develop a foundation from which to move on. However the practitioner needs to listen carefully to the pace at which all concerned can contemplate the idea of themselves in a new context. This is not a static process; a child's sense of identity and belonging is a changing, evolving process that families need to be attending to.

Children in the childcare system have not only suffered abuse and neglect but often numerous changes of placement, carer and social worker. Thus children may arrive at adoptive families with little hope that these people will commit to them. This is in sharp contrast to the hopes and expectations of the adoptive parents. This mismatch of hopes and expectations can lead to disappointment and difficulty in understanding each other's responses. In our experience, the wish to move forward quickly and forget the past can result in the child feeling unable to tell their story, or the child's past being seen as the only reason for current difficulties. The skills of a multidisciplinary team are essential to dealing with this process.

When new families experience difficulties it is not uncommon for everyone to feel responsible. Parents can feel they have failed and children that they are irreparably damaged by their past and intrinsically unlovable. The net result can be a fear that talking will lead to further damage. Much of our work is in creating a context where stories can be shared safely. For many of the children we see, their stories feel fragmented and incoherent and they often do not have the language to describe their experience. It takes more than the telling of a new story to help them develop a new description of themselves. We have to provide the opportunity for all aspects of children's communication to be attended to. In our experience this process takes time and can be facilitated by beginning with small questions, which give children the idea that their past is part of who they are. Adults often need practice in listening to children and can be helpful in helping them to anticipate and voice anxieties such as how to answer questions at school about whom they live with.

Other elements enter these complex relationships in kinship care. This can provide greater continuity and sense of commitment for children, but can also lead to complicated relationships within the extended family that require careful management. These include issues of divided loyalty, resentment about taking on another family member's responsibilities, and guilt about the role the carer feels they might have played in the biological parent's upbringing. In our experience children find it particularly difficult to talk about their biological parents because they feel disloyal to their carers. Children may have been the main carers of siblings and even their parents, making it difficult for them to allow themselves to be cared for. Our work involves helping children talk about or demonstrate through their play their experience of life with their biological parents and to relinquish the idea they were responsible for their parents' behaviour.

A narrative approach can be helpful in enabling children, young people and families develop a sense of the past as well as writing possible new stories they can all contribute to. It is also an approach that can help unpick some of the assumptions and beliefs about themselves, previous carers, their biological family and families in general that may be resulting in 'stuckness'. In all the work described in this chapter we endeavour to create a safe context for children and carers in order to undertake therapeutic work with them. This often includes working closely with the professional network that surrounds the family.

Acknowledgements

We would like to thank the families we have worked with for teaching us so much and for giving us permission to describe our work with them in this chapter. We also thank our colleagues in the fostering and adoption team at the Tavistock Clinic for their contribution to our thinking and to their support in our work. All clinical information in this chapter has been anonymised and, where appropriate, permission to use material has been sought and granted.

Chapter 10

Parenting adult children

A project combining narrative, clinical and empirical methodologies

Myrna Gower, Emilia Dowling and Irvine Gersch

> To stop contact would be like changing the locks on a door to which children are born with a lifetime key.
>
> (Irma Kurtz 2003)

The beginning of the story

Our interest in this topic was initiated a few years ago when two of us (MG and ED) met at a narrative conference. Unexpectedly, we began to share stories as mothers of young adult children and laughed at the competing anecdotes emerging in our conversation. We may have been thinking about this for some time on our own, but it somehow became articulated in the conversation in a way that surprised us both.

It is not quite clear what it was that made this conversation unique – it may have been many things. What seems the most significant was our pleasure in discovering that we shared a secret rebellion against what we perceived to be a dominant cultural narrative, namely that independence, separation and leaving home are crucial evidence of successful adult parenting.

Subsequently, ED and IG met and again the topic of adult children emerged against a background of grown up children and their flat hunting. This time the conversation included a father's perspective. All three of us then got together and decided to explore this transition by conducting research on the subject and writing about it. We have come together to explore this topic, maximising our distinct traditions in clinical psychology, systemic psychotherapy and educational psychology.

From those conversations onwards, we began to listen differently to other conversations in both the personal and the professional domains. We could not find words that accurately defined 'an adult child' and noted that the experiences of parenting adult children were under-represented in the literature that we reviewed.

This chapter is our attempt to capture what we have heard and learned so far, and outline our work on a project which we have entitled 'Parenting adult children'. The project combines three methodologies: narrative, clinical and empirical. Our microscope has, in a sense, three lenses.

The changing world

As preamble it is worth noting some apparent key economic, demographic and cultural changes that provided the background to our current experience of parenting adult children.

- People are living longer
- Many people are marrying later
- Young adults are leaving home later
- Parents are often involved in many complex ways in the lives of their adult children
- Many parents look after their grandchildren
- Parents wish to lead separate lives from their children
- People are fitter and younger looking than previous generations and want to have active lives
- Divorce rates are increasing
- There is an increase in interfaith and intercultural marriages (Marriage, Divorce and Adoption Statistics Series FM2 2003).

Aim of the chapter

The aim of this chapter is to examine the parenting task once children become adults and to describe some of the processes involved in this transition and beyond. The dominant themes in the family therapy literature tend to emphasise separation, leaving home and the 'empty nest' for parents as main features of their children's transition to adulthood.

Some useful concepts from the literature

In reviewing David Olsen's large normative study of family development, Falicov (1988) highlights the lack of descriptive information about the processes that occur at different stages of the *family life cycle*. Falicov further noted that Hill's significant life-cycle research (Hill and Rogers 1964) did not seem to focus on the processes involved in each stage of the family's evolution. For example, Hill and Rogers (1964) located staged divisions in the family, focusing on the *ages* of children and on corresponding changes that the family encountered as children mature. The seven stages suggested by Hill and Rogers are:

- Stage 1: Young couples without children
- Stage 2: Families with pre-schoolers (ages 0–5)

- Stage 3: Families with school-age children (ages 6–12)
- Stage 4: Families with adolescents (ages 13–18)
- Stage 5: Launching families (first adolescent; age 19)
- Stage 6: Empty-nest families (all children gone)
- Stage 7: Retired couples (male over 65).

The family life cycle framework as described by Carter and McGoldrick (1980) offers a developmental model for looking at the life stages from a multi-generational perspective. This framework stresses the significance of families moving successfully though various key stages of their life. 'Family life cycle passages are concerned with shifting membership over time and the changing status of family members in relation to each other' (1980: 12). In this model a new life cycle begins at the stage when an unattached young adult forms a stable relationship. Interestingly, Carter and McGoldrick warn that 'adequate completion of this task would require that the young adult separate from the family of origin *without cutting off* or fleeing reactively to a substitute emotional refuge' (1980: 3, our italics). Clinicians have often seen psychological symptoms as an expression of getting stuck at key transitions.

We are proposing that *Parenting adult children* be included as an ever-present stage in the family life cycle to be viewed as a lifelong process. Our ongoing research with parents of different ages supports a further proposal for acknowledging *several* stages in the process of parenting adult children. For example, parenting newly launched children; parenting middle-aged children; parenting older children, and grandparenting. Such a framework will need to incorporate changes in the parents' lives to include transitions such as separation and divorce, re-partnering, retirement, grandparenting, illness, loss and death as well as other significant life events. This richer tapestry illustrates the interdependence of the life cycle stages and the continuing impact of changes in one generation on another. We believe that this new formulation will have significant implications for the understanding of family functioning and the assessment and treatment of clients and their families. We also believe families have to be understood within the context of appreciating cultural diversity.

Attachment theory provides a useful model for understanding emotional development and John Bowlby's ideas have had a crucial impact in terms of understanding the effect of relationships on relationships. Attachment theory postulates that the relationship a child develops with his or her mother or caregiver is crucial to the development of future relationships. We know from the attachment research (Bowlby 1988) that the more secure the relationship with the caregiver, the more the infant is able to explore the world around him or her in the knowledge that there is a 'secure base' to which to return.

Mary Main, a prominent attachment researcher (Main *et al.* 1985) has used the notion of *internal working models* to explain how young children represent and construct the experience of a relationship. She argues that the internal working model of the young child's relationship with a parent will be formed out of a history of the parent–child interaction, including the child's efforts to regain the parent even when the parent is absent. The *working model of the relationship* will not reflect an *objective picture of the parent* but the *history of the perceived responses to the child* (Dowling 1993). Therefore, a child whose parents are perceived as being available and helpful is likely to construct a model of self as not only coping but also worthy of help. Children who experience their parents and other significant adults as lacking in response or as being unavailable, may tend to build a story about themselves as unlovable and unworthy (Bowlby 1977).

If parents are to provide children with a secure base from which they can develop emotionally and socially they need:

- to understand that a child's wish for proximity, attention and responsiveness is not naughty, demanding or unreasonable, but is rather an expression of developmental needs. The more such needs are rejected or unmet, the more the demand will increase and eventually feelings may be expressed in the form of physical or psychological symptoms;
- to recognise that the most common source of a child's anger is the frustration of the desire for love and care, and that anxiety usually reflects the uncertainty as to whether parents will continue to be available;
- an appreciation of the idea that children who are securely attached are able to explore the world, safe in the knowledge that reliable adults will be available when needed, especially when the children are anxious or distressed.

Attachment theory postulates that if children grow up in an environment where not only their basic physical needs, but also their emotional needs, are met, they are likely to develop secure attachments to their caregivers and gradually evolve a narrative about themselves as loveable and likeable, which will form the basis of further positive relationships. The impact of transition and change will be different in different contexts and at different developmental stages. Transitional experiences are very important in this theory.

Systems theory focuses on interactions between people rather than on the individual's inner world. It represents a paradigm shift from *linear* to *circular* causality. Clinicians have moved from asking questions beginning with *why* to *how* relationship patterns develop. The emphasis has shifted from the *causes* to the *effects* of individual behaviour on others. The systemic stance acknowledges that the observer is part of the system, and both influences and is influenced by the system. An emphasis on understanding the meaning of behaviour and the underlying beliefs is an important ingredient of a systemic approach.

Relationship between systems theory, attachment theory and narrative theory

A major contribution that *systems theory* has made to attachment research is the recognition that attachments to other family members develop at the same time as the primary attachments to parents. Caffery and Erdman (2003) suggest that the shift in the focus of attachment research towards the dyadic and then the family relationships was influenced by recognition of the systemic nature of the attachment relationship. The focus of interest moves away solely from the child's attachment to the parent, towards a more complex set of influences, emanating from the wider relational context of the growing child eventually entering young adulthood.

Byng-Hall (1995) acknowledges that the ideas of attachment theory have only lately begun to be applied into systems theory and hence into the construction of family groupings. He defines a secure family base as 'a family that provides a reliable network of attachment relationships which enables all family members of whatever age to feel sufficiently secure to explore relationships with each other and with others outside the family' (p. 104), and emphasises the term 'network' implying that anyone who needs assistance can be offered care.

In a recent attempt to conceptualise attachment processes within the family, Hill *et al.* (2003), highlighted the links between systems theory, attachment theory and narrative theory. They refer to the importance placed by systemic theorists on clarity of communication, distance versus proximity and the organisation of the system as relevant factors influencing families' ability to negotiate developmental tasks. Narrative theory in their view has 'highlighted the manner in which families construct a system of joint meanings that informs a family's understanding of itself' (p. 211).

Anecdotal evidence suggests for example, that the 'gap year' between school and university is becoming popular in some sectors of society in the UK and there is plenty of cogent advice available on planning and encouraging successful adventures 'away'. Moving away for work reasons is also increasingly common and choosing to live near the nuclear family may be viewed somewhat sceptically and with reflective doubt, such as 'he will never learn to manage on his own'. Such 'independent exploration' is now applauded as a way of building the template for a full adult life.

It is possible to speculate that sometimes these journeys are filled with difficulties that are easily linked to 'separation anxieties' and young adults with experience of disruption of their attachment patterns are likely to be more vulnerable in those circumstances. The desire for contact on the part of the young adults can be described or interpreted by the parents as 'lack of independence' or 'failure to let them go'. This deficit discourse can induce guilt on the part of the young, anxiety on the part of the adult parent and as a result secrecy of mutual needs may prevail (Royal College of Psychiatrists Council Report 2003).

Social constructionist and narrative influences

One of the basic tenets of the social constructionist world-view is that reality is constructed in interaction, through language. Hoffman (1990) has highlighted the interactional emphasis of social constructionism. Realities are organised and maintained partly through stories. Within a social constructionist world-view, it 'is important to attend to *cultural* and *contextual stories* as well as to individual people's stories' (Freeman and Combs 1996: 31). Therefore, it is important to recognise that the construction of the transition to adulthood in terms of independence, separation and leaving home, is a predominantly western construction, in particular an *Anglo-American construction*.

Multiple voices, multiple perspectives

Freeman and Combs (1996) describe the process of *deconstructive listening* as seeking 'to open space for aspects of people's narratives that haven't yet been storied' (p. 46). They talk about how the process of deconstructing problem-saturated narratives and the constructions of preferred stories often go hand in hand. We find this definition very helpful, as often in our interactions with people around the subject of parenting adult children, we initially encounter an apologetic opening statement as if the only permissible story is one of separation or independence. 'I am afraid my 23-year-old is still living at home. There must be something wrong with me.' 'I haven't managed to make them independent'.

It is as if the discourse of parental failure is automatically linked with the 'failure of the young adult to separate'. We often find that there seems no other way to articulate their story. As the conversation continues, and we share our curiosity about the *relationship* rather than the separation, new descriptions begin to emerge. These narratives often encompass pleasures and connections as well as irritations but what recurrently occurs is this sense of confusion and not knowing whether the submerged narratives can be acceptable or are even 'normal'. For example, 'It is weird', said the mother of a 22-year-old, 'but I am really delighted she is living at home at the moment, I can relate to her as an adult, she comes and goes as she pleases and so do I.' By prefacing it with 'it is weird', the mother communicated a sense of being unusual, perhaps feeling what she wasn't supposed to feel.

Using a narrative approach as the focus of intervention, we are aware that when we are listening to a story it will be from one person's perspective. Decisions about who to invite to an interview or a meeting and *who* we listen to may be based on this one perspective and this therefore may determine whose voice might remain unheard. There is always a danger that we might privilege some voices or perspectives over others.

'The central tenet of narrative theory is that the self is constructed, and storied through interaction with others and that in this context language produces meaning and does not just reflect experience' (Burck 1997: 64). Social constructionism proposes a fluidity of narratives of self as the theory suggests that identity is constructed through interaction and new realities are constructed through language. These theories propose that the stories we develop about ourselves do not encompass all our experience. There may be other, submerged stories that would also fit, and would be more liberating and helpful.

One key principle of narrative therapy (and indeed of systemic therapy) is that *the problem is the problem . . . the person is never the problem*. One of the most important aspects of our professional intervention is to facilitate a move away from limited, problem-oriented narratives towards a richer story which is co-constructed, incorporating new but less well known and obvious ideas, skills and abilities since they do not form part of the dominant discourse. In our experience, families with adult children show obvious relief when they discover it is permissible to incorporate a new discourse of connectedness.

We need to be curious about *who* has been silenced and *whose* voices have become marginalised. How are we, through the process of consultation, going to empower those voices to emerge and be heard?

Descriptions of parenting adults frequently have a negative bias and can be dominated by the belief that parents have to come to terms with significant loss at this time. In western cultures, narratives of dependency, over-involvement and enmeshment (lack of boundaries) often punctuate stories about parenting adults.

Our alternative perspective is that parenting is a lifelong process, with many joys and potential joys as well as anxieties.

This chapter challenges predominantly negative descriptions and offers a different perspective of the transition. It illustrates some new and richer narratives that have evolved in our work with families, during and in the aftermath of transitions. The chapter acknowledges the different stages of family life cycle development but begins to include the continuity of the parenting task into early adulthood and thereafter as a normative notion. Parenting of adult children is rarely directly discussed and it is proposed that this topic merits further research if we are to consider its position both in the clinical situation and in our lived experience.

Our parenting adult children project

Starting proposition

There are insufficient descriptions of the processes involved in parenting and being parented from the age of 18 onwards and the ways that these relationships are re-constructed and renegotiated. There needs to be a challenge to established notions such as 'empty nest' and 'fleeing the nest'. There are of course many reasons for young people leaving home, including leaving in order to escape abuse. New (non-pathologising) ways must be found to describe the processes that move away from negative constructions towards descriptions of parenting adults as part and parcel of normal ongoing family relationships.

Some commonly held assumptions

- Notions of parenting are culture bound
- Dominant discourses in the Anglo-American literature put a high price on being independent adults and on being independent adult children
- 'Independent' could mean 'not requiring of parenting'
- 'Good parenting' is synonymous with having 'independent' adult children
- Adult status is generally perceived as being reached at 18. (It is in fact 19 for young people with special educational needs.)

Narratives from clinical practice

The following themes have emerged as distinct patterns in the different discourses we have encountered in clinical practice (names and details have been changed to respect confidentiality).

It doesn't matter what they do, so long as they are happy

Rose, 38, lives with Jack, 20 years her senior. Jack has been married twice before and has five children ranging in age from 19 to 37. Rose and Jack have lived together for 9 years and themselves have two children, aged 7 and 4. Rose came for help at the point at which she has met a man and wishes to leave Jack. When asked in therapy what advice her parents have for her, she replied 'my parents say they just want me to be happy'. She said that while she does not want them to interfere, she does not find the position they take helpful. She explained that she needed more engagement with her dilemma. She needs them to debate her complex situation with her and challenge her.

The need to be ill in order to remain connected

'As soon as he is better, he will have to find somewhere else to live as it is best for him to leave home and be independent.' In a family where the dominant discourse had been that of independence, self-sufficiency and managing on your own, this young man found a way of returning to the parental home to be cared for. However, the only legitimate route to do so was that of vulnerability expressed through physical or mental illness.

Parents need to be free

'I am tempted to change the locks', 'It is time I had a life', 'It is my turn now'. The construction of the relationship only in terms of dependence resulting in lack of freedom for the parent is often coupled with the social pressures to *lead one's own life*. It is as if remaining connected is somehow incompatible with pursuing new interests and pathways. A rigid 'either–or' position develops where the only choices that can be contemplated are between total sacrifice of the parents' wishes or a distancing process which would result in a fractured relationship.

Returning to the parental home represents failure

Violet, a 30-year-old professional with a history of hospitalisation was referred on account of depression. She felt ashamed to return to her parents' home, the place where she feels safest and is able to steady her mood state. In order to preserve her professional and social integrity (as she saw it), she purchased an apartment in the city (her parents live in the country). Unhappy and lonely, she returned to the parental home. In spite of the parents' reassurance and Violet's acceptance that this arrangement works well, the same pressures came to bear. She sold her flat in the city and purchased an apartment near the parental home. Once again her mood deteriorated.

The therapist saw Violet with her mother who was most affirming of her daughter. It became apparent that, at the time, the only solution to Violet's obvious dilemma was to set up home and live alone. An exploration in the therapy enabled us to widen the narrative, to incorporate Violet's worry that she was not in a relationship with a man. Part of her narrative was that living alone was the template for the rest of her life, which she feared.

It is not fair to worry the children; they have lives of their own

Mr and Mrs Brown are in their 60s and both have significant health problems. Mr Brown had to be hospitalised suddenly for exploration of the return of cancer. Despite his longing for support from his children due to his sudden relapse, he was reluctant to seek any help from them and even drove himself to hospital for admission in order 'to protect them in case they got upset'.

Protecting the children through keeping secrets

I did not tell them that my mother favoured my brother. I do not talk to my brother since my mother died. I feel very depressed about it all but I try to make sure that this does not affect the children (adults). I do not cry in front of the children. They might know that something is wrong but they do not know how I suffered. This mother remains adamant that she will protect her children from her anguish by preserving their separateness. This mother's emphasis remains focused on the preservation of independence, precluding options that could enhance the adult attachments between her and her grown up children.

The need for independence

'He needs to be independent', 'It's about time he managed on his own', 'I dread him coming back'. These parents expressed helplessness about how to assist their son any further. They had given him endless loans as he convinced them of his imminent business success, only to realise he was soon in debt again. They said that they were apparently unable to talk to him and to get him off their backs, but they usually relented to his pleas for money. He would then not contact them for some time.

Adult children have obligations towards parents

'She has to look after me', 'Daughters look after parents. It is my turn now'. This widowed mother cared for her own mother who developed Alzheimer's some 10 years prior to her demise. Her daughter came for help when she was at her wits end as no matter what she did for her mother, it did not seem good enough. Her mother was constantly critical and she, the daughter, found herself withdrawing more and more. This had led to an escalation in her mother's fury towards her.

A clinical case illustration

Remaining connected (with one's family) while being different

Mrs S was concerned about her 20-year-old son Ravi who, in her words, had not 'grown up'. He had dropped out of college, was unemployed at the time and was living at home with his mother. Mrs S said that 'he was not really trying to sort himself out'. Mrs S believed that parents should be there to help their children for as long as it takes to get them to 'stand on their own two feet'. She had done so with her other three and it had paid off.

Mrs S and her four adult children attended the first session. We learned that Sami, the eldest son had recently left home to live 'on and off' with a partner, and his life style was causing distress to several members of the extended family.

Nabil, the second son, had recently moved out to live with his girlfriend. Neeta, the only daughter, was still living at home. Although she had a good job at the time she wanted to go abroad in the future.

The main challenge for this family was how to remain together support-ively while allowing for diversity of views and life styles. Mrs S firmly believed that if she helped her children financially, this would entitle her to have a say in the way they ran their lives. She said she did it for 'their own good'.

Sami felt his mother had supported him when she found out about his life style but was reluctant to accept that this had caused her any pain. Nabil felt very caught between the beliefs of his girlfriend's family (basically live and let live) and the pull towards his own. Neeta declared that she didn't want a life like her mother's. In her view Mrs S had worked too hard and suffered too much. Ravi agreed with the family's narrative that he was the 'odd one out, good for nothing, and had failed in his studies'. This negative description paralysed him and at the time he was choosing to do nothing.

During the session, it emerged that the men in the family had not had an opportunity to really appreciate the hard life that their mother had had and the current dilemmas that their sister faced. The work with this family focused on finding ways for each member to be different while still being able to remain connected to the family. Gradually, they began to take risks in terms of pursuing their own life styles. The therapy sessions provided an arena for family members to continue to communicate and discuss between them the consequences of their decisions.

Ravi got a temporary job and moved out of the family home to share a house with friends. He and his mother were encouraged to talk together about Ravi's plans and aspirations for the future. Mrs S gradually accepted that, at present, Ravi was not going to pursue his studies, but that he was determined to support himself and show his mother that he could succeed at what he was doing.

Neeta decided to go abroad for a period. During subsequent family sessions she shared her excitement and for the first time got support from her mother and brothers about her plans. As the work progressed, Sami became more integrated into the extended family and was welcomed at social events.

The work centred on the dilemmas and tensions generated by the different beliefs and decisions of the children and their mother. A new discourse emerged that held high the value of remaining connected, promoting com-munication, mutual respect and tolerance, and ultimately enabled this family to move themselves forward.

Emerging themes from non-clinical data

We have collected empirical data from a non-clinical population who offered a wealth of experiences and stories about rearing their adult children. We remain concerned more with the ordinary rather than with a pathological description of the phenomena. Consequently, the presence of a non-clinical population is regarded as crucial to the contribution and naming of these constructions and how they develop over time.

We have collected information, through questionnaires, from three different sources: a Jewish cultural group, a postgraduate student group and a social science practitioner group. In all 80 questionnaires were completed.[1]

A rich and substantial collection of data has resulted. We have amalgamated the data from the three studies. For the purposes of this chapter we have limited our report to main themes emerging from some responses to the questionnaire. More detailed findings will be reported elsewhere (Dowling, Gersch and Gower work in preparation).

The joys of parenting adult children from the parent perspective

- Pride (e.g. achievements, friends, lifestyle):
  - Seeing them do well
  - I am proud to claim them as 'mine' – seeing my sons able to make their own choices and seeing their growing determination to be happy adults
  - Pleased he has not got into drugs or in any trouble with the police
- Leisure/fun:
  - To have fun together and still have a strong family unit
  - Visiting them and sharing things in common such as books, films, etc.
  - Being on holiday together
  - Enjoying grandchildren – all the fun and no responsibility
  - They make me laugh
- Remaining connected:
  - Having adult conversations.
  - They still give me respect, they are people with whom I can be entirely myself
  - Enjoying them wanting to tell me about their lives or ask my opinion (as a dad) which dress to wear
- Independence, growth and change (including friendship and expressions of love):
  - Enjoying the look and feel of them as adults – so different from how they were as children
  - I enjoy the move from being their mum when they were children to being their friend

    – I value the opportunity to get to know them differently as adults and go on developing the relationships

The joys of being an adult child from the adult child perspective

- Pride (e.g. achievements, friends, lifestyle):
  - Feeling that my parents can discuss their problems openly with me and my being able to help
  - Having my parents talk about me with pride in my achievements
  - Not feeling embarrassed to talk to them about any topic
  - Talking as equals about current affairs and politics
- Leisure/fun:
  - I look forward to the pleasure my children will bring my mother
  - I enjoy treating my parents e.g. inviting them round to my and my fiancé's house for dinner rather than always going there
  - Going home for Christmas
  - The joys of spending holidays with her [my mother]
- Remaining connected:
  - My parents are there for me now
  - Being able to support them when they need help
  - Knowing there is someone to turn to if everything goes horribly wrong I can go home
- Growth of independence and change (including friendship and expressions of love):
  - Having 'adult' conversations with my parents and spending quality time with them
  - Now being able to make positive decisions with limited challenges from parents
  - Independence but support when I need it
  - Having a better relationship with my parents

Most difficult areas in parents' relationships with adult children

- Not knowing how much to be involved:
  - Watching them be affected emotionally and struggling to overcome difficulties in their lives. Not knowing how much to be involved
  - Sometimes not knowing how much or how little to be involved in their life choices and life issues
  - My daughter's suppression of negative feelings during her teenage years surfaced in an emotional 'attack' on me
  - I found it difficult to balance the needs of my adult children at the same time as managing my elderly parents
  - Letting go

- Financial dependence/independence:
  - My son's dependence on me financially. He seems to think I will bale him out without thinking what impact it has on me
- Letting go:
  - Providing endless financial support
  - I feel resentful that my husband cannot let them go to live their lives. Our daughter is a single mother and I feel he has to have a 'hold' on them financially and he tries to take on the father role for the baby
- Communication – telling them what you think:
  - Dealing with my daughter in relation to future sexual relationships
  - My 18-year-old daughter left education and home to live with a 39-year-old partner who is divorced with children he does not see. Our relationship remains close but there are areas we do not discuss
  - Relationship between sisters. How to discuss this as a family in a constructive way
  - Most difficult is speaking honestly to my children about my and their relationship with their mother from whom I am now divorced. I don't want to stretch them between my ex-wife and me
- Having limited influence:
  - Loss of a child
  - My child overdosed
  - Coping with my child's involvement with a cult

The most difficult areas for adult children in their relationship with their parents

- How to renegotiate my relationship with my parents:
  - Being able to have a meaningful relationship with both parents at the same time. It took the death of my mother for me to have a relationship with my father
  - Working out how to rebel in a way that my parents (especially mother) will approve of
  - Caring at a distance for my elderly widowed father
- Uncertainty about becoming an adult:
  - How to be different and adult while still wanting to behave like a vile 14-year-old
  - Feeling easily criticised by my parents
  - Gaining independence while maintaining connectedness
  - Being asked for advice and support by my parents realising that I have become an adult
  - Struggling for independence
  - Being respected as an adult in my own right

- Communication – telling them what you think:
  - Family breakdown, cut off due to differences
  - My mother died when I was 15. I remained with my father until he died when I was 25. It was difficult to find a language – words or touch – to express the love we knew
  - Coming to terms with how my adult brother communicates and respects my parents – not to the same standards I would
  - Negotiation. Father thinks he is right most of the time and doesn't want to accept that he is wrong at some points. However he is improving in these areas

Discussion

Thus far, we have found the research to be well received. Both clinical and non-clinical groups have indicated that this topic has rarely been discussed in spite of its importance in everyday life.

The *joys of parenting adult children* were enthusiastically reported. Parents mentioned the joy of seeing their grandchildren, seeing their children happily married and doing well in their businesses and careers. Many reported the joy of seeing their own values being carried on to the next generation.

The most frequent joy reported by adult children was their being able to help and contribute to their parents. Adult children repeatedly indicated the importance of remaining connected with their parents. Many different examples acknowledged these adult attachments and their continuity in adult life.

Side by side were the many expressions of personal pleasure in adult children's own evolution into adulthood where their relationship with their adult parents had now transformed at the same time. Respondents enjoyed having 'adult conversations' with their parents. They enjoyed receiving advice and discussion on major life events and in particular, valued the 'friendship' of their parents. It is of particular interest that many of the adult children's joys as noted still identified their pleasure in being watched over, valued and appreciated, and ultimately their relief that, no matter what their age, they could still turn to their parents.

Not knowing quite how much to be involved with their adult children remained the overwhelming debate for parents. How to communicate ideas, whether continuing guidance was still appropriate and just how best to honour attachments seemed the most difficult elements reported of parenting adult children. Adult children indicated their worries about 'growing up'. Many introduced the notion of independence as a dilemma in itself.

Some parents spoke of the importance of not interfering too much in their adult children's private lives or friendships, trying not to intrude but being available when needed and when invited.

Conclusion

Why is it important to look at parenting adult children? Current assumptions often rely on exit, separation and independence as the keys to the narratives that inform this process.

Our preliminary research reports support our contention that it is time to study a shift in pattern away from 'independence' towards a paradigm of the continuous connectedness of parents and children throughout the life cycle.

Thus far we have found that parents and adult children are concerned with when and how to let go, who is responsible for what, how best to communicate with each other and how to remain related and connected. A high value seems to be attached to *negotiation* about beliefs, behaviours and expectations in the changing relationship. In addition, the noting of specific markers of achievement seems significant as a measure of the ongoing parenting process. Many parents take pride in their adult children achieving financial autonomy, separate homes and partners, and enjoy sharing leisure time together, while at the same time respecting each other's working lives.

In our clinical conversations, narrative theory contributed much to our work in studying the process of parenting adult children and indeed our preliminary findings, some of which are reported here, underline the importance of the stories of families, and their unique perceptions.

As clinicians we propose to invite more questions regarding what part these descriptions and uncertainties about adult parenting play in conversations with adult children. We are interested in the meanings ascribed to the attachment between parents and their adult children. We want to focus on following the developmental path this attachment has taken and what the implications will be for present and future relationships. The research will continue to explore the stories that people (from both clinical and non-clinical populations) tell about these connections. The purpose of this chapter and future study is to explore specific narratives of parenting adult children over time from the standpoint of both clinical and non-clinical contexts. So far we are intrigued by the different stories revealed in clinical conversations when adult parenting is explored and the interesting avenues this has opened both for us and for the families with whom we have talked.

It is likely that many further unexpected discourses will arise. The major contribution of this work would be to highlight a new description, and a rethinking of the family life cycle as we currently know it.

Part IV

Narratives in special contexts

Chapter 11

Whose story is it anyway?

Children involved in contact disputes

Kirsten Blow and Gwyn Daniel

'Parents will be parents'.
(13-year-old Martin whose separated parents argued constantly over him and his siblings)

Working with children whose parents are engaged in contact or residence disputes leaves us feeling as if we are right at the heart of all the diverse and frequently contradictory societal, cultural and personal narratives of family life and parenthood, and indeed of childhood itself. Intense emotional processes are activated in relation to loss and to the terror of loss, to the different entitlements of fathers and mothers, and around what parents owe children and what children owe parents. Despite the fact that divorce and separation are now so common as to be conceptualised in terms of 'family life cycle' narratives (McGoldrick and Carter 1989; Robinson 1991) the intensity of individual feelings of abandonment or of outrage at the disruption of hopes and dreams for permanence or security seem to be as raw as ever for parents and children alike. Parents' fear of loss of their child/children can propel them into vicious fights with each other over residence and contact. While we have written elsewhere about the dynamics of such conflicts between the adults (Blow and Daniel 2002), our focus here is on the impact of these fights on the children.

The view that in contact disputes, children's rights, needs and interests are paramount and that their voices should always be heard is an undisputed narrative for professionals and parents alike. It is part of the rhetoric employed by everyone involved, however misguided or harmful their actions might be judged to be by others. Children too are increasingly conscious of how their rights need to be respected (Lyon *et al.* 1998; Smart *et al.* 2001; UN Convention on the Rights of the Child – UN 1990).

However we are aware that, even in the context of this wider discourse, children's voices continue to be unheard and decisions taken which are more in line with being fair to adults than emerging from a thorough consideration of the child's position. The more compromised children's narratives are seen to be by the drama of their parents' battle, the more, paradoxically, they are likely to remain silenced. A practical example of this is the reluctance of many child and adolescent mental health services (CAMHS) to see children who are referred when their parents are in the middle of a legal battle.

The work discussed in this chapter is carried out in a private therapeutic service, offering systemic therapy to individuals, couples and families. Over the years our service has come to be seen as a valued resource for solicitors, members of CAFCASS and the Family Court and we receive an increasing number of referrals requesting our input when the legal professionals have reached an impasse. In this work, focused around assessments, we enter into children's lives for a very brief period of time and, inevitably, in a context in which their parents are in dispute. While our contract is generally for assessment and not for therapy, we always aim to make a difference; however we are never sure what difference children may think we have made. We may only meet them three or four times and do not always learn the outcome of our intervention. Indeed, it is often more important for us to focus on creating some processes that may influence the narratives children can have in the future rather than expecting change to happen in the short term. This may involve introducing some more complex, less blaming or judgemental ideas, creating opportunities for a parent who has left their child with intensely painful feelings to apologise, or creating contexts for children to experience more agency. We will give examples of these processes.

In our work with children who are caught up in the divorce process, we aim to suspend blaming and taking sides. We make it explicit that we know that children may have different ideas from their parents about what is best for them. Most importantly we make it explicit that we know that they have a mind of their own. Our aim is to access the children's understanding of the impact parental separation and divorce has had on them. How do they understand the past and the present and what agency do they think they have to create their future within this new context? All the children we see have found it hard to be heard by their parents as they themselves become embroiled in the adversarial process. In fact most of the children we talk with are pessimistic that they will ever be heard. They fear this process will go on and on. They have talked to other professionals who have told them they wanted to hear what the children thought would be best for them, only to be disappointed. How, they ask, are we going to be different?

One problem is that many of the adults involved in finding the solutions for the children think they know best. Each parent might think they know the child's mind better or question if the child has a mind of her or his own, because they may feel so strongly that a child is merely parroting the views of the other parent. Disagreement is also present in the professional system concerning issues of how to understand children, and especially about when they can be seen to have a mind of their own. Our ideas about children and the nature of childhood influence the way we talk with children and the relationship we, as professionals, can have with them. The UN Convention on the Rights of the Child (1990) has prompted professionals to reflect on our understanding of childhood and children's development beyond relying on traditional developmental psychology in which children are seen as having to progress through defined stages before developing into 'real' people (see classical developmental theories like those of Piaget 1932; Freud 1959 or Erikson 1950). The discourse of the rights of the child – especially the right to be heard – gives us an opportunity to question the received wisdom of seeing children as invisible or inferior (Smart *et al.* 2001), and to see children as active and serious practitioners of social life (Sommer 2001). Children know the social world that they share with the adults in their life.

Looking for guidance to research into the consequences of divorce reveals a similar picture of disagreements over what is best, and selective research findings can be utilised by a political group to justify a particular point of view (Gorell Barnes *et al.* 1997; Rodgers and Prior 1998). It is also important to reflect on how even commonplace professional narratives may be in tension. Although ascertaining children's wishes is embedded in good professional practice, this often clashes with a narrative about the importance for children's later development of having contact with both parents. This may be a particularly salient narrative in relation to boys having contact with their fathers.

How does the narrative approach help us? In 'Frozen narratives' (Blow and Daniel 2002) we discuss narrative and systemic therapy at some length. While 'narrative therapy' (White and Epston 1990) clearly has some limitations within the assessment context, we find it invaluable to hold onto the narrative metaphor in this work. We have found that holding all the family members' narratives in mind enables us to conceptualise the pressure on each one. These family members have to hold on to being the lead actor in their own narrative about the past and the future while at the same time being asked to take a supporting role in other narratives. Being invited to take a supporting role in someone else's narrative is the fate of many children; worse still they are often asked to take the supporting role in two, if not more, competing narratives. Ideas from the narrative approach help us to engage with children in the exploration of other possible narratives with different outcomes (Gorell Barnes and Dowling 1997; Dowling and Gorell Barnes 2000).

We engage with children first to give voice to the story they have, and then to explore with them how their story will serve them. We look at consequences for this in the immediate and longer-term future. We explore who is most likely to challenge their story. We explore how sticking with their story might affect their lives in the context of siblings, the extended families, school and friends. We endeavour to make new connections and create different contexts in which children can learn about themselves, thus freeing them from the tyranny of the present. Through our therapeutic assessment process (working in pairs) we take care to ensure that the voice of the child is the dominant one. Restoring the children's confidence in their own agency is central to our work with them. We may do this through reflecting conversations between us where we might discuss likely outcomes or remind ourselves of other children's experiences. We may rehearse difficult encounters or dramatise feared scenarios.

As we have worked with these processes with many different families, we notice two related dilemmas that recur when we consider children's narratives. These represent particular 'edges' that we always need to be aware of in our work and they also provide challenges to any simplistic ideas about creating new or more coherent narratives.

The first is how constrained children's narratives are likely to be in the context of their parents' polarised versions of reality. It is as if children's stories are intensely 'politicised'; they are at the centre of a battle for their hearts and minds with no neutral territory. To use a legal metaphor, children will probably be well aware that what they say is likely to be taken down and used as evidence (usually against the other parent). It is therefore essential to be aware of how these constraints influence what children can and cannot say both to their parents and to professionals. Additionally, as we have said, the process of a legal battle will augment parents' tendency to go for certainty about what the children *really* think. Indeed, in a context where it is very easy for professionals too to assume that they can find out what children *really* think, want and need, the only certainty we freely allow ourselves is that of assuming that children's narratives are richer and more complex than either parent gives them credit for. We need to convey to children our understanding that the narrative they have constructed is one which takes into account the relational possibilities and that these possibilities may seem very limited. We therefore need to walk the therapeutic tightrope of respecting what children are actually saying but simultaneously attempting to de-construct and contextualise their narratives without undermining them.

The second and related dilemma is how to assume agency on the part of children. It is one of the truisms of professional narratives and also a mantra of sensitive parents when they tell their children about an impending separation, that this is not the children's fault, they have done nothing to cause it and they are the innocent victims of their parents' failed relationship. The short step to constructing children in terms of a victim narrative can, however, restrict clinicians from appreciating children's agency. While children have generally been powerless to prevent parental break-up (although it is important to bear in mind those children who actively long for their parents to separate and are relieved when it happens) we need to appreciate and highlight their role as actors.

Martin, Leo and Denise's story, part 1

Martin, Leo and Denise aged 13, 11 and 8 who were referred to us for an assessment of contact arrangements, told us how, before the separation, they had been worried about parental violence. Their parents worked together and there had been one episode where their father had violently pushed their mother in the office, which was attached to the house. They told us how they had developed a strategy whereby two of them would stand at the bathroom window, which had a view down to the office. If they thought things were getting out of hand they would call down to the third sibling who would phone the office and shout down the phone 'Stop fighting!' It is of course possible to regret that children have to take on this kind of responsibility, or to describe them as being inappropriately 'parentified'; however, while holding onto these ideas as perfectly valid, the narrative we chose to develop with these three children was that of their excellent teamwork.

Emphasising children's agency in relation to the decisions they themselves make about contact is another ambiguous process. Sometimes it is as if children are not expected to judge relationships and find them wanting in the way that parents have given themselves permission to. A separation carries with it the inevitable message that a relationship or an individual has been judged to be not good enough and that the solution is to end it. For children this carries with it, possibly for the first time, the idea that taken-for-granted relationships are in fact contingent and that the survival of the relationship depends on what each person does rather than on some immutable quality in the relationship itself. Research interviews with children from families where their parents have separated have shown how they will often construct family membership in terms of what adults actually do rather than any automatic inclusion based on biological ties (O'Brien *et al.* 1996). However this knowledge can be unpalatable and its implications hard to assimilate. The other truism spoken when parents separate is: 'Although Mummy and Daddy don't love each other anymore, we both still love you; we are not leaving you but only [the other parent] and *our* relationship will not be affected; we will go on seeing each other.' It can carry the implication that children will not have views of their own about this. The vast majority of children do, of course, want to stay in close contact with both parents. However in the context within which we work, a parent fearing loss or the influence of the residential parent may not allow themselves a realistic understanding of how angry and judgemental a child might be in their own right.

Danny's story

We asked 9-year-old Danny, whose father had suddenly and, from his point of view, unexpectedly, left the family, what reason his father had given him when he asked why. 'Well', said Danny, 'he gave three reasons and two of them were pathetic!'

When parents are fighting through the courts, frequently because a child has declared reluctance to see a parent, the antipathy between the parents can make it harder for anyone to accept that the child has ideas and agency of their own and parents' narratives may end up predominating. When we are assessing children in this context it is thus important to hold the edge between children's right to make a decision and our knowledge of how complex are the pressures that might be acting on them.

Barney's story

Nine-year-old Barney told us that he did not like going on contact visits with his father because his father would never allow him to phone his mother and he would never tell Barney or his mother where they were going. It turned out that Barney had witnessed a terrifyingly violent attack by his father on his mother in which he had tried to intervene but had felt completely powerless. This experience had never found its way into the narrative developed within the legal system, which tended to support the father's story that the mother was instilling anxiety into her son because of her own antipathy to contact. In fact Barney's mother was trying to persuade him to go with his father because she feared imprisonment if she flouted the court order for contact. We saw Barney becoming increasingly angry and frustrated with both parents because he did not think that anyone was listening to his story. He told us that he thought his mother was too weak to stand up to his father over contact just as she had not been able to protect herself from his violence.

Children's positions

We have identified a number of recurring ways children respond to repeated legal disputes between their parents and we describe how we explore these with children in terms of a narrative that makes sense and confers agency.

Choosing silence

Children who refuse to talk invite parents, professionals, friends or neighbours to have their own interpretation about why the child takes this position. When entering this territory it can be quite seductive to join in the competition for the 'best' explanation of why.

Jo's story

We were asked to help find the best solution for contact between Jo and her father Ken. By the time Jo had reached the age of 10 her parents had been involved in endless litigation, with each parent using the court to mediate between them. Jo's parents had lived together for a short time but separated 1 month after Jo was born. Shortly after Jo's third birthday, an Order was made for regular contact between Jo and her father, including overnight stays, on the advice to the court of Jo's social worker. From the court papers it looked as if all requests by both parents to change this level of contact between Jo and her father were justified by claims of neglect or abuse by the other parent. Each time the court got involved an attempt was made by a professional to find out what Jo wanted. Jo never openly expressed a wish and this left professionals guessing. Jo herself thought that she had told one social worker that she was frightened of her dad. She became sad and less willing to talk when this was not conveyed to the court.

When we became involved Jo was still seeing her father every second weekend and staying overnight at his house. Hand-over took place on the village green with Jo walking alone across the green from one parent to the other. In her letter of instruction the solicitor stated that we had to make an application to the court if we deemed it necessary to meet with Jo.

Our meeting with Ken and Tracy, Jo's parents, helped us to appreciate just how hostile the relationship between them was. We also understood that in this battle of control over who had the right to know what is best for Jo, Jo had to be seen by both her parents as having no mind of her own. Sadly, this almost became Jo's solution too.

Early on in our first session with Jo we used puppets to demonstrate how we understood Jo's dilemma. Jo joined in, and was able to make comments on our performance. Showing Jo that we understood her predicament, but in a context of make believe and inviting her to join in by directing us, reassured her. This enabled us to ask her questions and to act out different scenarios with the puppets. In later sessions Jo made several animal puppets through which she let us know what she wanted. Her confidence in herself and in us enabled her to tell Ken that she was frightened of him and that she did not want contact to continue. She trusted us when we told her that no harm would come to her even though we had to insist that she told her father directly. Jo understood that if we recommended direct contact to stop, then Ken would challenge our recommendation using her 'not having a voice and a mind' as justification.

In our last meeting with Jo, after contact with her father had been suspended, she was able to tell us more about what she wanted. She said: 'If I don't have to see my dad I can think more, I can go to school and not worry all the time.' When we asked 'Why?' Jo said: 'I can't think because I worry about whether he is going to hurt me. Sometimes he hits me hard on my shoulders.

I don't want to see my dad ever again.' She added 'I don't want to think because I'm busy sleeping. I am happy when I sleep – good dreams like sitting on the beach and my family is with me and it's a nice time.' At the end of the session she told us more about the narrative she had created to protect herself.

She said: 'I am half a dragonfly and half a lizard. I have magic powers. I live in the jungle. It's a very dangerous jungle. My magic can only do good. Sometimes people come in. If dad came I would destroy him with fire. If mum came I would make her the same as me.' Using her idea of magic we said: 'If we were going to make ourselves into fairy godmothers who gave you three wishes, what would they be?' Jo answered: 'I would get rid of dad, we would live in another place like Africa and I would be rich.'

Rigid or blaming stories

We are frequently involved in cases where one parent has lost contact with his or her children and where the children or one of the children are adamant that they do not want to resume contact. This is most frequently the father; however we include here two cases where the mother is the non-residential parent. While it is beyond the scope of this chapter to describe the implications of gender and cultural discourses in these cases, we pay great attention to this dimension in the work. It is easy to get caught up in a battle of rights, especially in having to agree with perceived hierarchies of rights. We struggle in our endeavour to be non-partisan and to be seen by all parties to be so. All the fathers we have met have found it difficult to believe that their child/children are refusing contact with them; all prefer to think that their mother is behind the children's refusal to have contact. Fathers' conversations with their children therefore often get focused on blaming the mother, rather than on their relationship with their children.

Anna and Jenny's story

Anna and Jenny's parents' separation was nasty. Their father Tim responded violently when Liz, his wife, left him. Liz had planned the separation in secret and had also managed to keep her affair a secret from her husband and his family. Liz was young when she met Tim; his family never really accepted her because their affair led to Tim's divorce from his first wife. In the chaos that followed the break-up of the marriage, little thought was given to where the children should live. Anna stayed with Tim and Jenny stayed with Liz. Anna felt that her father did not appreciate all she did for him and decided to leave and stay with her mother. Jenny, who was her father's favourite, was confused about the arrangement and probably felt let down by her father. Anna's reason for not wanting to see her father was much more to do with her own needs and feelings than with a need to show loyalty to her mother. She had a more complex, interactional understanding of her parents' marriage than Jenny. Jenny was passionate to show her mother that she wanted to be with her and she publicly denounced Tim and expressed her worries that Liz would be unable to stand up for herself. For different reasons Anna and Jenny refused to meet with their father during our assessment or with both their parents together. We were concerned that Anna and Jenny were unable to meet with their father to tell him of their hurt and suggested in a meeting with Tim and Liz that they, as parents, should write a narrative to their daughters about the life of the family. This they did in a session with us. This task proved very important for Tim. It gave him a sense of being understood; and an opportunity to apologise to his daughters for having hurt them and to let them know how much they enriched his life. This enabled him to abandon further court proceedings. He understood that to continue would not bring his daughters back to him. On the contrary, to proceed along these lines would only confirm their belief about him. We do not know if we created a new narrative for Anna and Jenny. We used a narrative approach at a different level and this led to Tim taking a new position. It may have given Anna and Jenny the possibility to understand Tim in a new way and to understand their relationship with their mother outside the context of their father's influence.

We have found it difficult to help children relinquish rigid stories about parents. We have met with a number of children for whom holding on to their judgemental criticism of a parent and blaming them for all problems seems to be the only position they feel they can take. It is as if giving up on this explanation would be unsafe and possibly lead to chaos. It is in such encounters that holding all the family members' narratives in mind helps us to refrain from being judgemental and to remain interested in understanding the contexts in which such stories develop and are supported.

Vijay and Hitesh's story

Nine-year-old Vijay and his younger brother, Hitesh, aged 7, were reluctant to see their mother, Reena, for contact visits. Reena had left the family home after bitter arguments with her mother-in-law who lived with them, in which the father, Ravi, would usually take his mother's side. In our sessions with the boys they both, but especially Vijay, blamed their mother for everything that had gone wrong in their lives, stating that she had never loved them, never looked after them and that they could not visit her at home because they did not trust her. Vijay would reluctantly agree to meet his mother at a restaurant but would refuse to eat any food and would phone his father to come and take them home early. Hitesh appeared more able to enjoy himself with his mother but could not say so in front of his brother.

While there was no evidence that Reena had been a neglectful or unloving parent, the fact that she worked full time and left most of the care of the children to her parents-in-law had become a reason to blame her. We came to understand Vijay's position as feeling that he had to choose between his mother and his grandmother and that he was not free to love them both. Given that living in a multi-generational household with strong attachments to both parents and grandparents is culturally normative, we explored the particular dynamics in this family that made it problematic. Vijay appeared to despise his father for continuing to try to keep in contact with his mother. We had some painful sessions when both he and Hitesh poured out all their resentment at their mother and she listened to their narrative without contradicting them or blaming her husband or mother-in-law. This was very helpful in that we saw that both boys gradually became more lively and relaxed in the joint sessions with their mother. However this did not translate into progress on contact visits. It became clear that Reena could no longer bear the rejection that her children showed to her and she decided to withdraw from the court proceedings. In our report we tried to weave this into a narrative that reflected on the dilemmas for everyone in the family of this decision. While we thought it important to accept that no one, least of all us, could compel Vijay to enjoy seeing his mother, we were worried about the power that this might accord him or whether it might leave him trapped in a rigid and judgemental attitude to others which could be a drawback in developing friendships. We were concerned that Hitesh would be deeply hurt by his mother's withdrawal as, when she was pressing for the court-ordered contact, he had evidence of her love for him, and he could go and see her because both he and his brother 'had to', and we were not sure if he would feel strong enough to go voluntarily for contact in the face of his brother's disapproval. We also reflected on the losses for both parents, as we knew that Ravi wanted his sons to see their mother but had never felt able to challenge his older son's rigid story about his mother and grandmother. We were aware that Reena felt she now needed to move on in her life but knew how important it was for her sons to have continuing evidence of how deeply she went on thinking about and loving them.

In another family, where a seemingly devoted mother suddenly left without saying anything, we had to work at the edge of two very rigid and blaming narratives.

Kate and her children's story

We were asked to help facilitate contact between Kate and her four children, Nadia aged 18, Jemala aged 16, Hanna aged 14 and Bassam aged 12. Kate had left the family home without telling anyone or saying goodbye to her children. Jemala could not understand how her mother could endure changing from seeing her children 24 hours a day to only 3 hours a week – even less how she could stay away from them for a fortnight when she first left. She was sad and angry and wondered how much she meant to her mother. Nadia focused more on Kate's disloyalty to her family of creation and saw this as having been engineered by Kate's mother. Kate's family had never accepted Hassan, her husband. All the children spoke very articulately about their loss and their hurt at not having been prepared for this change.

Kate could not understand that her children could not see that she had to make this move in secret. How else could she have left Hassan, she asked her children? It was as if Kate thought that her children would understand, perhaps even welcome, the new family structure. Kate had taken sole control of the creation of her new narrative – her living in the family home with Nadia, Jemala, Hanna and Bassam and with Hassan moving out of the home. Nadia, Jemala, Hanna and Bassam felt as if they were given a part to play in someone else's story. All of them said that they were unable to trust their mother. Kate found this hard to understand as 'she had done it for them as much as for herself'. She continued to be defensive when the children questioned her. For Kate, it appeared that her experience of being the victim of Hassan was so powerful that it was very hard to engage with the idea that she had hurt the children. For all the children, there was a sense of having been duped, perhaps of having misunderstood the past, and now not knowing what to believe. This may be why they came to think that the safest position for them to take was to trust only in their own perceptions.

Holding out for your own mind

We do, however, meet many children who, despite their parents' conflict, are determined to hold onto a less blaming narrative and to make this as different from the processes between their own parents as they can.

Hannah's story

Ten-year-old Hannah, originally referred for therapy, was living with her father and had decided that she wanted to return to live with her mother. The father had gained residence because her mother had had a number of serious depressive breakdowns. Neither parent was able to restrain themselves from hostile and critical talk about the other in Hannah's presence. Hannah had decided to take a position where she would never ever be involved in this; she hated it when her parents 'slagged each other off' and would stonewall either parent when they started to do this. Managing the decision to change residence was agonising for Hannah as her father contested it through the court and her mother was terrified that she would be humiliated by references to her 'mental illness' as had happened last time. Also, during the previous court appearance, Hannah felt that she had been misrepresented by the court welfare officer who she felt had manoeuvred her into a position where she was seen as having chosen one parent over the other. This had a devastating effect on her mother and she did not want either parent to experience this again. Thus, while Hannah's mother provided a narrative about the father's unsuitability to have residence because of his heavy drinking, his domineering ways and the fact that they lived in temporary accommodation, Hannah refused to say a word against him. She instead chose to put the emphasis entirely on other advantages of the move, such as the different school and the opportunities for sport and social life. Her immersion in her social world also gave her multiple opportunities for other narratives about her situation and this may also have helped her, as an only child, to hold onto her own mind. When she was asked by the therapist what she would like to go into her court report, she said that it must not contain anything either parent could read as criticism. This was obeyed; however the therapist could not resist putting at the end that both parents could perhaps learn something from their daughter's example!

Single children

For other only children at the centre of contact disputes, there may be less opportunity to make strong connections outside the family and no close neutral person in whom the child can confide. The conflict itself may make this less likely as each parent may wish to maximise the time they spend with the child. It is important for us to find creative ways of accessing children's ideas outside the constraints of 'Mum's and Dad's stories' so that there is the possibility for a less polarised framework of thinking.

Jools' story

Jools was 9 when we saw him. His parents had been involved for years in acrimonious disputes. They disagreed about everything. Helen, his mother, felt she had been duped by Edward, her husband, into agreeing to be the breadwinner when Jools was born. She felt that Edward had undermined her confidence by talking to her and about her as if she was losing her mind. Jools showed a great deal of insight into the dynamics between his parents and was able to relate positively to each of them. He was sad that his parents were so unwilling to talk constructively to each other, especially as they knew how much their fighting hurt him. We wondered if being an only child added to his burden. So, in order to make our session with him less centred on him alone, we developed a scenario of 'what if he had an older brother and a younger brother'. 'What were the questions he would ask of his older brother and what did he think were the questions his younger brother would ask of him?'

He said: 'I would ask my older brother why don't Mum and Dad get on? Why do they both want me to themselves? Why can't I do what I want? Why does Dad say Mum is crazy?' He thought his little brother would want to ask him: 'Why don't they live together any more? Will Mummy and Daddy get back together again?' We saw his use of language as a sign of how engaged he was with the task. We noticed that he called his mother and father 'Mum and Dad' when talking to his older brother, while his little brother called them 'Mummy and Daddy'. Creating siblings for him enabled us to make use of their voices throughout our sessions with him, and perhaps he could make use of his 'brothers' at home when he was trying to understand what was going on.

Understanding siblings' positions

We find that seeing siblings together can be enormously helpful in building a sense both of their shared experience and of their different ways of responding to this experience.

Talking with children in the presence of their parents can also give each parent the freedom to develop new ideas and experiences without having to engage directly with the other parent. It is often easier with sibling groups than with only children to be playful about their perceptions of the adults' inability to collaborate. We might give children tasks such as making a list of what everyone in the system, including themselves, could do to make contact easier. We write these down and send them out in a letter to all concerned. We might ask the children to rate the level of their parents' degree of collaboration throughout the assessment and invite them to be our consultants.

Martin, Leo and Denise's story, part 2

In the work with Martin, Leo and Denise (see part 1 of their story) our task was to assess the potential for improved arrangements with their father. In the course of this work we had several sessions with them alone, one with them and each parent, and one with them and both parents. One of the themes we developed was their excellent teamwork and their ability to be a resource for each other.

This idea was expanded into the different positions they chose, and how that allowed the others to take the positions they did. Martin, who had moderate learning difficulties, had become much more connected to the world of school and sport. He had made a den for himself in the garden and spent a lot of time on what could quite literally be seen as 'neutral territory'. His attitude towards his parents was cynical and he detached himself from their arguments. Leo was the one who expressed most worry about the potential for violent conflict and took a protective position towards his mother. He became very anxious in our session with his father that they would be late back home and their mother would be worried and cross. Both he and Martin would often insist on editing the e-mails their parents sent to each other to make them less inflammatory! Denise was the one who wanted more contact time with the father; she felt that he was more likely to stick up for her if her brothers bossed her around than was her mother. She worried about her father living on his own and all three children agreed that he had been most upset by the marriage ending whereas their mother had grown in self-confidence. What was interesting was that, although each child took a very different position, they were able to support rather than disqualify the perception of relationships on which each position was based.

When we met with the children and parents together and some of their narratives were highlighted, both parents seemed to experience a sense of relief and pride at how impressed we were by their thinking skills, their ingenuity, and their ability to care for each other and for each of their parents. Given that part of the conflict was their unbearable fear that they had let the children down or damaged them, a fear that was quickly transposed into blaming the other, this session had a powerful impact.

Working with very young children

For very young children (many of whom we never meet) involved in contact disputes, our aim might be to help the parents create the possibility for a coherent narrative for their child, or at least to avoid a fragmented one.

If relationships between parents are very fragile, hand-over may take place in a neutral context such as the nursery school or through intermediaries such as grandparents. As a result children as young as 2 or 3 may have to cope with worlds that are quite split off from each other, where they may rarely, if ever, see their two most important attachment figures together. In these circumstances we try to connect parents with the hope for the future that is vested in the child and talk about how to protect the child's emotional wellbeing in the future. Sharing with parents some of our professional knowledge base about young children's cognitive and emotional development is often helpful here.

We may encourage parents to keep a diary that goes with their child so that the other parent can have an understanding of how the child has spent their time, can be informed of any health problems and can comment on milestones the child has achieved. The child can then have the experience that, when they are with one parent, they are in the other parent's mind, because that parent can convey to the child some understanding of the other context. Of course when relationships are very fraught this may seem risky, but in the context of an agreed aim of putting the child first, it can be achieved and indeed would be one of our ways of exploring, within an assessment context, how far parents are able to do things differently in the interests of their child.

Jamie's parents' story

In work with Melanie and Bob, the parents of 3-year-old Jamie, the book initially took the form of Melanie, the resident parent, writing lists of instructions to Bob for contact weekends, which he would interpret in the light of his story of Melanie as 'control freak' and would then disregard. However, through work with the parents, Bob was able to see how he too could use the book to inform Melanie and an important marker was achieved when she was able to acknowledge some advice he gave as having been helpful. The importance of this type of parental communication seems to be that very young children do not have to protect their world by developing fragmented narratives.

The risks of disregarding the emotional impact on very young children of contact arrangements made by the courts with the apparent aim of being fair to warring parents who are unwilling or unable to communicate or negotiate was highlighted in the case of Jo (discussed earlier).

When we work directly with young children, we may be faced with the dilemma of talking with children who have been frequently subjected to interviews by adults in order to get to the 'truth' of an experience.

Tracey's story

Four-year-old Tracey was referred to us for a court report after her mother, Lisa, had stopped unsupervised contact because she alleged that the father's partner, Donna, had hit Tracey. The father, Dave, denied that Tracey had ever met Donna and the 'truth' of the matter had never been resolved. Tracey had been interviewed a number of times by CAFCASS and by social services; by the time we met her, the incident was a year old and it was clear that, although Tracey repeated to us that Donna had hit her, we were never going to know for certain what had happened. Dave and Donna had since split up and were no longer in contact.

In meetings with Dave, Tracey was relaxed, playful and affectionate; however she became extremely anxious when her parents were seen together and was preoccupied with secrets and being called a liar. She conveyed the strong impression that her dignity had been affronted by the suggestion that she was lying. While she told us she wanted to see more of her father, she never said this in front of her mother. In our report we recommended that, because of the circumstances, the extremely volatile relationship between the parents, and Tracey's age, contact should continue to be supervised for another 6 months until we reviewed the situation.

At the court hearing 6 months later, the solicitors, barristers and the therapist all agreed that Tracey must be released from any further interrogation. However neither parent would budge from their positions; Dave that Tracey had never met Donna and Lisa that he would have no more contact until he admitted what had happened (she had never suggested that Dave had harmed Tracey). We developed a ritual, in the form of words that Dave would say to his daughter at a meeting to be arranged at our Institute. Both parents and a rather bemused judge accepted this as a way forward. At the meeting with us, Tracey was brought by her maternal grandmother, with whom we had developed a good relationship. Tracey initially played happily; when Dave mentioned Donna's name she became very distressed; however when Dave apologised to her for ever having implied that she was a liar because he knew that she was not a liar, her whole demeanour changed and she appeared relaxed and happy again. We wondered whether, for Tracey, even at her age, it meant a lot to have her position publicly acknowledged, so that she was seen as an important player rather than a pawn.

Conclusion

In the present climate where the rights of mothers and fathers are aired so publicly, and where we are invited to understand the plight of parents who separate in the context of right and wrong/good or bad, it becomes all the more urgent to find ways to hear children's voices and to understand children's dilemmas outside the adversarial domain.

When an agreement is reached in court we know that our work has been successful enough to stop the legal fight between parents, but we do not know how our conversations with the children have helped them, if at all. The inability to get feedback at this level means we can only guess. We have cases where we are tempted to ring someone up to find out how children experienced and used our input. This is often in cases where we have been challenged to find ways to create a new narrative. As systemic therapists we also know how important feedback is for our own learning. Perhaps, then, the next task for us is to develop a larger narrative in which we can all be curious about the kind of input that facilitates resolutions.

Chapter 12

Narratives of attachment in post-divorce contact disputes

Developing an intersubjective understanding

Gill Gorell Barnes

Assessing the nature of children's wishes to see their fathers in cases of protracted litigation where violence, accusations of sexual abuse or issues of mental health are involved, is a complex process. Fathers, pursuing contact with their children, are often also in pursuit of a missing part of themselves, and irrational, passionate and extreme narratives and behaviours are commonplace; as the activities of the organisation 'Families need Fathers' have shown us. The Court however, asks for an assessment of whether contact is in the child's best interests, not the father's.

The ways in which narrative is used as a frame for thinking about processes of communication between people, as well as a frame for providing information about an individual and their state of mind, will undoubtedly receive multiple descriptions within this book. In this chapter the sources of my thinking about narrative can be found in three places: first, from my own clinical work (Cederborg 1994) and later from work with families living through and after the direct experience of divorce and family transitions (Gorell Barnes and Dowling 1997). Second, from attachment research and the varying use of narrative descriptions that have evolved from the use of attachment as a frame in relationships between men and women (Fonagy 1999), as well as between parents and children and the family as a whole (Fonagy *et al.* 1994; Hill *et al.* 2003) and third, from the literature that has evolved from the study and analysis of everyday language and text (Bruner 1987a, 1987b; Ochs and Taylor 1992; Ochs *et al.* 1992).

In the child and family department at the Tavistock Clinic, from 1992 to 1998, Emilia Dowling and I carried out an in-depth action research project working with children and parents making the family transitions that follow a decision by one or other parent to divorce. The children seen by us were referred in the context of psychological distress bringing them to the attention of a professional person in their lives, usually the GP or their school. The work, maintained over a period of 6 years, allowed us to consider the effects of ongoing conflict-laden relationships on children's immediate development. This included thinking about the effects of different kinds of interparental discourse as well as personal narratives (Gorell Barnes and Dowling 1997; Dowling and Gorell Barnes, 2000).

While narrative was not our primary frame for considering our work, the appeal of linking presentations of distress in children to certain different types of family narrative, qualitatively different from one another, grew as the years passed. We characterised three groups of narrative among the parents that we saw. The first group contained ongoing conflict-oriented narratives. In these a parent sought to be seen to triumph in an imaginatively constructed battle that displayed their 'superior' parenting qualities. Such narratives often disqualified the child's experience in favour of a personal slant. In these situations children were found to modify their own narratives to fit with each parent when they spend time with them. Children often expressed a loyalty dilemma as to which parental narrative to believe, and often could not reconcile accounts that they experienced as inauthentic. The second group of parents lacked a common narrative about the divorce process itself, the children being unclear about whether their parents were still together or not. Parents, or one parent, would remain silent about the divorce, often refusing to discuss any change that children might themselves have observed in the family, and blanking or refuting children's own attempts to develop explanations about the processes they could experience and witness taking place around them. The absence of any shared narratives between parent and child about their daily lived experience, contributed to confusion in the child's mind. A third group consisted of parents who, while acknowledging the divorce, remained entangled with their ex-partners and were constantly preoccupied or indeed obsessed with concerns about the care offered to 'their child' by the other parent. Current failures of parental care towards the children were often translated in their narratives into earlier subjective narratives of personal neglect by a former partner. The wish to reform the ex-partner remained a motivating force in their lives.

Initially we took as a central goal of our work the concept of developing a coherent story or shared family frame of reference about the meaning of family before and after the divorce, on behalf of the child – an idea which, as we progressed through the project, became modified to attempting the reconciliation of multiple differing stories in which the main element of positive coherence was each parent's desire to do the best for their children. In linking problematised behaviours to collective stories maintained by one or both parents, we attempted to see how qualitative changes could be generated in those processes in the course of our clinical work. We worked with a number of families for one or more years looking at how the expression of this desire often changed from cooperative to competitive; competition which in diverse ways could develop into hostility, accusation and counter-assertion and different forms of power play.

In the course of this work, as with other intimate intense therapeutic encounters with couples who are still married, I have found myself focusing more tightly on the hierarchies of discourse within the spoken repertoires of couple or family life, as these are reported to me in a professional context. The ways in which certain stories about the lives of children, parental functioning and intention come to fill the narrative space and dominate over other potential stories which in turn become marginalised, silenced or submerged, requires careful scrutiny. Privileging certain 'truths' over others can be found in the nuances of language, the ways repeated beliefs, words and phrases become arranged in the telling of stories. In the divorce project, because we worked with families over 1, 2 or even 3 years, such narrative arrangements and their tendency to rigidify in negative ways or to remain open for more flexible positions to develop, were available for scrutiny and intervention, the results of which could be assessed. Stories driven by self-allocated power in which a parent asserted their moral superiority could be countered by our own experience of the 'other' parent. Oppression created by silence and omission of information, which did not allow a child to think or to process their own experience, could be challenged by our own shared knowledge of the child's experience and gaps in the dominant narrative explored and filled in. Helping children voice their own experience or 'find their own voices' was an important component in developing new family narratives that took into account both difference in generational position as well as the importance of thinking about a co-constructed parental future on behalf of the children.

Work with families in the context of Court assessments

In the last 6 years I have continued to work with a number of post-divorce family structures in the context of entrenched parental disputes over children's contact with one of the parents. About one third of these have been in the context of legal proceedings. (Out of twenty-four families it has been the father seeking contact in twenty-two of them.) My role, appointed as 'expert witness' by the Court, has officially been to do an assessment of whether it is in the child's best interests for a parent to pursue contact often after long absences of 2 or more years. The Court often allows a flexible interpretation of 'assessment' in which the possibility of proceeding to a supervised contact within the remit of the order, depending on the experts' therapeutic judgement as to the advisability and usefulness of this, can be part of the remit. Usually the allegations against the father by the mother have included violence, and sometimes in addition inappropriate sexualised behaviour, on which it has not always been possible for the Court to make a clear finding. In many of these cases separation between the parents took place before the child was 3 years old, and contact ceased before the child was 5 years old.

Where a father has been excluded from the life of his child for a number of years other powerful issues come into play that may have a bearing on whether there is a likelihood of a successful relationship being re-established. Five issues that I will explore briefly in this chapter include:

1   The way attachment is expressed by the parent seeking contact: is the attachment primarily directed towards the child or is it towards the former partner?
2   The way in which attachment is expressed by the child towards the absent parent.
3   The capacity of a father to work on understanding the potential effects of former or current violence in the parental relationship on the child, as well as on the mother's concerns about his future contact with the child.
4   The ability of either parent to work towards at least a minimal position of understanding of the other parent's position in the service of promoting the child's best interests in developing a relationship with both their parents in the future.
5   The child's wish to reconnect.

It is the accurate assessment of these elements, preceding any direct contact itself, that is likely to inform the Court as to the advisability of contact being instigated successfully.

The clinical setting and the Court assessment process – differences and similarities in working with families where there has been violence

The clinical setting, because it is more open ended, offers more potential for multiple narratives to evolve. We found that for parents to narrate their stories of divorce in a therapeutic context offered ways of moving between past, present and possible family futures considering different possibilities as they talked. In families where violence had been experienced within the couple relationship, the consideration of a future working relationship on behalf of the child covered the spectrum from 'totally impossible' to dramatic shifts taking place in the context of our working time with the family. These families required a longer commitment, usually 2 or more years, more frequent interviews and more individual time for the children.

The context of assessment for the Court, in families where there has been violence, involves meeting with parents whose position regarding each other and the children's relationship with the 'other' parent has rigidified often over 2 to 3 years or more, in the context of allegations, refutations, affidavits and counter assertions; sworn statements of oppositional positions that have necessarily been taken in order to further a particular goal. The Court process itself may become construed as essential to the preservation of some key definition of self as a good or bad parent. By implication, the definition of the 'other parent' as good or bad has become part of this self-definition and the child becomes in part a hostage to these parental self-definitions, often at the expense of their own development. The emphasis placed by the Children Act on the 'child's best interests' can be directly placed before each parent as an alternative position, strengthening the focus on the child but also as a freestanding 'metaposition' neutral to parental parties. The process authorised by the Court is time limited and has cost implications, and is in its construction open to scrutiny by all parties involved. In this pressured transparency there is a therapeutic possibility in the tension created which lends itself to more direct exploration as well as provocation of both curiosity and the posing of different kinds of possibility of thought and action for the parties to consider. The value of asking questions about alternative storylines which might lead to different possible futures can be of great value in shaking up cherished arguments that have become set 'in stone' as well as genuinely creating new conversations about ways of going forwards. Future-oriented questions inviting parents to consider the well-being of the children in 5 years time; when they are old enough to seek a parent out for themselves, or when a current parent might find themselves in a new role as grandparent, assists in creating a longer term developmental perspective that can take some of the tension out of the current cramping preoccupation with achieving or preventing a goal of imminent contact. The ability of a parent to set aside their own grievances and consider the potentially different positions of their child in relation to the dispute, as well as the possible effects on the child of the dispute, is always a useful indicator of likely future dispute resolution.

In the clinical setting I believe that a common therapeutic goal would be to contribute to parents moving from a reactive to a more reflective narrative about self and other in which a balance between hostility and some recall of tenderness or recognition of the good qualities of a former partner could be included. The notion of reflective self-function (Fonagy *et al.* 1994; Fonagy 2001), the ability to take into account the mental states of others, is important for the success of future parenting, and has been found to have a predictive value for secure attachment in children. As professionals intervening in the current context of a child's life, developing in dramatically changed circumstances following parental separation, we used our positions as clinicians to develop settings within the family for more reflective conversations to take place. Working towards a milieu where discourse could replace monologue, where thinking openly about changing life experience replaces making it taboo, can create significant differences in moderating discord and denial.

The Court framework does not make such issues a requirement of the assessment process but they nonetheless have relevance. The context, though not one of therapy, does not preclude therapeutic possibilities developing. Three that I would always try to build into the process include first, on my part an explicit expression of empathic understanding of the pain and passion experienced by a parent who has been cut off from their child; second, on the part of the parent seeking contact, increasing an understanding of children as unique beings, who while still dependent and developing, carry their own repertoires of making sense of the world around them, and seeing where their understanding promotes or hinders their goal of developing contact. Third, developing each parent's ability to understand and interpret the behaviour of the other in terms of possible mental states underlying the behaviour, or at least to develop willingness to attempt this. These three processes combined with much greater attention to the effects of violence on a family system can all play a key part in negotiating successful contact.

I have found that a systemic approach, in which the mutual influence of the parties involved is openly looked at, makes sense to a family in entrenched dispute. For a father, willingness to understand the child's mind necessarily will include an understanding of how the children's thinking is likely to be linked to their mother's thinking (and maybe to the thinking of her extended family). To access the goodwill of his child a father will necessarily need to take into account the child's capacity to work out his own intentions towards and understanding of the child's mother. A child's readiness to meet with a long absent father is in my experience directly affected by the child's beliefs about how the father himself is holding both the child and his mother in mind. And even after one or two meetings the question of 'how he was horrible to my mum' can arise as a serious concern that has to be addressed.

The problem for very young children in this situation is how to retain their own positive memories of their father. Where a mother has emphasised negative aspects of a father's behaviour or intentions to her children, consciously or unconsciously over the years, the children will need to have a legacy of good memories or a source of stories about the good aspects of a father to construct an alternative narrative that will take them through the anxieties attendant on Court proceedings to the meeting point itself. Similarly, where a child has directly witnessed violent or verbally abusive behaviour from father to mother he will need a significantly different range of personal experiences of father inside himself to counteract the behaviour he has witnessed and the effects it has created. Many children may have these positive experiences submerged from former living alongside their fathers or from former contact; but such experiences may not be languaged in the domain of the child's own home. In the assessment process the complexity of these levels of feeling and knowing about both parents can be discussed in a more neutral way and the ambivalence children may feel towards a direct contact that they may simultaneously construe as disloyal to their mother can be voiced without assignment of blame.

Aggression and young children

Following many years of detailed research that corroborates and amplifies clinical experience, we now have greater understanding of the effects of marital conflict on children and their adjustment (Cummings and Davies 2002). It is important to listen to the way children narrate the effect of specific stimuli in particular contexts (i.e. doorstep violence, letter box violence or kitchen sink violence); the specific characteristics of what has gone on (i.e. did father break a pane of glass); with what intention did he break it (violence to objects); did he break a corner cupboard with mum's treasured tea set in it (violence towards loved objects), or did he break glass to threaten mum with it (violence towards the key loved person in the child's life)? It is important to set the responses of children in the specific context of each child, their particular family history and prior histories of violence. The attributed or assigned meanings and the former narratives evolving from violent episodes will affect the way the child perceives and interprets what is going on at the present time.

For illustration I have selected here two families where father was seeking contact following a break in direct contact of 3 or more years. In each case the mother and father separated when the child was under 3 and contact ceased when the child was under 5. In each family the children had witnessed violent behaviour from their father towards their mother on more than one occasion prior to and following separation. However the way in which the children subsequently assigned intention to their father's behaviour differed in a number of ways; as did the alternative stories of positive experiences of life lived with their father before and after parental separation. The issue of 'parental alienation' – a process by which a mother is alleged by the other party to have constructed a story deliberately influencing the child against their 'other parent' – is not easy to assess when a child was very young at time of parting. In my experience it is most usefully looked for in comparisons between the mother's narrative about the father and the child's own narrative, the repetitions, freedoms and constraints within the child's narrative, and the willingness of the child to explore alternative ideas about their father put to them in the assessment process.

It is now widely accepted that past histories are likely to affect how children of any age appraise and respond to interparental conflicts. The effect on a child of any particular piece of conflict will therefore relate to their former exposure to such episodes and their interpretations of them, as well as the current climate of available understanding they are living within. If we take an example of violence common to each of these two cases, the breaking of a pane of glass in the front door, one child of 7 years old, Paul, who had previously been having regular good contact with his father, was able to voice a belief that his father had been angry at the time because his mother had not let him in to collect the children. He could retain an idea that held a positive intention by father in order to contextualise the violent episode. However a similar episode when her father had broken a pane of glass and tried to get in was interpreted by Roseanne, also aged 7, as one only of threat. This was first, because her father had previously tricked her by getting her to give him the key through the letter box, following which he had 'burst in and flown at her mother'; second, because of the former episodes of fighting she had seen between her father and her mother, and third, because her expressed belief was that he might try to kidnap her, a belief based on threats he had uttered in temper on previous occasions. Children also note expressions of fear from either parent as particularly distressing and, whereas Paul's mother did not express fear but rather anger, Roseanne's mother had acute anxiety attacks following episodes such as these.

In reflecting on the goals that guide children's appraisals of violence between their parents, Cummings (Cummings and Davies 2002) concluded that children form representations based on a composite perspective of the socio-emotional climate in the home, in turn drawn from their experiences in multiple family systems. Thus what grannies, uncles and aunts say about what is going on can elaborate understanding or corroborate negative perspectives. In Paul's family a robust maternal grandmother took a general position that men could be rubbish (having divorced her own husband) but nonetheless maintained an alternative perspective on Paul's situation, as 'boys need their father when they're growing up'. Roseanne's grandmother not only maintained that her dad was a threat to family security but also gave several instances of how, in her view, he had never shown much affection to Roseanne when he was still living in the home, describing episodes where he had smacked her, leaving granny 'all of a tremble'. To this view of the danger of fathers Roseanne added her own experience of watching East Enders, describing her father as 'worse than C who had put the iron on his wife'. The meanings or truths embedded in these long past events became hostage to the constructions put on them by different family members and their narratives about the events repeated over time.

Negative appraisals and expectancies about what may take place in the future evolving from personal and extended family narratives about the past will inevitably fuel a child's negative reactions to a father seeking contact. The emotional arousal created by demands for contact and by Court processes exploring earlier painful episodes replete with violent emotion, may bring into play former cognitive negative representations of a father, and may motivate a child to reduce their own emotional arousal through avoidance strategies that help them cut off from painful feeling. Children often escape into other areas of their lives to avoid the topic of their absent parent but again there is variation in the degree to which they do this. Paul said 'I just get on with it . . . that's what most people do isn't it'; whereas Roseanne said with a greater show of agitation 'I won't look at a photo of him because of the bad dreams.' She refused to open cards or letters from her father or to receive birthday or Christmas presents because what she wanted to do was forget the effect of his presence in her life.

Factors influencing a decision to take up a relationship with a parent after a long absence should not be generalised or over-simplified. However considering the different experience of Paul and Roseanne through their own differing stories of: (1) their earlier attachment to their father; (2) their understanding of his aggression; (3) the narratives of their father's understanding of them as unique children with their own thoughts and wishes; and (4) father's understanding of the potential effects of disruptive experiences on their lives, indicates some key differences.

Paul and Kelly and their parents Ted and Anna

Paul and Kelly's parents separated when Paul was nearly 4 years old and contact with their father began when Anna was still breastfeeding Kelly who was under a year old. A Court order had been made for there to be overnight contact with their father, Ted. Anna's anxiety about handing over her girl baby for overnight contact was acute and was likely to have been conveyed nonverbally to Paul as well as affecting her ability to calm and soothe Kelly. Neither parent had been prepared for it to be more difficult to effect such handovers as Kelly got older, rather than less difficult. Solomon and George (1999) in a study of infants between 12 and 20 months found that conditions affecting their secure contact with fathers included the conditions of handover and return, and the degree to which mother felt under threat from father and the effect this had on her own ability to soothe and comfort her infant. Anna's experience of being rendered powerless on behalf of her own infant and her anger at having her pleasure in her baby daughter spoiled was powerfully expressed 3 years later. Her belief that Ted may have been harmful to Anna arose in the earlier context of this long mistrust of enforced contact procedures.

At the point of my involvement 3 years later Paul retained affectionate memories of his father. These were however in conflict with his observation of his mother's expressed anger with his father and his own memories of his parents being angry with each other at point of handover. He also feared that his father might have harmed his little sister because his mother appeared to believe this. Anna at this point in the Court process alternated between agreeing that she may 'have been mistaken' and also asserting aloud that Paul would not want contact with his father if 'he believed his father had hurt his little sister'.

At the start of working with this family Ted believed that Anna had turned the children against him; Anna believed that Ted would always stalk her, criticise her handling of the children and damage Kelly her daughter in non-specific ways due to his incompetence with females. However she also persisted in her spoken belief that a 'boy needs his father as he grows up' just as her own mother did. In placing myself in the lives of the children I established why, in their minds, we were meeting. Paul thought we were meeting because the Court said we should meet. He then introduced the notion of 'justice' into our shared discourse. His mother took this up in terms of the judge had asked me (Gill) 'to get them to help it happen that they would see their dad again'. Thus the Court process allowed the issue of 'meeting their dad' to be moved outside the personal domain of mother's control and sanctioned a joint endeavour between the children and me. Paul took this forward in terms of the judge as 'someone who decides if wrong has been done and who decides what they are going to do about it'. On being asked, Paul did not think anyone in his family had done anything wrong but agreed that someone might have thought so once.

We discussed the long and confusing process of Court procedures in which both children had been involved and I asked a question I always find a way of introducing: 'What differences are there between the way it was before dad left the house and after he had left?', and also: 'What do you remember of things that had been upsetting going on between mum and dad following the separation?' Paul responded vigorously to this and described a particular incident on his birthday when he had not wished to leave his mother's house but his father had insisted that the time was 'due to him' and he had to leave the house kicking and screaming. He correctly dated this event to 30 months earlier. Other features of Paul's narrative included his protectiveness of his little sister in relation to his father's care of her. I introduced the subject of difficulty in looking after little babies and Paul allowed us to discuss the possibility of doubt in the attribution that his father had hurt Kelly: 'in looking after babies it might be possible that dad had been rough with Kelly and not meant to'. I then directly addressed Anna's expressed ambivalence contained in the statement that if Paul knew dad had hurt Kelly he would not want to see him, and asked Paul if he felt that his mother had given him permission to see his father. He indicated that he was not sure, so I invited Anna to repeat in the room what she said they had discussed in the car. Anna said clearly that she knew Ted loved Paul and she thought Paul should feel he could see his dad whenever he wanted to. The value of such open statements in the Court process is that they are spoken in the knowledge that they will become information for the other party: an issue which is more ambiguous in the clinical process.

Subsequently I invited Ted to write a letter to the children and enclose a range of photos of things they had done together. I suggested that he include an expression of any regret he might feel for harm that had been done to the children by the parental proceedings as well as assurance of his continuing love for them. The photographs were intended to elicit memories of the times he had spent with them, which I believed might have been suppressed in their minds in the context of the acrimonious proceedings. Ted's letter, which became the first part of the shared narrative subsequently developing between himself and the children, managed to resist any insinuation of blame of Anna and sent a strongly worded message of love and continuity to the children. The higher authority of the Court as a place where things could be sorted out was once again referred to in this letter, as it had earlier been by Anna and by

Paul. Ted then went on to remember shared events of his time with the children and included many relevant photographs. In the following session the combination of the letter and the photos evoked a very personal response from Paul, memories of his own, laughter and some wistfulness. At the end of that meeting he said he would like to meet his dad if I was there all the time. This meeting took place the following week, fully supported by Anna. In this meeting the same photos acted as a bridge between the 'taboo' of a past when dad had been a legitimate part of the children's lives, a visual assurance that there had been good times with father which did not need to be denied, and led to discussion about a shared possible future, 'maybe you could come and help me finish the pond in the garden/come and have a holiday in the caravan again next year'.

It is important to note how powerful the taboos against loving memory can become in the minds of children. For all the reasons outlined, the powerful affect aroused by remembered experience in a context where such remembered experience seems to run contrary to the wishes and possibly the well-being of the parent with whom the child has residence, may make it easier to deny such a parent than maintain the wish to see them as a living reality. In a subsequent meeting with Kelly, who now wanted to meet her dad because Paul had met him and there had been no negative effects in the family household, she was very active in trying to remember what he was like, although the only memory she could produce was that his 'chin was prickly'. My job at this point seemed to be to keep the possibility of a safe father alive in the room, given the 3 years of uncertainty she had lived through. I checked many times on this reality before I accepted that she would really like to meet her father, double-checking on the fact that mother's wishes might still influence her one way or the other, 'If I am talking to mummy and she asks me about whether you want to see daddy if I am here with you, am I still to say you said "yes"?' The meeting took place the following week and it was as though it had only been the previous week they had parted, with a warm physical contact initiated and reciprocated on both sides in an appropriate and direct manner.

Dave, Roseanne and Fleur

In this second family example the father, Dave, was unable to accept either that the acts of violence had actually been committed or the potential effects of these on his former wife and daughter, which compounded the effects of the violence. Fonagy (1999) has written cogently about the ways in which violent acts towards women are often committed by men whose capacity to mentalise has been damaged by their own earlier experiences of abuse (also see Goldner et al. 1990). In Dave's earlier life there had been much confusion, deprivation and some ill-treatment. The execution of violence towards a partner with whom a man has been intimate and with whom he has brought up young children necessarily suggests an impaired capacity to 'mentalise' at the time such acts take place. Such impairment is usually amplified and extended by post-divorce hostilities, especially in my view where a father has experienced through his child the possibility of repairing aspects of his own damaged childhood self. The experience of 'growing through your child' which many men who are cut off from their children come to narrate with passion, is truncated. 'When you lose an adult you love, the experience gets better over time, when you lose a child it gets worse', as one father reported. A double loss is experienced – the loss of the child herself and the loss experienced through that part of the self which was being nurtured by the experience of looking after the child. The desperation engendered by this often creates a narrative in which the reality of the child and their own experience is obliterated by the personal pain and rage experienced and expressed by the father. Dave's narrative was of this kind. He had left to live with another woman at a point where he later described himself as lonely because Fleur was too wrapped up in her job and in Roseanne. However in his story this was only a temporary affair, designed to show Fleur what he was missing in the marriage. He claimed that he had been astounded when she did not want him back, and he had pursued her with intensity, following her everywhere to get her to see his point of view. This became obsessive stalking, corroborated by various independent witnesses. This in itself had become frightening to Roseanne as well as to Fleur as Dave had attempted to 'bump' their car on several occasions, and had also turned up in school from which the headmistress had to have him forcibly removed. Unlike Ted, who had been able to maintain recognition that his children had their own experience to bring to the current 'knot' in the multipositional drama of contact proceedings, Dave predominantly expressed his own sense of injustice and upset. He constantly positioned himself as the victim rather than the perpetrator of violent episodes and saw the Court procedures as organised around righting the wrongs done to him rather than taking the best interests of the child as the highest context marker. 'I wasn't allowed to know my dad when I was her age, I tried to get to see him when I was 16, but it was too late. A child needs their dad.' In his narrative 'the child' who often featured in the welter of words he poured out was his own childhood self in whose best interests contact with his former wife and his daughter were desperately needed.

I felt moved by Dave's desperation, but frustrated by his inability to 'see' the consequences of his own failed attempts to achieve recognition from his wife and daughter over the 3 years of Court proceedings. In encouraging him to think about his daughter's point of view I invited him to write her a letter in which he showed he could recognise some of the effects of the violent episodes, of the stalking and shouting and of the police being called to their home on several occasions. In my letter to him I wrote:

> the question for Roseanne is, how is she to understand these events? It appears that she has chosen to withdraw from the relationship with you

rather than face again some of the emotions that may have been aroused in these contexts over the years. In order for her to have any possibility of being interested in meeting with you again it is important that you try to address her beliefs and whatever beliefs her mother may have about the potential threat that you posed.

In a valuable judgment made by Dame Elizabeth Butler Shloss in the Court of Appeal she laid out principles on which the restoration of contact in cases where children had been affected by exposure to high acrimony or violence would be based. It includes reference to the Children Act, to the centrality of the child and to the promotion of his or her mental health, and states that the purpose of contact must be clear and have a potential for benefiting the child. It points out that the risk of promoting direct contact includes the risk of promoting a climate of violence around the child which can undermine the child's general stability and sense of emotional well-being. If the Court were to go against a child's expressed wish for no contact they would look for the following indicators: first, that there might be some prospect of the child changing his or her view as a result of work done by a third party (such as myself); and second, that there is a history of meaningful attachment and a good relationship which can once again be brought into play between parent and child. In Dave and Roseanne's story the relationship that he clung to so dearly in his own mind was based on his time with her before she was 3 years old, and had been seriously eroded by subsequent violent events as well as by the family and friends' discourse contextualising the events. As with Ted, I suggested Dave's letter to Roseanne should include some acknowledgement of the violence that had taken place, particularly in relation to those events that she herself had described. Even though these were differently accounted for in his own narrative he should offer some explanation of how these sequences had developed using language and ideas that Roseanne could understand. Also, there should be some acceptance of responsibility on his part for the distress these had caused her, as well as an expression of his genuine interest in Roseanne and a future commitment to her well-being in which he did not make any conditions about his rights as a father such as those he had tried to insist on in the past. I again suggested I could use any photographs he could find as backup for his assertions of happy times spent with her, and emphasised how we could only proceed to direct contact if he could create a climate in which she accepted his continuing wish to stay as a part of her life. At the present time even indirect relationship between himself as an absent parent and his daughter, had broken down.

When I received the letter I was to read to Roseanne it was clear Dave himself had not written it. The fluency of thought and ideas in the text in no way resembled his normal speech pattern, so that any resonance between the text and fond memories the child might have had of him could not be brought into play through the rhythms of the language itself. Also Dave had no photos of himself with his daughter since she was a baby, and no photographs of him doing anything with her independently. The images he had were based around Roseanne and her mother Fleur. Unlike the images of 'doing everyday things with dad' that Ted was able to bring to the process of re-establishing contact, there were no scenarios that could be called to mind through images. Nonetheless Dave had tried to identify some specific memories – time spent eating boiled eggs and toast fingers together, time spent at the zoo, and time spent playing in a toy car that Roseanne had been able to ride in and drive herself.

When I showed Roseanne the photos that contained her father, with her mother and herself as a baby, she looked at them in a very fixed way, that is, she made herself look at them because I had asked her to and then quickly took her eyes away. She said that looking at him scared her because it brought back the bad dreams; specifically a dream based on him staring through the letterbox when he was shouting at her to give him the key to let him in after he had left the home. She had been determined not to let him in because on a previous occasion he had tricked her into letting him in and he had then 'gone for mummy'. He seemed to leap from the door to her in a second and got her by the neck. Roseanne said, 'I was shouting "leave mummy alone, leave mummy alone", I have bad dreams about him coming to the house and shouting at mummy, so when I hear someone at the door I hide under the cupboard downstairs just in case.' She also asserted that 'it's not true that we did together those things that he says we did'. In response I told her that I understood these would have taken place when she was very small and it was possible that she might not remember them any more, 'sometimes when you are little, memories can be rubbed out'. Roseanne replied, 'I try not to think about him', which we agreed might contribute to the memories not being there now. I went in detail through each of the pleasant examples of things they had done together that Dave had given, but she denied remembering any of the pleasant things. She did remember the toy car but had no memory of him playing in it with her. Roseanne and I became engaged in a lively discussion about memory and how it works. She consistently brought up memories of being scared rather than any memories that related her to Dave in a positive way, giving examples of other occasions when she had hidden at hearing the noise of a car outside the house, saying 'I was scared he might get in and come and take me away'. Roseanne further asserted that she would not want to meet him 'even if there were a whole room of people . . . if I did have to see him again I would be frightened that he might shout a lot'. She added, 'I'm sure that if I was ever on my own with him again he would do it again, be angry with me again.' Roseanne also said that Dave used to smack her for small things like 'spilling my drink' but she said the 'shouting was worse', and the fact that 'he used to shout at my mum and hit her. Mummy and he were always having arguments and mummy was scared.' I asked if she had ever tried to stop him when he was shouting at mum. She said 'if I was bigger I would stop him but I was too little then'.

In an earlier interview Roseanne had told me a story of an occasion when she had kicked Dave because he was holding a knife to mum at the sink. This incident, which had formed a central part of mother's own narrative, had been repeated to many people and was denied by Dave himself. The story sounded 'often told' and had a fixed quality of description in it as though it could have been brought forth specifically to 'discredit' her father. However the fears expressed by Roseanne in relation to the letterbox incident and Dave taking her away seemed to have a current vividness about them which was different in quality to the fixed pattern of words surrounding the memory of the 'knife' incident where Roseanne and Fleur's descriptions used identical phrasing.

When I asked Roseanne if thinking forward into the future there was a way in which she might like to maintain some indirect contact with Dave, she replied 'tell him I'm not really interested because I know that you were bad in the past and I know that if I was alone with you, you might do it again'. She said that she did not want presents or cards:

> I don't want him to write daddy on it because he was bad to mummy and made her cry. Tell him I don't think I will want to see him in the future. Mum has a new boyfriend now and I feel safer. I just want to get on with being in this family.

In these circumstances, using the criteria of the Butler Shloss judgment, it seemed that no progress to contact could be made. The possibility of a 'transformative process' in which qualitative changes in the stories one party (the child) held of another party (her father Dave) could not be made in spite of the work of a third party (myself). Similarly while there had been some attempts to move towards a more intersubjective understanding on Dave's part, this had come too late in the story of the repeated frightening episodes to create any new influence on his daughter's beliefs.

The complexities involved in mitigating the effects of violent episodes in this family illustrate some of the difficulties inherent in the pursuit of contact following a long absence where a child has been separated from her father at a very young age, and the separation has been compounded by violent attempts by a father to restore a relationship with his wife and child. The negative influences generated in stories about the hostilities amplify the emotional effects of the violent episodes themselves. Where the context in which the child lives and develops her own story is permeated in this way by actions and the words of others about those actions (Bakhtin 1984), it will inevitably mitigate against the likelihood of a positive story of an absent parent being held in mind.

In the context of Court proceedings where violence has played a part in the past, both during the marriage and in the post-separation experience, the importance of the child having a reservoir of positive attachment links to the absent parent as a source of developing attachment in the present is highly consequential, as perhaps is the presence of a trusted person who can bring alternative stories to bear about the absent person. Equally the capacity of a father to bear in mind the child as a separate being and the complexity of the child's position, and for him to acknowledge, even while not agreeing, the importance of the child's understanding of the mother's and the father's position in relation to one another is likely to make a key difference to the instigation of contact as well as to the successful maintenance of contact once it has been generated.

For Ted, Anna, Paul and Kelly the contact, once instigated, continued, because there was enough positive feeling generated by the initial meetings for any subsequent hitches to be overcome. Anna, seeing her children's enjoyment of meeting with their father, was able to relax much of her prior anxiety and later to meet with Ted to discuss the children face to face. As she said on this occasion 'we will never be in each other's fan club'. I responded 'nonetheless you each need to be able to hear positive comments from the other inside your own head' and she concurred with this, saying 'it may be more important to have them inside our heads than to hear them outside'.

In recent research Hill *et al.* (2003) have suggested that the key elements of attachment processes within the family are affect regulation, interpersonal understanding and the provision of comfort within intimate relationships. All these may be threatened by the processes of parental divorce, but can be maintained on behalf of children where parents make it explicit that they will work together to do so. The concept of shared frames or representations of emotions, cognitions and behaviours as these affect the children, can be transformed to evolve alongside new family structures, and parental narratives about the care of children and the importance of both parent's having a part in the child's life which honour this concept can be developed. However where violently oppositional stances develop between two parents, family processes threaten individual security and undermine the ecology of an attachment relationship. Work in the Court process can strengthen or rekindle attachment, but a realistic assessment has to be made as to whether a prior relationship was sufficiently strong and is still sufficiently alive, even though submerged, to overcome the processes of negative influence that may have intervened. It is in these situations that a therapeutic service relating to Court procedures and to the best interests of children could be usefully developed further in the future.

Chapter 13

Narratives in primary care

John Launer

Introduction

This chapter has three main purposes:

- To give an impression of the lived experience of working in primary care.
- To provide readers with an understanding of primary care as a context for eliciting and developing the stories of children and their families.
- To demonstrate the opportunities for practising as a narrative practitioner with children and families in primary care, and the constraints on doing so.

Throughout the chapter, I use the term 'primary care' to mean general practitioners (GPs) and those who generally work alongside them, including practice nurses, health visitors and district nurses.

Socially, culturally and politically, primary care is constructed as the principal 'open space' that is accessible to the entire population, 24 hours a day, regardless of their age or health status. For most people, including children and their families, it is one of the first places to take narratives of distress, whether these concern minor and transient physical symptoms or matters of multiple loss. For some people, it is the only such space, since other arenas such as mental health services or social services may be seen as too inaccessible or stigmatising, or may operate in ways that effectively exclude some of the most needy members of the population by virtue of ethnicity, language, mobility, domicile, and so on. On average, someone living in the United Kingdom will see their GP three or four times a year, the equivalent of nine or ten consultations per household, and an astonishing one million consultations per day done by GPs alone. Around 20 per cent of these consultations will be focused on children's problems, but children are also likely to be present in a considerable number of adult consultations, for example when their mothers visit doctors.

Conventionally, about a third of consultations in primary care are said to centre around emotional or psychosocial issues, and around a fifth of attenders are reckoned to have diagnosable mental disorders (Goldberg and

Huxley 1992). In reality, however, many GPs and primary care professionals would probably regard such estimates as arbitrary. The stories that people bring to primary care often range in an undifferentiated way across bodily discomfort, personal unhappiness, disharmony in relationships or families, and economic or social deprivation. The encounters that arise as a result cannot easily be squeezed into the kinds of taxonomies that will satisfy specialists or statisticians. In spite of this, GPs and primary care nurses receive the majority of their mental health training solely through exposure to hospital-based psychiatry. The style of thinking in that setting is largely linear and positivistic, and the treatment is mainly pharmacological. The emphasis is almost entirely on adult mental health, with children virtually always invisible in both the literal and metaphorical sense.

Once working in primary care, most doctors and nurses probably learn to reorient themselves from a biological to a biographical perspective, and from an individual perspective to a family one. The reality of primary care is that several family members are often registered with the same practice. Even nowadays, many doctors will find themselves looking after three or even four generations of some families. However, there is no obligation for medical or nursing practitioners to undertake specific training in counselling, family therapy or any other talking treatment, or in addressing the mental health needs of children and their families as identified groups. As a result, the vast majority never actually undertake such training. If clinicians in primary care do discover how to listen empathetically to people's stories, or to pay attention to the mental health needs of families and of children, it is probably through working alongside good role models, through their own personal and professional growth, or through their experience as parents.

Helping primary care practitioners to hear the stories of children and families

Over the years a number of attempts have been made by various therapists and educators to bridge the chasm between the Cartesian abstractions of much medical education and culture and the complex narratives that are brought to primary care. Perhaps the best known of these attempts was the movement founded by the psychoanalyst Michael Balint in the 1950s (Balint 1957). Balint took patients' stories – and the stories told by doctors about their patients – very seriously, and he regarded them as sources of vitally important information about the doctor–patient relationship. Balint's thinking and that of his followers has been deeply influential in primary care but has also had significant limitations. Its epistemology is explicitly psychoanalytic, and mainly oriented to thinking about individuals rather than families, and adults rather than children. Some critics have also argued that it has made GPs more inclined to make psychologising or presumptuous interpretations of their patients' problems.

In recent years another highly influential group of north American educators have been promoting the notion of 'patient-centred medicine' (Stewart *et al.* 2003). Drawing on consultation research from the social sciences, they have developed training methods to strengthen the ability of clinicians to elicit such things as patients' illness beliefs, feelings, fears, and wishes. Patient-centred medicine has made an important contribution to sensitising doctors to the issues that affect people's lives beyond their symptoms and diseases. However, it too has its limitations. Patient-centred interviewing usually appears to treat the 'patient's agenda' or 'the patient's story' as if it has a prior, static and rather concrete existence rather than as something fluid and open to continuous co-construction with the clinician. In addition, patient-centred medicine does not seek to ask any challenging questions of scientific medicine itself, nor to offer a critique of the patriarchal and adult-centred practices that are widespread within health services. It too is largely adult centred, and individual centred.

In the last decade, a quite different movement has arisen at the intersection of social sciences and health care: narrative-based medicine (Greenhalgh and Hurwitz 1998). The people involved in this movement have come from a range of backgrounds including sociology, anthropology, medical humanities and medical ethics. They have come with a number of perspectives including feminist and postmodern ones. Part of their driving force has been a reaction against the unbalanced hegemony of 'evidence-based medicine', with its backers in the pharmaceutical and molecular genetic industries. There has also been support from patient and consumer groups, who increasingly want their voices and their stories to be heard in ways that are individualised rather than collectivised.

What is new about narrative-based medicine is that it does not necessarily take the authority, rationality or objectivity of medicine as an indisputable given. It has the capacity to see within conventional medicine a 'dominant discourse' or 'meta-narrative' that must be willing to enter into dialogue with other discourses and other narratives. Narrative-based medicine also offers a reconceptualisation of medical encounters as an essentially story-making activity, in which elements such as suspense, character, plot, chance and morality all play a part. On the other hand, narrative-based medicine does not claim to offer any particular guidance as to the conduct of the medical consultation itself. It draws scarcely any of its ideas from the variety of narrative approaches to individual and family therapy that have grown up in the last two decades. What is rather peculiar from a therapist perspective, is that narrative-based medicine has so far been largely concerned with research rather than with bringing about any widespread change in medical practice itself.

Developing a narrative-based approach to primary care

For several years a group of systemic psychotherapists at the Tavistock Clinic in London have taught a regular course for GPs, nurses and other clinicians from primary care (Launer and Lindsey 1997). We come from several different disciplines including general practice, child psychiatry, clinical psychology and social work. We have been influenced by the ideas of a number of different groups involving both primary care clinicians and family therapists, including the 'Thinking Families Network' in Britain, and the Collaborative Healthcare Coalition in the United States (Launer 1995; Bloch and Doherty 1998). Our aim has been to use systemic ideas to look at a wide range of primary care work – not just family work but also everyday consultations with individuals, as well as interactions with practices and teams. We offer specific skills training as well as opportunities for theoretical and case discussion. We place particular emphasis on gender and ethnicity, and we pay specific attention to the need to hear and incorporate the voices of children in primary care.

Over the time that the course has been running, we have developed both our thinking and our approach to teaching in a number of ways. One of the principal changes has been from a largely systems-oriented approach to one based on narrative ideas. In undertaking such a change, we have been influenced both by the 'narrative turn' within family therapy, and by the emergence of narrative-based medicine as a distinct voice in its own right. In a sense, what we have done is to complete the triangle between medicine and narrative studies from the social sciences by adding a third element: systemic therapy (Launer 2002).

Looked at in narrative terms, primary care can be seen as a place where patients and families bring stories that contain puzzles, questions, or things that do not yet make sense. They want professionals to try to help them to pull together a new and more coherent story. There may be a need for some practical and technical solutions – such as a prescription, injection or hospital referral. However, patients are unlikely to accept any advice or treatment unless it also makes sense as part of a new narrative. One of the key themes of our teaching is therefore a reorientation from a 'normative' style of interviewing to a 'narrative' one. This reorientation goes beyond 'patient-centred' medicine since it affords primacy not just to the hopes, fears and beliefs of the patient but to the exact logic of their narratives as they present them in the surgery.

Our objective in these courses is to train primary care clinicians to let go of conventional styles of medical interviewing, and any consultation guidelines they might have learned previously, and instead to follow feedback constantly, tracking the exact words and phrases used by the patient, and making enquiry into these. We teach them a questioning technique that is largely based on Karl Tomm's notion of 'interventive interviewing' although we prefer to use the description 'conversations inviting change' (Tomm 1988). We also encourage interviewers to try to interpolate any biomedical questions only at moments in the conversation that fit the narrative logic too – in other words, not to interrupt the patient's narrative development unless there are compelling or urgent reasons for doing so. Initially our aim is to promote effective interviewing with individuals since this is the dominant mode of primary care consultation, and because the opportunities for other kinds of consultations in general practice in particular are often limited. However, later on we use role play in order to encourage participants to take advantage of the many opportunities that arise naturally in primary care to work with parents and children together, with couples, and with families. We then encourage them to create further opportunities for this kind of work by inviting different family members along together for extended consultations, and hope they will become emboldened in making interventions with children and families as a routine part of their work (Asen *et al.* 2003).

Three case examples

I now want to use three case vignettes to illustrate the opportunities and constraints of using such an approach in primary care. All the vignettes concern families I saw in my own surgery as a GP, although I have altered identifying details to preserve anonymity.

I have intentionally taken as my starting point an encounter not with a family but with an adult. This is because most GP consultations are with adult individuals, and children generally play a part in such consultations only as offstage characters. This patient turned out, quite unexpectedly, to be the parent of children who were obviously at great risk in many ways.

The first case

I was approaching the end of my morning surgery, having already seen fourteen patients, with two more to go. I checked my computer screen and saw that the new patient was someone who had just registered that morning and had never been seen at the practice before. I went into the waiting room and called her in: she was a black woman in her early 40s, somewhat overweight and with a sad and distracted expression. She told me that she had hurt her bottom the previous day, and simultaneously took out of her handbag a number of packets of medication to show me what she was currently taking.

I asked her how she had hurt her bottom and she told me that she had fallen. I enquired a bit more about how this happened, and she said that her fiancé had pushed her. When I questioned her further about this, she said they had been arguing in the car, she had got out, and he had followed her and pushed her over on the pavement. I asked if this happened a lot and she said yes it did, mainly because of her drinking. She had been an alcoholic for some time but was now trying to give up. I asked if she was getting any help for her alcohol problem and she said no, but she was a mental patient and had been getting help with her mental problems until recently when she moved away into our area.

I asked her to tell me something about her mental problems and she said she got hallucinations, hearing and seeing things that were not there. When I enquired if she had ever been admitted to hospital because of these, she said no but she had been in hospital for a few weeks during the summer for another problem. When I questioned her about this, she told me that she had a tumour. I enquired where the tumour was, and she said it was in her brain. At this point I thought that the tumour might be a delusion, so I asked her if she could show me the scar. She showed me a fresh but well healed scar behind her right ear that was entirely consistent with recent brain surgery. She then told me that it had been a 'meningi-something', and when I suggested the word 'meningioma', she said yes that was it. She told me the name of the consultant she was seeing for this, a neurologist I know. At the same time, I was examining the packets of medication she had laid out on my desk, and some of these were anti-epileptic pills. (The others were a type of sleeping tablet, and beta-blockers which might have been for anxiety, or for raised blood pressure or migraine.)

I said to her that it sounded as if her life was very difficult at the moment, and I wondered if there was anyone at home who was looking after her. She said that her fiancé did not live with her, but her children were at home. I asked her how many children she had and she started to cry, saying that she had had five children but only three were alive now. When I asked her how this came about, she told me that her first child had died soon after birth, having been born very prematurely. However, her main cause of grief was the murder of her eldest son, aged 24, which had happened 2 years ago. I expressed my sympathy, and then asked her how old her surviving children were. She explained that they were 15, 7 and 1 year old respectively.

Having gained all this information, I suggested that we should attend to the problem she had originally brought to me, namely her painful bottom. I examined her briefly, reassured her that she had only been bruised, and at her request prescribed some painkillers that would not interact with her other medication. I suggested that she should make a follow-up appointment in a few days time with the GP in the practice she would be registering with. (I now only work part-time in the practice and felt that I could not offer the kind of continuity of care needed by someone with such multiple and complex needs.) I also suggested that I should book her in to see our attached community mental health nurse. She agreed with both suggestions, and I gave her a written slip to hand in at the desk to fix this up.

After she left the room, I wrote up the consultation notes on the computer, and sent an internal e-mail to the doctor who would be seeing her next week, drawing his attention to my notes and suggesting that he might want to make contact with the health visitor before seeing her to enquire if anything was known about the infant. I also sent a note to the community mental health nurse, and another one to the practice secretary asking her to enter the patient's name on a list of patients for discussion at the next primary care team meeting. Having done all this, I went out to fetch the last patient of the surgery; an Albanian refugee with a history of depression who had recently been knocked down by a lorry in London and was suffering flashbacks and insomnia. The consultation, record-keeping and communication took, in all, about seventeen minutes.

Commentary

The first thing that may strike the reader about this consultation is its overwhelming, even devastating, quality. Clearly not every consultation in primary care is like this. Yet many are, and every GP, practice nurse or health visitor will be exposed on an almost daily basis to narratives that unfold a succession of losses and tragedies in the way that this one does.

Professionals from child and adolescent mental health services (CAMHS) are often tempted to challenge GPs with questions that draw attention to the enormous opportunities in primary care for identifying child mental health problems, and with how poorly these opportunities are generally taken up or exploited. The account of this consultation may indicate in some ways the difficulties that surround such 'opportunities'.

For a start, none of the patient's children are actually present at this consultation, and it was only after a specific enquiry that their existence was even revealed. When adults come to the surgery unaccompanied by their children, their focus is on their own needs. Indeed, that rare privilege may be one of the main attractions of the setting as far as they are concerned. When they do bring their children, it is likely to be with such problems as acute febrile illnesses, where it may be neither possible nor appropriate to explore any issues other than the child's symptoms and the parents' anxiety. If, as is commonly the case, parents see their usual doctor in a booked appointment for their own problems but ask to be 'fitted in' with a locum, assistant or duty doctor each time a child becomes acutely ill, it may not be possible for any single professional in the practice to hold in mind both the social and medical narratives, nor indeed necessarily to be aware of everyone's kinship. In these circumstances, it is not surprising that children and their mental health problems slip into everyone's peripheral vision, or never emerge from there to start with.

One of the things I tried to do in this consultation was to track the patient's narrative as closely as possible. As each event emerges in her account, in a sequence that is so dramatic that at one moment I believe it to be implausible, I try to help her draw out her narrative thread in a way that will hopefully allow me to understand (in the limited time available) the largest number of contexts for her distress. In doing so, I am consciously – and with some effort – striving to resist all the instinct for convergent enquiry that has been instilled in me by my training as a doctor and by medical culture itself. Almost subversively, I am having to relinquish the familiar professional syntax of 'history – examination – investigation – diagnosis – treatment' in favour of a narrative epistemology.

In that context, it may seem almost shocking that I made a choice to bring the consultation back at the end to the relatively trivial presenting symptom which began her narrative; the painful bottom. Having created what is possibly for her an unprecedented space to express her story in a way that is not constrained by the categories of one medical speciality or another, I intentionally foreclosed our encounter, and her story, at a point where I experienced the pressure (both of time and emotion) to be as much as I could bear. It was at this point, perhaps inevitably, that my own professional contexts moved into the forefront of my consciousness. These included the need to exclude the possibility (however slight) of a serious injury, and the need to document an assault that might later become the subject of a police enquiry or litigation. I was also preoccupied with the need to withhold my resources in a work setting where I cannot offer everything to everybody. I am a trained family therapist, but in my surgery I cannot be a family therapist to the sixty or so people I see in a day, nor would such pretensions be welcomed by the other members of the team who properly hold responsibility for this woman's problems – her own GP and health visitor, and the community mental health nurse.

Within the limitations imposed by such constraints, however, I believe it is possible to apply systemic thinking, and narrative ideas in particular, both humanely and realistically. First, it is possible to abandon the rather rigid enquiries that prevent professionals from hearing patients' stories with any degree of fullness, and to use specific techniques that will elicit a different kind of narrative: tracking language, following feedback and using circular and reflexive questions. It is possible to work instead from a stance of curiosity, neutrality and reflectiveness, in order to counter the objectifying tendencies that may have come with professional acculturation. Second, it is possible to reconceptualise the primary care consultation as a therapeutic encounter during which, in however limited a way, patients do have the opportunities to elaborate their stories in a way that is directed by their own preoccupations and sense of self rather than by some external and imposed conceptual framework brought by the professional.

It is also possible for practitioners to make the choice of enquiring as a matter of routine into some of the subjugated dimensions of people's medical stories, and this can perhaps especially include their identity as parents. Even if there is rarely time to elicit anything like a comprehensive genogram in most primary care consultations, it is rarely difficult to ask a few simple questions that will allow one to sketch at least a two-generation genogram on a piece of scrap paper.

Finally, primary care affords many possibilities for communication and teamwork that could be exploited far better than they often are. Paradoxically, the arrival of sophisticated computer networks in almost every surgery in the country has meant that one can rapidly draw the attention of a network of colleagues to any case that is causing concern. Unlike what often happened in the past, patients such as this woman and her family can hopefully become the recipients of collaborative and joined up care. My hope is that the effect of the consultation for this woman is twofold: a psychological experience of being permitted to tell her own story in her own manner without being boxed in by medical constructions of the world, and a practical experience of being linked with multiple sources of potential help.

The second case

This patient was an 8-year-old Ethiopian boy. He came into the room with his mother and his 5-year-old sister. Saying nothing, he tugged at my arm, and kept tugging. It seemed as if he wanted me to get up, and so I wondered if he wanted to sit in my chair. I got up and offered him the chair but, still in silence, he pushed me over to another empty chair in the room, an upholstered chair with wheels that I do not particularly like to sit in but is clearly meant to be 'the doctor's chair'. He sat me down in this and wheeled me over to face my desk, at the correct angle rather than the more informal one I usually adopt. At this point I realised he was trying to turn me into 'a proper doctor'. I glanced at his summary on the computer screen and was not surprised to see the diagnosis: autistic spectrum disorder.

He then started to organise his mother in a similar way, but placing her in what was clearly an appropriate chair, and an appropriate position, for a patient. She smiled at me, and seemed to appreciate my willingness in letting him use me in a sculpt. She told me that he had been complaining of a sore throat, and she had been worried that he would not let me examine him, but as she was speaking he sat down meekly in her lap and opened his mouth wide for me to look in. The serious bit of preliminary theatre had meant he could now take his allotted role too, as the cooperative patient.

In the 8 minutes that followed, we held a conversation that moved in and out of three quite separate domains: the boy's sore throat, his autism and its management, and the family's experience as asylum seekers. I established that the sore throat was minor and did not need treatment. I found out that he is being well cared for at a specialist school for autistic children, although his mother finds the school holidays particularly taxing as a single mother with a younger child too. I also found out that they have managed to achieve asylum status in Britain but the mother remains anxious about being able to bring her husband over here, which is proving much more difficult. He is in

Saudi Arabia and they have been apart for just over 5 years, which means that he has never seen his daughter. She cried as she told me this, but recovered herself quickly as if to let me know that the tears were always close but she also needed to maintain control over them in order to manage. I turned to the daughter and we had a short conversation about daddy. She has seen photos of him and they sometimes talk on the phone, but she is sad that he cannot come over here and does not understand why they will not let him on a plane to fly here. Her mother seemed appreciative that I took the trouble to hold this conversation, but also seemed keen to finish the consultation too since I had dealt with the matter of the sore throat.

Commentary

Like most practices in inner London we have a large number of asylum seekers and their families registered with us. Many do not speak English and we sometimes use interpreters for up to a third of all consultations in any surgery, but in this case the mother and daughter spoke good English, although the boy remained silent. It is always a dilemma knowing how much one should address the issues of asylum and displacement in any consultation, particularly when meeting a family for the first time. Since they play such a large part in family narratives, it can be gross to ignore them, even in the context of minor illness. On the other hand, families like these also want to lead normal lives and it may feel intrusive or oppressive if well-meaning professionals make enquiries about these issues on every occasion.

The same dilemma also holds in respect of a diagnosis like autism, and indeed with other conspicuous handicaps such as learning disabilities or congenital abnormalities like Down's. If such diagnoses are excluded from the narrative during the consultation it can seem as if the doctor is embarrassed or uncaring, but equally parents may feel that they cannot ever share the normal experience of taking a child to the surgery with a minor illness in order to be reassured.

In practice, many doctors and nurses in primary care become adept at weaving the kind of conversation I attempted to hold with this family. Such conversations are inevitably limited in length and also in the scope of their enquiry. However, they provide opportunities to acknowledge the things that most dominate people's lives without dwelling on them when not invited to do so. Just as important, they provide a chance of letting children know that their voices and their narratives matter, and that adult figures of authority are capable of paying attention to their suffering and understanding it.

For such conversations to take place with the right balance of curiosity and tact, people who work in primary care need to be able to follow both verbal and nonverbal feedback attentively, and to respond appropriately. I hope that this Ethiopian family, in their single encounter with me, felt that the many dimensions of their experience were being noted and respected, without imposing an additional burden of pathologisation.

The third case

The appointment had been booked for a boy aged 2. When I called the name out in the waiting room, I was followed back to my room first by the boy, then by his big sister aged about 7, then his mother. When I sat down, the boy came right up to me and held onto my knees. I was surprised. Although this kind of immediate physical contact seems to be quite common with Afro-Caribbean children, this was a white family, and although I have known the children since birth, I was still surprised. The girl sat herself quietly down on a chair on the corner, and the mother sat in the patient's chair facing me. I asked her why she had brought the boy along, and she said he complained of being tired all the time. Once again, I was surprised. Adults very often come to general practice complaining of being tired all the time, and doctors often write simply 'TATT' in the notes. However, I cannot ever remember a small child using these words.

I asked the mother if perhaps he was echoing words that she was using, and she said that she herself did not use the phrase, but she admitted she did feel tired a lot of the time. (I should say that the boy, who was still holding my knees, looked the picture of health but his mother looked drawn and rather burdened.) I asked the mother why she was tired, and she said that actually the boy always kept her awake. He found it hard to go to sleep at night and would only do so in her arms on the sofa in the living room. When she finally took him to his bed, he slept for a while but usually woke up about one or two in the morning and insisted on coming into her bed. He spent the rest of the night there, but was restless and she often never got back to sleep properly once he was there. I asked her how long this had been going on for, and she explained that it had started when her husband left about 6 months previously to go and live with another woman. This was unknown to me. Although she has been my patient for more than a decade, this was the first news I had had from any source of what had happened. I offered my sympathy and asked if this departure had been a surprise to her. She said yes, but she was coping and had a lot of support from her own family and from friends. She was not tearful.

I turned to the girl and asked what it was like now that daddy had gone. She said she was sad, she missed him. I asked if she saw daddy sometimes and she said yes, they went to stay with him and his girlfriend at weekends. Her mother interrupted to say that this was now becoming less common, and sometimes he did not keep to the arrangement. She feared he was losing interest in the children and might reduce his contact with them even further, especially if his girlfriend got pregnant.

I asked her if she was getting any help from the practice or elsewhere with all the issues that she must be having to think about: managing on her own with the children, managing their distress about their father moving out, and so on. She said no, but repeated that there was a lot of support around her and she did not really want help for herself. All she really needed was advice about how to help with the boy's sleeping problem. I asked her what advice she had already been given about this. She said that it varied. Some of the friends were saying that she should be tough and take the boy back to his bedroom immediately if he climbed into her bed. On the other hand, her own mother had said that she should be tolerant and allow him to stay there because he was still likely to be very distressed about the break-up of his parents. She asked me what I thought of the two different approaches.

I said that I thought both approaches had advantages and disadvantages. The 'tough' approach was likely to work if she really stuck to it, but she might have a week or so of hell while the boy adjusted to the new regime, and also it might make her feel guilty as she knew why he needed to come to bed with her. At the same time, she also needed her own sleep so that she could function and also do all the things that she had to do as a mother. I said I thought there was no easy answer – it was a difficult dilemma. She seemed happy with my formulation, and not disappointed that I had avoided going one way or the other. Encouraged by this, I suggested that she might set a date in advance (such as the boy's third birthday) when she would expect him to sleep all night in his own bed again. Perhaps she could discuss this with him in advance and maybe even set in place a system of incentives or rewards for this. She said she thought this was a good idea and would discuss it with her mother.

I asked if there was anything else she wanted to raise in the consultation. She said no, her daughter was sad as she had told me herself, but was sleeping all right and was doing well at school. It was miserable for them both that their father was no longer at home, but she thought they were doing pretty well in the circumstances. Time would help. I asked if she wanted to book a follow-up appointment with me in a couple of weeks to let me know how things were going but she said no, what I had said was really helpful and it was enough to be getting on with. She knew where I was and would come and talk about herself or the children when she needed to. The consultation lasted about 12 minutes.

Commentary

This consultation, in contrast to the previous one is much more explicitly 'therapeutic'. With the tacit consent of the mother, I used questions to lead the conversation almost immediately away from physical symptoms in one of her children to a shared distress – that of separation – experienced by the whole family. The nature of their loss, though devastating in itself, is apparently uncomplicated by other dislocations, traumas or life-threatening illness.

It is, in other words, much closer to some of the more straightforward kinds of cases that reach child and adolescent mental health services. It is also, for the same reason, manageable as a piece of therapeutic work within 10 minutes or so. In addition, it affords me as a GP an opportunity to harness my social authority in order to normalise reaction to distressing events, and effectively to offer permission for the mother to follow a range of possible responses.

This in itself raises some interesting questions. Many CAMHS professionals, on hearing about this kind of case, would identify the family as 'an ideal referral', but this is open to challenge in many ways. The scale of need represented by the patient in the first case (and her children) is almost certainly far greater than the family in the third, and yet it is the latter who are far more likely to be picked up as 'a good case'. This is a compelling example of the 'inverse care law', so familiar to those in primary care, whereby the neediest patients are the ones for whom it is often hardest to connect with appropriate resources, because their problems cross so many boundaries that their care either becomes hopelessly fragmented or is entirely disqualified by the rules and rigidities of welfare state bureaucracies.

Another paradox of this situation is that the 'ideal' CAMHS case represented by this family is perhaps the one that can most readily be addressed by a GP or health visitor in a short space of time, and perhaps quite effectively. Without underestimating the effect on this family of their abandonment by the father, it could be argued that the effect of such a common experience can best be dealt with by the first professional to whom it is disclosed, and at the moment of disclosure. In the non-stigmatising context of the surgery, the natural conversational way in which the story can be elicited, and the potential for integrating the events into the evolving life cycle to which the practitioner or practice team may bear witness, may be superior in many ways to the facilities offered by even the most sophisticated CAMHS team. Indeed, the delays, distance, formalities, rituals and aura of the CAMHS clinic may all handicap the kind of effective work that can be done succinctly and opportunistically in the surgery or health centre. Certainly, the feedback from this mother suggests that a brief family intervention in the surgery met her needs as fully as she wished, and that 'making too much of it' through a referral might have been counter-productive.

It may appear surprising that I did not act more forcefully by suggesting that she should come back, perhaps for a series of appointments with and without the children. From a CAMHS perspective this is certainly what one might be expected to offer in the context of a marital break-up. In primary care, it feels important to respect distance as well as to offer intimacy. One may need to let the narrative evolve over multiple small episodes at irregular intervals chosen by the patient and family. I have been at the practice for 21 years and may well stay there until I retire. Probably I will have plenty of opportunities to have conversations with this mother and with her children as they grow up. Elsewhere, I have called this kind of work 'ultra-brief, ultra-long therapy' (Launer 1996).

Conclusion

These cases highlight the opportunities that arise every day in primary care for working with children and families using a narrative approach. Perhaps more important, each of the cases also draws attention implicitly to the need for close collaboration between primary care and local CAMHS services.

Sessions in the GP surgery can help therapists to learn, perhaps with a shock, about the scale and complexity of the distress among children and families in the community, and about how it is skewed towards those population groups they may never have encountered – such as the housebound, the deaf, or those who do not speak any English. They will also learn how people bring entirely different narratives to primary care: narratives that are perhaps constrained by time, but also freed up by the informality and familiarity of the setting, and where the coexistence of both physical and emotional symptoms provides an extra dimension. This kind of exposure can enable CAMHS therapists to adapt and develop their own skills, including the ability to deliver brief and opportunistic interventions in the same way that GPs, primary care nurses and health visitors often have to do, so that they can offer help more equitably and more effectively.

The benefits to the primary care team can also be great, especially if CAMHS professionals are willing to give training and supervision to their primary care colleagues, and to help them to be more alert to child and family mental health issues, or more courageous in their willingness to offer interventions. In the end, we may only be able to bring forth new stories among the families who attend primary care if we can stimulate enough dialogue among primary care professionals and CAMHS therapists to bring forth a new narrative of what primary care is, and what it ought to become.

Chapter 14

Narratives of young offenders

Rudi Dallos

In discussing this work two main strands of ideas will be considered: first, that approaches from narrative therapy can be effective in helping young people to shape more constructive as opposed to destructive stories about their lives; second, ideas will be woven in from attachment theory and research on the development of narratives to consider the structure of these young people's stories. In effect the first strand concerns the content and meaning of their stories, and the second the form or structure of the stories. Importantly this second emphasis on structure tries to take account of the learning and development of the 'skills' required to place our experiences into narrative. Arguably, this is not simply an inherent human skill but an ability which needs to be developed and carefully fostered. In fact therapy can be seen not only as a context where the content of ideas is shaped, examined and co-constructed but also as an 'educational' experience where the abilities required to create a story for one's life are encouraged and developed. Perhaps it is worth adding that for many young people in the 'offending' context, words, literacy, use of language and, even more broadly talk, present difficulties and can be experienced as aversive activities.

This chapter starts with an exploration of ideas from developmental narrative research and attachment theory. These strands are then woven together to suggest how narrative approaches can be shaped to fit work with young people in the context of a Youth Offending Team. Some common aspects of the experiences of the young people are offered as a window into the sorts of lives and circumstances in which they live.

Narrative therapies – some problems with narrative approaches

In our work with young offenders we have employed two principal orientations from narrative therapies: (1) re-storying – exploring and resisting dominant discourses of deviance; and (2) externalising – exploring unique outcomes and attempting to reduce the dysjunctions between how these young people feel they are seen and how they would like to be seen. However, before turning to a discussion of how narrative therapeutic approaches can be employed with these young people, I want briefly to review a number of issues regarding narratives. First, it is interesting to consider how the narratives develop and the ways in which there are commonalities between the lived experiences of these young people and the narratives of self and others that develop. Second, I want to consider the structure of these narratives. This has typically been discussed in terms of the concept of coherence but I want to suggest that there is also an element of acquired 'skill' in the ability to articulate one's life in terms of a coherent narrative.

Development of narratives

Content

It is not evident from the narrative therapy literature (White and Espton 1990; White 1995; Sluzki 1992) where narratives come from and how they develop. In our experience, many of the young people we work with have 'real' lived experiences involving violence, abuse, deprivation and neglect. These present themselves in terms of the actions and scenes which make up the stories of the protagonists. Arguably, there is only so much flexibility available in the way we can weave such experiences into a life story rather than an infinite range of stories that we can make up. In addition, this story-making process is shaped by wider culturally shared discourses – to use a familiar example, 'problem families' with bad blood and feckless and irresponsible fathers. Importantly, it is also shaped by broader images of masculinity regarding emotional toughness, self-reliance, and so on. These elements often combine to shape stories of lives of brutality, failure and lack of respect for self and others. Overall there can be a sense of hopelessness about the future. Yet, this may also be flavoured with a sense of risk and 'devil-may-care' fun for many young people, which may be a combination of their natural energy along with a belief that life owes them something. This sense of entitlement to something more pleasurable can combine with the desire to generate 'fun', which others may instead regard as deviant and anti-social.

Narrative as 'skill' – coherence

It is not only the content of the stories the young people develop that is important, but also their ability to create stories to place their lives into a narrative. Two strands of research offer some insights here. Research on the development of narrative abilities or skills (Baerger and McAdams 1999; Habermas and Bluck 2000) indicates that the ability to author our lives in terms of a coherent story is a highly complex 'skill'. Initially it seems that stories of young children around the age of 7 are relatively concrete, immediate and episodic. Their narratives do not span extended periods of time. Initially they hold relatively simple and concrete explanations for why people act in certain ways (Piaget 1955). When asked to talk about themselves, they tend to refer to immediate events, today or yesterday, to relate the concrete aspects of what happened, to talk in terms of physical features of the participants and perhaps describe people's actions in terms of simple traits such as 'nice' or 'horrible' or 'very clever' (Habermas and Bluck 2000). This does not mean that they do not understand more about themselves and others than this, but that they may not yet have the language skills to express such understanding (Donaldson 1978). It seems that the ability to develop sophisticated narratives starts around adolescence (Habermas and Bluck 2000). Much of the work exploring narrative development has focused on the concept of *coherence* in narratives. This is seen to involve a number of components: setting the story in context, causal connections between events, an evaluation of events and a sense of purpose or a point to their lives. This also needs to make reference to culturally shared ideas of normative development of people's lives, transitional markers and expectations. For example, in adolescence there are culturally shared expectations of increasing independence, decision-making about careers and education, and sexual activity. The connecting of events requires an ability to think about other people's intentions and internal states and to stand outside our stories and reflect on inconsistencies, gaps and details.

As in language development generally, part of it is linked to the neurological development of the brain. Increasingly more sophisticated operations become possible as the complexity of the neuronal connections develops. However, the development is a complex interplay between nature and nurture. The biological development at the same times requires practice and encouragement, and a conducive emotional environment. An important basis or 'scaffolding' for this skill for children arises out of the nature of the conversations with their parents. This requires parents to engage in conversations with their children to help teach them how to make sense of their lives, to connect events over time and to be able to weave together a thread of events being linked in a causal way. As a simple example, a study by McCabe and Peterson (1991) revealed that mothers' narrative styles could shape their young children's abilities to link events causally over time, as well as the level of detail and elaboration in their narratives. When assessed at 27 months two infants had very similar abilities. Their respective mothers had different styles regarding the way they spoke to their infants, one emphasising details in stories and the other causal connections. Eighteen months later the infants showed concomitantly striking differences in the way they told stories about things that had happened to them, the differences between them matching their mothers' styles.

Narrative skill and attachments

However, these studies tend to underplay the emotional contexts and forces in the young people's lives. Attachment theory also proposes that the interactions and communications between a child and his or her parents are vital in shaping how their narrative abilities develop. Bowlby (1969) argued that it is particularly important how the parents react when the child is distressed or frightened. If the child experiences that others can be relied on for support and reassurance when he or she is frightened or distressed then a 'working model' is seen to develop which predicts that the world is relatively safe and that the child is worthy of love and care. This is typically described as a 'secure' attachment model. Alternatively, if parents cannot be relied on, or the child is discouraged from showing his or her feelings, or even punished for doing so, then an 'insecure' model is seen to evolve. Initially, for a young child this 'working model' is nonverbal and is based predominantly on feelings, actions and visualisation. By analogy we can think of how animals, for example dogs, can learn to trust or distrust their owners. Essentially the development of the 'working model' is based on repeated interactions and communication between the parent and the child. Initially this communication is nonverbal but as the child grows the interactions are shaped not just by nonverbal communications but also by language.

Attachment theory suggests that there are significant variations in the ways parents respond to and communicate with their children. In studies employing the Strange Situation (Ainsworth *et al.* 1978) it has been found that parents differ not only in how they react to their infant's distress when separated from them, but also in the nature of the play that they engage in with their infants prior to the separation. For example, parents of children that are classified as 'insecure' generally are less attuned to their child and slower to respond to their distress. Crittenden (1998) has extended this work by employing video-tapes of interactions between infants and their mothers which reveal that there are wide variations in how attuned, consistent, coercive and sensitive they are able to be.

These differences appear to be linked to the content and coherence of narratives that children subsequently develop. There is a wide range of evidence, for example studies employing the Separation Anxiety Test (SAT), in which 6-year-old children are asked to respond to six pictures showing a child of the same age and sex as themselves in various situations depicting separations. These vary in intensity from mild – being tucked up in bed – to extreme – parents going away for 2 weeks. The children are prompted to talk about what the child in the picture might feel and why, and what they might do. They are also asked what he or she might do in a similar situation. Studies such as these repeatedly show that the children differ, and not just in the content of their answers. For example, children who had years earlier been classified as secure in infancy were able to state that the child in the picture might feel sad or worried, but that the relationship with the parents was warm, the child was seen as valuable and help would be given when it was needed. By contrast, children who had been classified as insecure were also able to say that the child was sad, but they had less positive views of the child and less faith that the parents would be available to help them. Often they were silent regarding what might happen to the child. The children differed in the nature or coherence of their stories, with the insecure children being less able to be open and to offer details of what the children felt, why they felt as they did and how the story might end. In addition they were less able to connect these with how the child in the story might feel and how they themselves would feel. In effect their stories were less coherent in terms of explanations for how and why people were acting and also in terms of consistency between their own and others' feelings.

Communication, attachment and narratives

In one important study (Main *et al.* 1985) the children's responses to these separation pictures and stories were also compared to the recorded conversation between the child and his or her mother following a 1-hour separation. Where the child's stories had been classified as secure the child and the mother were able to freely discuss a wide range of topics, including relationships and feelings. By contrast, where the children had been classified as insecure, their conversation with the mother was restricted, impersonal and showed little elaboration, and the mothers tended to ask closed as opposed to open questions. These studies suggest that as children develop their abilities to put their experiences into narratives, this varies in terms of the content and the coherence of their stories. In turn, the kind of scaffolding that the parents are able to offer to the young child to foster their narrative abilities appears to vary according to the nature of the parent's attachment style.

Oppenheim and Waters (1985) suggest that, rather than thinking about attachment narratives as predominantly internal representations, it is important to think about them as communicational processes:

> Some of the most powerful discriminations between secure and insecure children come from judging individual differences in ease, openness, and coherence of emotional communication and from examining how children construct narratives about attachment themes and communicate them to others.
>
> (Oppenheim and Water *et al.* 1985: 205)

This view is consistent with Bowlby's original emphasis on the importance of parent–infant communication. Moreover, recent research has confirmed that almost as soon as children become capable of talking they engage in conversations about feelings with their parents (Bretherton 1985; Fivush and

Fromhoff 1988). Children's abilities to talk about emotional and interpersonal issues emerge in the context of conversations with their parents. Hence their abilities to make sense of their own feelings and others' feelings – distress, sadness, loss, anger as well as positive feelings – and to generate stories involving explanations and reasons for people's actions, depend on the support that their parents and carers can provide. We have already seen that narrative skills, for example to develop detailed, consistent, causal stories about how and why people act, are related to the style of their parents' conversations (McCabe and Peterson 1991). These studies suggest that the narrative skills children develop in 'normal' secure attachment situations may vary considerably according to differences in the parents' styles of conversing with the child.

But what about family situations where there are significant difficulties, stresses and distresses? Bowlby (1969) argued that the extent to which communications between child and parent are free as opposed to restricted was extremely important to the healthy development of the child. He argued that particularly harmful were situations where the child's accurate perceptions of painful events related to the self and others are negated or distorted by the parents. In effect the child might be told what he or she 'should' feel rather than what the child sees to be true. One of the most vivid examples of such a process is the distortion involved in sexual abuse, where a child may be told that she imagined it, or that she had initiated and was therefore responsible for it, by the abusive parent. Other examples may be where the child learns from the parents that they should not talk about a loss, for example the death of the other parent. Such instruction may be largely nonverbal, for example the facial expression and emotional withdrawal by the parent. It may also involve the parent changing the topic of the conversation rapidly or directly instructing a child not to discuss the loss or show their feelings about it.

From such communicational sequences with adults children may learn that they should not communicate about these feelings. They may also lack the emotional scaffolding – the support to help them make sense of these feelings. This means that not only do they have difficulty in communicating to others but they are less able to communicate with themselves, to have inner dialogues to help them make sense of the events. Especially for young children, their abilities to talk with themselves are shaped from the conversations with and around them (Vygotsky 1962). In effect they need help to learn to think about emotion and to put their experiences into coherent stories. They also learn both whether they can and should talk with others and how to do this. Constructive conversations with others involve a co-creation of narratives and this in turn involves turn-taking, listening to and building on others' stories, linking others' experiences with one's own, being able to contemplate how others might see things differently, and so on. A child growing up in a family where this rarely occurs may lack the sense of permission, skills and confidence to engage in conversations which can help him or her elaborate on their narratives.

Narrative therapy with young offenders

Youth Offending Teams (YOTs) are multi-disciplinary and include the police, social services, youth service, education and health services. Set up just over 5 years ago their remit was to offer early intervention to help youngsters who engaged in criminal activities to avoid becoming entrapped into criminal identities and careers. The service operates at a number of levels, starting from offering final warnings to avoid further prosecution on the condition of engaging in various types of work such as counselling, reparation and group activities, which look at offending behaviour and motivation to change, among other things. Further down the line young people convicted of offences may be given various supervision orders by the courts instead of custodial sentences. These can also involve reparation, therapy and group activities and in some cases can include parenting orders whereby parents are required to engage in 'counselling and guidance' activities to assist them in the care of their children. This is a very brief thumbnail sketch of this innovative service which attempts above all else to avoid the use of custodial sentences whereby many young people graduate from prisons to become more persistent and devious offenders.

In our work as a clinical psychologist and a parenting coordinator with this service we offer assessment and therapeutic input, as well as consultation with case workers. Each young person is allocated one key case worker who offers a variety of interventions, including managing their reparation work, counselling, work with their families, orchestrating input from education, assisting employment, and working with the police and the courts. It is necessary to describe this context a little in order to make sense of the kinds of stories that evolve for these young people. Let us start with a brief story about one young man, Adam. I have chosen Adam because his story encapsulates many of the experiences and circumstances that we have encountered in our work with young people in this service. However, this does not include all the variations and differences that are to be found. For example, not all the young people we work with have experienced physical violence or poverty and deprivation. However, these do seem to be common significant ingredients. Even in families who are relatively financially secure we see and hear stories of contradictions, inconsistency and criticism in their lives, often spanning several generations.

Adam

Adam was referred by his key worker for a psychological assessment and possibly therapy. He had been given a final warning by the police for a violent assault on a victim who was unknown to him. He was drunk at the time and subsequently it was discovered that he regularly drank heavily. His key worker was concerned that he was also engaging in self-harming behaviour – smashing his head and hands into doors and walls – and was frequently angry and also very depressed. She felt that this may have been an indication of a deep level of distress and possibly a high level of risk of serious harm to himself and others. She felt that he was using cannabis and ecstasy to manage his feelings. The intentions of 'final warnings' are to allow some early intervention to occur and hopefully offer an alternative to an escalation into further offending. Also, since they do not incur a criminal record, it is also hoped that they avoid stigmatisation and promotion of criminal identities. Adam was living at a residential college during the week and with his mother at weekends and holidays. His older sister had recently left home.

The approach we have developed, and which was being formed at the time of the work with Adam, was that we would attempt to build on the relationship that the key worker started to establish. In this case there had not been much contact but we made it clear to Adam that we would be in communication with his key worker. We came to an agreement that he could read our notes at any time and could request that we did not pass some information on if he was unhappy with this. He had sessions with me as well as joint sessions with me and my colleague. Later these included a session in which we introduced a teacher from the Team to him and a YOT worker who would help him to find accommodation. As many of these young people have experienced being passed from one person to the next, these others were introduced in the context of our relationship with him. In our view it takes a substantial period of time for trust to develop and once it has we try to build on it rather than introduce a sequence of new people outside the context of an established relationship.

I read Adam's case notes and created a mental image of him. This was based on the 'shorthand' version of a young man who was 'depressed, angry, self-harming, using cannabis and ecstasy, and drinking heavily', who had received a final warning for common assault while drunk. He was in fact a pleasant looking young man, dressed in a designer jacket, softly spoken, often smiling, polite, not overly physical but looking reasonably fit and healthy. On the surface he was in control and quite relaxed. But this was not in fact the case. A brief mental health inventory (BSI: the Brief Symptom Inventory) revealed that he had quite frequent suicidal thoughts, he was depressed, he had trouble sleeping, he used alcohol and cannabis to help him relax, and he feared that his temper was out of control.

He told me quite a bit about himself in the first session which was elaborated in subsequent meetings. His life story in brief was that his father had disappeared from his life before he was born. Until recently he had lived with his mother and his sister, but his sister had left home 3 years earlier when she was pregnant. When Adam was 8, his mother married another man. She was preoccupied and insecure with the relationship and did not respond to Adam when he was bullied at school and beaten by older boys. Both she and his step-father called him a 'mummy's boy' and a 'baby' when he cried, and his step-father decided to make a 'man' of him. In an attempt to please him, Adam aged 11 started to stand up to bullies and often got into fights. He was aware that his mother was drinking a lot and was caught up in her ambivalence towards him – 'I love you, I care, come on, give us a cuddle / you're a bastard, you're the worst thing that ever happened to me' – his anger and growing depression offering him some sort of clarity in its familiarity. Alongside this he experienced more and more abuse and frequently witnessed his step-father's violence towards his mother. Adam came to fear and resent him and was glad when he eventually left.

Adam's wish had always been to live with his father, but he had rejected Adam many times. This included after his grandmother's funeral, when he and his mother got into a fight because Adam had not cried.

He told me a story of a Dr Jekyll and Mr Hyde transformation in his life as he grew up. As his mother's drinking increased, Adam began to do the same. He hated seeing her drunk and hated himself for doing likewise. He also described to me how his new violent character, like Mr Hyde, came to dominate more and more. He sometimes went looking for fights in pubs and clubs, but felt no pain, because it was numbed by adrenalin. However, Adam's Mr Hyde had strict rules: no hitting women, no hitting children, no hitting his parents, it has to be a fair fight, not premeditated, he does it on his own, he never walks away from a fight, no kicking people in the head, if people are down let them get up and no trying to deliberately injure people. Above all he said what he wanted was respect and power, which he had never had. We called these his Marquis of Queensbury rules.

Narratives of offending: commonality and uniqueness

When we listened to Adam's story this triggered memories of similar features from the stories of many of the young people with whom we had worked. Members of the Youth Offending Team value young people as unique individuals and adopt a respectful position towards them. At the same time they acknowledge that it is important to recognise the common features and events that shape the lives of these young people. This recognition helps us to be more sympathetic and to work alongside them in order to resist the potential blaming and marginalisation that can occur if these commonalities are overlooked. A striking example is that over 90 per cent of the cases we work with are males and it is widely established that young men are much more likely to engage in offending behaviours than young women. Gender, and in particular masculine identity, appears to play a major part in their stories. Frosh *et al.* (2002), in a major study of identities of young men, have discussed extensively how their sense of who they are, how they should act and what it is to be a man, are constructed from dominant narratives or discourses. Typically these feature notions of toughness, assertiveness, action rather than emotion, and independence and physical courage. Arguably, even when young women offend their actions are often shaped by discourses of male identities. This chapter, as is the book, is about narratives and their use in therapeutic work with children and young people. We want to suggest that these narratives have both commonalities and uniqueness, in terms of their structure as well as their content. It is also possible to consider a developmental perspective to examine how the content and structure of these narratives develop. To start with we can consider some common aspects of the narratives of these young people.

Self

- I'm not good enough, I'm bad, I can't control my anger, I can't be trusted and I don't trust anybody, they say I'm just like my dad, I don't give a toss about my dad, you've got to be hard, I don't take any shit.

My life

- I've seen a lot of shit, my dad used to hit my mum, my mum gets stressed out, she gets pissed, she gets depressed, she takes it out on me, my dad abandoned us, we don't really have anybody to rely on, if people wind me up, do my head in, take the piss then you've got to fight, I've got no life ahead of me really, hate school, crap at reading and exams, just want a job and have some money and have my own place. I feel best with my mates having a few beers, getting stoned, having a laugh.

Others

- You can't trust anybody, except some of my mates, my brother and sister a bit.
- My dad/step-dad is a bastard and he doesn't care about me, he is violent, he drinks, he hits/used to hit my mum.
- My girlfriend is OK but sometimes she winds me up.
- My mum – she does my head in going on at me all the time, she is a silly cow for getting together with my step-dad.
- My step-dad, he was OK at first, but he doesn't like me now and I don't like him, he says my mother is too soft on me, what does he know?
- Social workers, police, psychologists – they all try to tell you what to do, I especially hate shrinks they try to tell me I'm loony.

We can predict with some certainty that a good proportion of these common elements have been/will be present in the work with most of the young men we meet. Interestingly, many of these components also exist in the stories of the young women. When assembled together they add up to a narrative of life on the edge, of deviant outsiders to be feared by society. In pointing to these commonalities we are not seeking to perpetuate stereotypes, nor to make these young people appear stupid. They are not. However, they share many common experiences, such as witnessing violence, living in deprived circumstances, separations and little contact with their fathers or father figures. These factors have been well documented in the research on young offenders (Hollin and Howells 1996). These experiences, it can be reasonably argued, are likely to predispose the development of their stories about the world.

Narrative therapy

Narrative therapies do not constitute a body of techniques but more an orientation to therapy which attempts to be emancipatory, empowering and non-expert or prescriptive. Fundamental is the view that we live in and through the stories we hold about our lives. These stories both describe, but also construct, our experience and our domain of choices – our possibilities. A story serves to connect up the pieces of our experiences over time and helps shape these into a narrative in which 'I' stands as the central character. Importantly, consistent with a social constructionist position, narrative approaches view that dominant cultural discourses have a powerful impact. These contain ideas about what it is to be 'healthy', 'normal', 'successful', and 'worthy of respect' as a human being. Whether they are aware of it or not, families are influenced, for example, by ideas from television, advertising, films and newspapers about how they 'should' be and what they 'should' strive to be (Gergen and Davis 1985). Furthermore, such ideas are continually played out more locally in conversations with friends, family, at school and in the pub. It is here in what Goffman (1959) calls the 'interactional order' that in conversations dominant discourses are given further personal impact. For young offenders this conversational space with their mates is very important. It is where ways of gaining respect and acknowledgement are worked out.

Approaches from narrative therapy

Dominant stories – content

Among the most widely used approaches employed in narrative therapies are the search for unique outcomes, externalisation, exploring alternative stories, exploring stories about ideal and actual self, exploring dysjunctions between preferred and actual, and exploring dominant discourses which shape these ideas of a preferred self.

As we saw in the initial example of Adam's life, many young men hold stories about how they should be which involve narrow and stereotypical ideas of masculinity. To be acceptable as a young man you need to be 'hard', 'unemotional', 'not frightened' and 'not vulnerable'. Added to this there are frequently ideas that are more specific to an offending sub-group, such as 'willing to take risks', 'not afraid to break the law' and 'not a nark'. This involves a loyalty to the code of not 'grassing' or telling the authorities about crimes that others have committed even when they may involve violence to oneself. This constellation of ideas can be seen as a dominant story of masculinity. One of the powerful aspects of such dominant discourses is that they may appear to young people to be just 'obvious', 'natural', 'what everybody thinks'; that is, they are powerful partly because they are invisible and therefore not questioned or contested. An important aspect of work with young offenders, including young women is, by contrast, to raise these implicit beliefs and stories to consciousness and explore their implications.

Part of this exploration can involve looking at how the young person may experience pressure to conform to the imperatives of these discourses. One approach to this can be to draw up a list of the pros and cons of how they see themselves at the moment and how they would like to be and what helps or hinders them making the changes that they would like to see in their lives. This can be fostered by a discussion of exceptions or 'unique outcomes' – any times that they were able to think, feel or act differently. Particularly helpful can be an analysis of what prevents change. This can utilise the idea of externalising the problem/s, especially in terms of how the problem maintains itself. Such a discussion can help consideration of ideas of resistance, starting with what makes it hard to change. Some young people can benefit from the metaphor of the problem as an entity which has ways of tricking and trapping them. The older ones sometimes find that this works better if it takes a less metaphorical form in a discussion of social contexts, events, beliefs, relationships, and so on.

We drew up a table with Adam regarding his drinking, which contains many ingredients of a narrative approach (see Table 14.1).

As we can see in Table 14.1, Adam is able to point to some exceptions to his drinking, to identify what helps him to resist and what pulls him back into drinking. Alongside these details it is also possible to see a dominant story of masculinity. His girlfriend's ex-partner needs a 'good hiding', she 'pisses him off' when she is 'nagging' and overall Adam has learnt essentially two ways to deal with his distress, one involving drinking and the other fighting his way out: both examples of traditional notions of a macho, hard-drinking, hard-fighting masculinity. However, one of the contradictions for him is that his mother also drinks very heavily and perhaps this association of drinking with an emotional, vulnerable femininity is one of the pressures for change for him. He said he hated seeing his mother drunk and hated himself for being like her.

Table 14.1 Narratives of choice regarding Adam's drinking

What helps me to stop drinking	What pulls me back into it
Some friends, older, more mature, no hassle	Some friends, younger, fun but stupid
Girlfriend, nice asks me not to do it	Girlfriend, when she pisses me off, nagging
Occupied – work, going out, videos	
Not bored or frustrated	Ex-boyfriend texts her, they have a kid, pisses me off, I want to attack him, he needs a hiding, don't trust him, hate him
Seeing dad's relatives	
Memory of mum doing it – makes me want to not get in that state	Police harassing me, want to get away from it
	Seeing mum's side of the family, temptation, join in, in your face socialising

Structure and coherence

Adam was an extremely articulate, bright and cooperative young man in our sessions. However, what became increasingly apparent was that this activity of reflecting on his life, of considering ideas about who he was and what he wanted to be, the nature and implications of his stories, where they evolved from and possible alternatives, was a novel activity for him. It was also clear from his descriptions of his childhood that he had rarely had the opportunity to engage in conversations with his parents about his thoughts and feelings. Instead, what he had witnessed was that feelings in the family were very much regulated by alcohol or violence or both. He did suggest that there may have been some times when things were different, for example when he and his sister lived alone with his mother and times spent with his sister, although he described how she too was a heavy drinker and could be very violent. Several sessions into our work together he revealed in a matter of fact manner that he was quite severely dyslexic. His mother knew little about this and he had coped at school by remembering what was said in class rather than being able to write very much down. This vividly illustrates the problem for Adam and many other young people we have worked with: he had a structural difficulty with language. Although he was bright and able to think clearly he had difficulty in expressing himself in written form and also in verbal form. This was not to imply that he was inarticulate – far from it. But his ability to articulate aspects of his life and place these into a coherent narrative about himself appeared to be held back.

As we have seen earlier, research on the development of narrative suggests that coherence consists of a number of components: causal connection, temporal connections, cultural awareness, thematic coherence, reflectivity. What is frequently apparent in work with these young people is that many of these elements are disconnected or fragmented. Importantly, there may be particular problems in terms of an ability to reflect on their stories or to contemplate alternatives. The latter can be seen in terms of an awareness of culturally dominant stories.

Attachment theory

The difficulties concerning coherence can be seen to reside particularly in emotional domains. Adam for example was able to speak in a coherent way about a range of topics and had succeeded at school, despite his dyslexia and had done well on a college course. However, he appeared to be much less coherent when trying to make sense of his own emotions, particularly anger, and his relationships.

Attachment theory suggests that broadly the two insecure attachment patterns differ in the way emotional events are processed (see Table 14.2).

Adam expressed themes of violence and drinking in his life and could see patterns across the generations in his family. He was also able to map out the temporal connections in terms of a sequence of events in his family continuities over time. He was able to articulate the sequence of events of his early childhood, such as being close to his mother and being called a 'mummy's boy' by his step-father. It is possible that his accounts implied that he was aware of causal connections between his violent actions and the experiences of taunting from his step-father, and the domestic violence he had witnessed. However, this was not clearly articulated by him. Instead, he appeared to find his own drinking and violence to be a mystery and his descriptions seemed to cast him as a victim to powerful forces that would come over him:

Table 14.2 Attachment patterns

Insecure: ANXIOUS-AVOIDANT	Insecure: AVOIDANT
Overwhelmed by feelings, preoccupied by emotional states with a tendency to flit between descriptions of episodes without an ability to weave these together into a coherent account in terms of temporal and causal connections between events	The accounts lack details of emotions and feelings, as if these have been censored out. Typically this leads to a bland, robotic sounding account which is overly rational
A sense of distrusting words and explanations	These accounts in effect seem to distrust feelings in a dismissive 'whatever' sort of way

I can't control it, I get a shaky, tingling feeling, and I have to smash something, I smash my hand in the wall, look it's been broken, even my head, I don't give a fuck, I've got to do something.

Adam's account appeared to embody an attempt to make sense of his experiences in terms of a form of biological or medical narrative, along the lines that there was something seriously wrong with his head that needed to be fixed. The idea that alternative stories were possible and that these could be explored calmly in conversation was not something he appeared to have experienced. As has been suggested, the family environment can shape a child's understanding of what he or she feels it legitimate to communicate. In turn this not only influences the opportunities to practise such communication and to evolve coherent narratives, but also may shape the form of a young person's internal conversations. Prohibitions or patterns of managing conflict and distress may lead to acquired internal conversational habits. For example, Adam appeared to lack the ability to use internal conversations to soothe himself, specifically, to explain events in terms of other painful thoughts of rejection and attack, and confusion.

Reflectivity

In order to develop coherent accounts we need to be able to stand back from our stories, in effect to be 'outside' them, to be able to consider what parts may be inconsistent, whether we have been over-selective in our focus on specific events and whether alternative explanations make better sense of the events. This also involves being able to take the position of the listener – to see how others might interpret what we are saying – and possibly see it differently. This activity requires having had an experience of safe, secure environments where such reflection can occur. Where the environment is chaotic and dangerous, a child's thinking is taken up with ensuring his or her own safety, and that of others close to them – survival. This requires rapid reflex responses when danger is imminent (Crittenden 1998). From Adam's accounts it seemed likely that such calm conversations and a sense of being listened to had rarely occurred for him. Instead, his thinking seemed to embody the family environment of overwhelming emotions, especially anger – reactive as opposed to contemplative action.

Therapy: individual and family work

What are the implications of these two strands of research for work with young offenders?

From the discussion of Adam's life and the framework presented we can see that the work involves an integration of attempts to work both with the individuals and with their family and relational system. The narratives that the young people hold are seen to have developed within their family systems and as they reach adolescence the influence of peers becomes increasingly important. Both the content and the structures of their narratives can also be seen to be shaped by current circumstances and patterns. For example, Adam described that he found being with his mum 'did his head in'. He felt he could not think and that they 'wound each other up'. Partly this led him to drink more as a way of coping. He mentioned that when he was away from his mother they both drank less. Towards the end of our work together he decided to move out, partly at his mother's request, although he agreed that it was a good idea.

In our work, in many cases we saw the young people with their families and not infrequently we ended up, having seen the young person once, doing most of the work with the parents without the young person being present! In Adam's case he did not want his mother to be involved but wanted a chance to talk on his own, in part because he felt the problems were his own. However, the most common pattern was that we worked in pairs, with some time spent conjointly with the family, and also with one of us working individually with the young person and one of us with the parents. This often reassures the parents that the young person is 'getting help' and acknowledges their story that he or she 'needs help'. Likewise it also acknowledges the young person's beliefs that their parents need to do some work, as it is they and not just the young person who have problems! In cases where the parents attended alone, we wrote a letter or had telephone contact with the young person to reassure them that the sessions were not about blaming them. Our impression was that many young people were deeply reassured that their parents were sorting out their problems without continuing to pull (triangulate) them in. As the parents become more able to explore their ideas, consider alternative stories, look at their own past and expectations, reflect on their own assumptions and integrate previously inconsistent aspects of their lives, this seemed to have a powerful effect on their children.

Within this systemic framework there are two broad strands to the work: first, there is an emphasis on the content of narratives and how these construct identities; and second, a concern with the structure of narratives and in particular the extent to which young people possess the skills to be able to place their experiences into coherent narratives. Therapy can be seen as consisting of a four-stage approach: creating a secure base; developing narrative skills; exploring narratives and exploring alternatives. These four stages are discussed next.

Creating a secure base

Typically young offenders are used to being required to talk about their problems and in particular to offer justifications for their actions. Moreover, they are encouraged to show contrition and empathy for their victims. It can be helpful in building a relationship to discuss with them that this is important, but also to acknowledge their anger and consequent difficulties in showing empathy for others' feelings. There is a delicate balance between fostering abilities to think about others' feelings and also accepting and validating their feelings. Veering too much on one side can feel like 'finger-wagging' accusation which they are likely to resist, and on the other collusive acceptance of destructive views of others and themselves. Establishing some clarity about this is an important starting point, and from it can result a more genuine attempt at considering the perspective of victims. Issues of confidentiality also need to be discussed and exactly what might be shown to the courts.

Bearing in mind that many of these young people have found that they cannot trust people and cannot rely on what people say, it is helpful to acknowledge this from the start. Also, given that conversation has often been difficult for them, or that even to talk about their feelings and intentions is a relatively new experience, it is helpful to acknowledge this and to offer reassurance that they will not be required to talk about difficult and painful feelings unless and until they may want to do so. Many youngsters show considerable fear and shame about having to talk to a 'shrink' and would not want their mates to know.

Above all, a context needs to be constructed of emotional safety, one in which it will be safe to talk about difficult issues and where revelations of genuine feelings, especially negative ones, will not incur punishment or rejection. Clear agreement about confidentiality can be very important to reassure the young person that, for example, accounts of weakness and vulnerability will not be mocked or revealed publicly.

Developing narrative skills

This starts with a recognition that placing their experiences into coherent narratives is a difficult experience for young people in general, and perhaps particularly so given the lack of encouragement and facilitation of these skills for many young offenders. Therefore these two strands – exploration and facilitation of narrative skill – need to run side by side. We have found a number of approaches useful here.

Scaffolding

Therapy needs to involve a process whereby young people are assisted to build stories to encompass their experiences. This may be assisted by offering a structure for them in terms of setting out a framework for the basis of a story. For example, to offer the beginnings of a story: 'I've heard so far that this is what has happened in your life . . .' and invite them to add and elaborate, or to offer explanations for why certain events took place, what people were feeling and intending.

Modelling

Self-disclosure – we offer stories about our own experiences, how we made sense of these and the struggles we had to do so.

Visual aids

- Life-lines where key events in the young person's life can be plotted along a line with accompanying feelings and thoughts.
- Sociograms – mapping the key people in their lives and their closeness and connections with them.
- Genograms – depicting the composition of their family and indications where there has been separation, for example father moving away.

Focusing on specific incidents

It can be helpful to deconstruct particular situations they may have experienced as difficult and explore causal, thematic and temporal connections, for example:

- Themes of confrontational situations with people, what they have in common as opposed to differences.
- How the events can be understood in terms of causal sequences – what led to what – and temporal connections in terms of what typically follows which event.
- Circularities – it can be helpful to depict incidents in terms of patterns of events over time. These can be mapped collaboratively with young people to help to integrate causal, temporal and thematic aspects of their narrative. As an example we might track the patterns of actions that occurred the last time a confrontation occurred, such as when the young person came home late.

Exploring narratives

There is of course an overlap between these aids for developing narrative skills and an exploration of the content. It can be helpful to comment in this exploration on what the young person is thinking and feeling now as they are telling the story and how they felt at the time. Often there is a minimisation or avoidance of feelings in this process. We may prompt this by suggesting how we might feel in that situation or by making connections, finding similarities with our own experience. Also it can be useful to offer stories about other people who may have had similar experiences and tell what happened to them – to extend the story into the future. In some rare cases young offenders are able to put their narrative into a written form but in our experience this is exceptional. However, our verbal accounts or narration of their life are something that they did seem to appreciate and were often received with silent appreciation. Many of the young people have problems with literacy and their way of engaging with ideas and stories is through television and music. At times we have been impressed by young people spontaneously bringing along song lyrics that summarise their thoughts.

Many of the young people have a sense that their experiences are 'strange', 'mad', 'weird', 'unusual'. Without negating the uniqueness of their stories it can be useful to make connections with similar themes in the lives of other young people with whom we have worked. A frequent example is that of absent fathers who are described, particularly by their mothers, in negative terms as irresponsible, uncaring, violent and abusive. Frequently the young person is seen as physically similar, which makes the belief that they are also psychologically similar all the more compelling: 'You're just like your father'. This story places the young person in a potentially very difficult narrative. They feel rejected by their father and frequently state that they 'don't give a fuck' about him, 'he's a bastard', but at the same time are aware of being seen as just like him. Underneath this they often desperately want to know about him and to know that he does care. In effect their own story is intertwined with that about their father.

Exploring alternative narratives

It may be provocative to suggest that for narrative therapy this is an aspiration but not one that is often truly realised! As we have seen, even to move towards a coherent story about our life is a huge undertaking. To contemplate how it might be different is an even more massive accomplishment. In our experience, rather than contemplating different narratives, it is a substantial step for young people to view aspects of their experiences in different ways. Part of the issue here is that the process of creating new narratives is simply not in their grasp. This process is subject to the vicissitudes of meanings ascribed by family members, peers, the legal system, and so on. In our work with young offenders we invariably work with family members to co-construct new narratives (Vetere and Dallos 2003). However, young people can be assisted to contemplate different meanings to their lives so far, and the possibility that the future can be less bleak than they had imagined. One helpful approach can be to consider their life in terms of an accumulation of learning, that through adversity they have grown stronger. Surprisingly perhaps, many young people engage in hypothetical conversations about what advice about 'life' they might give to their own future children.

Conclusions

The experience of working with young offenders has revealed contrasting dominant stories: of young people whose anti-social behaviour is a real threat to the security and peace of mind of their families, their communities and society, alongside stories of lives of rejection, abuse, humiliation, neglect, violence and failure. It is not difficult to become drawn into their sense of anger and rebellion at people's tendency to label them as deviants. This is not to deny the reality of the experiences of victims or to be naïve and romantic about the effects of their offending behaviour. However, the real experience of many of these young people suggests a life suffused with difficulties. This is not necessarily to blame the parents. Often the stories we heard were of mothers on their own trying to manage financial, emotional and interpersonal difficulties with little support, doing their best against all the odds. Or of parents with little or no experience of being cared for themselves, perplexed by the behaviour of their teenagers' aggressive and apparently callous lack of respect in a world that is constantly changing. Arguably, the stories that the young people develop are not distortions – overall they fit the facts. However, for those who have courageously begun the process, their ability to develop, reflect on and contemplate alternatives is a skill that needs to be nurtured. In our experience this nurturing, along with a validation of their own experiences, can help equip them with the tools to develop new ways of looking at themselves, the world, and the future – including their own future families.

Acknowledgement

The material for this chapter is drawn from an approach developed collaboratively with my colleague Linda Staines. She was a source of great inspiration, creativity and humour throughout the period of our pioneering work with young people as part of our roles with the Youth Offending Team. I would like to thank Linda for her inspiration and enthusiasm and for her astute comments, editing and additions to this chapter. On behalf of Linda and myself we also thank Linda Barnett (Manager of Somerset Youth Offending Team) for her support of the development of this approach to working with young people and for her encouragement for this publication.

Chapter 15

Narrative work in schools

Patsy Wagner and Chris Watkins

This chapter offers an account of the use of narrative ideas and approaches by two practitioners in different but overlapping relationships with schools. We describe some of our understandings and practice, and propose that the particular stance on narrative we adopt has transformational potential, a capacity for making connections, and the power to illuminate core processes of schooling.

Since 'the narrative turn' in the human sciences, we find the term narrative used in very many ways, but with significant differences. We position the particular stance on narrative which best describes our understanding and our intentions on the following brief map of the field. Uses of the term vary in two aspects: location and level. First, location: by this term we aim to highlight the different 'places' where authors and practitioners seem to think narrative is located. We suggest three places – in texts, in accounts, and in all life and action.

Literary texts have long been analysed for their construction through various types of narrative, its components and devices. Locating narrative in texts is not limited to literary theory. The story telling of young children across countries and cultures displays different narrative conventions, which are viewed as reflecting qualitative differences in children's life worlds (Carlsson *et al.* 2001). And this overall stance has been applied to professional life, suggesting that, for example, social work may be analysed in terms of the way that its texts are constructed (Hall 1998) or that medical knowledge may be understood in its narrative structure (Hunter 1993). Helping interventions based on the 'narrative in texts' stance include bibliotherapy where others' texts are selected and recommended for their therapeutic potential.

Narrative is sometimes located in a writer's account of their experience (in contrast with others' experience or fictional accounts). Examples include life-history accounts, the lives of children (Engel 1999) and teachers' lives (Thomas 1995). On a smaller scale the professional lives of school psychologists, as reflected in narrative journals, have been analysed in themes of affiliation and isolation (Henning Stout and Bonner 1996). Helping interventions from this stance on narrative utilise the increased reflection which can follow the writing of accounts.

The third location for narratives is in all life and action. This stance is reflected in phrases such as 'the storied nature of human conduct' (Sarbin 1986). Here the focus is not a text, nor a separately analysed account of experience, but the idea that all human experience is understood through stories and enacted through stories. Bruner (1987b) uses the phrase 'life as narrative' to indicate the view that we organise our experience of human happenings in the form of narrative. Story telling is life making – we are our stories: 'a life as led is inseparable from a life as told' (Bruner 1987b: 31). The way that human intelligence is organised in terms of stories is one of the major understandings to emerge from decades of research on artificial intelligence (Schank 1995). The stance, which may be abbreviated as the narrative construction of reality, is a special case of the wider perspective called social constructionism. This perspective holds that knowledge, social relations and life forms are created through human interaction rather than being provided by some external reality or based on some objective view. It stands in contrast with dominant ways of thinking, and Bruner (1985) proposes that narrative modes of thought are irreconcilable with the dominant categorical modes of thought. White (2001) describes his narrative stance as non-structuralist and contrasts the terms by which an individual is understood in contrast to the dominant, structuralist ideas of the twentieth century (see Table 15.1).

Helping interventions which adopt this stance are likely to stand alongside White's (1995) phrase of 're-authoring lives' and to adopt narrative therapy's key orientations and practices (e.g. notions of voice and power, influence mapping, problem externalisation, exception stories, audiencing). These will be illuminated later.

Table 15.1 Terms for describing individuals

Structuralist identity categories	Non-structuralist identity categories
Behaviour	Action
Needs	Conscious purposes
Properties	Commitments
Personality	Values
Assets, strengths	Dreams
Motives	Hopes
Weaknesses, deficits	Visions
Attributes	Intentions
Drives	Preferences
Resources	Plans
Characteristics	Aspirations

Our second dimension for mapping the various uses of narrative is that of level. Here we value the fact that the term narrative is sometimes applied to an individual (as in life-history), sometimes to a family, sometimes to an organisation, and sometimes to large social groups such as 'children' or to whole societies. What is to be made of such diversity? One answer is to embed individual in family or organisation and then again in society. The hazard here is to invoke an unanalysed notion of hierarchy, where 'larger' levels are subtly attributed larger power and even homogeneity. The constructive alternative may be developed from the work of Pearce and Cronen (1980). That is to say, in any utterance or collection of utterances it should be possible to listen for narratives at any level – individual/family/organisation/ culture – and it is not necessary to place these in a relationship of hierarchical power. All of us are multivoiced and can speak with the voice of family, organisation, and society (both dominant and non-dominant modes). So each of these levels can be viewed horizontally, that is, as contexts for one another (Hoffman 1992).

In our practice we adopt the ubiquitous multilevel stance on narrative, and consider this choice no coincidence given the context of our work with complex human systems and their values.

The educational psychologist (PW) and her context

Educational psychologists (EPs) working in local education authorities describe their role as applying psychology to finding solutions to complex questions in educational settings. Such questions are often presented by schools and teachers as problems residing in individual children or young people, sometimes in groups and less often as concerns at the organisational level. Yet these levels are embedded and replicated one in the other and are most usefully conceptualised when those connections are made overt. The family, however, is often seen as the origin of problems of individual children in schools. Government initiatives encourage the identification of individual children for special provision or programmes, so that individuals become the centre of attention, explanations that are within-the-person come to predominate and deficits and labels abound. In such a context, concepts of narrative and related practice are immensely powerful in creating alternative viewpoints and realities.

My teaching experience, training as an EP at the Tavistock Clinic, and further training at the Institute of Family Therapy in London, has led systemic thinking to be an important part of my way of trying to make sense of concerns that arise in social systems, whether schools, classrooms or families. The inter-relating systems of school, family, local education authority, local community, and local services and agencies within the wider political, social and technical system make up my context and, consequently, systemic thinking in particular has been significant in providing a guiding framework

(Wagner 1995). Collaborative, solution-focused consultation based on inter-actionist and systemic understanding has been a grounding for my engage-ment as an EP in my consultation work with schools, teachers and families (Wagner and Gillies 2001), and post-structural narrative developments have added significantly to my thinking and practice. Ideas about narrative described by Bruner (1986b) and about social constructionism (Burr 1995 and Gergen 1999), developed in practice by White and Epston (1990), Nylund (2002) and Morgan (1999a, 1999b), have all been inspirational.

The narrative metaphor proposes that everyone lives a multi-storied life. Consequently, no *one* story can speak the totality of a person's lived experi-ence. However, single stories can come to dominate and these single stories are often problem-saturated stories about loss, incompetence, vulnerability, and so on. They can then come to constitute the totality of a person's life in a way that creates a dead-end and a restriction. Narrative work aims to uncover the stories of skills, competence, resilience and strengths so that a person can tell themselves a different story and in so doing bring to light that different story and see themselves differently. The act of deconstructing the dominant story of deficit and uncovering and celebrating a more explicit story about competence is crucial. In this way, narrative therapists focus on the construction of reality moment by moment in interaction.

Alternative stories of competence are often needed when working with school-based difficulties. Terms such as low self-esteem, attention seeking, dysfunctional, disruptive, hyperactive, disaffected, depressed, anti-social, at risk, vulnerable, have become common currency in our schools. This dis-course of deficit discredits the individual, drawing attention to problems, shortcomings, weaknesses or incapacities, which then attract a corrosive and spiralling process of negative attributions. In this course of events, expec-tations are reduced and disapproval increases. Teachers and parents have often been inducted into such negative terms, and the thin stories that accompany them, and the children and young people who are the subjects of such labels and stories have little power to reverse the story that is told. A social con-structionist stance holds that a discourse of deficit promotes continuing and escalating difficulties, whereas a discourse of competence, strength and resili-ence promotes the amplification of those very qualities. Narrative therapy provides key practices for uncovering stories of competence and skill, and then thickening those stories. The processes of externalising the problem and developing alternative stories of competence are crucial in the following story of a consultation in which the initial concern focused on an individual. Although the example I have chosen for this chapter to illustrate the narrative approach is one which focuses on an individual child, in my practice as an EP the example could have been of a group, a class or an organisational issue: the stance and the process are the same.

A thin story of boredom, disaffection and dyslexia versus a story of engagement and success

Dion was raised as a concern in consultation with the school's EP when he was 8 years old, after a term in Year 3. He had joined the nursery class aged 3½ years and was described then as settling well into school. He was one of a few children of Afro-Caribbean heritage in an Inner London school with an ethnically mixed population. The school was appropriately welcoming of pupils and families of all ethnicities and pupils achieved well. Dion was considered to be a child with an advantaged background, an active, bright, verbally articulate and happy child who loved construction, music and stories. In reception class Dion's teachers were puzzled, as he did not progress as they expected in literacy skills. When he was in Year 1 Dion's parents separated, and put in place cooperative arrangements for sharing care of Dion and his brother. Concerns in school continued to mount in Year 1 and Year 2, and by Year 3 the teachers felt that something more needed to be done because Dion was not making progress as expected, especially in reading and writing. His teachers viewed him as fast becoming a disaffected child, who did not seem interested in class-based learning. By this time, Dion had been given substantial amounts of additional help in class as well as sessions out of class to help him with his reading, with a teacher who had a qualification in teaching children who had a diagnosis of dyslexia. The school reported that Dion's parents were keen to be very supportive to Dion and the school, and they too were of the view that Dion might have dyslexic-type difficulties, especially since his father had had difficulties in learning to read. Dion's younger brother had joined the nursery class and was progressing well and finding reading easy. It seemed, therefore, that the difficulties were specific to Dion. He was not making progress and had become more and more 'switched off' in class, to the point where his behaviour was becoming a cause for concern.

Up to this time two stories had developed in school to 'explain' Dion's difficulties. One was the 'dyslexic story', supported by the view that Dion's father had literacy difficulties in school. However, investigation of Dion's literacy difficulties was inconclusive, other than showing he was, clearly, very behind. In that sense at least, everyone agreed that he was dyslexic. The other story was one of 'disaffection'. Added to this were parental concerns about what would happen as Dion got older and went to secondary school. At this point there was little that illuminated Dion's competencies and skills in a positive light and more of an emphasis on his difficulties, which were seen as dyslexia, and on his ability to avoid learning and create disruptive effects in class, which fed the disaffection story. There was a depressed air in the stories about Dion that forecast a school career of prolonged failure and disaffection, and a view developing that a formal statement of special educational needs would be required.

The process and effects of self-defeating stories that make problems appear to be insoluble seemed to be operating. Dion appeared to have taken somewhat of a stance against the dyslexic story, by rejecting the attribution of reading difficulties. He said he did not care about reading, that it was 'boring' and not for him. This could be seen in systemic terms as creating a supportive link with his father and providing a bridge between his estranged parents, which brought them together as caring and cooperative parents over the concern about Dion's reading. In areas such as practical construction, story telling and music making, Dion had a very positive view of himself, but he rejected the one thing that did not make him feel good about himself. Dion's disengaged approach to anything to do with reading and writing meant that he could not progress in a school system predicated on those skills.

Systemic and interactionist practice aims to take account of the perspectives of all the key players: the school, the family, the individual, and other agencies as appropriate. It aims to bring together these perspectives and to develop alternative explanations of the concern by exploring stories of competence and possibilities that construct a different reality. On this occasion the school and family meanings for dyslexia were important, as was the way they might have helped as well as hindered progress. It became clear that the label 'dyslexia' (which stood for a difficulty in learning to read) had, indeed, been helpful to the school, the parents and to Dion, since it helped everyone feel that Dion's difficulties were not due to any fault on his part, but to his dyslexia. This meant that no one felt blamed. The down side was that everyone now accepted that Dion's dyslexia explained his lack of progress in spite of skilled help in school, which meant he would continue to progress very slowly and he would need very skilled help for this to happen.

In class, Dion was not acting as an engaged and active learner when the learning involved anything to do with literacy. He tended not to start unless prompted by an adult and then he acted as if he thought he could not do what was presented to him, even though it was within his current capacity. He tended not to get involved with other children in talking about the topic when any reading or writing was involved and, at those times, he seemed generally uninterested. As a result, he was not motivated by learning with other children; and, as a way of engaging with other children, he tended to distract them when they were absorbed. This strategy of social engagement was causing difficulties in his social relationships with the other children in class, as well as with his class teacher because it was hindering the planned learning. When asked about his learning, Dion told his teacher that he was mostly bored in class.

When a child says 'It's boring' or 'I'm bored', the tendency is for this to be viewed as a pejorative statement which is then sometimes taken as a comment on the teacher, the teaching style, the curriculum and curriculum differentiation, as well as on the learner and his approach to learning. In any blame game around boredom, however, there is a tendency for the pupil to come out with a label of lazy, or worse!

The practice of externalising the problem aims to separate the problem from the child. Once everyone involved can see the problem as the problem, rather than the child being seen as the problem, then blame becomes less important and tends to evaporate. Dion was already clear that he was bored in class, so externalising the problem as boredom was not difficult. Once the problem has a name then questions can help to separate it further from the child and help the child to see its effects and then begin to work out how to avoid it, trick it, or otherwise overcome it. For example:

- 'So, how long has boredom been around?'
- 'Can you spot boredom coming? How? Does it creep up on you slowly or spring up suddenly?'
- 'What does boredom look like?'
- 'How does boredom distract you when you're in class?'
- 'What does boredom tell you to do . . . not do?'
- 'How do you feel when boredom is around you?'
- 'Is there ever a time when boredom isn't around, what's it like then?'
- 'Has there been a time when you've been able to ignore boredom? How did you do that?'

Children seem to find it very easy to externalise a problem and to discuss how such a problem can then be tackled. Dion described boredom as slipping into the room and then sitting like a dark cloud on top of him, which made him feel 'not very happy'. When he felt this way he did not want to do what the teacher was asking him to do, but he still wanted to talk with the other children. Dion liked the idea of thinking about the things he could do to stop boredom from getting to him and was creative in thinking about ways to outwit it. This process helped Dion to establish more personal agency and control and, most importantly, it removed blame and deficit from the picture and pitted Dion with his teacher and his classmates against boredom. Involving Dion's teacher and parents in this was an important part of the process, so that they too could engage with him in externalising conversations, and help him to review the success of his strategies. The approach that was developed involved all the children in the class in constructing positive stories about their own learning. This meant that Dion was not singled out in his class, but was part of a whole class initiative to reflect on and improve learning about learning.

Developing alternative stories of competence

The practice of developing alternative stories of competence is crucial in deconstructing negative stories. Winslade and Monk (1999) describe this as carefully assembling, with the client, a story line that is invigorating, colourful and compelling. The alternative story becomes more compelling and convincing when all the key players who share the concern are involved in its development. In a school context this includes the child, the people who work most closely with the child, and, ideally, the parents/carers. In this case, assembling a story of competence started with Dion's teachers and with Dion himself, and then continued with his teachers, parents and Dion all together.

Dion already had a lot of success in focused and engaged learning. These occasions, however, had been overlooked by the school and the family, as they were not occasions when traditional literacy skills were very evident. However, they were excellent examples of when Dion showed his capacity to be an active learner and to avoid any hint of boredom in class. By exploring these alternative stories about imagination, creativity, ingenuity, concentration and effort it was possible to build up a picture that began to challenge the power of the story of boredom and disaffection. Narrative work is very explicit about uncovering the events that help to create alternative stories of competence and skill. This practice is referred to as re-storying, a process through which alternative stories and rich pictures emerge via questions which reduce the potency of thin stories of deficit. White and Epston (1990), following Bruner (1986b), describe two overlapping categories of questions in the process. The first is *Landscape-of-action questions*. These seek to identify exceptions to the problem story, and comprise mainly 'when?' and 'how?' questions, which are addressed to all the people involved, including the child, for example:

- 'When does Dion show that he is able to keep himself interested?'
- 'What does he do to show that he is interested?'
- 'How do you explain that he is able to do that?'
- 'What might you or others be doing on those occasions to help him to be more interested and engaged?'

Questioning for exceptions resembles the practice of solution-focused brief therapists (de Shazer 1982) and helps to convey that there are times when the problem is not present and that the child, therefore, has the power to overcome the problem. Asking school staff these questions about when and how Dion managed to focus his attention/avoid boredom helped to elucidate that he had these skills and capacities. Asking Dion similar 'when?' and 'how?' questions helped him to clarify that he had many ways of being interested in class and that he could keep 'boredom' away when he wanted to. Exploring Dion's competencies and skills with his parents and the school together helped richer joint stories of competence to emerge.

The second category of re-storying questions is *Landscape-of-meaning questions*, which 'encourage children and families to reflect on and give meaning to the positive developments that have occurred in the landscape of action. By asking the client to address, specifically, the meaning they are making about themselves or new events, we underscore the meaning of the new story and further expand the client's experience of their preferred identity' (Nylund 2002: 132). These questions are even more meaningful and compelling when used in joint meetings with school staff and parents/carers. For example:

- 'What does it tell you about Dion that he is able to be so very focused in class on certain occasions?'
- 'What abilities and capacities do you see in Dion when he engages so positively?'
- 'What do you feel about Dion when you see him acting this way?'

Through these practices the emerging story of competence and effort helped reduce the power of the boredom and disaffection story. They also help adults and family members connect with their feelings of affirmation and pride over the child and when this happens with the child present the effects are very powerful indeed.

The third element in re-storying is *Re-membering*, which places the child outside the problem identity, in this case 'Dion is a disaffected and dyslexic child'. Although the 'dyslexia' story had helped everyone not feel blamed, its simplicity also veiled important ideas. As Ravenette (1968: 22) puts it: 'For every child with a specific handicap who cannot read, there are plenty more with the same handicap who can.' Ravenette proposes that reading difficulty must be understood in terms of the child's construing of reading, of the reading task and of himself as a reader. Through the process of re-membering it became clear to all concerned that Dion was a competent learner who had the attributes of what makes a good reader.

At this stage an important part of the family story emerged that helped everyone to make sense of how Dion's difficulties may have started. When Dion was a very small baby, his parents had separated, his mother returning to her home country, France, with Dion, who was brought up for the next 2 years speaking only French. French was, therefore, his first language. The family got back together later in England. Dion quickly picked up English so that by the time he started in nursery class he appeared fluent. Consequently Dion did not receive help with English as an additional language. It was not surprising, therefore, that Dion's literacy skills in English – especially those of reading and writing – did not emerge as quickly as some of the other children in his class who had English as a first language. The fact that Dion's little brother, who was born and brought up in England with English as his first language, found learning to read very easy compounded the difficulty for Dion. Added to all this, Dion's father, determined that Dion would not experience the difficulties he had experienced in learning to read, had alighted on ways of helping Dion that they both found stressful, as well as unsuccessful.

The last strand in putting together a different story about reading for Dion was to help Dion reclaim reading and writing as something that could be pleasurable, and which he could share with his parents as a competent reader. This was achieved by taking a language experience approach (Goddard 1974), which utilised Dion's personal interests and enthusiasms to create books from stories which he dictated to a learning support assistant who had been trained in the approach. He was then able to learn to associate what he had said with the written word and could read the story to others, to his teachers, classmates and parents, because the story was *his* story. In his way Dion could show he was not only a reader, but also an author. This was the last piece in the story of developing competence that helped Dion become a successful reader and, subsequently, to progress well in school.

From this account of narrative work in consultation we now turn to consider the wider narratives that circulate in school contexts.

Addressing the narratives of schooling

As someone with a training in school counselling and a great interest in systemic intervention, narrative has formed an increasingly important part of many aspects of my practice and my theorising of the core processes of schools. The idea that narrative is the only form that humans have of relating lived experience (Ricoeur 1989) has informed my now everyday use of the term 'story'. When meeting teachers applying for a course, my request, 'Tell me the story of how this application came about', gives rise to a more holistic and human account than anything created in response to clever interviewer questions. When helping teachers find their voice in the unusual activity of writing, the prompt, 'Tell me the story of how the writing's going', provides a smooth entry into their priorities and challenges. Here the non-technical use of 'story' seems perfectly acceptable and does not activate the voice of doubt, 'it's only a story', which sometimes arises when adopting narrative as a research method.

Narrative concepts are of great value when viewing schools as human institutions as constructed by their members (Campbell 2000) – even for illuminating what the forces of opposition are to that project! Twenty-first-century schools display many tensions in the stories they use to construct themselves as organisations and to maintain their daily practices. Recent decades have witnessed a new powerful voice in the picture, that of government control and specification. The effect has been that the stories of classroom life now show greater resemblance to those from the earliest known classrooms in Sumerian society 5,000 years ago (Kramer 1963): teacher control, learner passivity, pupil conflict and other phenomena associated with hierarchical control – people acting strategically in order to look good in the eyes of the surveillance agents.

But there is a better way, and it involves focusing on the very narratives of learning which are generally silent in classrooms. For organisations that are sometimes referred to as 'seats of learning', the narratives of learning in schools are predominantly 'thin'. By this I mean they are of low complexity and low status. Because of this, to focus on narratives of learning is difficult at first. Within this focus the complex interplay between individual, familial, organisational and cultural narratives of learning is soon apparent. But the complexity is easier to embrace, and becomes empowering if placed in the context that our professional purpose is to help people get the most from themselves and their worlds – then it is bound to challenge the patterns of privilege and power which the dominant narratives play a part in maintaining. My interest is, therefore, to highlight and enrich the narratives of learning which circulate in individuals, classrooms and schools.

Three major narratives of learning

Many (but not all) young people start school with little explicit narrative for learning. Perhaps families tell their young people 'you'll learn when you get to school' – another version of a 'blank slate' metaphor. Schools are likely to compound this stance, since as the first socialising agency outside the family their practices are designed to help young people reproduce the routines of classroom life, and may underplay the role of a learner. Thus the dominant conception of learning is born: *'learning = being taught'* (Watkins 2003). This conception is often clear when asking someone to tell you their story of an experience of learning: they tell you an experience of being taught and focus their story on what the teacher (or equivalent person) did. In this way the role of the teacher is privileged and the role of the learner is underplayed: learners become passive and ineffective, saying things about themselves such as 'The best way I learn is by listening to the teacher but if there is noise around, the teacher's words just go through one ear and out the other' (Hamza, 11 years). This view in the voice of the learner is maintained by the dominant practices of school in the later years, in which teachers decide and plan the themes and processes of teaching, which create the regular patterns of classroom experience. The story of 'transmission', that children learn what teachers tell them, is embodied in views of curriculum and learners' narratives such as 'I learn quickly and it stays in my head' (George). In this example the individual notion of the head as a container for learning is no coincidence; it is a key metaphor in the transmission view of things.

'Learning = being taught' is an example of a story which is both thin and stuck: it downplays and discredits the activity of the learner yet has managed to maintain itself over millennia, probably supported by cultural assumptions about the relative roles of young and old, power relations, and so on. As we examine the multiple layers of schooling we notice the systemic isomorphisms of this story: in the same way that teachers treat their pupils as passive recipients, so are teachers in their turn treated by policy makers as infants (or passive deliverers). As Sarason puts it: 'Teachers regard students the way their superiors regard them – that is, as incapable of dealing responsibly with issues of power, even on the level of discussion' (1990: 83). Under these conditions the experience of classroom learning is disempowering for all, for not only are the role and uniqueness of the pupil disregarded, so is the role of the teacher in human relationships dishonoured.

Learners who somehow start to notice and tell the story of their learning in terms of their own processes soon move on from the dominant cultural narrative and into individual empowerment: 'The way I learn is to work it out by myself' (Emily). The act of focusing attention and meaning on one's own lived experiences of learning and one's own actions within them positions the learner in the centre of the narrative. In this way the learner becomes an active agent.

The narrative *'learning = individual sense-making'* highlights the human capacity for making meaning, and that of standing back from experience, so that reflection and review are important. Thinking about thinking (metacognition) becomes an element, as does the wider capacity for learning about learning (meta-learning): both of these support the self-determining learner. Teachers who develop classroom practices along these lines become more 'guide on the side' than 'sage on the stage'. Their actions can generate increased tension with dominant cultural narratives. This may arise in relation to the voice of the pupil: 'Why don't you give us the right answer?', to the voice of the parent 'Just tell them when they've got it wrong', to the voice of the organisation 'That class is getting noisy', or to the wider system of surveillance 'You have not complied with delivering the prescribed curriculum'. Some teachers maintain resilience in the face of these tensions by knowing that the voice of research during the latter half of the twentieth century provided ample evidence that the narrative 'learning = sense-making' is more powerful than everyday discourse in explaining the phenomena of learning (Bruner 1995).

The third narrative of learning is probably evident even less frequently in classrooms yet is evident in most elements of learning outside school and throughout life, including teachers' working lives. I abbreviate this to *'learning = building knowledge as part of doing things with others'*. Although the title may seem cumbersome at first, adults soon recognise this as describing key features of their richest learning, in which the construction of new knowledge occurs in non-linear often unpredicted ways, resulting from interaction with others on a task which was not chosen for learning something – a teachers' working group creating a policy, a group of photocopier technicians fixing a new model without ever opening the manual, a team of professionals devising new practice in relation to changing conditions, two people learning about mig-welding as they fix a Land Rover. And on a wider scale this narrative describes the cumulative processes of scientific communities, with their more formally agreed approaches to the testing of truth claims.

Occasionally young learners narrate the core process of co-construction: 'You learn more [when working with others] because if you explain to people what to do you say things that you wouldn't say to yourself, really. So you learn things that you wouldn't know if you were just doing it by yourself (Annie, 10 years). Or more prosaically 'Learning is cooperating' (William, 5 years).

Knowledge in this conception is much more linked to its location than is suggested by the depersonalised and decontextualised version found in school curricula, yet there are classrooms in which this third narrative operates, and they address current curricula in a more successful fashion, with improved achievement, more engaged behaviour and more pro-social moral development (Watkins 2004). It is no coincidence that the richest learning narratives are associated with the notion of a learning community: enriched narratives honour more people, embrace diversity and support community processes.

How do learning narratives develop? Strategies for enrichment

To some degree the experience of schooling and the maturational processes which promote greater agency in growing children, may contribute to learners taking more charge of their learning, and increasingly recognising the role of collaboration with others in it. But this seems to happen mainly for those children who have always been privileged by schools, and cannot be attributed to the experience of classroom life when we know that a focus on learning may be happening at most 2 per cent of the time. So classroom practices are needed which help pupils (a) notice, (b) discuss, (c) reflect on, and (d) experiment with their lived experience of learning. These not only satisfy the drive for better results (Watkins 2001) but also contribute to the development of classroom life along lines which may honestly be described as learning communities. In such settings pupils' narration of their own learning becomes richer, more complex, and more reflexive, as with the 10 year old girl who said:

> I think learning is . . . you watch, and you teach yourself sometimes or other people or other objects help you, and you like listen, you watch, and you like add to what people say.

Within the creation of a broadly dialogic stance, strategies from narrative therapy take a key place. The very act of focusing on stories of lived experience forms an important antidote to the categorical forms dominantly used to describe learners (Bruner 1985). Finding the exceptions to the thin stories individual learners tell of themselves (White and Epston 1990) is a challenge which teachers embrace. The process of externalising difficulties (Huntley 1999) is liberating for learners, and combats the worst effects of the 'right answer' culture as told by the classroom poster from an Ealing school 'Mistakes are our friends: they help us learn'.

Barriers to narrative practice

Barriers to the wider adoption of a narrative stance exist, and I find it useful to think about them as yet another set of narratives. Given the power and dominance of categorical thinking, deterministic assumptions, and the idea of depersonalised knowledge, it would be unusual if there were no barriers to change. Often the processes of self-handicapping operate, as when teachers adopt the voice of disqualification to downplay their local knowledge of classroom life, and their stories of change and resistance: 'It's not important', 'It's only an anecdote', 'It doesn't prove anything'. Beyond these, I meet two particular sorts of stories that teachers tell (to themselves and to others) which stop them experimenting with alternative classroom practice:

1 'I'll be caught out'
   – by a noisy classroom, by not looking like a teacher should look, by not 'covering the curriculum', by my class getting poor measured performance
2 'It will all fall apart'
   – I'll lose control of the classroom; this learning-centred is laissez-faire and has no role for the teacher, . . .

Each shows the ways in which the voice of fear does its life-negating work through exaggeration, over-stating the likelihoods of 'you'll get caught' and 'it will be dreadful', and creating a story that masks the real evidence. Nevertheless teachers do experiment, with support and with the vision that classrooms have to change. Such teachers may seem to others to be acting confidently, but they are not immune to the voice of fear: they have learned that confidence is continuing to act in accordance with your principles while in the presence of the voice of fear.

The final barrier is an understandably powerful one – it is to go silent on learning and the developmental voicing of learners' narratives, so that the status quo returns. This would be a more common occurrence if it were not for the transformational effect which comes through teachers experiencing the process themselves, noticing more about their own learning, putting aside the voices of judgement, and talking it over with their pupils. As an experienced teacher wrote last week: 'You've helped me reinforce the belief that I can achieve success in learning. Your "effective learning" course has increased my general confidence immensely. When I started I didn't believe that learning could change you as a person, but I do now!!!' From individuals to families, organisations and wider systems a post-structuralist stance on narrative can prove transformational, and can offer an entry into addressing wider societal difficulties today (Smith 2004). With awareness of the role of dominant narratives in society, a practice which is 'against the grain' becomes more appropriate and more achievable.

In this chapter we hope to have conveyed something of our developments of narrative in particular aspects of the worlds of schools. The stance on narrative that we have described as ubiquitous and multilevel could clearly be applied to a much wider range of themes and examples than portrayed here. We regard such a stance as productive in addressing the disconnected and repetitive patterns which so often characterise school practice. At the same time we have learned that dominant discourses often act to undermine, disqualify or marginalise such narrative ideas and practices. Ultimately the co-construction of alternative stories through conversations that make a difference is, we believe, the educator's prime task.

Chapter 16

Narratives of school exclusion

Sue Rendall

This chapter discusses narratives of pupils who have been permanently excluded from school, and of their parents and head teachers. The source of these narratives is a study investigating factors relating to exclusion from school from a systemic approach (Rendall 2000).

The place of narrative theory in a systemic framework

The fact that this study applied narrative theory within a systemic framework might evoke questioning from some quarters of systemic purists. Minuchin (1998) accused narrativists of having moved away from systemic principles, claiming that they focus on the individual rather than on social relatedness, and have become preoccupied with the power of cultural discourses at the expense of family process. Minuchin also argues that narrativists have lost the systemic approach since typically they interact with each member of the family in turn as individuals, and no longer focus on interactional patterns of behaviour. It is appropriate in this chapter therefore to consider how one-to-one work with individuals stands up under the systemic microscope. Within the context of individual work the therapist and client are working in the interactional space between them to identify new narratives. The problem-determined system of meanings within existing stories is likely to be maintained by interactions with significant others (present or absent, alive or dead) that serve to sustain a problem. A systemic approach requires a focus on that interactional world. In individual work this can be achieved through working with the client's internalised voices of significant others (Tomm 1998) thus having a focus that is described by Anderson (1999) as not the person, but the person-in-relationship.

Exploring the perspective of these inner voices and how, in verbal or nonverbal ways, they communicate and feed back to the individual's core self, is a systemic way of working. However, in contrast with the Milan systemic approach, the therapist is interacting not with the family out there, but with an internalised version of that family (or equivalent, e.g. school, group, organisation) within one individual. Not all narrativists who work with individuals stress the use of internalised voices. White (1995), emphasises other techniques that are not in themselves systemic, such as 'identifying unique outcomes', so among narrativists who work with individuals, some do so in a more systemic way than others, particularly those who make active use of working with the idea of internalised voices.

Further support for a narrative approach having a solid place within a systemic framework is underlined by Sluzki (1998) who refers to 'narrative based systemic practices'. Even though family interactions are not the direct focus of attention, as Minuchin would require, the beliefs that drive these interactions certainly are, and narrativists particularly focus on those beliefs that are incorporated from the cultural context in which the family lives (Schwartz 1999). Tomm (1998) emphasises the fundamental importance of family members (or equivalent) in the generation and maintenance of specific meanings within narratives.

Narrativists stress that new narratives will create a different system of meanings for the family, which may then be influenced by feedback loops in much the same fashion as is the case with the Milan approach, where the system of beliefs sustaining the problem is also central. Indeed one of the main similarities between the Milan approach and narrative work is that both give prime importance to systems of meanings which sustain problems; the differences between the two approaches relate more to the level of meanings that are focused on, and to the techniques used to bring about helpful change.

Personal stories as an interactional process

Narrativists see the development of personal stories, including problem-sustaining stories, as an interactional process. The family (or school) is held to have an important role in this process, especially through the way it plays out wider cultural discourses such as gender roles and positions of influence and power. In bringing out new and previously marginalised stories, interactional techniques are used. It is clear therefore that narrativists rely on systemic theory in the way they interactionally work with meanings, and in the way they create circumstances whereby interactions in the meaning systems of the family can occur. Their work with families is consistent with systemic ideas, even though their techniques, which do not focus on interactions within the session, are clearly different from those of Minuchin.

The application of narrative theory within a child, family and school context

The data (narratives) presented in this chapter have been elicited through semi-structured interviews which were employed to hear the stories, or narratives, of two pupils who had been permanently excluded and their parents and head teachers, all of whom took part in the larger study referred to at the beginning of this chapter. The study was not concerned with the 'truth' or with the facts, but with the perceptions and memories of the participants, and comparing the differences in the accounts which each gave of the same incident and event. Reissman (1993: 64) emphasises that 'the historical truth is not the primary issue. Narrativization is a point of view'. Individuals do present different narratives about the same event, using facts and interpretations to shape new facts and new interpretations. This is particularly shown in this chapter where different stories of exclusion are presented by the pupils, parents and head teachers.

Through the presentation of these narratives this chapter demonstrates how it is possible to gain a greater understanding of how pupils who have been permanently excluded from school, their parents and their head teachers, have similar and different stories to tell, and attribute different meanings to the same event.

It was made clear to the participants of the study that participation would not result in reinstatement to school or in the exclusion being overturned. What they were told was that it can often be helpful to talk about difficult times, and to share feelings with a third, independent party. Only twenty-three parents and pupils needed to be approached in order to find the twenty required for the study. Of the three who were approached but did not participate, one refused because her son had recently been offered an appointment with a child psychiatrist, and she did not want him to be involved with too many people, and the other two parents did not reply at all to my request. Given that there was no incentive to take part in the interviews, other than to have an opportunity to tell their side of events (to tell their story) there is strong evidence that these parents and pupils welcomed this opportunity and gave it some importance. Indeed, the parents of eighteen of the twenty pupils interviewed said that it was the first time that they had been given an opportunity to tell someone about their experiences of the exclusion.

Philip

Philip is a 15-year-old (Year 11) white boy, living with both parents and two sisters of primary age.

Philip's story

Philip talked about his first fixed-term exclusion from school, when he was accused of setting off a fire alarm during a school fete. He explained that later the school found out that it was not him who had done it. It was clearly important for Philip that his 'truth' be established early in his story. He said that he had had to meet the governors after this and he was given another chance. Philip described that when he returned to school after his exclusion teachers treated him differently and the head teacher 'kept having a go at me'. Philip said 'it just built up and built up'.

He said that he was finally permanently excluded because he hit a boy – 'the head teacher saw me and just came up to me and said he'd seen me smoking and he was chucking me out'. Philip said that he felt 'pretty gutted'. He said that one of the teachers who did help him 'got chucked out of the school herself'. This seemed to me to be an example of Philip making a connection between himself and another 'victim' of what he understood to be his school's unfairness. Again, here, the 'truth' is not what is being sought. I have no idea if such a teacher was 'chucked out of school' – in professional terms it is unlikely – she may have been a student in placement, or a supply teacher, or she may have left for other reasons, but in Philip's mind she was helpful and had been unfairly treated. He said that he was not surprised about the exclusion. He thinks that his mother has been affected the most in the family – 'she cares a lot and doesn't want me to turn out a yob'. He was not sure what his father thinks. Philip said that he found some of the work at school difficult and that he only got help for his English. He said that he could have done with more help. He wanted to return to his school and said that he would try very hard to stay out of trouble. He said that he would ask for more help, but did not believe that he would ever get back into another school.

Mr and Mrs F's story (Philip's mother and father)

Mrs F said that they received a series of letters from the school 'about a lot of little things'. Mr F had been into the school about a year earlier as Philip was 'getting in with the wrong crowd'. He then described a 'major problem' when they had to meet the head teacher. Mr F explained that he had an agreement with the school that they would keep them in touch with what Philip was doing. He said that the school had been very good and that he sees his job as a parent to 'bring Philip into order without physical discipline'.

Mr F explained how they had tried to support the school by grounding Philip when he had been in trouble. He said that he and his wife both felt that some people at the school had tried very hard to help Philip but that one or two teachers, including the headmaster, were 'the complete opposite'. He felt that some people gave them a lot of support and others, including the head, were not helpful at all.

Mrs F described an earlier short-term exclusion which Philip had received for setting off a fire alarm at the school fete. It was discovered that Philip had not been to blame. The final permanent exclusion followed this incident 3 weeks later, and was because Philip had smashed a door in the corridor. Mr and Mrs F said that it had been an accident when Philip had been running away from some boys who were chasing him. Mr F felt that this incident gave the head teacher an opportunity to 'have another go' at Philip.

Mrs F said that the head teacher had always said that he liked Philip and that was why he had given him a second chance after the fete incident. Mrs F said that the head had told her that Philip was not like other boys and that although he was always cheerful and pleasant 'he had something in him'.

Mr F said that the head teacher had told him that Philip was disruptive in some classes and this was stopping other pupils from learning. The school had said that it would be 'better all round if Philip wasn't there so that the other kids could learn'.

Mrs F had talked to Philip about his disruptive behaviour and he had told her that he was only disruptive in lessons he found difficult. Mr F said that Philip had difficulty with learning. They said they did not get any help from the school after Philip had been permanently excluded. Mrs F had been told by the head of year that she would arrange for some work to be sent home for Philip, but none had arrived. They had heard nothing from the school since but had received a letter from the Education Authority.

Mr and Mrs F and Philip attended the governors' meeting and Mrs F said that she had pleaded with them to give Philip another chance, particularly as he had difficulties with reading and writing, and had only one more year left at school. Mr F had also hoped that he could persuade the governors. Mrs F said that she was very upset and felt that although Philip did not behave at school, he had never been violent and really wasn't 'a bad lad'.

Mr F described the governors, at the exclusion meeting, saying 'they were all right but you were made to feel as though you'd killed somebody'. His is an example of what Anderson (1999) calls focus as the person-in-relationship. Mr F's account is one of feeling powerless and guilty. He described how a list of Philip's misdemeanours had been read out and everything was logged, including the fact that he had been caught chewing gum. The reasons for the final exclusion were given as 'caught smoking and being off the school premises at lunchtime without permission'. This had confused Mr and Mrs F as they had thought it was because Philip had smashed a school door, and Philip had thought that it was because he had hit the other boy.

Mr F remembered how there were two teachers present at the governors' meeting who had 'spoken up' for Philip, but that he felt that the head teacher was 'dominant and made his feelings known that he'd had enough'. Both Mr and Mrs F had felt that there was a good chance that Philip would be reinstated. They had to wait a couple of weeks before they received the letter saying that Philip was permanently excluded. Both parents described feeling very upset and Mr F felt annoyed. They felt that because of the way the head teacher had spoken at the governors' meeting the governors had to support him. They also recalled that Philip had not spoken up when the governors asked him a question at the meeting. Mrs F said that they had probably thought that he was being 'ignorant' but that she had known how nervous he was in front of the governors.

After the exclusion Mr F rang the education office and was told that someone would come to the house to teach Philip and that he would be found another school. Mr F thought that this would be good, but 3 months had passed and Philip had received no education, neither at home nor at another school.

Mr and Mrs F felt that they had tried very hard to support the school. They thought that Philip had not received enough help with his learning difficulties. Mrs F said that they had no help when Philip was excluded – she said 'they're so quick to throw them out and so slow to help afterwards'.

Mr F explained that they as parents had to do 'all the work' after the exclusion. Both parents wanted Philip to go to another school but they thought that this would not happen. They discovered a week ago that they could have appealed against the exclusion, but that this had to be done within a set period of time, and the deadline had now passed. They wished that they had known at the time that they could appeal. Mr F said that they would definitely have appealed but that it was too late now.

Philip's head teacher's story

Philip's head teacher started his story of Philip's exclusion by stressing how sorry he felt for Mr and Mrs F. He said that they had been very supportive parents and they had worked together with the school. He said that Philip was 'not a truly bad lad' and that he was 'more a cheerful and likeable rogue'. He explained that he had given Philip more chances than he had given other boys but that 'in the end there were no more chances left'.

He explained that he was personally very distressed if he had to permanently exclude a pupil, and that he always sought advice from senior staff and his Chair of Governors whenever he was considering it. He said that excluding Philip had been a particularly difficult decision because his parents had been so supportive and because he was in his last year at school and would now be unlikely to do his exams.

He said that he knew Philip had some learning difficulties and that his exam results would have been 'poor' and he felt that 'in reality it had not mattered too much that he didn't do his GCSEs – except perhaps to his parents'. This view powerfully highlights a difference between the beliefs and ethos of the school's culture and those of Philip's family (Schwartz 1999). The head teacher explained to me that at the governors' meeting Philip 'didn't do himself any favours', and explained that what he meant was that Phillip had not told the governors that he had wanted to stay in the school, and they had been left with the impression that Philip didn't care.

Philip's head teacher said that he believed that it was in Philip's best interests to be excluded. He said that he probably should have excluded him earlier as he might have had a better chance of getting into another school. He knew that Philip was not in another school. He felt that he now could offer no more help to Philip or his parents and that it was now 'over to the LEA to sort out'. During the interview Philip's head teacher repeated several times how much he regretted having to exclude pupils and said 'it is the worst part of my job'.

Discussion

There is agreement in the accounts of Philip's parents and head teacher that the parents had been very supportive of the school, and that they had been kept informed of the difficulties which the school was having with Philip. There is also agreement that Philip experienced learning difficulties. Philip and his parents shared the view that staying on at school and taking his GCSEs was important for him, but his head teacher took the view that this would not have been helpful for Philip as his results would have been poor, although he acknowledged that it mattered to Philip's parents that he took them.

There is further agreement that Philip is 'not a bad lad' and that he was likeable and cheerful. There is evidence of contradiction and confusing messages, and/or ambiguity in the stories, with the parents believing that the head teacher 'liked Philip' and the head teacher's descriptions of Philip as being 'a likeable rogue', and Philip's comments that his head teacher 'kept having a go' at him, and Mr and Mrs F's comments that the head teacher was 'no help at all'. There is also a sense from Philip and his parents that they believed that the head teacher was the dominant voice at the governors' meeting, and that the final decision to exclude Philip was his. There is further confusion about why Philip was finally excluded. Philip believed that it was because he had hit another boy; his parents thought that the final exclusion followed an incident when Philip had smashed a door. The reason for the exclusion as read out at the governors' meeting was 'caught smoking and off the school premises at lunch time without permission'.

Both Mr and Mrs F and his head teacher referred to Philip not speaking up for himself and not doing himself 'any favours' at the governors' meeting. This connects with Tomm's (1998) notion of the fundamental importance of the maintenance of specific meanings within the narrative through the generations of the family (in this case the generations of the school). The head teacher reported that the governors had interpreted Philip's lack of response as not caring, but Mrs F offered a different explanation, saying that he had been very nervous at the meeting. In his account Philip made no reference to the governors' meeting.

David

David is a 13-year-old (Year 8) Anglo-African Caribbean boy living with his white mother and African-Caribbean step-father and 11-year-old white half-brother.

David's story

David could not remember the actual day when he was excluded or the reason for the exclusion. He remembers being sent out of the class to report to the deputy head teacher, who had talked to his teacher and returned to David telling him they would have to permanently exclude him. David said that he did know that this meant that he was excluded forever. He said that he was given a letter to take home to his parents but he had not given it to them and did not tell them about the exclusion, as he did not want to get grounded. He said that the school sent another letter home and his parents were 'pretty angry' with him.

David later thought that the final incident was because he let a fire alarm off. He said that he and his friends were messing about. He said that as soon as the alarm went off he told a teacher that he had done it but that it was not intentional. He remembers the deputy head saying to him 'well I knew it would be you David, you're the only one stupid enough to do such a thing'. David said that he remembered saying to her 'what, no one else in the school has ever done this? I'm the only stupid one?' He said that she hadn't answered him. He remembered feeling angry because she had called him 'stupid', and it had been an accident and he had owned up to it, but he was still in trouble. David said that when the deputy head had said that he was excluded from school he had 'begged her' to take him back and he remembers being really upset. He thought that the governors might have allowed him back, as they had done a friend of his earlier in the year. David said that he had never liked the atmosphere of the school.

He could think of no good things about being excluded and that the bad things were not getting an education and not 'knowing what's going on'. He thought his mother had been most affected by his exclusion, although he thought his Dad was also upset. He said his mother had cried and this had made him feel upset and guilty.

David believed that he could behave at school and that he often did, but that he had got a bad reputation and 'the deputy head really hated me – she's a racist'. He could not think of anything which he could have done differently which might have prevented his exclusion. He described himself as 'a nice guy but just don't get on the wrong side of me. I stand up for my rights'.

Mr and Mrs G's story (David's mother and step-father)

Mrs G said that she was first told in a telephone call from the deputy head that David was being sent home. She was told there had been a minor incident and they were sending him home for a short time until the school had investigated the incident. After speaking to David, Mrs G decided to make an appointment with the headmaster but was told that he did not get involved at this stage, but that she could see the deputy. When she met with the deputy head teacher the next day Mrs G was given a slip of paper which said that there would be a special governors' meeting the next day where it would be decided whether or not to permanently exclude David. Mrs G said that she was very shocked and confused and at first thought that David had not told her the whole story.

Mr and Mrs G told me that they had attended the governors' meeting but that they still didn't know on what grounds the school wanted to permanently exclude David. He described attending the meeting as 'like going into court unprepared'. Mrs G explained that they were presented with a dossier of all the things David was supposed to have done over the past 2 years. She said that they were given 5 minutes to read it and were then expected to defend themselves and David. Mr G was angry to read in the dossier a reference to someone ('a lady') seeing 'someone who resembled David in the park and acting as though he was on drugs'. This had been on a day when David had been unwell and at home. Mrs G remembered telephoning the school that day to report his absence due to illness. Mr and Mrs G described several other references in the dossier which they considered to be untrue, inaccurate or unfair. Mrs G said that she was 'horrified' to read in the dossier that David had been admitted to hospital having taken an overdose of tablets. She explained that a girl at David's school had had an argument with him and told a teacher that David had taken a 'load of pills'. David had denied this but was taken to hospital, where it was shown that he had not taken anything. He was then sent home. Mr G said that with these inaccuracies in the dossier 'it did look bad for David'.

Mr G described another incident when David had been beaten up in school by the 22-year-old uncle of another boy. The police had been called to the school and David had been taken to hospital unconscious. Mrs G was called to the hospital and described David as being 'all smashed up'. Mr and Mrs G had received a telephone call from the head teacher telling them to keep David out of school 'for his own safety'. No prosecution followed the incident and David returned to school 3 weeks later. This had happened 6 months before David's final exclusion. The incident was documented in David's dossier and Mr and Mrs G felt that it was recorded as though 'David was the perpetrator and not the victim'. Mrs G said that she very strongly felt that the school and the governors were accusing them of lying. The governors said that they would not take into account any of the incidents in the dossier, but that they were going to base their decision on David's entire school career. Mr and Mrs G were confused by this. Mr and Mrs G acknowledged that David had been disruptive at school and had 'bunked off school' sometimes, but they felt that the school had not kept them informed and they had only learnt about some of these things from David himself.

Mr G said that children at school don't have a voice and that 'if teachers have it in for certain kids, the kids don't stand a chance'.

Mrs G thought that the main reason David was permanently excluded was because he had 'a run in with the deputy head who had it in for David and is a racist'. David had lied to the deputy head and had admitted this. The headmaster was quite new to the school and Mr and Mrs G believed that he had taken the deputy's recommendation to exclude David, and the governors agreed. Mr and Mrs G felt that 'the teachers were believed and that children do not get heard'.

Mr and Mrs G said that they were told nothing about being able to appeal against the exclusion. A few weeks after the governors' meeting they received a letter explaining that the Education Department was upholding the governors' decision to exclude David permanently. Mrs G emphasised strongly that she believed the deputy head to be a racist.

Mrs G said that David was off school for 8 weeks before she realised he could have tuition while they looked for another school. It was when she contacted the Admissions Department that she was told about her right to appeal. Mrs G explained that she had to keep telephoning the Education Department and eventually found a 'very helpful lady' who told them about the appeal system but by then they were out of time.

Mr and Mrs G felt that as far as the school was concerned David was always lying and other pupils were always telling the truth. They believe that it was more likely to be 'six of one and half a dozen of the other'. They considered that 'the teachers cover their backs and cover up for each other'. They said they were only told that David hadn't been doing his homework when they read it on his report. Mrs G said the only time the school wanted to work with parents was when things were going wrong. She did not feel that she was welcomed in the school, even when she was 'called up to go in'. She felt that she was treated like one of the naughty children, 'even by the school secretary lady'.

Mr G acknowledged that teachers have a difficult job and he believes that they are not trained properly to deal with adolescents.

Mr and Mrs G thought David's permanent exclusion was the result of his bad relationship with the deputy head and a bad record. They said they felt let down by the school and that children, particularly David, are not believed. Mr G said that 'schools take the easy way out when they exclude'. Mr and Mrs G are very concerned that David's younger brother will be affected by David's exclusion, as he attends the same school.

David's head teacher's story

David's head teacher explained that he had not been working in the school for very long when David was excluded, and he thought that David was probably his first exclusion. He said this was his first headship, but in his previous school as deputy head he had been involved in excluding pupils, 'although not many'.

He recalled being told by certain staff that David had a history of being a troublemaker, and when he had looked up his records he was surprised that the school had not excluded him before. He said that, according to the records, after David took an overdose his parents had been told that he should see a psychiatrist, but as far as he was aware, they had not arranged this.

The head teacher described David as being 'street-wise' with a bad reputation. He thought that Mr and Mrs G 'can only see the good side of David' and he and his staff had found them to be 'confrontational and not easy to work with'.

The head teacher explained that his deputy head had mainly dealt with David's exclusion, and he totally trusted her judgement. He said he had no reason to doubt that she had dealt with things properly, including giving Mr and Mrs G all the information they needed. He said that in hindsight, now he was 'more established', he would 'look more carefully into a pupil's record' and would be 'more in charge' but he doubted that in the case of David the outcome would have been different.

Discussion

In the stories of David and his parents, David is portrayed as a victim in every incident which they recalled and described, although Mr and Mrs G did say that it was likely to be 'six of one and half a dozen of the other'. His parents reported things they considered to be inaccurate and untrue. David did not report these things and it was unclear from his account as to whether or not he knew about the dossier to which his parents referred.

The head teacher acknowledged not having been in the school for very long when David was excluded, and that he had learnt about David from his school record. As it was difficult for Mr and Mrs G to accept the accuracy of the school records, it is likely that they would consider that the head teacher was basing his knowledge of David on inaccuracies.

The deputy head teacher, in the two stories, is given a strong and influential position. Mr and Mrs G and David describe her as 'the main reason' why David was excluded, and that it was she who had made the final recommendation. Both Mrs G and David talked about the deputy head being 'a racist'. The head teacher described his total confidence in the deputy head and acknowledged that she had probably been in charge of the situation at the time, as he was so new to the school. It is interesting to note here that, in his story, the head teacher had referred, unsolicited, to his previous post in a different school, where he had held the position of deputy head teacher. It is possible that he was trying to communicate that he fully understood the position of his own deputy head, and held some respect and empathy for the current post holder in the light of his previous experience.

Mr and Mrs G presented as feeling very angry with the school about the way they were treated and about the way David's exclusion was handled. They felt they had been seen by the school and the governors as 'liars'. The head teacher described that he had found Mr and Mrs G 'confrontational and not easy to work with'. The parents considered they had not been given all the information to which they were entitled, until they spoke to 'a very helpful lady' in the Education Department. The head teacher described that he had confidence that his deputy would have provided Mr and Mrs G with all the information they needed and the procedures required.

Making sense of similar and different narratives

The examples of Philip and David, their parents and the head teachers, demonstrate how individual stories are likely to have similarities and differences but which, together, form a 'whole system story'. A head teacher may hold the most powerful formal position in the relationship between pupils, parents and schools (although in some situations parents may hold the more dominant position). The fact that each individual story contributes to the system story means that even the story of the least powerful member of the system holds a prominent place in understanding the interrelationships of the system members.

One of the most common responses from the excluded pupils and their parents in the study, when asked what might have helped in the relationship between the school, the parents and the pupils prior to and after the exclusion, was that teachers should listen more to pupils. When asked to comment on this, many of the head teachers interviewed held the view that pupils *were* listened to. They reported that a pupil's account had often differed from that of other children and staff, inferring that the pupil was telling lies and giving unreliable accounts to avoid blame. Further discussion with the head teachers suggested that when the pupils were asked about 'what had happened' it had been for the purpose of eliciting 'the truth' – the facts about an incident. There was no acknowledgement that there may be more ways to 'listen' to individual stories than to listen for corroboration of a collective 'truth'. The differing accounts of other children and teachers might be more about differing perceptions of the same event than about intentionally changing the facts to avoid blame. A pupil who claims he hit out at another child because he was being taunted, may genuinely believe in the taunting. The fact that others observing the incident did not perceive the behaviour in that way does not negate the fact that it was perceived and felt to be taunting.

Information regarding the emphasis each narrator gives to an incident can be understood by what is included and what is left out of the story. In the case of David it was only David and his mother who referred to the white deputy head teacher as being racist. This does not mean that they were right or wrong, or that only they had considered this as a possibility. One meaning might be that this had been an important part of their own construction of the events, which they had been able to name. From others in the story, that is, David's black step-father and white head teacher, racism was not mentioned. David's step-father referred to the 'school having it in for certain kids'.

What understanding can we gain from listening to differing stories of the same event? Most of the head teachers in the study described in this chapter genuinely believed they had listened to pupils and parents, yet those pupils and parents, equally genuinely, by and large had not felt listened to or heard. Being given an opportunity to describe and give an account of how we experience a particular incident does not mean that we will not ultimately be held accountable for any wrong doing. The telling of the story can be used as an opportunity to reflect on our part in the incident, and to see our own behaviour in the context of the whole. To hear another's story of the same incident will help us put ourselves into that different position, to empathise and to see it from another's position. A parent will have a different, usually protective, relationship towards their child; a teacher will have a relationship which will see that child in relation to the other children in the school, and possibly in relation to their own job satisfaction and career success. One position is no more or less legitimate than the other, but unless each is able to listen and understand the other's position the result is likely to be unhelpful, with the pupil stuck between the two.

Applying a narrative approach to therapeutic effect in work with pupils, families and schools

Applying a narrative approach to work within an educational context is not the sole domain of the researcher. Teachers, learning mentors, connections workers, education welfare and social workers, school nurses, school counsellors and educational psychologists can all appropriately and valuably employ a narrative framework in their work with vulnerable and troubled young people.

It is important that the invitation to pupils and parents to tell their story is made in a non-judgemental manner, and not used to confirm or refute blame. In some cases this might only be achieved through a third party, where there are not the issues of power relationships or hierarchy which inevitably exist in school, parent and pupil interactions. A legitimate third party could be an educational psychologist or school nurse, who is part of neither the school nor the family system, but who has training and a formal role to support parents, children and schools in their relationships. From interviews with different members of the school and family systems of the excluded pupils, many important issues which had a bearing on the pupils' behaviours came to light, most of which had been unknown to others in the system. In most cases this information did not excuse or condone the behaviour, but did serve to understand it, and through this understanding, enabled pupils, parents and teachers to gain a greater understanding of each other, and to develop 'non-blame' relationships to supporting each other. It takes time to truly listen, and to feel listened to. We tend to hear what we have time to hear, and what we have time to deal with and respond to. In schools there does not seem to be the luxury of the quiet, peaceful calm of the closed clinical setting. Interviews with parents and children can be interrupted by the change of lesson bell, the teacher needing to go off to another task, or someone else needing to use the room. These are the realities of school life. An interruption in the telling of a story will affect its depth, richness and flow. It may be impossible to repeat the conditions which prompted the story – the moment may have passed. These are things which are important for professionals to understand and plan for when they say to pupils 'tell me what happened'.

Children and parents in the narratives presented in this chapter expressed the view that they needed to be listened to. They did not say that they needed to be agreed with, nor that they needed to have their own way in all matters, only that they wanted to be listened to. The implication for professionals working with pupils and parents is that we need to develop ways of facilitating conditions in which they can feel not only listened to but heard.

Chapter 17

Narratives of hope

Alan Carr

Introduction

The principles for an integrative approach to the practice of family therapy are presented here (Carr 2000b; Carr and McNulty in press a). This approach to practice, particularly the formulation of exceptions, has been informed by the literature on resilience (Haggerty *et al.* 1994; Luthar 2003; Luthar *et al.* 2000; Luthar and Cicchetti 2000; Rutter 1999, 2000) and developments within the positive psychology movement (Carr 2004; Snyder and Lopez 2002). The way this approach helps parents develop hopeful narratives about themselves, their children and their lives is shown, and the chapter closes with an example of family work which illustrates this approach.

An integrative approach

The variety of traditions, schools and models of couples and family therapy may be classified in terms of their central focus of therapeutic concern and in particular with respect to their emphasis on:

1   Repetitive problem-maintaining behaviour patterns;
2   Constraining narratives and belief systems which subserve these behaviour patterns; and
3   Historical, contextual, and constitutional factors which predispose families to adopt particular narratives and belief systems and engage in particular problem-maintaining behaviour patterns.

In the same vein, hypotheses and formulations about families' problems and strengths may be conceptualized in terms of these three domains. Also, interventions may be classified in terms of the specific domains they target. Our integrative model of couple and family therapy (Carr 2000; Carr and McNulty in press a) which rests on these insights, draws on a wide range of family therapy theory, practice and research (Carr 2000; Gurman and Jacobson 2002; Liddle *et al.* 2002; Pinsof and Wynne 1995; Sexton *et al.*

2003). Formulation is central to this integrative approach and it is to this that we now turn.

Formulation of problems and exceptions

For any family problem, an initial hypothesis and later formulation may be constructed in which the behaviour pattern that maintains the problem is specified, the constraining narratives and beliefs that underpin family members' roles in this pattern are outlined, and the broader contextual factors that predispose family members to have these beliefs and behaviour patterns are given. For example, in the case presented in the second half of this chapter, our initial hypothesis was that the family became involved in regular conflictual patterns of interaction in which the children's expression of their needs, the father's anger control problems and the mother's panic attacks might have played a part. Our second hypothesis was that the narratives and beliefs which underpinned their roles in these interaction patterns involved the father having views about being entitled to certain things from the mother (in their marital relationship), and to the mother believing that she was either in danger or powerless. Our third hypothesis was that these beliefs and behaviour patterns were intergenerational and had their roots in adverse family-of-origin experiences.

Strengths may be conceptualized as involving exceptional interaction patterns within which the problem does not occur, empowering narratives and beliefs that inform family members' roles within these interaction patterns, and broader contextual factors that underpin these competency-oriented narratives that provide a foundation for resilience. For example, in the case study presented in the second half of this chapter, our first strengths-oriented hypothesis was that occasionally the mother and father became involved in cooperative patterns of interaction. Our second hypothesis was that the narratives which underpinned their roles in these interaction patterns involved the couple's commitment to their marriage and to raising their children together. Our third hypothesis was that these narratives and behaviour patterns had their roots in positive family-of-origin experiences and positive experiences within the family of procreation.

Three categories of interventions

In the light of formulations of families' problems and strengths, a range of interventions which address interaction patterns, narratives, and broader contextual factors may be considered. Those which fit best for clients, make best use of their strengths, and for which there is best evidence of effectiveness may be selected. Some interventions aim primarily to disrupt problem-maintaining interaction patterns. In the example of family work presented later in the chapter, the self-regulation work we did with the father, the graded challenges work we did with the mother and the parenting skills training we did with the couple fall into this broad category. Other interventions aim to help couples evolve more liberating personal and family narratives. These include reframing the family's difficulties in interactional rather than individualistic terms, externalizing the problem, pinpointing strengths, and building on exceptions. A third group of interventions aim to modify the negative impact of broader contextual factors, or draw on positive historical, contextual or constitutional resources and factors that may promote resilience. In the example of family work presented later in the chapter, building support is an intervention that falls into this category.

Stages of therapy

Couples and family therapy is not always straightforward. Sometimes clients have difficulty engaging in therapy. In the example of family work presented later in this chapter, the parents probably would not have attended therapy at all without careful planning about who to invite to the initial sessions and what the focus of these meetings should be. Furthermore, many families show marked improvement following assessment only. That is, once they develop a shared understanding of their difficulties and exceptional situations where their problems were expected to occur but did not, they spontaneously avoid problematic interactions and engage in exceptional non-problematic interactions instead. Finally, some families come to therapy with one problem, such as parenting difficulties, and when this is resolved request therapy for other difficulties, such as sexual problems. To address these various challenges, the process of therapy is conceptualized as a developmental stagewise process.

The first stage is concerned with planning, the second with engagement and assessment, the third with treatment, and the fourth with disengagement or recontracting for further intervention. At each stage, key tasks must be completed before progression to the next stage occurs. Failure to complete the tasks of a given stage in sequence or skipping a stage may jeopardize the consultation process. For example, attempting to conduct an assessment without first contracting for assessment may lead to cooperation difficulties if the couple find the assessment procedures arduous or threatening. Failure to complete assessment before treatment, compromises decision making about goal setting and selecting specific therapy strategies. Therapy is a recursive process insofar as it is possible to move from the final stage of one episode to the first stage of the next.

Problems and strengths

Throughout the history of family therapy, different traditions have placed more or less emphasis on clients' problems and strengths. Structural, strategic, systemic behavioural and psychodynamic traditions have highlighted the importance of the role of systemic factors in the formation and maintenance of problems. Solution-focused and narrative traditions have privileged the importance of emphasizing solutions, strengths, exceptions, resilience and potential for growth in therapy (Carr 2000).

Therapeutic conversations which focus on the role of systemic factors in the formation and maintenance of problems have many benefits for clients. They invite clients to recognize, and by implication avoid re-enacting, problematic behaviour patterns. They allow clients and non-systemically oriented colleagues to understand problems in contextual rather than individual terms. They also provide opportunities for clients to process painful emotions associated with the development of these problems at earlier stages of the lifecycle. However, exclusively problem-focused therapeutic conversations have one major drawback. They privilege deficit-oriented personal and family narratives. They invite clients to think of themselves as members of problem families or members of families that cope with problems. When families become involved with therapists in these problem-saturated narratives, they may feel demoralized, despondent, and pessimistic. This in turn may compromise the therapeutic alliance and the possibility of therapeutic progress.

Indeed, this very difficulty has been an impetus for the development of theories and practices that focus on strengths. Where strengths and solutions are privileged in therapeutic conversations, important possibilities emerge. Clients may come to recognize exceptional circumstances in which problems were expected to occur but did not, by implication pointing to exceptional patterns deserving re-enactment. Personal and family narratives and belief systems that underpin such exceptional non-problematic transactional patterns may come to the fore, and these may come to supplant deficit-oriented stories about the self and the family. So clients may come to describe themselves as members of strong families, loyal families, families with special talents, skills and potentials. Therapeutic conversations premised on the search for strengths, may uncover or bring forth historical, contextual and constitutional factors that form the bedrock of clients' resourcefulness and resilience in the face of adversity. Clients may come to talk about the good things they have learned from past generations, the supports they receive from their networks, and the personal attributes that make them the sort of people who keep going where others might fall by the wayside. However, exclusively strengths-oriented therapeutic conversations have their shortcomings too. They close down opportunities for developing systemic framings of problems and opportunities to process traumatic emotions and 'unfinished business'. When clients notice these avenues being closed off, they may feel unheard. They may feel that in the urgent pursuit of solutions, the therapist has failed to take their problems seriously. This in turn may compromise the therapeutic alliance and hinder therapeutic progress.

A central challenge in family therapy practice is to balance the focus on problems with the focus on strengths. In the integrative model of practice described here, the use of problem and exception formulations is one practice that facilitates this balance and the development of narratives of hope.

Exception formulation, resilience and positive psychology

The literature on exception formulation in family therapy and the related literature on the applications of findings from studies of risk and resilience (Haggerty *et al.* 1994; Luthar 2003; Luthar *et al.* 2000; Luthar and Cicchetti 2000; Rutter 1999, 2000) and positive psychology is relatively sparse and has only recently come to the fore (Carr 2000, 2004; Carr and McNulty in press b; Snyder and Lopez 2002). Key findings from this literature that may be incorporated into exception formulations are sketched in the sections that follow.

Exceptional behaviour patterns

Hypotheses and formulations about exceptional behaviour patterns may include a description of what happened before, during and after the problem was expected to occur but did not. Commonly, the exceptional pattern will also include positive feelings. These offer clues as to how the exceptional pattern may be strengthened. For example, in our family example the good feelings that followed cooperation offered a reason for Tom (the father) and Sue (the mother) to cooperate more in future. Exceptional behaviour patterns are often characterized by effective problem-solving and clear communication. They usually entail a higher rate of positive, supportive rather than negative, critical exchanges. A clear expression of needs, particularly attachment needs, a degree of psychological intimacy, and greater balance in the distribution of power (within the cultural constraints of the family's ethnic reference group) are common features of exceptional behaviour patterns, particularly within the couple subsystem. Exceptional patterns of parenting typically involve consistent, authoritative, cooperative co-parenting. Exceptional family behaviour patterns often involve emotional support and flexibility about rules, roles and routines. Within professional networks, exceptions tend to occur more commonly when there is good interprofessional coordination and cooperation between families and professionals.

Exceptional narratives

Exceptional non-problematic behaviour patterns may be subserved by a wide variety of positive personal and family narratives. These narratives often entail acceptance rather than denial of the problem, a willingness to accept responsibility for contributing to problem resolution, and an interactional rather than an individualistic framing of the problem. Commitment to resolving the problem and conviction that one is competent to so do are common features of positive narratives. When family members have useful and empowering stories about the nature of the problem and its resolution, exceptions may also occur. The occurrence of exceptional behaviour patterns may be associated with the development of the belief that the advantages of resolving the problem outweigh the costs of change. Clients may construct narratives in which once feared consequences associated with their presenting problems come to be seen as not so dreadful or likely after all. Exceptions may occur when family members have positive and empowering narratives about their relationship and about their roles in the family. This may include a realization of how much family members care for each other and how important it is to be loyal to the family.

Exceptions may also occur when family narratives entail benign beliefs about the intentions and characteristics of family members and where the prevailing view is that family members are good people who are doing their best in a tough situation rather than vindictive people who are out to persecute others. An optimistic attributional style may also underpin exceptional, non-problematic behaviour patterns and typify empowering narratives.

When exceptional behaviour patterns occur, sometimes they are associated with the use of healthy defence mechanisms to manage anxiety arising from conflicting desires to follow a course of action but also avoid rejection or attack from others. Healthy defence mechanisms include self-observation, looking at the humorous side of the situation, being assertive about having one's needs met, and sublimation of unacceptable desires into socially acceptable channels such as work, art or sport.

Contextual factors associated with resilience

Exceptional behaviour patterns and the hopeful narratives that subserve them arise from protective factors which foster resilience. These protective factors may be rooted in family members' constitutional characteristics, the family's broader social context, or their historical family-of-origin experiences. Important personal characteristics which contribute to resilience are physical health, high intelligence, specific talents, creativity, wisdom, easy temperament and positive personality traits. Such traits include emotional stability (as opposed to neuroticism), extraversion, openness to experience, agreeableness and conscientiousness.

A good social support network including friends and members of the extended family and low extrafamilial stress enhance a family's chances of resolving the problems they bring to therapy. Well balanced home and work roles, moderate or high socio-economic status, a positive parental work environment, positive preschool or educational placements for children, and empowering cultural norms and values also contribute to resilience in the face of adversity (Carr 2004).

Positive family-of-origin experiences and positive family-of-origin parent–child relationships lay the foundations for resilience in later life. Good parent–child relationships characterized by secure attachment, authoritative parenting and clear communication in the family of origin foster later resilience and strength. Successful experiences of coping with problems in the family of origin and the current relationship, flexible organization in the family of origin, good parental adjustment and a positive relationship between parents in the family of origin may also engender later resilience.

In the light of this brief sketch of our integrative approach to practice, let us turn to a case example which illustrates key features of the model. See Carr (2000b) for further discussion of this approach.

An example of couple/parent work

Tom and Sue, a couple in their mid-20s, were referred by a social worker for therapy at a psychology clinic attached to a general hospital. From an ethnic and socio-economic perspective the couple were white, working-class people living in a market town in the UK. In the referral letter the social worker said that the couple had multiple problems. Tom had an explosive temper, which was frightening for Sue and her two children. Sue, who had a history of panic attacks, had developed a constricted lifestyle because of fears of having panic attacks when away from home. The couple argued constantly. Although no actual violence had occurred, the potential for violence was the central issue leading to the referral. The case was referred to social services by a health visitor who became concerned for the welfare of the couple's children, Maeve (4 years) and Mike (1 year), when conducting a routine developmental assessment visit with Mike around the time of his first birthday. The social worker visited the couple at their home and met with a frosty reception. The couple initially insisted that everything was all right and that no family evaluation and support were required. The social worker explained that she had a statutory obligation to evaluate the capacity of the parents to provide a safe and secure home environment for the children. In the conversation that followed the social worker formed the opinion that the couple frequently argued about how best to care for the children and indeed many other issues. These arguments often escalated in intensity and rarely led to shared decisions with which both partners felt comfortable. One recommendation arising from the social worker's assessment was that the couple complete a programme of therapy to address the conflict between them, since this was interfering with their capacity to cooperate to meet their children's needs.

Contracting for assessment

Because of the couple's ambivalence about attending therapy, invitations to an initial contracting meeting were sent to the referring social worker and the couple, with a request that the social worker arrange transportation for the couple to attend our clinic. In the intake meeting the couple expressed their ambivalence about attending therapy, but the social worker pointed out that if they decided not to attend, then their children's names would be placed on an at-risk register held in her department. In light of this information, the couple agreed to attend two sessions during which an assessment would be conducted. If that indicated they were suitable for therapy a contract for a further ten sessions of therapy would be offered.

Formulation of problem episodes

In the assessment sessions it became clear that during episodes of couple-conflict Sue would not do something that Tom aggressively demanded, such as soothing the children or being attentive to his needs. In response Tom would criticize her, and she would initially argue back, but eventually withdraw into silence or, following stressful exchanges, have a panic attack. Tom would then back off. The couple would then not be on speaking terms for a few days. Gradually they would have increasingly more contact until the next episode. Sue's personal narrative, which underpinned her behaviour in these episodes, was that the demands of life, her children and her partner were too great for her to manage and she would usually fail. In this story she saw herself as a helpless victim. She also believed that arguments between couples were competitive exchanges that were won or lost. She believed she could never beat Tom in an argument and that was why she gave up each time, a process that reinforced her beliefs in her own lack of power to influence Tom. Also, when she became frustrated she believed that her increased physiological arousal was a sign that she was about to have a heart attack, a belief that often preceded her panic attacks. It seemed Sue had learned this pessimistic narrative from her mother, who had longstanding depression, and from observing her parents' very unhappy marriage. Tom behaved as he did during problematic episodes because his personal narrative entailed the view that Sue was being deliberately uncooperative to punish him and that it was unfair that she did not cherish him, because he was devoted to her. Another aspect of his personal narrative was the belief that others were trying to take advantage of him – a hostile attributional bias – which it seemed he had learned from his father. Tom had a conflictual relationship with his father, who treated his mother as Tom treated Sue. In developing this problem formulation, we both interviewed Tom and Sue about such episodes, and also observed them directly interacting with the children over two 90 minute assessment sessions. The observations of family interaction were made during enactments in which we invited the family to reach agreement on how best to schedule regular periods of positive family interaction. During these enactments it was clear that Tom's aggression was commonly expressed when Sue had difficulty being attuned to her children's needs and responding to these in an effective way. Our sensitivity to the children's positions was informed by attachment theory (Bowlby 1969, 1973, 1980, 1988).

Formulation of exceptional episodes

In contrast to these problematic episodes, there were exceptional episodes in which the problem was expected to happen but did not. During these episodes, Tom helped rather than criticized Sue when she was having difficulty soothing the children or cooking his dinner, doing the washing or some other household job. In response, she smiled at him and good feelings between them followed. Tom had learned from his mother that 'a little kindness goes a long way' and it was this story that underpinned his generous behaviour. Tom's mother was well disposed towards the children and both she and her husband valued them highly, since they were their first grandchildren. Sue had learned that 'one good turn deserves another' from her dad with whom she had a good relationship and this story underpinned her good feelings when Tom was kind to her. Both Sue's father and mother valued the children highly, since they were their first grandchildren. This formulation of exceptional episodes was based on interviews and observations of family interaction mentioned in the previous section.

Contracting for treatment

On the basis of the assessment and the problem and exception formulations, the couple were offered and accepted a contract for ten sessions of therapy. The overall goal for therapy agreed between the couple, the referring social worker and the therapist, was to help the couple reduce the level of conflict in their home and increase the safety of the children's parenting environment. The children attended five of the ten sessions.

Therapy

The ten sessions of therapy covered the issues that follow.

Interactional reframing

In the early sessions of therapy the problem formulation was revisited repeatedly. The couple's difficulties were reframed as an interactional problem rather than as a reflection of personal psychological or moral deficits. There was a gradual move away from the dominant narrative that each of them suffered from individual psychological problems. This narrative, couched in deficit discourse, entailed the view that the main problem was either Sue's 'bad nerves' or Tom's 'short fuse'. Instead the couple came to understand the family's difficulties as a problematic interaction pattern, in which a central concern was how to respond cooperatively to the children's needs (Dowling and Gorell Barnes 2000).

Externalizing the problem

In the early sessions of therapy the couple's difficulties were externalized and framed as peripheral to the core of their essentially positive relationship. They were invited to name their problem in a metaphorical way, and in response they began to talk about their problematic episodes, as 'the North Wind that blew through their house'. They began to monitor the occurrence of problematic episodes and to withdraw from these if they spotted themselves contributing to them. They referred to this as 'closing the shutters to keep the North Wind out of their house'.

Pinpointing strengths

Reframing the problem in interactional rather than individual terms, externalizing the problem, naming it in a metaphorical way, and adopting joint ways of combating it offered many opportunities to highlight Tom and Sue's personal strengths (for example, thoughtfulness, courage, persistence) and strengths that characterized their family relationships (for example, loyalty, warmth, sensitivity, steadfastness). Through naming these strengths, Tom and Sue began to develop a more hopeful narrative about their relationship, and a more positive view of themselves as parents.

Building on exceptions

The therapy also involved revisiting the exception formulation. The couple were repeatedly invited over the course of therapy to remember and recount, in emotive detail, many exceptional episodes in which the problem was expected to occur but did not. Invitations to give accounts of such episodes initially focused on the pattern of interaction, then on the underlying personal narratives, and finally on the constitutional, historical and contextual factors that underpinned the positive personal narratives. Then the similarities between these and other similar past episodes were explored. The couple were also invited to consider what the occurrence of these episodes said about them as a family and how they expected such episodes to recur in the future. Through this process, the couple developed a narrative about their relationship and their family marked by kindness, concern, sensitivity, warmth, closeness, understanding, compassion and many other positive qualities, which they recognized had always been there and would probably persist into their future and the future of their children. In this way the seeds for a narrative of hope were sown.

Tom's challenge: self-regulation

Another aspect of the therapy focused on helping Tom to define himself as a man who was engaged in learning to identify and express his attachment needs in a direct way. He came to talk about himself as a man who was learning to soothe his own sense of panic or anger when he feared his attachment needs would not be met by Sue immediately. In developing this new narrative about the sort of man he was, Tom gradually gave up the story that Sue was to blame for his aggression. He adopted a more hopeful narrative about himself as a man in charge of his own feelings, responsible for his own behaviour and able to challenge intergenerational legacies for men. Some skills training was offered to Tom to help him identify and state his needs, and to monitor and contain rising frustration if his needs were not met.

Sue's challenge: being courageous

A further aspect of the therapy focused on helping Sue to define herself as a courageous woman who was learning to accept that a racing pulse and sweaty palms were signals to relax, not panic. To help her revise her personal narrative, Sue was invited to set herself challenges in which she made her pulse race and her palms sweat, and then to deal with these challenges by using relaxation skills and support from her partner. She and Tom planned and completed a series of graded challenges. Earlier challenges involved containing and soothing Sue's increased physiological arousal in the therapy sessions. In later challenges the couple travelled away from the house for gradually increasing distances, until eventually they both went on a date in the city. This was a major achievement for the couple. It consolidated Sue's optimistic story about herself as a courageous woman who was increasingly ready to take on greater challenges in her life.

Managing resistance

Progress in therapy was intertwined with periods of slow movement, and ambivalence about change. Managing resistance was the main therapeutic activity during these periods. Indeed, as part of the contracting process, we explained to Tom and Sue that ambivalence about change and resistance were an inevitable part of therapy and to be welcomed, since they are an indicator that the therapy is working and change is really happening. Resistance showed itself in many ways. Here two examples will be mentioned.

While Tom was moving towards defining himself as a man who was engaged in learning to identify and express his attachment needs in a direct way rather than to blame Sue for his aggression, progress was not straight-forward. He would occasionally doubt that the benefits of defining himself in this new way outweighed the costs of giving up the view that Sue, and not he, was responsible for his aggressive and violent outbursts. When this occurred, we invited Tom to address his personal dilemma about the costs of maintaining the status quo and the costs of changing his situation. He came to see that if he maintained the status quo he could preserve a story about himself as a good man provoked to aggression by Sue, but he would have to give up any hope of a truly intimate and loving relationship with her and the two children. This, we suggested, was because Sue could not be fully intimate with a man who attacked and blamed her for things that she had not done.

Similarly, progress was far from straightforward when Sue was learning to define herself as a courageous woman. She would occasionally doubt that the benefits of defining herself in this new way outweighed the costs of giving up the view that she was a helpless victim who could justifiably remain cocooned at home forever. When this occurred, we invited Sue to address her personal dilemma about the costs of maintaining the status quo and the costs of changing her situation. She came to see that if she maintained the status quo she could avoid the terror of facing her fear, but she would have to give up any hope of defining herself as a powerful woman in her own right, a competent role model for her daughter, and an equal partner for Tom.

For both Tom and Sue, the theme of abandonment underpinned the cata-strophic narrative that fuelled their ambivalence about change. Tom's per-sonal narrative was that if he accepted full responsibility for his anger and angry behaviour, then this meant he was not a good man, and so Sue would have to leave him. Sue's personal story was that as long as she was a helpless terrified victim, Tom would remain to protect her, but if she showed signs of sustained courage and strength, he would leave her to fend for herself. To address these catastrophic narratives, Sue and Tom were invited to explore alternative and more hopeful narratives of the future in which Tom could allow himself to be forgiven and accepted by Sue and Sue could allow herself to be on an equal footing with Tom (rather than in a one-down position). The pessimistic narrative of abandonment and the related ambivalence about change receded over the course of therapy as Tom and Sue's more hopeful story about their lives came to the fore.

Parenting

Therapy also focused on inviting the couple to explore their story about themselves as good-enough parents. Parenting issues were addressed in all sessions, but were the central focus of four sessions in particular. Invitations were offered to them to describe ways in which they successfully met their

children's needs for safety, security, nurturance, control, intellectual stimu-
lation, and age appropriate responsibilities. Through describing many
examples of good-enough parenting and enacting these within conjoint
family sessions, Tom and Sue developed a story about themselves as competent but not perfect parents. This hopeful parenting narrative led them to
ask us for expert advice on parenting skills so they could improve the way
they managed the challenges of child-rearing. It was into this context that
behavioural parenting skills training was offered. This covered all the usual
skills to enhance parent–child interactions, increase positive behaviours and
extinguish aggressive and destructive behaviours. The couple incorporated
these skills into their own parenting styles and into their own story about
themselves as good-enough parents. This skills training involved direct
coaching during conjoint family sessions. During these sessions Maeve (aged
4), began to describe herself as a more 'grown up' girl, as viewing her father as
a 'gentle daddy' rather than a 'cross daddy', and her mother as 'more fun'.

Building support

The couple were invited in the middle and later stages of therapy to
strengthen their ties with their families of origin. This was not an easy
invitation for the couple to accept. Over the years both partners had become
increasingly distant from their own parents, because in each of their families
they felt triangulated. During her teens Sue had gradually become a confidante
for her father and was estranged from her depressed mother. Tom, in contrast
had become a confidante for his mother and had frequent conflicts with his
father. In both Tom and Sue's families of origin their parents were locked into
rigid, close, conflictual patterns of marital interaction. Despite all this, as
Tom and Sue's narrative about their own relationship became more hopeful,
they became more understanding of their parents' difficulties and were prepared to visit their families of origin more frequently. They let their parents
know that they had come through difficult times, but were now hopeful
that there were better times ahead, and that they were strong enough to build
a good family. This admission of vulnerability and declaration of hope
strengthened ties between Tom and Sue and their families of origin. Also
the grandparents, Roger and Teresa, and Conor and Rachel, welcomed
the opportunity to spend time with their grandchildren, Maeve and Mike.
This created a context within which they could be more supportive of Tom
and Sue.

Disengagement

The first six sessions were held at weekly or fortnightly intervals. As the
family began to make progress, the final four sessions were spaced at 3 to 5
weekly intervals. Much of the therapy in the last three sessions focused on

helping the couple make sense of the change process, develop relapse management plans, and understand the process of disengagement as the conclusion of an episode in an ongoing relationship with the clinic rather than the end of the therapeutic relationship. Tom and Sue were invited to forecast the types of stressful situations in which relapses might occur, their probable negative reactions to relapses, and the ways in which they could use the strengths they had discovered in therapy to deal with these relapses.

After ten sessions a review conducted with the referring social worker indicated that the family was doing much better. The social services department decided that frequent monitoring of the family was no longer necessary. At the review, the following specific treatment gains were noted. In the social worker's view the conflict between the couple no longer placed the children at risk. The frequency of episodes of conflict between Sue and Tom had reduced from five to one per week and the couple was confident that these arguments would never become violent. Both children were healthy, well adjusted and were being well cared for. There were marked improvements in Tom's anger management and Sue's panic disorder with agoraphobia. The couple said their marital satisfaction improved. Supportive links with each of their families of origin were strengthened. In short, the therapy goals had been attained.

Relapse management

A relapse occurred a couple of years later at a time when Sue began working outside the home for the first time since the birth of the first child. After two sessions in which the couple explored ways that they could use their strengths jointly to manage the new challenges in their lives, the frequency of the couple's unproductive arguments reduced again.

Dilemmas in the therapist's narrative

There were three dilemmas central to the therapist's narrative in this case. First, there was the issue of 'customerhood'. Clearly, the main customer initially was the referring social worker, not the family. We addressed this issue by conducting a careful network analysis and inviting the social worker to bring the family to the contracting session and explain the implications of accepting or rejecting an offer of therapy. Second, in this case there was a statutory requirement to monitor the risk that the parents posed to the children's welfare, and the conflicting requirement for the parents to engage in a trusting therapeutic relationship to reduce this risk. We addressed this dilemma by agreeing that the referring social worker would adopt the statutory risk-monitoring role, and the therapist would adopt an exclusively therapeutic role. A third issue in this case was making space for attending to the needs of the children while being mindful of the narratives of the parents.

The needs and welfare of the children Maeve and Mike, both of whom were under 5 years, were paramount in this case. But the parents, Tom and Sue, were also 'needy clients' with limited personal coping resources. Throughout the therapy, we were mindful of balancing the needs of the children and the needs of the parents. This was challenging because Tom and Sue's stories were well articulated, but specific steps had to be taken to make the experiences of Maeve and Mike more salient. We did this during the assessment sessions through facilitating enactments and commenting on episodes in which the parents made good-enough or ineffective attempts to be attuned to the children's needs and cooperatively meet them. Throughout the ten sessions of therapy, parenting issues were addressed, and parent training was a central focus of four sessions. Our approach to parent training involved helping Tom and Sue become attuned to the needs of Maeve and Mike, and in doing so to be able to listen to their implicit, unarticulated and future narratives. In this sense Maeve and Mike were central to the success of this episode of therapy. The therapy as a whole was very demanding. The management of the dilemmas described in this work was addressed in peer supervision, and in so doing, we were able to respond appropriately to the children's needs.

Summary

In the integrative model of couple and family therapy presented in this chapter, therapy is conceptualized as a developmental and recursive process involving the stages of planning, assessment, treatment and disengagement or recontracting. Therapeutic interventions may be classified in terms of problem and exception formulations, with some interventions targeting behaviour change, some targeting narratives and beliefs, and others focusing on contextual risk and protective factors. A central challenge in family therapy practice is to balance the focus on problems with the focus on strengths. The use of problem and exception formulations is one practice that facilitates the development of narratives of hope. Key findings from positive psychology have been incorporated into the exception formulation model used in this approach to practice.

Epilogue

Emilia Dowling and Arlene Vetere

The wider context: the National Service Framework for children, young people and maternity services (DoH 2003)

At the time of writing this book (summer 2004), the emerging findings of the children's task force and their recommendations for the implementation of the UK National Service Framework (NSF) for children have just been published (DoH 2003). As Professor Aynsley Green observes in the preface 'The children's NSF offers an opportunity to improve the lives and health of children and young people through the development of effective, evidence-based and needs led services' (p. 2). The document states that 'Children's Mental Health is everyone's business', and sets as one of its targets the provision of a comprehensive service by all child and adolescent mental health services, including health promotion and early intervention, by 2006.

The NSF document estimates that 12 million children are living in England, of whom 60,000 are in the Looked After System, and one-fifth have ethnic minority backgrounds. It quotes evidence that:

> up to 2 million under 16 year olds in England may require help at some time, of whom about half suffer from mental health disorders and a smaller number have severe mental illness. Mental health problems in children are associated with educational failure, family disruption disability, offending and antisocial behaviour, placing demands on social services, schools and the youth justice system. *Untreated mental health problems create distress not only in the children and young people but also for their families and carers continuing into adult life and affecting the next generation.*
>
> (DoH 2003: 32, our italics)

It mentions further evidence about the needs and underachievement of children in special circumstances, such as looked after children, children of problem drinkers, children in domestic violence refuges and young people within the criminal justice system – highlighting the high levels of unmet mental health needs (p. 15).

The Children's NSF, which effectively is government policy informed by professional advice is recommending among other things: Child-centred services *taking into account the views of young people, children, their families and carers*. In other words the young people will have a say in what services are provided and how they are delivered. Their voice will be heard. Parents, when asked, emphasise the need to see their child as an individual, within the contexts of school, family and community. These developments are taking place in the context of a focus on children, a shift in the balance of power, emphasis on decentralisation and delivery of services at a local level. There are proposals afoot for the establishment of Children's Trusts and a forthcoming Green Paper on services for children at risk. The emphasis is on prevention and early intervention, and the delivery of more closely integrated services: multi-disciplinary teams and interagency working – organisations that learn from each other!

The theoretical framework and the ideas as well as the different accounts of professional practice contained in this book are particularly relevant in this wider context which emphasises proposals and, hopefully, implementation of crucial changes for the resourcing and delivering of Mental Health Services for children, adolescents and their families.

Notes

2 Narratives and phantasies

1 'I take the constructivism of social psychology to be a profound expression of democratic culture' (Bruner 1990; 30).

2 Bauman's critique was put in its strongest terms in his *Modernity and the Holocaust* (1989).

3 In the new translations of Freud's writings which are being undertaken under Philips's editorship, diversity of interpretation and plurality of voices are celebrated, in contrast to the aim of the original *Standard Edition*, to be a canonical and correct representation of Freud's thought.

4 The recognition of the partial shaping of social life through culture took place within the Marxist historical and social scientific tradition some decades before its celebration in post-modernism. See for example the work of Antonio Gramsci, Edward Thompson, Raymond Williams and Stuart Hall. This insight subsequently developed as the full autonomisation of the culture and cultural explanation, freed from all material or social constraint.

5 On various aspects of narrative, see Nash (1990).

6 Useful introductory essays and commentary are in Wood (1992).

7 The 'facts of life' set out by Roger Money-Kyrle (1978) proposed a comparable foundation for psychoanalytic reflection.

8 A psychologist who does so, with an argument similar to that of Ricoeur, is Jerome Bruner (1986a).

9 Generally systemic therapists refer to their clients, psychoanalytic psychotherapists to their patients. We use both terms in this chapter.

10 Joyce McDougall has developed a psychoanalytical version of a dramaturgical approach to the mind with great effect in her *Theatres of the Mind* (1986) and *Theatres of the Body* (1989).

11 The psychoanalytic consulting room has some of the attributes of an experimental setting. The constancy and reliability of many aspects of the frame (time, place, frequency, avoidance of intrusion, etc.) render the effects of unconscious phantasy more open to investigation than they are in more everyday situations (Rustin 2002a).

12 One could see these enactments in a therapeutic space as 'prophylactic' experiences of elements of the mental illness or problem, in a 'contained' setting where they can be learned from, and where they can do little harm.

13 Systemic therapists, partly because they have to cope with the inhibitions of members of a family group, adopt more active and interventionist techniques to encourage communication.

14 They have their analogue in the Lacanian psychoanalytic landscape of the real, the imaginary and the symbolic, though these terms map the territory of the mind in a different way.

15 Systemic family therapy also emerged in the 1970s, at a moment when reforms in social services in Britain called for a therapeutic discipline which could address systemic issues and not be confined to the 'normalising' (or pathologising) treatment of individual 'cases'. Family therapy offered a relevant new expertise in this context.

16 *Multiple Voices* is the title of a Tavistock Clinic book on systemic therapy (Papadopoulos and Byng-Hall 1997).

17 This can be seen in writings about adoption in these two traditions. For both, the whole situation includes the presence in mind of both biological and adoptive parents for a child, and adopted and unborn biological children for adoptive parents. For one tradition this is the whole family situation, for another it will include elements of unconscious phantasy. But for both, the important thing is hold all this complexity in mind and enable families to remain in touch with it too (Lindsey 1997; Rustin 1999).

18 Richard Rorty's critique of foundationalism is set out more fully in Rorty (1991).

19 Attachment theory, partly because of its origins in evolutionary biology, in fact has less affinity with social constructionism than the more 'mentalist' approach of contemporary psychoanalysis, although the elaboration of its idea of 'internal working models' has brought these perspectives closer to each other.

20 A similar approach, bringing together a psychoanalytic exploration of relationships within families with consideration of its societal context, is adopted in our *Mirror to Nature: Drama Psychoanalysis and Society* (Rustin and Rustin 2002).

4 Children's narratives of traumatic experiences

1 Diane Baylis (2004) gloriously demonstrates her similar passion for words.

2 Jim Wilson in Chapter 6 of this volume gives a clear example of this in relation to a teenage boy and his mother discussing the marital break up of 8 years previously.

3 Psalm 23 'The Lord is my Shepherd, I shall not want', *The Holy Bible* King James Version.

4 Presentation, 'Brothers, Sisters and the Legacy of Sexual Abuse', St Katherine's College, Oxford, 3 April 1996.

5 Dowse, A. (ed.) *Poetry in Motion*, Peterborough: Young Writers' Forward Press.

6 Although I am discussing primarily my work with refugee children in this chapter, it is based on my extensive work with children within the care system where life story work is such a crucial part of helping them to make sense of their experiences.

7 I remember vividly Emmanuela telling me that at the time she thought the people were lying down but with the benefit of hindsight and being older she now realises they were dead. This is a clear example of the protective benefits of denial and of knowing but not knowing simultaneously.

8 I have benefited enormously in my thinking around multilingualism by discussions with my multilingual trainees and colleagues – Nasima Hussein, Ramon Karamat-Ali, Kathleen Van de Vijer and Charlotte Burck.

9 A notable exception in my experience has been the violence and abuse perpetrated by nuns on children within the so-called 'Orphanages' in Ireland.

10 For example 'The AntiColouring Book', which offers prompts.

7 Narratives of fathers and sons

1 The word 'fabulous' has come to mean something wonderful, though it originally refers simply to what is told in fable or story; by implication fiction or myth. Therapeutic narratives are based on perceptions of real events. One woman took offence at my talking about her 'story', thinking that I was accusing her of lying. She had been sexually abused in childhood by her stepfather, and was not believed by her mother.

2 Even if they cannot forgive them. This is 'earned security' which they pass on to the next generation.

3 All the world's a stage, / And all the men and women merely players. / They have their exits and their entrances, / And one man in his time plays many parts. *As you like it*, 2.7.139.

4 As early as 4 months children can manage triangular relationships (Von Klitzing *et al.* 1999).

5 Girls' identifications, if smoother, are more complex because they have to distinguish themselves from mother's person but not from her gender. Paternal functions are just as important for girls, but that is another topic.

6 'If a male cannot tell when a female ovulates, he must tend her more or less continuously to be sure he sires her offspring' (Hinde 1982: 250).

7 'There is no such thing as a baby', said Donald Winnicott in 1940, perhaps the first to note the essentially systemic nature of the baby and mother couple. 'The infant and the maternal care together form a unit' (Winnicott 1960: 39). A father's function is equally dependent on the existence of the other two (Etchegoyen 2002: 34).

8 The Aka pygmies of Central Africa share parental care of infants, more than any other human group studied. There are no external enemies, so men are not needed as boundary keepers and protectors. 'Husband–wife reciprocity is most likely the prime factor that leads to increased paternal involvement' (Hewlett 1992: 171). Paternal investment is lower when the male has higher status, suggesting a link with non-human primate patterns in which males are more likely to care for children when they want to impress the female.

9 'The term coalition means a process of joint action *against* a third person . . . the problem is more severe when the coalition across generations is denied or concealed . . . when this act becomes a way of life the family is in trouble' (Haley 1976: 109). Haley, one of the great pioneers of early family systems therapy, did not acknowledging the Freudian origins of the pathological triangle.

10 'Enmeshment' here describes a harmful misconnection between parent and child which has been a focus of developmental psychology for at least 50 years; the double bind (Bateson *et al.*, 1956), maternal impingement (Winnicott 1960), anxious attachment (Bowlby 1973), invisible loyalty and parentification (Boszormenyi-Nagy and Spark 1973), enmeshment (Minuchin 1974), expressed emotion (Leff and Vaughn 1985), disorganised (Main and Hesse 1990) or unresolved/preoccupied attachment (Patrick *et al.* 1994), and failure of reflective function (Fonagy and Target 1997) or of attunement (Trevarthen and Aitken 2001).

11 'If the link between the parents perceived in love and hate can be tolerated in the child's mind it provides him with a prototype for an object relationship of a third kind in which he is a witness and not a participant. A third position then comes into existence from which object relationships can be observed. Given this, we can also envisage being observed. This provides us with a capacity for seeing ourselves in interaction with others and for entertaining another point of view whilst

retaining our own, for reflecting on ourselves whilst being ourselves' (Britton 1989: 87).

12 We might encourage fathers to bath their babies, but any *obligation* to do so will not necessarily help, and may backfire. Associations between parental behaviours and child outcomes can only show what happens when people make their own choices.

13 The more the task is shared, the more the children will see that gender roles are not fixed. This is regarded as an advantage by most therapists but not by all families. Some have very traditional views which have to be respected and explored in every case.

14 'A father who is dead may be carried within the child's mind as a very alive figure depending on the mother's way of talking about the father. . . . a father who is physically present might nevertheless be lived as symbolically lost, absent or dead in the child's inner world' (McDougall 1989: 209). 'The physical availability of the father may be neither sufficient nor necessary for triangulation to evolve. What does seem critical is a situation within which the child can envisage a relationship between the two other, emotionally significant figures' (Target and Fonagy 2002: 57).

15 or with a stranger: Hobson *et al.* (2004) show how maternal sensitivity is correlated with the 1-year-old child's capacity to engage more freely with other people. When father is non-resident, mother's relationship with him retains a strong influence on the quality of the child's relationship with him (Dunn *et al.* 2004).

16 Salomonsson (2004) describes psychoanalytic work with a boy who has attention deficits.

17 After some months of this work mother told me that she remembered seeing me 16 years ago with our then toddler-aged sons in a double buggy en route to the play group.

18 Overmeyer *et al.* (1999) show how tempting it is to lose interest in psychosocial narrative when a prescription is available.

19 Until they were confiscated at an airport security check.

20 Bateson frames the opening verses ('thunderous prose') of Genesis as a scientific statement about *order*: 'and God divided the light from the darkness . . . and divided the waters which were under the firmament from the waters which were above the firmament' (1973).

21 This discovery is, according to Lacan, 'the fundamental disappointment of the child' [*la déception fondamentale de l'enfant*] (1994: 81).

22 'Essentially, the task for the mother, father and infant involves tolerating the link between two people they desire and which excludes them. This situation cannot be harmonious' (Marks 2002: 95).

23 It would not be possible to present one particular case to illustrate this. It is not ethical to publish such clinical narratives without permission, nor is it ethical to ask.

24 In psychoanalytic therapy there is time, and a need, to challenge head on destructive motives arising, for example, from jealousy and envy. In work with families more strategic and indirect methods are usually required to avoid shaming one family member in the presence of others.

10 Parenting adult children

1 The research has followed the strict guidelines of the British Psychological Society and University of East London ethical committee, which has meant that

we were very clear in explaining the nature and purpose of the research, while ensuring that both confidentiality and anonymity were assured. We made it clear that participation was entirely voluntary and that respondents were free to withdraw at any point.

References

Ainsworth, M.D., Blehar, M.C., Waters, E. and Wall, S. (1978) *Patterns of Attachment: Psychological Study of the Strange Situation*, Hillsdale, NJ: Lawrence Erlbaum.

Allen, S.M. and Hawkins, A.J. (1999) 'Maternal gatekeeping: mothers' beliefs and behavior that inhibit greater father involvement in family work', *Journal of Marriage and the Family*, 61: 199–212.

Altschuler, J. (2002) 'Narratives of migration in therapy', *Clinical Psychology*, 17: 12–16.

Andersen, T. (ed.) (1990) *The Reflecting Team*, New York: Norton.

Anderson, H. (1999) 'Reimagining family therapy: reflections on Minuchin's invisible family', *Journal of Marital and Family Therapy*, 15, 1: 1–8.

Anderson, H. and Goolishian, H. (1998) 'Human systems as linguistic systems: preliminary and evolving ideas about implications for clinical theory', *Family Process*, 27: 317–93.

Anderson, H. and Levin, S. (1997) 'Collaborative conversations with children', in C. Smith and D. Nylund (eds) *Narrative Therapies with Children and Adolescents*, New York: Guilford Press.

Andolfi, M., Angelo, C. and De Nichilo, M. (1989) *The Myth of Atlas: Families and the Therapeutic Story*, New York: Brunner Mazel.

Angold, A., Costello, E., Messer, S. and Pickles, A. (1995) 'The development of a short questionnaire for use in epidemiological status on depression in children and adolescents', *International Journal of Methods in Psychiatric Research*, 5, 237–49 and 251–62.

Angold, A., Costello, E.J. and Worthman, C.M. (1998) 'Puberty and depression: the role of age, pubertal states and pubertal timing', *Psychological Medicine*, 28: 51–61.

Asen, E., Tomson, D., Tomson, P. and Young, V. (2003) *Ten Minutes for the Family: Systemic Interventions in Primary Care*, London: Routledge.

Baerger, D.R. and McAdams, D. (1999) 'Life story coherence and its relation to psychological well-being', *Narrative Inquiry*, 9: 69–96.

Bahktin, M. (1981) 'The dialogic imagination', in M. Colquitt (ed.) *Four Essays*, Austin: University of Texas.

Bakhtin, M. (1984) *Problems of Dostoevsky's Poetics*, Manchester: Manchester University Press.

Balint, M. (1957) *The Doctor, His Patient, and the Illness*, London: Pitman.

Barnes, J. (2003) 'Interventions addressing infant mental health problems', *Children and Society*, 17, 5: 386–95.

Bateson, G. (1972) *Steps to an Ecology of Mind*, New York: Ballantine.

Bateson, G. (1973) *Steps to an Ecology of Mind*, St Albans: Paladin.

Bateson, G., Jackson, D., Haley, J. and Weakland, J.H. (1956) 'Towards a theory of schizophrenia', *Behavioural Science*, 1, 4 (Reprinted in Bateson, G. (1973) *Steps to an Ecology of Mind*, St Albans: Paladin).

Bauman, Z. (1987) *Legislators and Interpreters*, Cambridge: Polity Press.

Bauman, Z. (1989) *Modernity and the Holocaust*, Cambridge: Polity Press.

Bayliss, D. (2004) 'A thousand words', *Context*, 71: 24–5.

Berger, J. (2001) 'Ape theatre', in G. Dyer (ed.) *Selected Essays*, London: Bloomsbury, p. 548.

Berg-Nielsen, S., Vikan, S.A. and Dahl, A.A. (2002) 'Parenting related to child and parental psychopathology: a descriptive review of the literature', *Clinical Child Psychology and Psychiatry*, 7, 4: 529–52.

Bertrando, P. (2000) 'Text and context: narrative, postmodernism and cybernetics', *Journal of Family Therapy*, 22: 83–103.

Bibou-Nakou, I. (2004) 'Parents' mental health and children's wellbeing', *Clinical Child Psychology and Psychiatry*, 9, 2: 309–12.

Bion, W.R. (1962) *Elements of Psychoanalysis*, London: Heinemann.

Bion, W.R. (1963) *Learning from Experience*, London: Heineman.

Birmaher, B. (1998) 'Psychometric properties of the screen for child anxiety related emotional disorders (SCARED): a replication study', *Journal of American Academy of Child and Adolescent Psychiatry*, 38: 1230–36.

Blake, A. (2002) *The Irresistible Rise of Harry Potter*, London: Verso.

Bloch, D. and Doherty, W. (1998) 'Editorial: the collaborative family healthcare coalition', *Families, Systems and Health*, 16: 3–6.

Blow, K. (1994) 'Old chestnuts roasted in systemic consultancy with teachers', in C. Huffington and H. Brunning (eds) *Internal Consultancy in the Public Sector*, London: Karnac.

Blow, K. and Daniel, G. (2002) 'Frozen narratives? Post divorce processes and contact disputes', *Journal of Family Therapy*, 24: 85–103.

Boal, A. (1979) *Theater of the Oppressed*, London: Pluto Press.

Boal, A. (1992) *Games for Actors and Non-actors*, London: Routledge.

Boal, A. (1995) *The Rainbow Of Desire*, London: Routledge.

Booth, A. and Amato, P.R. (2001) 'Parental predivorce relations and offspring post-divorce well-being', *Journal of Marriage and the Family*, 63, 1: 197–212.

Boszormenyi-Nagy, I. and Spark, G. (1973) *Invisible Loyalties: Reciprocity in Intergenerational Family Therapy*, Hagerstown, MD: Harper & Row.

Bowlby, J. (1969) *Attachment and Loss*, Vol. 1, London: Hogarth Press; New York: Basic Books.

Bowlby, J. (1973) *Attachment and Loss, Vol. 2: Separation, Anxiety and Anger*, London: Hogarth Press; New York: Basic Books.

Bowlby, J. (1977) 'The making and breaking of affectional bonds', *British Journal of Psychiatry*, 130: 201–10 and 421–31.

Bowlby, J. (1980) *Attachment and Loss: Vol. 3: Loss, Sadness and Depression*, New York: Basic Books.

Bowlby, J. (1984) 'Violence in the family as a disorder of attachment and caregiving systems', *American Journal of Psychoanalysis*, 44, 1: 9–27.

Bowlby, J. (1988) *A Secure Base: Clinical Implications of Attachment Theory*, London: Routledge.

Brent, D., Holder, D., Kolko, D., Birmaher, B., Baugher, M., Roth, C., Iyengar, S. and Johnson, B. (1997) 'A clinical psychotherapy trial for adolescent depression comparing cognitive, family and supporting therapy', *Archives of General Psychiatry*, 54: 877–85.

Bretherton, I. (1985) 'Attachment theory: retrospect and prospect', in I. Bretherton and E. Waters (eds) *Growing Points of Attachment Theory and Research*, Monographs of the Society for Research in Child Development, 50: 1–2, Serial No. 209.

British Crime Survey (1996) *Home Office Statistical Bulletin, Issue 19/96*, Croydon: Home Office.

British Crime Survey (2000) *Home Office Statistical Bulletin, Issue 18/00*, Croydon: Home Office.

Britton, R. (1989) 'The missing link: parental sexuality in the Oedipus Complex', in J. Steiner (ed.) *The Oedipus Complex Today: Clinical Implications*, London: Karnac.

Britton, R. (1998) *Belief and Imagination: Explorations in Psychoanalysis*, London: Routledge.

Britton, R. (2003) *Sex, Death and the Superego: Experiences in Psychoanalysis*, London: Karnac.

Browne, K. and Herbert, M. (1997) *Preventing Family Violence*, Chichester: Wiley.

Bruner, J.S. (1985) 'Narrative and paradigmatic modes of thought', in E. Eisner (ed.) *Learning and Teaching the Ways of Knowing*, Chicago, IL: University of Chicago Press.

Bruner, J.S. (1986a) *Actual Minds, Possible Worlds*, London: Harvard University Press.

Bruner, J.S. (1986b) *Acts of Meaning*, Cambridge, MA: Harvard University Press.

Bruner, J.S. (1987a) 'The transactional self', in J. Bruner and H. Haste (eds) *Making Sense: The Child's Construction of the World*, London: Methuen.

Bruner, J.S. (1987b) 'Life as narrative', *Social Research*, 54, 1: 11–32.

Bruner, J.S. (1990) *Acts of Meaning*, London: Harvard University Press.

Bruner, J.S. (1995) 'The cognitive revolution in children's understanding of mind', *Human Development*, 38, 4–5: 203–13.

Burck, C. (1997) 'Language and narrative: learning from bilingualism', in R.K. Papadopoulos and J. Byng-Hall (eds) *Multiple Voices: Narrative in Systemic Family Psychotherapy*, London: Duckworth.

Burck, C. (2003) 'Explorations of life in several languages', unpublished PhD thesis, The Open University, Milton Keynes.

Burr, V. (1995) *An Introduction to Social Constructionism*, London: Routledge.

Byatt, A.S. and Sodré, I. (1996) *Imagining Characters: Six Conversations about Women Writers*, New York: Vintage.

Byng-Hall, J. (1995) *Rewriting Family Scripts*, New York & London: Guilford Press.

Byng-Hall, J. (2002) 'Relieving parentified children's burdens in families with insecure attachment patterns', *Family Process*, 41, 3: 375–88.

Cabrera, N.J., Tamisk-LeMonda, C.S., Bradley, R.H., Hofferth, S. and Lamb, M.E. (2000) 'Fatherhood in the twenty-first century', *Child Development*, 71: 127–36.

Caffery, T. and Erdman, P. (2003) 'Attachment and family systems theories: implications for family therapists', *Journal of Systemic Therapies*, 22: 3–15.

Campbell, D. (2000) *The Socially Constructed Organisation*, London: Karnac.

Campbell, D., Bianco, V., Dowling, E., Goldberg, H., McNab, S. and Pentecost, D. (2003) 'Family therapy for childhood depression: researching significant moments', *Journal of Family Therapy*, 24: 417–35.

Carlsson, M.A., Samuelsson, I.P., Soponyai, A. and Wen, Q. (2001) 'The Dog's Tale: Chinese, Hungarian and Swedish children's narrative conventions', *International Journal of Early Years Education*, 9, 3: 181–91.

Carr, A. (1999) *Handbook of Clinical Child and Adolescent Psychology: A Contextual Approach*, London: Routledge.

Carr, A. (ed.) (2000a) *What Works with Children and Adolescents?*, London: Routledge.

Carr, A. (2000b) *Family Therapy: Concepts Process and Practice*, Chichester: Wiley.

Carr, A. (ed.) (2002) *Prevention: What Works with Children and Adolescents*, London: Brunner-Routledge.

Carr, A. (2004) *Positive Psychology: The Science of Happiness and Human Strengths*, London: Brunner-Routledge.

Carr, A. and McNulty, M. (in press a) 'Couples therapy', in A. Carr and M. McNulty (eds) *Handbook of Adult Clinical Psychology: An Evidence Based Practice Approach*, Hove, East Sussex: Brunner-Routledge.

Carr, A. and McNulty, M. (in press b) *Handbook of Adult Clinical Psychology: An Evidence Based Practice Approach*, Hove, East Sussex: Brunner-Routledge.

Carter, E.A. and McGoldrick, M. (1980) 'The family life cycle and family therapy: an overview', in E.A. Carter and M. McGoldrick (eds) *The Family Life Cycle*, New York: Gardner Press.

Cecchin, G. (1987) 'Hypothesising, circularity and neutrality revisited: an invitation to curiosity', *Family Process*, 26: 405–13.

Cecchin, G., Lane, G. and Ray, W. (1992) *Irreverence: A Strategy for Therapist's Survival*, London: Karnac.

Cecchin, G., Lane, G. and Ray, W. (1994) *The Cybernetics of Prejudices*, London: Karnac.

Cederborg, A.C. (1994) *Family Therapy as Collaborative Work*, Linkoping Studies in Arts and Sciences 106, Sweden: Linkoping University Department of Child Studies.

Cederborg, A.C. (1997) 'Young children's participation in family therapy talk', *The American Journal of Family Therapy*, 25: 28–38.

Combrinck-Graham, L. (1985) 'A developmental model for family systems', *Family Process*, 24, 2: 139–50.

Cooklin, A. (2001) 'Eliciting children's thinking in families and family therapy', *Family Process*, 40, 3: 292–312.

Coulehan, R., Friedlander, M.L. and Hetherington, L. (1998) 'Transforming narratives: a change event in constructivist family therapy', *Family Process*, 37: 17–33.

Council of Europe (1986) *Violence in the Family*, Strasbourg: Recommendation No R(85)4 adopted by the Committee of Ministers of the Council of Europe on 26 March 1985 and Explanatory Memorandum.

Coyne, J. (1990) 'Interpersonal processes in depression', in G. Keitner (ed.) *Depression and Families: Impact and Treatment*, Washington, DC: American Psychiatric Press, pp. 33–53.

Crittenden, P. (1998) 'Truth, error, omission, distortion, and deception: an application of attachment theory to the assessment and treatment of psychological disorder', in S.M. Clany Dollinger and L.F. DiLalla (eds) *Assessment and Intervention Issues Across the Life Span*, London: Lawrence Erlbaum.

Crossley, M.L. (2000) *Introducing Narrative Psychology: Self, Trauma and the Construction of Meaning*, Buckingham: Open University Press.

Cummings, E.M. and Davies P.T. (2002) 'Effects of marital conflict on children: recent advances and emerging theses in process oriented research', *Journal of Child Psychology and Psychiatry*, 43, 1: 31–63.

Dallos, R. (1997) *Interacting Stories, Narratives, Family Beliefs and Therapy*, London: Karnac.

Davidson, D. (1982) 'Paradoxes of irrationality', in R. Wollheim and J. Hopkins (eds) *Philosophical Essays on Freud*, Cambridge: Cambridge University Press.

Dawe, S., Harnett, P.H., Staiger, P. and Dadds, M.R. (2000) 'Parent training skills and methadone management: clinical opportunities and challenges', *Drug and Alcohol Dependence*, 60: 1–11.

de Shazer, S. (1982) *Patterns of Brief Family Therapy: An Ecosystemic Approach*, New York: Guilford Press.

De Zulueta, D. (1984) 'Connecting linguistic capacity and affective connexions – the implications of bilingualism in the study and treatment of psychiatric disorders: a review', *Psychological Medicine*, 14: 542–57.

Department of Health (1991) *The Children Act 1989*, London: HMSO.

Department of Health (2000) *Caring about Carers: A National Strategy for Carers*, London: Department of Health.

Department of Health (2003) *Getting the Right Start: National Service Framework for Children: Emerging Findings*, London: Department of Health.

Diamond, G. and Siqueland, L. (1995) 'Family therapy for the treatment of depressed adolescents', *Psychotherapy*, 32, 1: 77–90.

Donaldson, M. (1978) *Children's Minds*, New York: Norton; Glasgow: Fontana.

Dowling, E. (1979) 'Co-therapy: a clinical researcher's view', in S. Walrond-Skinner (ed.) *Family and Marital Psychotherapy: A Critical Approach*, London: Routledge and Kegan Paul.

Dowling, E. (1993) 'Are family therapists listening to the young? A psychological perspective', *Journal of Family Therapy*, 15: 403–11.

Dowling, E. and Gorell Barnes, G. (2000) *Working with Children and Parents through Separation and Divorce*, Basingstoke: Macmillan.

Duncan, S. and Reder, P. (2000) 'Children's experience of major psychiatric disorder in their parents', in P. Reder, M. McClure and A. Jolley (eds) *Family Matters: Interfaces between Child and Adult Mental Health*, London & Philadelphia: Routledge.

Dunn, J., Cheng, H., O'Connor, T.G. and Bridges, L. (2004) 'Children's perspectives on their relationships with their nonresident fathers: influences, outcomes and implications', *Journal of Child Psychology and Psychiatry*, 45, 3: 553–66.

Earley, L. and Cushway, D. (2002) 'The parentified child', *Clinical Child Psychology and Psychiatry*, 7: 163–78.

Engel, S. (1999) *The Stories Children Tell: Making Sense of the Narratives of Childhood* (reissued edn), New York: WH Freeman/Worth Publishers.

Epston, D., White, M. and Murray, K. (2002) 'A proposal for re-authoring therapy', in S. McNamee and K. Gergen (eds) *Therapy as Social Construction*, London: Sage.

Erikson, E. (1950) *Childhood and Society*, New York: Norton.

Etchegoyen, A. (2002) 'Psychoanalytical ideas about fathers', in J. Trowell and

A. Etchegoyen (eds) *The Importance of Fathers: A Psychoanalytic Re-evaluation*, Hove, East Sussex: Brunner-Routledge, pp. 20–41.

Falicov, A. (ed.) (1998) *Crossing Bridges. Training Resources for Working with Mentally Ill Parents and their Children*, London: Department of Health.

Falicov, C.J. (1988) *Family Transitions, Continuity and Change over the Life Cycle*, New York: Guilford Press.

Feldman, R. (2003) 'Infant–mother and infant–father synchrony: the co-regulation of positive arousal', *Infant Mental Health Journal*, 24, 1: 1–23.

Figley, C.R. (ed.) (1995) *Compassion Fatigue: Coping with Secondary Traumatic Stress Disorder in those Who Treat the Traumatised*, New York: Brunner-Mazel.

Fish, A. and Spiers, C. (1990) 'Biological parents choose adoptive parents: the use of profiles in adoption', *Child Welfare*, 64, 2: 129–40.

Fivush, R. and Fromhoff, F.A. (1988) 'Style and structure in mother–infant conversations about the past', *Discourse Processes*, 11: 337–55.

Focht-Birkerts, L. and Beardslee, W. (2000) 'A child's experience of parental depression: encouraging relational resilience in families with affective illness', *Family Process*, 139: 417–34.

Fonagy, P. (1998) 'Prevention, the appropriate target of infant psychotherapy', *Infant Mental Health Journal*, 19: 124–50.

Fonagy, P. (1999) 'Male perpetrators of violence against women: an attachment theory perspective', *Journal of Applied Psychoanalytic Studies*, 1, 1: 7–27.

Fonagy, P. (2001) *Attachment Theory and Psychoanalysis*, New York: Other Press.

Fonagy, P. and Target, M. (1997) 'Attachment and reflective function: their role in self-organization', *Development and Psychopathology*, 9: 679–700.

Fonagy, P., Steele, M., Moran, G., Steele, H. and Higgitt, A. (1993) 'Measuring the ghost in the nursery: an empirical study of the relationship between parents' mental representations of childhood experiences and their infants' security of attachment', *Journal of the American Psychoanalytical Association*, 41, 4: 957–89.

Fonagy, P., Steele, M., Steele, H., Higgitt, A. and Target, M. (1994) 'The theory and practice of resilience', *Journal of Clinical Child Psychology and Psychiatry*, 35: 231–57.

Fonagy, P., Target, M., Cottrel, D., Phillips, J. and Kurtz, Z. (2002) *What Works for Whom?* New York: The Guilford Press.

Fraiberg, S., Adelson, E. and Shapiro, V. (1975) 'Ghosts in the nursery; a psychoanalytic approach to the problems of impaired infant–mother relationships', *Journal of the American Academy of Child Psychiatry*, 14: 387–422.

France, A., Bendelow, G. and Williams, S. (2000) 'A "risky" business: researching the health beliefs of children and young people', in A. Lewis and G. Lindsay (eds) *Researching Children's Perspectives*, Buckingham: Open University Press.

Fredman, G. (1997) *Death Talk: Conversations with Children and Families*, London: Karnac.

Fredman, G. (2002) 'Co-ordinating cultural and religious stories with stories of identity', *Clinical Psychology*, 17: 29–32.

Fredman, G. and Fuggle, P. (2000) 'Parents with mental health problems: involving the children', in P. Reder, M. McClure and A. Jolley (eds) *Family Matters: Interfaces between Child and Adult Mental Health*, London & Philadelphia: Routledge.

Freeman, J. and Combs, G. (1996) *Narrative Therapy: The Social Construction of Preferred Realities*, New York: Norton.

Freeman, J., Epston, D. and Lobovits, D. (1997) *Playful Approaches to Serious Problems: Narrative Therapy with Children and their Families*, New York: Norton.

Freud, S. (1920) 'Identification', in *The Standard Edition of the Complete Psychological Works of Sigmund Freud*, Vol. XVIII, London: The Hogarth Press, 1955, p. 105.

Freud, S. (1959) in J. Stachey (ed.) *The Standard Edition of the Complete Psychological Works of S. Freud*, London: Hogarth Press.

Frosh, S. (1997) 'Postmodern narratives: or muddles in the mind', in R. Papadopoulos and J. Byng-Hall (eds) *Multiple Voices: Narrative in Systemic Family Psychotherapy*, London: Duckworth.

Frosh, S., Phoenix, A. and Pattman, R. (2002) *Young Masculinities: Understanding Boys in Contemporary Society*, London: Palgrave.

Garmezy, N. (1993) 'Children in poverty: resilience despite risk', *Psychiatry*, 66: 127–36.

Gelles, R. and Cornell, C. (1990) *Intimate Violence in Families*, Newbury Park, CA: Sage.

Gergen, K.J. (1992) 'Reflection and reconstruction', in K.J. Gergen and S. McNamee (eds) *Beyond Narrative in Negotiation of Meaning*, London: Sage.

Gergen, K.J. (1999) *An Invitation to Social Construction*, Thousand Oaks, CA.: Sage.

Gergen, K.J. and Davis, K.E. (eds) (1985) *The Social Construction of the Person*, New York: Springer-Verlag.

Gergen, K.J. and Kaye, J. (1992) 'Beyond narrative in the negotiation of therapeutic meaning', in K.J. Gergen and S. McNamee (eds) *Therapy as Social Construction*, London: Sage.

Goddard, N. (1974) *Literacy: Language-experience Approaches*, London: Macmillan.

Goffman, E. (1959) *The Presentation of Self in Everyday Life*, London: Penguin.

Goldberg, D. and Huxley, P. (1992) *Common Mental Disorders*, London: Routledge.

Goldner, V., Penn, P., Sheinberg, M. and Walter, G. (1990) 'Love and violence gender paradoxes in volatile attachments', *Family Process*, 29: 343–64.

Goldstein, M.J. (1988) 'The family and psychopathology', *American Review of Psychology*, 39: 283–99.

Gorell Barnes, G. (1995) ' "The little woman" and the world of work', in C. Burck and B. Speed (eds) *Gender, Power and Relationships: New Developments*, London: Routledge.

Gorell Barnes, G. and Dowling, E. (1997) 'Rewriting the story: children, parents and post-divorce narrative', in R.K. Papadopoulos and J. Byng-Hall (eds) *Multiple Voices: Narrative in Systemic Family Psychotherapy*, London: Duckworth.

Gorell Barnes, G., Thompson, P., Daniel, G. and Burchardt, N. (1997) *Growing Up in Stepfamilies*, Oxford: Oxford University Press.

Gosse, E. (1908) *Father and Son: A Study of Two Temperaments*, London: William Heinemann (Reprinted London: Penguin Classics, 1988).

Greef, R. (2001) 'Family dynamics in kinship foster care', in B. Broad (ed.) *Kinship Care: The Placement Choice for Children and Young People*, London: Russell House Publishing.

Greenhalgh, T. and Hurwitz, B. (1998) *Narrative-based Medicine: Dialogue and Discourse in Clinical Practice*, London: BMA Books.

Greenson, R. (1968) 'Disidentifying from mother: its special importance for the boy', *International Journal of Psychoanalysis*, 49: 370–74.

Grossmann, K., Grossmann, K.E., Fremmer-Bombik, E., Kindler, H., Scheurer-Englisch, H. and Zimmermann, P. (2002) 'The uniqueness of the child–father attachment relationship: fathers' sensitive and challenging play as a pivotal variable in a 16-year long study', *Social Development*, 11: 307–31.

Gupta, S. (2003) *Re-reading Harry Potter*, Basingstoke: Palgrave.

Gurman, A. and Jacobson, N. (2002) *Clinical Handbook of Couple Therapy* (3rd edn), New York: Guilford Press.

Habermas, T. and Bluck, S. (2000) 'Getting a life: the emergence of the life story in adolescence', *Psychological Bulletin*, 126, 5: 748–69.

Haggerty, R., Sherrod, L., Garmezy, N. and Rutter, M. (1994) *Stress, Risk and Resilience in Children and Adolescents: Processes, Mechanisms and Interventions*, Cambridge: Cambridge University Press.

Haley, J. (1976) *Problem-solving Therapy*, New York: Harper & Row.

Hall, C. (1998) *Social Work as Narrative: Storytelling and Persuasion in Professional Texts*, Aldershot: Ashgate.

Harre, R. and van Langehove, L. (eds) (1999) *Positioning Theory*, Oxford: Blackwell.

Harris, R. and Lindsey, C. (2002) 'How professionals think about contact between children and their birth parents: a qualitative study', *Clinical Psychology and Psychiatry*, 7, 2: 147–61.

Harter, S. (1999) *The Construction of the Self: A Developmental Perspective*, New York: Guilford Press.

Henning Stout, M. and Bonner, M. (1996) 'Affiliation and isolation in the professional lives of school psychologists', *Journal of Educational and Psychological Consultation*, 7, 1: 41–60.

Hesse, E. (1999) 'The adult attachment interview', in J. Cassidy and P.R. Shaver (eds) *Handbook of Attachment: Theory, Research and Clinical Applications*, New York: Guilford Press, pp. 395–433.

Hester, M., Pearson, C. and Harwin, N. (2000) *Making an Impact: Children and Domestic Violence*, London: Jessica Kingsley.

Hewlett, B.S. (1992) 'Husband–wife reciprocity and the father–infant relationship among Aka pygmies', in B.S. Hewlett (ed.) *Father–Child Relations: Cultural and Biosocial Contexts*, New York: Aldine de Gruyter, pp. 153–76.

Hill, J., Fonagy, P., Safier, E. and Sargent, J. (2003) 'The ecology of attachment in the family', *Family Process*, 42, 2: 205–21.

Hill, R. and Rogers, R. (1964) 'The developmental approach', in H. Cristensen (ed.) *Handbook of Marriage and the Family*, Chicago, IL: Rand McNally.

Hinde, R. (1982) *Ethology: Its Nature and Relations with Other Sciences*, Glasgow: Fontana.

Hobson, R.P., Patrick, M.P.H., Crandell, L.E., Garcia Pérez, R.M. and Lee, A. (2004) 'Maternal sensitivity and infant triadic communication', *Journal of Child Psychology and Psychiatry*, 45, 3: 470–80.

Hoffman, L. (1981) *Foundations of Family Therapy*, New York: Basic Books.

Hoffman, L. (1990) 'Constructing realities: an art of lenses', *Family Process*, 29: 1–12.

Hoffman, L. (1992) 'A reflexive stance for family therapy', in S. McNamee and K.J. Gergen (eds) *Therapy as Social Construction*, London: Sage.

Hoffman, L. (1993) *Exchanging Voices*, London: Karnac.

Hoffman, L. (2002) *Family Therapy: An Intimate History*, New York: Norton.

Hollin, C.R. and Howells, K. (1996) *Clinical Approaches to Working with Young Offenders*, Chichester: Wiley.

Hunter, K.M. (1993) *Doctors' Stories: The Narrative Structure of Medical Knowledge*, Princeton, NJ: Princeton University Press.

Huntley, J. (1999) 'A narrative approach toward working with students who have "learning difficulties" ', in A. Morgan (ed.) *Once Upon a Time: Narrative Therapy with Children and their Families*, Adelaide: Dulwich Centre Publications.

Jaffee, S.R., Moffitt, T.E., Caspi, A. and Taylor, A. (2003) 'Life with (or without) father: the benefits of living with two biological parents depend on the father's antisocial behavior', *Child Development*, 74, 1: 109–26.

Karamat-Ali, R. (in press) 'Bilingualism and systemic psychotherapy: some formulations and explorations', *Journal of Family Therapy*.

Kelly, G.A. (1955) *The Psychology of Personal Constructs*, Vols 1 & 2, New York: Norton.

Kelly, J.B. (2000) 'Children's adjustment in conflicted marriage and divorce: a decade review of research' *Journal of the American Academy of Child and Adolescent Psychiatry*, 39: 963–73.

Kim Berg, I. and Steiner, T. *Children's Solution Work*, New York & London: Norton.

Kitzinger, C. and Wilkinson, S. (1996) 'Theorizing representing the other', in S. Wilkinson and C. Kitzinger (eds) *Representing the Other*, London: Sage.

Koenen, K.C., Moffitt, T.E., Caspi, A., Taylor, A. and Purcell, S. (2003) 'Domestic violence is associated with environmental suppression of IQ in young children', *Development and Psychopathology*, 15: 297–331.

Kovacs, M. (1997) 'Depressive disorders in childhood: an impressionistic landscape', *Journal of Child Psychology and Psychiatry*, 38, 3: 287–98.

Kovacs, M. and Sherrill, S. (2001) 'The psychotherapeutic management of major depressive and dysthemic disorders in childhood and adolescents: issues and prospects', in I.M. Goodyer (ed.) *The Depressed Child and Adolescent* (2nd edn), Cambridge: Cambridge University Press.

Kraemer, S. (1991) 'The origins of fatherhood', *Family Process*, 30: 377–92.

Kraemer, S. (2000) 'The fragile male', *British Medical Journal*, 321: 1609–12.

Kramer, S.N. (1963) *The Sumerians*, Chicago, IL: University of Chicago Press.

Kuhn, T.S. (1962) *The Structure of Scientific Revolutions*, Chicago, IL: Chicago University Press.

Kurtz, I. (2003) 'Moving on: Letting go of the apron strings', *Times 2*, 20 September, p. 11.

Lacan, J. (1994) *Le Seminaire Livre IV: La Relation d'Objet*, Paris: Editions du Seuil.

Lamb, M.E. and Lewis, C. (2004) 'The development and significance of father–child relationships in two-parent families', in M.E. Lamb (ed.) *The Role of the Father in Child Development* (4th edn), Hoboken, NJ: Wiley, pp. 272–306.

Launer, J. (1995) 'General practice and primary care: the AFT special interest group', *Context*, 23: 27–8.

Launer, J. (1996) 'Towards systemic general practice', *Context*, 26: 42–5.

Launer, J. (2002) *Narrative-based Primary Care: A Practical Guide*, Oxford: Radcliffe.

Launer, J. and Lindsey, C. (1997) 'Training for systemic general practice: a new approach from the Tavistock Clinic', *British Journal of General Practice*, 47: 453–6.

Laws, S. (2001) 'Looking after children within the extended family: carers' views', in B. Broad (ed.) *Kinship Care: The Placement Choice for Children and Young People*, London: Russell House Publishing.

Leff, J. and Vaughn, C. (1985) *Expressed Emotion in Families: Its Significance for Mental Illness*, New York: Guilford Press.

Leverton, T.J. (2003) 'Parental psychiatric illness: the implications for children', *Current Opinion in Psychiatry*, 16: 395–402.

Liddle, H., Santisteban, D., Levant, R. and Bray, J. (2002) *Family Psychology: Science-based Interventions*, Washington, DC: American Psychological Association.

Lindsey, C. (1997) 'New stories for old? The creation of new families for old by adoption and fostering', in R. Papadopoulos and J. Byng-Hall (eds) *Multiple Voices*, London: Duckworth.

Luthar, S. (2003) *Resilience and Vulnerability: Adaptation in the Context of Childhood Adversities*, Cambridge: Cambridge University Press.

Luthar, S. and Cicchetti, D. (2000) 'The construct of resilience: implications for interventions and social policies', *Development and Psychopathology*, 12: 857–85.

Luthar, S., Cicchetti, D. and Becker, B. (2000) 'The construct of resilience: a critical evaluation and guidelines for future work', *Child Development*, 71, 573–5.

Lyon, C., Surrey, E. and Timms, J. (1998) *Effective Support Services for Children and Young People when Parental Relations Break Down: A Child Centred Approach*, Liverpool: Centre for the Study of the Child, the Family and the Law, University of Liverpool, UK.

Lysaker, P.H., Lancaster, R.S. and Lysaker, J.T. (2003) 'Narrative transformation as an outcome in the psychotherapy of schizophrenia', *Psychology and Psychotherapy: Theory, Research and Practice*, 76: 285–99.

McCabe, A. and Peterson, C. (1991) 'Getting the story: a longitudinal study of parenting styles in eliciting narratives and developing narrative skill', in A. McCabe and C. Peterson (eds) *Developing Narrative Structure*, London: Lawrence Erlbaum.

McCauley, E., Kendall, K. and Pavglidis, K. (1995) 'Developmental precursors of depression: the child and the social development , in I. Goodyer (ed.) *The Referred Child and Adolescent*, Cambridge: Cambridge University Press, pp. 46–78.

McDougall, J. (1986) *Theatres of the Mind: Illusion and Truth on the Psychoanalytic Stage*, London: Free Association Books.

McDougall, J. (1989) *Theatres of the Body: A Psychoanalytic Approach to Psychosomatic Illness*, London: Free Association Books.

McGoldrick, M. and Carter, B. (1989) 'Forming a remarried family', in B. Carter and M. McGoldrick (eds) *The Changing Family Life Cycle*, Boston: Allyn & Bacon.

McLeod, J. (1997) *Narrative and Psychotherapy*, London: Sage.

Main, M. and Hesse, E. (1990) 'Parents' unresolved traumatic experiences are related to infant disorganised attachment status: is frightened and/or frightening parental behavior the linking mechanism?', in M. Greenberg, D. Cicchetti and E.M. Cummings (eds) *Attachment in the Preschool Years: Theory, Research and Intervention*, Chicago, IL: University of Chicago Press, pp. 161–82.

Main, M., Kaplan, N. and Cassidy, J. (1985) 'Security in infancy, childhood and adulthood: a move to the level of representation', in I. Bretherton and E. Waters (eds) *Growing Points of Attachment Theory and Research*, Monographs of the Society for Research in Child Development, 50: 1–2, Serial No. 209.

Marks, M. (2002) 'Letting fathers in', in J. Trowell and A. Etchegoyen (eds) *The Importance of Fathers: A Psychoanalytic Re-evaluation*, Hove, East Sussex: Brunner-Routledge, pp. 93–106.

Marriage Divorce and Adoption Statistic Series FM 2 (2003) Available at http://www.statistics.gov.uk/glance/default/asp, last updated 22 July 2003 (accessed 7 June 2004).

Mas, C., Alexander, J. and Barton, C. (1985) 'Modes of expression in family therapy: a process study of roles and gender', *Journal of Marital and Family Therapy*, 11: 411–5.

Masten, A.S., Best, K.M. and Garmezy, N. (1990) 'Resilience and development: contributions from the study of children who overcome adversity', *Development and Psychopathology*, 2: 425–44.

Mead, G.H. (1934) *Mind, Self and Society*, Chicago, IL: University of Chicago Press.

Miller, M.L. (1999) 'Chaos, complexity and psychoanalysis, *Psychoanalytic Psychology*, 16, 3: 15–16.

Minuchin, S. (1974) *Families and Family Therapy*, London: Tavistock.

Minuchin, S. (1998) 'Where is the family in narrative family therapy?', *Journal of Marital and Family Therapy*, 24, 4: 397–403.

Mitchell, J., McCauley, E., Burke, P.M. and Moss, S.J. (1988) '10 major depressive disorders in adolescents – a district diagnostic entity?', *Journal of American Academy of Child and Adolescent Psychiatrists*, 27: 12–50.

Moffitt, T. and Caspi, A. (1998) 'Annotation: implications of violence between intimate partners for child psychologists and psychiatrists', *Journal of Child Psychology and Psychiatry*, 39: 137–44.

Money-Kyrle, R. (1978) 'Cognitive development' and 'The aim of psychoanalysis' (Chs 31& 33) in D. Meltzer and E. O'Shaugnessy (eds) *The Collected Papers of Roger Money-Kyrle*, Perthshire: Clunie Press.

Moran, M.H. (1991) 'Chaos theory and psychoanalysis: the fluidistic nature of the mind', *International Review of Psychoanalysis*, 78, 2: 211–21.

Morgan, A. (1999a) *What is Narrative Therapy? An Easy-to-read Introduction*, Adelaide: Dulwich Centre Publications.

Morgan, A. (ed.) (1999b) *Once Upon a Time: Narrative Therapy with Children and their Families*, Adelaide: Dulwich Centre Publications.

Morrell, J. and Murray, L. (2002) 'Infant and maternal precursors of conduct disorder and hyperactive symptoms in childhood: a prospective longitudinal study from 2 months to 8 years', *Journal of Child Psychology and Psychiatry*, 43, 7: 1–20.

Mufson, L., Aidala, A. and Warner, V. (1994) 'Social dysfunction and psychiatric disorder in mothers and their children', *Journal of the American Academy of Child and Adolescent Psychiatry*, 33: 1256–64.

Mullender, A., Hague, G., Imam, U., Kelly, L., Malos, E. and Regan, L. (2002) *Children's Perspectives on Domestic Violence*, London: Sage.

Nash, C. (ed.) (1990) *Narrative in Culture*, London: Routledge.

Nylund, D. (2002) *Treating Huckleberry Finn: A New Narrative Approach to Working with Kids Diagnosed ADD/ADHD*, San Francisco, CA: Jossey-Bass.

O'Brien, M., Alldred, P. and Jones, D. (1996) 'Children's constructions of family and kinship', in J. Brannen and M. O'Brien (eds) *Children in Families*, London: Falmer Press.

Ochs, E. and Taylor, C. (1992) 'Family narrative as political activity', *Discourse and Society*, 3: 301–40.

Ochs, E., Taylor, C., Rudolph, D. and Smithe, R. (1992) 'Story telling as a theory building activity', *Discourse Processes*, 15: 37–72.

Olson, D.H., Sprenkle, D. and Russell, C.S. (1970) 'Circumflex model of marital and family systems: cohesion and adaptability dimensions, family types and clinical applications', *Family Process*, 18: 3–28.

Oppenheim, D. and Waters, H.S. (1985) 'Narrative processes and attachment representation: issues of development and assessment', in I. Bretherton and E. Waters (eds) *Growing Points of Attachment Theory and Research*, Monographs of the Society for Research in Child Development, 50: 1–2, Serial No. 209.

O'Shaugnessy, E. (1994) 'What is a clinical fact?', *International Journal of Psycho-analysis*, 75, 5–6: 935–47.

Osofsky, J.D. (ed.) (1997) *Children in a Violent Society*, New York: Guilford Press.

Osofsky, J.D. (1998) 'Children as invisible victims of domestic and community violence', in G.W. Holden, R. Geffner and E.N. Jouriles (eds) *Children Exposed to Marital Violence: Theory, Research and Intervention*, Washington, DC: American Psychological Association.

Overmeyer, S., Taylor, E., Blanz, B. and Schmidt, M.H. (1999) 'Psychosocial adversities underestimated in hyperkinetic children', *Journal of Child Psychology and Psychiatry*, 40, 2: 259–63.

Palazzoli, M. Boscolo, L., Cecchin, G. and Prata, G. (1978) *Paradox and Counterparadox*, New York: Jason Aronson.

Palazzoli, M., Boscolo, L., Cecchin, G. and Prata, G. (1980a) 'Hypothesising, circularity, neutrality: three guidelines for the conductor of the interview', *Family Process*, 19, 1: 3–11.

Palazzoli, M., Boscolo, L., Cecchin, G. and Prata, G. (1980b) 'The problem of the referring person', *Journal of Marital and Family Therapy*, 6: 3–9.

Papadopoulos, R.K. and Byng-Hall, J. (eds) (1997) *Multiple Voices: Narrative in Systemic Family Psychotherapy*, London: Duckworth.

Patrick, M., Hobson, R.P., Castle, D., Howard, R. and Maughan, B. (1994) 'Personality disorder and mental representation of early social experience', *Development and Psychopathology*, 6: 375–88.

Pearce, W.B. and Cronen, V.E. (1980) *Communication, Action and Meaning: The Creation of Social Realities*, New York: Praeger.

Philips, A. (1997) *Terrors and Experts*, London: Harvard University Press.

Piaget, J. (1932) *The Moral Judgement of the Child*, London: Kegan, Paul, Trench, Trubner.

Piaget, J. (1955) *The Child's Construction of Reality*, London: Routledge and Kegan Paul.

Piaget, J. (1977) *The Development of Thought: Equilibration of Cognitive Structures*, New York: The Viking Press.

Pinsof, W. and Wynne, L. (1995) *Family Therapy Effectiveness: Current Research and Theory* (Special edition of *Journal of Marital and Family Therapy*, 21, 4), Washington, DC: AAMFT.

Pitcher, D. (2002) 'Placement with grandparents: the issues for grandparents who care for their grandchildren', *Adoption and Fostering*, 26, 1: 6–14.

Pruett, K.D. (1993) 'The paternal presence', *Families in Society: The Journal of Contemporary Human Services*, 74, 1: 46–50.

Puig-Antich, J. and Ryan, N. (1996) *Kiddie SADS Present and Lifetime Version* (4th working draft), Pittsburgh, PA: Western Psychiatric Institute and Clinic, University of Pittsburgh.

Quinodoz, J.M. (1997) 'Transitions in psychic structures in the light of deterministic chaos theory', *International Journal of Psychoanalysis*, 78, 4: 699–718.

Ravenette, A.T. (1968) *Dimensions of Reading Difficulties*, Oxford: Pergamon.

Reissman, C.K. (1993) *Narrative Analysis*, Newbury Park, CA: Sage.

Rendall, S.E. (2000) 'Factors relating to exclusion from school: a systemic approach', unpublished PhD thesis, University of London.

Renzetti, C.M. (1992) *Violent Betrayal: Partner Abuse in Lesbian Relationships*, Newbury Park, CA: Sage.

Ricoeur, P. (1984–8) *Time and Narrative*, Vols 1–3, Chicago, IL: Chicago University Press.

Ricoeur, P. (1989) *Time and Narrative* (trans. D. Pellauer), Chicago, IL: University of Chicago Press.

Ricoeur, P. (1991) In M.J. Valdes (ed.) *A Ricoeur Reader: Reflection and Imagination*, Hemel Hempstead: Harvester Wheatsheaf.

Riessman, C. (2003) 'Performing identities in illness narrative: masculinity and multiple sclerosis', *Qualitative Research*, 3, 1: 5–33.

Rober, P. (1998) 'Reflections on ways to create a safe therapeutic culture for children in family therapy', *Family Process*, 37, 2: 201–13.

Robinson, M. (1991) *Family Transformation through Divorce and Remarriage*, London: Routledge.

Rodgers, B. and Pryor, J. (1998) *Divorce and Separation: The Outcomes for Children*, York: Joseph Rowntree Foundation.

Rorty, R. (1980) *Philosophy and the Mirror of Nature*, Princeton, NJ: Princeton University Press.

Rorty, R. (1991) 'Freud and moral reflection', in *Essays on Heidegger and Others: Philosophical Papers*, Vol. 2, Cambridge: Cambridge University Press.

Rosenwald, G. (1992) 'Conclusion: reflections of narratives of understanding', in G. Rosenwald and R. Ochberg (eds) *Storied Lives: The Cultural Politics of Self-understanding*, New Haven, CT: Yale University Press.

Royal College of Psychiatrists (2003) *Being Seen and Heard: The Needs of Children of Parents with Mental Illness*, Training video.

Royal College of Psychiatrists Council Report (2003) *The Mental Health of Students in Higher Education*, Council Report CR 112, January, London: Royal College of Psychiatrists. Available at http://www.rcpsych.ac.uk/publications/cr/council/cr112.pdf (accessed 7 June 2004).

Rushton, A. and Miles, G. (2000) 'A study of the support service for the current carers of sexually abused girls', *Clinical Child Psychology and Psychiatry*, 5, 3: 411–26.

Rustin, M.E. (1999) 'Multiple families in mind', *Clinical Child Psychology and Pschiatry*, 4, 1: 51–62.

Rustin, M.E. and Rustin, M.J. (2001) *Narratives of Love and Loss: Studies in Modern Children's Fiction* (2nd edn), London: Karnac.

Rustin, M.E. and Rustin, M.J. (2002) *Mirror to Nature: Drama, Psychoanalysis and Society*, London: Karnac/Tavistock Clinic.

Rustin, M.J. (2002a) 'Give me a consulting room: the generation of psychoanalytic knowledge', in *Reason and Unreason: Psychoanalysis, Science, Politics*, London: Continuum.

Rustin, M.J. (2002b) 'Looking in the right place: complexity theory, psychoanalysis and infant observation', *International Journal of Infant Observation*, 5, 1: 122–44.

Rutter, M. (1985) 'Resilience in the face of adversity: protective factors and resistance to psychiatric disorder', *British Journal of Psychiatry*, 147: 598–611.

Rutter, M. (1999) 'Resilience concepts and findings: implications for family therapy', *Journal of Family Therapy*, 21: 119–44.

Rutter, M. (2000) 'Resilience reconsidered: conceptual considerations, empirical findings, and policy implications', in J. Shonkoff and S. Meisels (eds) *Handbook of Early Childhood Intervention*, New York: Cambridge University Press.

Rutter, M. and Quinton, D. (1984) 'Parental psychiatric disorder: effects on children', *Psychological Medicine*, 14: 853–80.

Rutter, M., Izard, C. and Read, P. (1986) *Depression in Young People: Development and Clinical Perspectives*, New York: Guilford Press.

Salomonsson, B. (2004) 'Some psychoanalytic viewpoints on neuropsychiatric disorders in children', *International Journal of Psychoanalysis*, 85: 117–36.

Sanders, C. (1985) ' "Now I see the difference": the use of visual news of difference in clinical practice', *Australia and New Zealand Journal of Family Therapy*, 6, 1: 23–9.

Sarason, S.B. (1990) *The Predictable Failure of Educational Reform*, San Francisco, CA: Jossey-Bass.

Sarbin, T.R. (ed.) (1986) *Narrative Psychology: The Storied Nature of Human Conduct*, New York: Praeger.

Schafer, R. (1992) *Retelling a Life: Narration and Dialogue in Psychoanalysis*, New York: Basic Books.

Schank, R.C. (1995) *Tell Me a Story: Narrative and Intelligence*, Evanston, IL: Northwestern University Press.

Schwartz, R.C. (1999) 'Narrative therapy expands and contracts family therapies horizons', *Journal of Marital and Family Therapy*, 25, 2: 263–9.

Selekman, M.D. (1997) *Solution-focused Therapy with Children: Harnessing Family Strengths for Systemic Change*, New York: Guilford Press.

Sexson, S. and Kaslow, N. (2001) 'Attachment and depression: implications for family therapy', *Child and Adolescent Psychiatric Clinics of North America*, 10, 3: 465–86.

Sexton, T., Weeks, G. and Robbins, M. (2003) *Handbook of Family Therapy: The Science and Practice of Working With Families and Couples*, New York: Brunner-Routledge.

Shepherd, R., Johns, J. and Taylor Robinson, H. (eds) (1996) *D. W. Winnicott: Thinking About Children*, London: Karnac.

Shotter, J. (1993) 'In search of a past', in J. Shotter (ed.) *Conversational Realities*, London: Sage.

Simonoff, E., Pickles, A, Meyer, J.M. *et al.* (1997) 'The Virginia Town study of adolescent behavioural development', *Archives of General Psychiatry*, 54: 801–8.

Sluzki, C.E. (1998) 'In search of the lost family: a footnote to Minuchin's essay', *Journal of Marital and Family Therapy*, 24, 4: 415–7.

Sluzki, C.S. (1992) 'Transformations: a blueprint for narrative changes in therapy', *Family Process*, 31: 217–30.

Smart, C., Neale, B. and Wade, A. (2001) *The Changing Experience of Childhood*, Cambridge: Polity Press.

Smith, C. and Nylund, D. (eds) (1997) *Narrative Therapies with Children and Adolescents*, New York: Guilford Press.

Smith, G. (1994) 'Parent, partner, protector: conflicting role demands for women whose children have been sexually abused', in J. Erooga, S. Morrison and B. Beckett (eds) *Offending Against Children: Assessment and Treatment of Male Abusers*, London: Routledge.

Smith, G. (1996) 'Brothers, sisters and the legacy of sexual abuse', paper presented at the Oxford Family Institute Conference, St Katherine's College, Oxford.

Smith, G. (2003) *Treating the Sexually Abused Child: A Training Programme for Foster Caregivers*, London: BAAF.

Smith, R.A.L. (2004) 'Poetic narratives and poetic activism: implications for improving school effectiveness for peace in Northern Ireland', unpublished EdD, University of London Institute of Education, London.

Snyder, C. and Lopez, S. (2002) *Handbook of Positive Psychology*, New York: Oxford University Press.

Sodré, I. (1999) 'Death by daydreaming: Madame Bovary', in D. Bell (ed.) *Psychoanalysis and Culture: A Psychoanalytic Perspective*, London: Duckworth.

Solomon, J. and George, C. (1999) 'The development of attachment in separated and divorced couples: effects of overnight visitation, parent and couple variables', *Attachment and Human Development*, 1, 1: 2–33.

Sommer, D. (2001) *At blive en person*, Kopenhavn: Hans Reitzels Forlag.

Spence, D.P. (1982) *Narrative Truth and Historical Truth: Meaning and Interpretation in Psychoanalysis*, New York: Norton.

Spencer, P. and Wollman, H. (2002) *Nationalism: A Critical Introduction*, London: Sage.

Stanislavski, C. (1937/1980) *An Actor Prepares*, London: Methuen Drama.

Steele, H. and Steele, M. (2000) 'Clinical uses of the adult attachment interview', in G. Gloger-Tippelt (ed.) *Bindung im Erwachsenenalter*, Stuttgart: Klett-Cotta, pp. 322–43.

Steele, H. and Steele, M. (2004) 'The construct of coherence as an indicator of attachment security in middle childhood: the friends and family interview, in K. Kerns and R. Richardson (eds) *Attachment in Middle Childhood*, New York: Guilford Press.

Steele, H., Steele, M., and Fonagy, P. (1996) 'Associations among attachment classification of mother, fathers, and their infants', *Child Development*, 67: 541–55.

Stewart, M., Brown, J.B., Weston, W.W., McWhinney, I., McWilliam, C.L. and Freeman, T.R. (2003) *Patient-centred Medicine: Transforming the Clinical Method* (2nd edn), Oxford: Radcliffe.

Stith, S.M., Rosen, K.H., McCollum, E.E., Coleman, J.U. and Herman, S.A. (1996) 'The voices of children: preadolescent children's experiences in family therapy', *Journal of Marital and Family Therapy*, 22: 69–86.

Stratton, P. (2003) 'Causal attributions during therapy: responsibility and blame', *Journal of Family Therapy*, 25, 2: 136–60.

Straus, M.A. and Gelles, R.J. (1990) *Physical Violence in American Families: Risk Factors and Adaptations to Violence in 8,145 Families*, New Brunswick, NJ: Transaction Publishers.

Strickland-Clark, L., Campbell, D. and Dallos, R. (2000) 'Children's and adolescents' views on family therapy', *Journal of Marital Therapy*, 22, 3: 324–41.

Sween, E. (1999) 'The one-minute question: what is narrative therapy? Some working answers', in D. Derborough and D. White (eds) *Extending Narrative Therapy: A Collection of Practice-based Papers*, Adelaide: Dulwich Papers Publications.

Target, M. and Fonagy, P. (2002) 'The role of the father', in J. Trowell and

A. Etchegoyen (eds) *The Importance of Fathers: A Psychoanalytic Re-evaluation*, Hove, East Sussex: Brunner-Routledge, pp. 45–66.

Thomas, D. (ed.) (1995) *Teachers' Stories*, Buckingham: Open University Press.

Tomm, K. (1988) 'Interventive interviewing: part III. Intending to ask lineal, circular, strategic or reflexive questions?', *Family Process*, 27: 1–15.

Tomm, K. (1998) 'A question of perspective', *Journal of Marital and Family Therapy*, 24, 4: 409–13.

Trevarthen, C. and Aitken, K.J. (2001) 'Infant intersubjectivity: research, theory and clinical applications, *Journal of Child Psychology and Psychiatry*, 42: 3–48.

Tribe, R. and Raval, H. (eds) (2002) *Working with Interpreters in Mental Health*, Hove, East Sussex: Brunner-Routledge.

Trowell, J., Rhode, M., Miles, G. and Sherwood, I. (2003) 'Childhood depression: work in progress: individual child therapy and parent work', *Journal of Child Psychotherapy*, 29, 2: 147–69.

Turgenev, I. (1861) *Fathers and Sons*, Oxford: Oxford World Classics, 1998.

United Nations (UN) (1990) *Convention on the Rights of the Child*. New York: United Nations.

Vetere, A. and Cooper, J. (2001) 'Working systemically with family violence: risk, responsibility and collaboration', *Journal of Family Therapy*, 23, 4: 378–96.

Vetere, A. and Cooper, J. (2003) 'Setting up a domestic violence service', *Child and Adolescent Mental Health*, 8: 61–7.

Vetere, A. and Dallos, R. (2003) *Working Systemically with Families: Formulation, Intervention and Evaluation*, London: Karnac.

Von Klitzing, K., Simoni, H. and Bürgin, D. (1999) 'Child development and early triadic relationships', *International Journal of Psychoanalysis*, 80: 71–89.

Vygotsky, L.S. (1962) *Thought and Language* (2nd edn), Cambridge, MA: MIT Press.

Vygotsky, L.S. (1978) *Mind in Society*, Cambridge, MA: Harvard University Press.

Wachtel, E.F. (1994) *Treating Troubled Children and Their Families*, New York: Guilford Press.

Wachtel, E.F. (2001) 'The language of becoming: helping children change how they think about themselves', *Family Process*, 40, 4: 369–84.

Wagner, P. (1995) *School Consultation: Frameworks for the Practising Educational Psychologist*, London: Kensington and Chelsea EPS.

Wagner, P. and Gillies, E. (2001) 'Consultation: a solution-focused approach', in Y. Ajmal and I. Rees (eds) *Solutions in Schools: Creative Applications of Solution-focused Brief Thinking with Young People and Adults*, London: BT Press.

Walker, J.P. and Lee, R.E. (1998) 'Uncovering the strengths of children of alcoholic parents', *Contemporary Family Therapy*, 20, 4: 521–33.

Walsh, F. (1998) *Strengthening Family Resilience*, New York: Guilford Press.

Walters, J. (1997) 'Talking with fathers: the inter-relation of significant loss, clinical presentation in children and engagement of fathers in therapy', *Clinical Child Psychology and Psychiatry*, 2, 3: 415–30.

Watkins, C. (2001) *Learning about Learning Enhances Performance*, Research Matters Series No. 13, London: Institute of Education School Improvement Network.

Watkins, C. (2003) *Learning: A Sense-maker's Guide*, London: Association of Teachers and Lecturers.

Watkins, C. (2004) *Classrooms as Learning Communities: What's In It for Schools*, London: Falmer-Routledge.

Weingarten, K. (1997) 'From "cold care" to "warm care": challenging the discourses of mothers and adolescents', in C. Smith and D. Nylund (eds) *Narrative Therapies with Children and Adolescents*, New York: Guilford Press.

Weingarten, K. (1998) 'The small and the ordinary: the daily practice of post modern narrative therapy', *Family Process*, 37: 3–14.

Werner, E. (1993) 'Risk, resilience and recovery: perspectives from the Kauai Longitudinal Study', *Development and Psychopathology*, 5: 505–15.

Whitaker, C. (1977) 'Symbolic sex in family therapy', reprinted in J.R. Neill and D.P. Kniskern (eds) (1982) *From Psyche to System: The Evolving Therapy of Carl Whitaker*, New York: Guilford Press, pp. 277–82.

White, L. (1999) 'Contagion in family affection: mothers, fathers, and young adult children', *Journal of Marriage and the Family*, 61, 2: 284–94.

White, M. (1995) *Re-authoring Lives: Interviews and Essays*, Adelaide: Dulwich Centre Publications.

White, M. (2001) *Workshop Notes: Narrative Therapy*, London: Brief Therapy Practice.

White, M. and Epston, D. (1989) *Literate Means to Therapeutic Ends*, Adelaide: Dulwich Centre Publications.

White, M. and Epston, D. (1990) *Narrative Means to Therapeutic Ends*, New York: Norton.

Wilson, J. (1998) *Child Focused Practice: A Systemic Collaborative Approach*, London: Karnac.

Wilson, J. (2000a) 'How can you tell when a goldfish cries? Finding the words in therapeutic stories with children', *Australian and New Zealand Journal of Family Therapy*, 21, 1: 29–33.

Wilson, J. (2000b) 'Child focused practice with looked after children', *Child Care in Practice*, 6: 4.

Wilson, J. (2003) 'Louie and the singing therapist', in 'Focusing Practice on Children', *Context*, 64: 1–2.

Winch, P. (1958) *The Idea of a Social Science and its Relation to Philosophy*, London: Routledge.

Winnicott, D.W. (1960) 'The theory of the parent–infant relationship', *International Journal of Psycho-Analysis*, 41: 585–95, reprinted in *The Maturational Processes and the Facilitating Environment*, London: Hogarth Press, 1965, pp. 37–55.

Winnicott, D.W. (1971) *Playing and Reality*, Harmondsworth: Penguin.

Winslade, J. and Monk, G. (1999) *Narrative Counseling in Schools: Powerful and Brief*, Thousand Oaks, CA: Corwin Press.

Wood, A. (1988) 'King Tiger and the roaring tummies: a novel way of helping young children and their families change', *Journal of Family Therapy*, 10, 1: 49–64.

Wood, D. (1992) *On Paul Ricoeur: Narrative and Interpretation*, London: Routledge.

Woodcock, J. (2001) 'Threads from the labyrinth: therapy with survivors of war and political oppression', *Journal of Family Therapy*, 23, 2: 136–54.

Wren, B. and De Ceglie, D. (1999) 'Children of transsexual parents: some principles of management', conference presentation at the European Society for Child and Adolescent Psychiatry, 11th International Congress, Hamburg, Germany.

Zimmerman, J.L. and Beaudoin, M. (2002) 'Cats under the stars', *Child and Adolescent Mental Health*, 7: 31–40.

Zoja, I. (2001) *The Father: Historical, Psychological and Cultural Perspectives*, Hove, East Sussex: Brunner-Routledge.

Index